COMMAND
AT SEA

Titles in the Series

COMMAND AT SEA

SEVENTH EDITION

ADM JAMES STAVRIDIS, USN (RET.)
RADM ROBERT GIRRIER, USN (RET.)
RADM FRED KACHER, USN

NAVAL INSTITUTE PRESS
Annapolis, Maryland

Naval Institute Press
291 Wood Road
Annapolis, MD 21402

Library of Congress Cataloging-in-Publication Data
Names: Stavridis, James, author. | Girrier, Robert, 1961– author. | Kacher,
    Fred W. author.
Title: Command at sea / Adm. James Stavridis, USN, Ret., Rear Adm. Robert
    Girrier, USN, Ret., Rear Adm. Fred Kacher, USN.
Description: Seventh edition. | Annapolis, Maryland : Naval Institute Press,
    [2022] | Includes bibliographical references and index.
Identifiers: LCCN 2022000688 | ISBN 9781682476130 (hardback)
Subjects: LCSH: Leadership. | United States. Navy—Officers' handbooks.
Classification: LCC VB203 .S73 2022 | DDC 359.3/3041—dc23/
    eng/20220131
LC record available at https://lccn.loc.gov/2022000688

♾ Print editions meet the requirements of ANSI/NISO z39.48-1992
(Permanence of Paper).
Printed in the United States of America.

30 29 28 27 26 25 24 23 22   9 8 7 6 5 4 3 2 1
First printing

All photographs are from official U.S. Navy sources.

Contents

Preface to the
Seventh Edition

First published in 1943, this book has served to aid officers in the preparation for and execution of command at sea. While much has changed over almost eight decades in terms of technology, technique, tools, and the geopolitical landscape, just as much remains timeless: the environment, seamanship, and leadership. *Command at Sea* blends these elements—reflecting a constantly evolving profession—while remaining anchored to fundamentals recognizable in the age of sail.

If you can find an original first edition of *Command at Sea*, written by Captain Harley F. Cope—perhaps in a used bookstore—buy it, read it, and cherish it. The book is a true classic of the seagoing community, written at the height of World War II by an experienced and combat-tested commanding officer. Terse and compact, it begins, "Every young officer who is worth his salt looks forward eagerly to his first command, whether it be a destroyer, a minesweeper, a submarine, a PT, or an auxiliary. There is a tremendous thrill in taking over your first ship." As we enter the third decade of the twenty-first century, these words ring as true as they did in the twentieth-century Navy of Captain Cope, and indeed in the eighteenth-century Navy of Captain John Paul Jones and Commodore John Barry.

Given the timeless quality of command at sea, one question then arises: Why are new editions of this classic required?

The reason is the relentless tide of change in much of the mechanics of how command at sea is executed and, equally as important, the context within which commanding officers work. Some of the changes since the sixth edition of *Command at Sea* was published in 2010 include the following:

- Publication of *A Cooperative Strategy for 21st-Century Seapower*—cosigned by the Secretary of the Navy, the Chief of Naval Operations, and the commandants of the Marine Corps and Coast Guard in 2015—focused on the warfighting capabilities of *deterrence, sea control, power projection*, and *maritime security*. The Tri-Service Maritime Strategy, *Advantage at Sea*, followed in 2020 and provides strategic guidance on how the sea services will prevail in day-to-day competition, crisis, and conflict.

- Publication of the *2018 National Defense Strategy*, which, noting the increasingly contested competitive advantage of the United States and its armed forces, declared the return of great power competition. In the Indo-Pacific, China's continued rise (and its considerable naval expansion) and a resurgent Russia's attempt to undermine North Atlantic Treaty Organization unity have challenged the global maritime primacy the U.S. Navy has enjoyed since the Cold War.

- Lessons learned from the collisions of USS *Fitzgerald* with the Philippine-flagged container ship ACX *Crystal* south of Tokyo Bay and, two months later, of USS *John S. McCain* with the Liberian-flagged tanker *Alnic MC* near the Strait of Malacca. These tragedies prompted the Navy to produce *Comprehensive Review of Recent Surface Force Incidents*, released in November 2017, which recommends significant actions pertaining to the training, operating, and equipping of surface ships and crews throughout the force.

- The novel coronavirus (COVID-19) pandemic, with cases first reported in China in December 2019 before spreading to more than 180 nations with tens of millions falling ill worldwide. This highly contagious—and deadly—illness has had profound impacts on societies, economies, and daily life throughout the world. As the United States grappled with this serious health crisis, our Navy began learning how to persist and operate globally in the face of this pandemic.

- Increased employment of maritime forces via joint and combined operations. Joint force commanders and their maritime components are involved in all manner of operations at sea and ashore. With this involvement comes a growing appreciation for coordination and cooperation with interagency players as well as nongovernmental organizations—both international and domestic. It has become clear that a "whole of government" and "whole of nation" approach is needed to address—and solve—today's security-related challenges. This realization extends to the coordinated efforts of allies, friends, and partners as well. Command at sea is embedded in this seascape.

- The continuing evolution of the fleet itself. In addition to improved baselines for cruiser-destroyer units enabling ballistic missile defense, newer classes have emerged. These include the littoral combat ship classes *Freedom* and *Independence*, the *Virginia* nuclear-powered attack submarines, as well as the F-35 Joint Strike Fighter variants and the P-8 maritime patrol aircraft—all representing improvement in combat capability (and in some cases stealth technology). Amid these new classes of aircraft and vessels, unmanned systems are now being introduced across undersea, surface, and air domains. Decommissionings have naturally accompanied these modernizations, seeing the end of service for several classes, including the guided-missile frigate FFG-7 *Oliver Hazard Perry* class. The fleet of ships and submarines is now below 300 from a high of around 590 in the late 1980s.

- The service of women in not only all Navy ships but also in command of ships, strike groups, numbered fleets, and submarines.

- The continuing growth of our fleet's bandwidth, leveraging netted systems, web-based services, and reach-back capabilities for planning, maintenance, data processing, afloat and ashore logistics, and communications/information/intelligence functions.

- The rising value of public affairs and strategic communications in the age of social media as well as the need for communications

discipline—both as a service and as individuals—as we welcome
a generation of sailors who have been raised as digital natives.
- In sum, the capacity to move and share information, which continues to increase by orders of magnitude.

The world moves on, and so there is much to revise in this edition,
but the continuing thread throughout all seven editions of *Command
at Sea* remains simply this: command remains the absolute heart of the
Navy, and whether you are involved in command of a ship, submarine,
or aircraft squadron, there are special challenges and rewards associated
with every aspect of that command.

Our hope is simply to continue the work begun by Captain Cope
more than half a century ago, bringing to this task the collected lessons
of the many superb officers who have worked on *Command at Sea* in the
intervening years, particularly Vice Admiral William P. Mack, USN
(Ret.), who was the lead author of several previous editions. In addition
to the wisdom already contained in *Command at Sea*, we have tried to add
contemporary lessons from today's Navy operating at sea, and we are deeply
grateful for Captain Jeff Heames and Captain Tom Ogden, who not only
provided lessons from their recently successful command tours but also
served as superb writing partners in their own right as they helped bring
this edition of *Command at Sea* to life. Like anyone else who has served at
sea, we have been particularly influenced by and must acknowledge several exceptional commanding officers under whom we have individually
been privileged to serve. Collectively, they include Captain Fritz Gaylord,
USN (Ret.), commanding officer (CO) in *Hewitt* (DD-966); Rear Admiral Ted Lockhart, USN (Ret.), captain in *Valley Forge* (CG-50); Captain
Larry Eddingfield, USN (Ret.), CO in *Antietam* (CG-54); and Admiral
Walter F. Doran, USN (Ret.), CO in *DeWert* (FFG-45). Among many
others, they stand out in their sharing of ideas and the setting of a fine
example in command at sea. We would also like to thank several serving
(and retired) flag and commanding officers for their thoughts and contributions on the subject of command at sea, including Admiral (Ret.) Sam
Locklear, Vice Admiral (Ret.) Thomas Kilcline, Vice Admiral (Ret.)
Derwood Curtis, Vice Admiral (Ret.) John Bird, Vice Admiral (Ret.)

Kevin Green, Vice Admiral Gene Black, Vice Admiral Lisa Franchetti, Vice Admiral John Nowell, and Rear Admiral (Ret.) Frank Drennan. It goes without saying that any errors of fact or judgment are ours alone.

An editorial note: A good bit of this seventh edition is still true to the earlier editions, and thus the reader will occasionally find the use of strictly masculine pronouns. Where these appear, it should be understood that they refer to both the men and women serving so well today in virtually all the warships of the U.S. Navy. In all the new and revised sections of the work, an effort has been made to refer to both genders, which is clearly appropriate in today's Navy.

Lastly, we would like to acknowledge the help and support of our families in this project, particularly three fine officers (two of whom have served as naval commanding officers during their distinguished careers): Colonel P. G. Stavridis, USMC (Ret.); Captain R. A. Hall, USN (Ret.); and Commander William H. Girrier, USNR (Ret.). To them, and to their generation of outstanding naval officers, we dedicate this volume.

In the end, we all know that command at sea is an art and that it is not fully learned by reading books such as this one. Rather, it is an art built on knowledge, study, and the practice of a great and important profession. We close therefore with the hope that this small volume may continue to be of help to all who accept the responsibility and accountability of command at sea in the ships, submarines, and aircraft squadrons of the twenty-first-century U.S. Navy.

—ADM JAMES STAVRIDIS, USN (RET.)
RADM ROBERT GIRRIER, USN (RET.)
RADM FRED KACHER, USN

Preface to the
First Edition

Every young officer who is worth his salt looks forward eagerly to his first command, whether it be a destroyer, a minesweeper, a submarine, a PT, or an auxiliary. There is a tremendous thrill in taking over your first ship. She is your ship—all yours—but the way to success is dotted with pitfalls for the unwary, the careless, and the diffident. From the moment you, as the new skipper, step aboard, you are on trial before your officers and men. Responsibility for the ship as well as for the crew is yours.

Particularly in time of war, when promotion is rapid and officers with comparatively little experience must frequently assume command, it is important that the officer have as complete an understanding as possible of the special duties and tasks with which he will be faced—the duties of both task force and independent naval operations, and the responsibility of maintaining a happy and efficient ship.

The officer with many years of sea experience has been afforded the opportunity to observe various commanding officers. Perhaps unconsciously he has thought to himself, "If I were skipper I would do it this way," and when command comes to him he has already made definite plans regarding the course he intends to follow. The inexperienced junior officer getting his first command often wishes that such opportunities had been afforded him.

There is no sure formula for success as a commanding officer. Some officers are natural leaders; others are not. Some have had the benefit of a long and good background of experience under competent commanding officers that others have not enjoyed. Some make mistakes, but it must be remembered that mistakes are greatly magnified if committed a second or third time, for one is expected to profit by mistakes.

In these pages, I have drawn from my experience and from the experience of others to present as fully and as specifically as possible the situation that will confront you as a commanding officer of your ship, and to suggest solutions to the problems which you will inevitably face.

—CAPT HARLEY F. COPE, USN

1

Taking Command

The Captain carried them all.
For him, there was no fixed watch, no time set aside
when he was free to relax and, if he could, to sleep.
He was strong, calm, uncomplaining, and wonderfully
dependable. That was the sort of captain to have.

—Nicholas Monsarrat, *The Cruel Sea*

Command at Sea

The experience of command of a ship at sea is unforgettable; it is without parallel or equal. The responsibility is heavy, but the rewards—which become embedded in the very fabric of your life—are priceless. The captain of the U.S. Navy warship stands as part of a long, unbroken line that stretches from the very founders of the Continental Navy through the great captains of America's wars at sea and on to the next generation of twenty-first-century leaders.

U.S. Navy Regulations, fully updated last in 1990, states that "the responsibility of the commanding officer for his or her command is absolute" and that "the authority of the commanding officer is commensurate with his or her responsibility." These are simple, clear, binding statements. No amount of explanation can alter their placement of ultimate responsibility—whether for success or failure—squarely on the shoulders of the captain in command.

In this respect, although the size of a ship may be important as a measure of her capability, durability, and endurance, the smallest mine countermeasure ship or coastal patrol boat is equal to the largest aircraft carrier in terms of responsibility and reward. The commanding officers (COs) of both are "captains," regardless of the number of stripes they wear on their sleeves. Each must ensure the safety of the ship and crew as well as the accomplishment of all assigned missions. Likewise, the skipper of an aircraft squadron assumes full and complete responsibility for the performance of a command at sea. *Navy Regulations*, in its chapter addressing COs (0801), continues, "In addition to commanding officers, the provisions of this chapter shall apply, where pertinent, to aircraft commanders, officers in charge (including warrant officers and petty officers when so detailed) and those persons standing the command duty."

Some thoughts from serving type commanders, from both Commander Naval Air Forces and Commander Naval Surface Forces, who have seen scores of commanding officers lead their ships through myriad challenges, provide valuable insight into what makes a successful CO.

Fig. 1-1. Taking command is a great moment for any officer.

Good COs can successfully translate policies to each individual in their command. They take care of their crew's well-being, ensuring they attend the right professional schools, are trained properly for their jobs, and take time for leave as appropriate. They provide opportunities and a development path for their crew members. They are the chief morale officer for their shipmates and their families, too. A good CO builds cohesion, afloat and ashore. Part of professional growth is the process of instilling high standards. Successful COs clearly articulate and enforce these standards in all areas: personal conduct, professional performance, material readiness, rigorous training, and, especially, crisp execution. They teach customs and traditions. Successful COs follow up, inspect, and hold crew members accountable in a disciplined manner. They provide feedback up and down the chain of command.

As COs become more senior, commanding larger vessels with crews from 2,500 to 3,000 personnel, their scope of responsibility naturally increases. More seasoned subordinates will serve in these larger ships, and successful COs adjust their leadership style to this reality. The most successful COs increasingly empower their subordinates as the size of their command grows. This requires good communication skills and the ability to connect in a broad context with the whole command as well as with each specific department and division. Successful COs are true professional experts within their commands—they lead from the air, and they lead from the bridge. They continuously teach and mentor. The crew must see this, as it reinforces the CO's credibility. Good COs are "out and about" as a matter of routine. They know their ship, and they know the environment. The crew will see this too, and this "full contact" approach will build trust.

Certain red flags mark an unsuccessful CO's behavior and consistently signal trouble. COs who fail to delegate responsibility and hold individuals accountable, or those who lead solely from their staterooms via a continuous stream of emails, will almost certainly flounder. When dialog between the CO and the crew becomes constrained, failure looms. Poor material readiness, low cleanliness standards, and lack of attention in the correction of deficiencies are telltale signs of a command's failing health. In rare instances, COs who fall short of the high standards expected of them in terms of personal integrity and individual conduct bring about their own failure while in command.

To achieve success in command, the captain must work through those whom he or she leads; little can be accomplished alone, no matter how brilliant one's individual talents. Admiral Chester Nimitz, on the occasion of a call by several of his captains, said, "Commanding a ship is the simplest task in the world, even if at times it seems complicated. A captain has only to pick good courses of action and to stick to them no matter what. If he is good and generally makes good decisions, his crew will cover for him if he fails occasionally. If he is bad, this fact will soon be known, and he must be removed with the speed of light."

The successful commanding officer, then, must learn to be as one with his or her wardroom and crew and to truly know their strengths and weaknesses, yet at the same time, he or she must remain above and apart. This unique relationship has been the subject of study and story for centuries. It changes, yet it remains timeless. It is a skill to be mastered in turn by each commander.

Two days prior to the Battle of Java Sea, in which HMS *Exeter* would be sunk in the dark early days of World War II in the Pacific, her commanding officer, Captain O. L. Gordon, Royal Navy, was having a late-evening drink at a Surabaya hotel with a group of young British and American junior officers. One of the American officers asked him how he felt about going to sea the next morning to meet the approaching Japanese naval force. Gordon knew that his ship would have little chance of surviving, but he smiled anyway as he said, "I would not trade all the Queen's jewels for the privilege of commanding *Exeter* tomorrow. I have the finest group of men ever to man a ship of war. They will not fail me, and they know I will not fail my Sovereign. We may not survive, but we will leave our mark." When the battle began, the gigantic battle ensign flown by the ship was an inspiration to the Allied ships that accompanied her. They knew she would be commanded well and therefore would fight well.

Even the realm of literature is full of allusion to the art of command. "The Prestige, Privilege, and Burden of Command," perhaps the best-known and most frequently quoted commentary on command at sea, was written by Joseph Conrad, who had himself commanded at sea as a merchant sailor:

Only a seaman realizes to what extent an entire ship reflects the personality and ability of one individual, her Commanding Officer. To a landsman this is not understandable, and sometimes it is even difficult for us to comprehend—but it is so.

A ship at sea is a distant world in herself and in consideration of the protracted and distant operations of the fleet units the Navy must place great power, responsibility and trust in the hands of those leaders chosen for command.

In each ship there is one man who, in the hour of emergency or peril at sea, can turn to no other man. There is one who alone is ultimately responsible for the safe navigation, engineering performance, accurate gunfiring and morale of his ship. He is the Commanding Officer. He is the ship.

This is the most difficult and demanding assignment in the Navy. There is not an instant during his tour of duty as Commanding Officer that he can escape the grasp of command responsibility. His privileges in view of his obligations are most ludicrously small; nevertheless command is the spur which has given the Navy its great leaders.

It is a duty which most richly deserves the highest, time-honored title of the seafaring world—"CAPTAIN."

Conrad's thoughts on command are echoed by one of fiction's great captains, Jack Aubrey, in Patrick O'Brian's superb series of novels about the nineteenth-century Royal Navy. Captain Aubrey's command philosophy is stated in a few sentences that are worth bearing in mind: "His idea of a crack ship was one with a strong, highly-skilled crew that could out-maneuver and then outshoot the opponent, a taut but happy ship, an efficient man-of-war—in short a ship that was likely to win at any reasonable odds."

A great deal has been written about command at sea over the years, but perhaps the thought that best sums up this most fulfilling assignment comes from another classic of sea literature, *The Caine Mutiny*. Herman Wouk's immortal character Lieutenant Keefer expressed it well: "You can't understand command till you've had it." And once you have had command, you are changed forever, marked as one who has stood in the long line of captains at sea.

The Accountability of Command

In navies in general, and in the U.S. Navy in particular, strict accountability is an integral part of command. Not even the profession of medicine embraces the absolute accountability found at sea. A doctor may lose a patient under trying circumstances and continue to practice, but a naval officer seldom has the opportunity to hazard a second ship.

There have been, at times, those who question the strict and undeviating application of accountability in the Navy, but those who have been to sea have always closed ranks against the doubters. In 1952, for example, the destroyer *Hobson* collided with the aircraft carrier *Melbourne* during night flight operations. Damage was extensive, and the loss of life was heavy. There were extenuating circumstances, but in May 1952 the *Wall Street Journal*, in a frequently quoted discussion of the disaster, concluded, "On the sea, there is a tradition older than the traditions of the country itself—it is the tradition that with responsibility goes authority and with them both goes accountability. It is cruel, this accountability of good and well-intentioned men. But the choice is that or an end to responsibility and finally, as the cruel sea has taught, an end to the confidence and trust in the men who lead. For men will not long trust leaders who feel themselves beyond accountability for what they do."

The enormous significance of this responsibility and accountability for the lives and careers of others—and often the outcome of great issues as well—is the reason for the liberality of orders to officers commanding ships of the U.S. Navy. The inexperienced officer may erroneously take this liberality to reflect vagueness or indecision on the part of superiors. Nothing could be further from the truth. It is provided to give the commander the flexibility necessary to carry out his or her orders.

One incident in the 1970s led ultimately to a reinforcement of the doctrine of the absolute accountability of command. The incident began with the collision of USS *Belknap* and USS *John F. Kennedy*, in which *Belknap* lost eight men and suffered $100 million in damages. The tragic results of the collision can be seen in the accompanying photographs.

The court-martial that followed caused many naval officers to reconsider the issues surrounding accountability of commanding officers. The Chief of Naval Operations (CNO), Admiral J. L. Holloway III, issued a

Fig. 1-2. The ultimate arena of responsibility, collision at sea. USS *John F. Kennedy*, shown here shortly after her collision with USS *Belknap*, suffered relatively little damage.

Fig. 1-3. *Belknap* suffered heavy damage and many casualties in her collision with *John F. Kennedy*. Her commanding officer was found to be responsible.

memorandum dated 2 October 1976 discussing the entire issue. This document, which sets forth the circumstances of the collision and of the consequent administrative and judicial processes, is presented in appendix 5.

In subsequent years, several additional cases of groundings, collisions, and fires at sea have further emphasized the complete accountability of the commanding officer for the actions of the ship. Of note in this regard—and worth reviewing with the wardroom on occasion—are the grounding of USS *Spruance* in the Caribbean in 1989, the collision of

USS *Kinkaid* with a merchant tanker in the Straits of Malacca in 1991, the collision of the aircraft carrier USS *Theodore Roosevelt* with the cruiser *Leyte Gulf* in 1997, the fire aboard the aircraft carrier USS *George Washington* in 2008, the hard grounding of the cruiser *Port Royal* in 2009, and the collisions involving USS *Fitzgerald* and USS *John S. McCain* in 2017. In each case—as well as in other instances of the mishandling of ships at sea—the doctrine of full accountability was strongly enforced in the U.S. Navy, and it will continue to stand at the very heart of command at sea.

Fig. 1-4. USS *Fitzgerald* returns to Yokosuka, Japan, after suffering heavy damage to her starboard side due to a collision with motor vessel *ACX Crystal*.

Fig. 1-5. USS *John S. McCain*, in a collision with motor vessel *Alnic MC*, suffered damage to her port side, resulting in the death of ten sailors.

The Independence of the Commander

Traditionally, American commanding officers have been directed to accomplish missions without being told specifically *how* to do so. Occasionally they may be referred to doctrine or example about how their tasks might be performed or how they have been carried out in the past. The choice of action, however, remains theirs to make; it is required only that their methods intelligently support the objectives of command.

In recent years, however, this traditional independence has been modified in practice. The issue today is not too much liberality, but rather a growing tendency of high command to exercise control in great detail. Several factors have contributed to this trend. First, command in the present-day atmosphere of worldwide political unrest requires extraordinary sensitivity to an extremely complex web of global relationships. The post–Cold War world has complicated the missions undertaken by individual ships, submarines, and aircraft squadrons. Second, the ability of global media organizations to place the spotlight on naval operations has increased exponentially over the past few years and will continue to do so. With network and cable news flying overhead, and the wire services constantly requesting and obtaining permission to visit U.S. Navy warships at sea, the latitude of the CO to act independently has been proscribed simply as a result of the unrelenting glare of publicity. Third, and most significantly, technological advances have given the entire chain of command the ability to track and direct virtually every aspect of naval operations at sea.

In this sense, technology has flattened the chain of command. The capabilities of our billion-dollar Aegis destroyers and cruisers illustrate this point more fully. A ballistic missile defense (BMD)–capable ship can simultaneously be involved at the tactical, operational, and strategic levels of warfare: tactically employed in a local anti-surface, anti-submarine, or anti-air warfare mission; operationally engaged in a theater missile defense mission; and strategically included as part of a multi–time zone BMD fire control system providing national defense to our homeland. Along with these high-tech capabilities is the need to synchronize and coordinate their employment. Coordination requires connectivity at multiple levels of command, and it should come as no surprise that providing missile defense to cities and population centers will invite senior-level scrutiny. Likewise, an amphibious ship—for example one engaged in humanitarian assistance and disaster response efforts at one moment and then rapidly shifting to duties as an afloat forward staging base for a joint task force elsewhere in a given theater—can operate astride a confluence of tactical, operational, and strategic missions.

In hand with the increased capability that technology brings is a complementary capacity for assistance via reach-back mechanisms that leverage staff expertise and compiled data from across the globe. This can be tremendously powerful, but also overwhelming if not managed properly. Notwithstanding all the "help" from outside sources, an extraordinary level of responsibility remains on the shoulders of the captain. The CO will make the decision whether to fire in an individual engagement; when and how to tactically execute boardings at sea; when and how to undertake a medical evacuation—indeed, the time, method, and ultimate execution of a thousand discrete decisions remain the responsibility of the captain. In most cases, higher authority will respect the judgment of the captain at the scene, and there is little likelihood of that changing in the near future.

Orders to Command

The day you receive orders to take command of a U.S. Navy warship or squadron will be a memorable one. You will probably sit back in your chair and reflect on the challenges and rewards that lie ahead. Normally, a considerable "pipeline" of training will precede your assumption of command, including a leadership course, training in your community (surface or submarine prospective commanding officer's course or refresher flight training), tactical study on the appropriate coast at either Tactical Training Group Atlantic or Pacific, and time with our evolving warfare centers of excellence if possible.

Once you have orders in hand, you should contact your relief to arrange your schedule and work out a turnover plan. Your initial contact is normally a letter, phone call, or email and should include your personal plans: when you will move your family, your housing plans in the homeport, the date you would like to report, and so forth. The officer you are relieving will work with you to decide on an appropriate plan for the turnover and a change of command date.

Bear in mind that the preparations for the turnover, the change of command, and the details associated with each are almost entirely under the direction of the incumbent commanding officer. Unless there is an overriding reason you cannot comply with the incumbent's wishes, you should accept them.

Once these matters have been settled, both officers can then begin preparations for the change of command. Appendix 1 includes material you will find helpful.

Preparations for Change of Command

Prior to reporting to your new command, and after having looked at the command's website, which in most cases includes considerable background information, it is appropriate to ask the current CO to send you a "care package" with basic information about the ship, submarine, or squadron. The key here is not to generate new work for the command, but rather to obtain "on the shelf" publications and products that will prepare you to hit the deckplates running. The following are some of the items you might find useful to review before stepping aboard to begin turnover:

- A ship's social roster of both officers and chiefs. Try to learn their names before you report and have a solid understanding of responsibilities and the chain of command. Some commands will put together a book with photos and biographies of the key leaders in the ship. This is very helpful, but it should be something voluntarily provided.
- A damage control handbook for the command.
- A copy of the operating schedule, both short and long range. This will be classified, so it should be sent to your current command or a pipeline school for your review.
- Copies of recent issues of the ship's newsletter and ombudsman helpline.
- An engineering handbook.
- CO's battle orders, standing orders, typical set of night orders, engineering orders, and any standard tactical maneuvering doctrine.

(Some of these may be classified but can still be forwarded via appropriate electronic means to your current duty station.) This applies to squadrons as well as ships and submarines.
- Anything else the incumbent thinks might be useful.

Navy Regulations, chapter 8, article 0807, and appropriate type commanders' instructions provide guidance for the change of command process. *Navy Regulations* requires that both officers inspect the ship, exercise the crew at general quarters and general drills, discuss any defects that may be present, and transfer all unexecuted orders, official correspondence, and information concerning the command and its personnel. Specific requirements include a current audit of the post office, turnover of magazine and other keys, and an inventory and audit of registered publications. The officer being relieved must complete and sign fitness reports, logs, books, journals, and other required documents. Each type commander requires some augmentation or variation in these basic procedures.

Generally, all of these requirements can be met on a conventionally powered vessel in about five days, regardless of the ship's employment. A relatively standard procedure in the fleet today is to have the prospective CO arrive on a Monday and take command with appropriate ceremony on Friday.

The turnover period should be long enough to permit the new commander to determine the combat readiness of the ship, primarily by observing appropriate general drills. Of particular importance is the damage control readiness of the organization, which is best ascertained by observing the efforts of the damage control training team, which should be well led by the executive officer (XO) and capable of conducting realistic, stressful drills "within the lifelines." Another key indicator of an efficient ship is the readiness and performance of the navigation team. Focus specifically on the ability to navigate and on damage control readiness; almost everything else can be quickly brought up to the mark if necessary.

As the relieving officer, you should carefully review the handling characteristics of the ship with the previous CO. Ask how she accelerates and handles in various sea states. If you are not familiar with the ship type from previous assignments, you will have to take much of this information on faith until you gain experience. It will be helpful to review some of the literature on your ship class, both in recent *Proceedings* articles and in the appropriate sections of the classic *Naval Shiphandling*.

Assuming you have a full five days for the turnover, you can augment the basics of shiphandling, navigation, and damage control. The next issue for a new commanding officer is the state of the combat system and the engineering plant. Both are critical components of your command's ability to fight and win at sea. Next in priority is a careful review of the supply status of the command. Spend half a day with each of your department heads—whether you are taking command of a ship, submarine, or squadron—and try to gauge the readiness, morale, cleanliness, and general state of their department. Each department head will probably give you a binder full of turnover information, from the biographies of the officers and chiefs to the inventory of critical bulkhead-mounted spares. Read the binder in the evening or after you assume command, and spend your turnover week walking through the hangars or on the deckplates getting to know your people.

The following are some additional items to concern yourself with *after* you have ascertained the navigation, damage control, supply, engineering, and combat systems status of your command:

- Read the fleet, type, and unit commander's instructions.
- Start the process for updating your security clearance, if this has not already been done.
- Forward a photograph and a short biography to the chief of naval information. This is in addition to the photo and biography required for the Naval Military Personnel Command.
- Review the last administrative inspection checklist; the last material, supply, and medical inspection checklists; the last engineering assessment checklists; the naval technical proficiency inspection results; and—for nuclear-powered ships—the recent Operational Reactor Safeguards Examination results. For a squadron, review the similarly key material and corrosion inspection results. Focus on trends.

- Study the ship's organization, the ship's orders, and the type commander's orders and manuals. Hopefully, you've already done this with your "read-ahead" package and during the pipeline training.
- Review financial areas, such as the wardroom mess and any small accounts. Trouble can often lurk here.
- Review the ship's classified files and methods of handling such items. A thorough review of all these areas is required by regulations. Ensure that it is complete and accurate by spot-checking a few areas.
- Review the status of the Maintenance and Material Management and Personnel Qualification Standards programs. Accompany your predecessor or the XO on several spot checks of both programs. You will make an instant statement about your standards with your comments during your first few spot checks, which should wait until *after* you take command.
- Review in detail the procedures associated with weapons release authority and the location and use of all firing keys in your combat system.

The key throughout the relieving process is remembering that you are being shown the ship by your predecessor. This is not the time or place to begin putting your own ideas, philosophies, or standards in place. There will be plenty of opportunity for that—after the change of command.

During the relieving process you should be alert, interested, and noncommittal. The crew will be observing you intently for the least reaction, and word will fly through the command about "the new skipper." Stay on an even keel throughout the turnover process, and politely take everything in—taking notes as required for follow-up after you've relieved.

Report of Transfer of Command

Navy Regulations requires that a letter report of the routine change of command be prepared and signed by the officer relieved and endorsed by the individual relieving. This letter should be addressed to your immediate superior, with copies sent to the CNO and others in the chain of command.

Give this letter report your careful attention. Be sure that all substantial deficiencies affecting the operational readiness and safety of the ship are listed. Key problems should be noted, but it is certainly not expected that all minor deficiencies will be listed. Use your professional judgment.

Bear in mind that the letter will immediately become a high-priority, high-visibility "to do" list for your entire chain of command. Be judicious in your comments, and recognize that you are not an inspector, but rather the new team captain. With that in mind, draft the letter accordingly.

The Change of Command Ceremony

Now that all examinations and inspections are complete, you are ready to take part in the traditional ceremony of the change of command. For your part, you should prepare a copy of your orders reduced to the most basic language, such as the following:

From: Chief of Naval Personnel
To: Commander John Paul Jones
Subject: Relief of Command

Proceed to the port in which USS *Stockdale* (DDG 106) is located and report as relief for the Commanding Officer.

You will also be expected to make *extremely brief* remarks upon assumption of command. The traditional formula is no more than two to three minutes in length and includes an acknowledgment of key guests and family members, a word of thanks to the crew for their hard work in preparing for and executing the change of command, a complimentary remark about your predecessor, and an enthusiastic comment about future operations with the command. Anything longer is simply not appropriate. This is the day for the outgoing CO to hold center stage. Your time will come all too soon.

Navy Regulations provides that at the time of turning over command, all hands should be mustered, that the officer about to be relieved shall read the orders of detachment and formally turn command to the successor, and that this officer should then read the orders in turn and assume command.

This is a simple and straightforward requirement. Prior to World War II it was usually carried out strictly as set forth with the simplest of ceremonies. Guests were seldom, if ever, invited, and usually the unit commander attended. Since the war, however, it has become customary to invite numerous civilian guests, family members, the chain of command, and the commanding officers of all ships present. The arrangements are entirely the prerogative of the incumbent CO, who schedules the ceremony, issues the invitations, and announces the time and place of the change of command. The oncoming CO merely sends an invitation list to the incumbent.

There is a growing trend in the fleet today to return to the simpler ceremonies of the past. This is particularly true when the ship's schedule is compressed, and the effort of staging an elaborate change of command ceremony does not fit well with the ship's schedule. This is completely a matter to be decided by the outgoing CO. There is a wonderful simplicity and elegance that goes with an at-sea change of command, which involves simply the ship, captain, and crew. Many officers feel that there is no better place to take command than on the rolling deck of a ship at sea.

A good reference on the entire process of the change of command is *Naval Ceremonies, Customs, and Traditions*, published by Naval Institute Press. In general, a change of command will be a full-dress affair, held in a dignified and ceremonious fashion. It is very much an all-hands evolution; all members of the crew not actually on watch should attend. The officers and enlisted personnel should be stationed, if possible, so that they and the two commanding officers are facing each other. The ceremony was established so that the outgoing commander could bid farewell to all of the officers and sailors attached to the crew.

The basic change of command ceremony and the layout of the ceremonial area are presented in appendix 2.

Courtesies Due a Relieved Commanding Officer

Remember that *Navy Regulations* provides that the officer relieved, although without official authority in the command from the moment of relief, is still entitled to all ceremonies and distinctions accorded while in command until actual departure from the ship, submarine, or squadron.

When departing, the outgoing CO should be given side honors appropriate to a commanding officer and should be offered the use of the gig. Some ships use officers and chiefs as side boys, a remnant of times past when officers rowed their old captain ashore.

The officer relieved should make every effort to depart promptly and completely. If possible, most or all of his or her baggage should be disembarked before the ceremony.

Upon Taking Command

When the relieved commanding officer and the guests have departed, your real work begins. The first requirement, once again—as it will always be—is to ensure that the ship and her crew are in safe condition and able to perform as required. There are also administrative matters to take care of, including the issuance of any new orders; new standing night orders or battle orders may be required.

The next item of business will be making calls. An officer assuming command shall, at the first opportunity thereafter, make an official visit to the senior to whom he or she has reported for duty. The circumstances of this call vary widely, depending on the ship's schedule, location, and the relationship with the senior. For a ship or submarine commanding officer, this typically will involve a call on the squadron commander. For the skipper of an aviation squadron, this will mean a visit to the commander of the air wing. Follow the traditions of your area, and don't hesitate to call the chief of staff for the squadron or the deputy commander of the air wing to obtain guidance. In general, you should make an appointment to pay a call the week following your assumption of command. Be prepared to give your new boss an assessment of your command, remembering that you were aboard not as an inspector, but as the new team captain. Don't ever portray the officer you have relieved in a bad light or complain about any aspect of your new command—but be honest in evaluating capabilities and readiness. If there are problems, state them and indicate your plan to improve them to standards. Your new senior will probably take the opportunity to give you a few words about squadron or air group philosophy, which will be very helpful.

You should also drop by the operations shop at the squadron or air wing as well as pay a courtesy call on the first flag officer in your chain of command; this will normally be the "group commander"—typically either the carrier strike group or expeditionary strike group commander.

It is a good idea to call on the senior officer present afloat (SOPA) as well. For example, if you are a destroyer captain tied up at a pier, the pier SOPA will normally be a cruiser skipper, and you should drop by for a cup of coffee and present your respects. In general, whenever your ship ties up at a pier in homeport you should see the pier SOPA; if at a naval station outside of homeport, it is customary to call on the CO of the station. If your ship ties up at a shipyard for repairs or alongside a tender, a call on the CO is also appropriate. Check local SOPA regulations for specifics.

Philosophy of Command

Throughout long years of preparation for command, every naval officer studies leadership techniques, observes senior officers in command, and gradually formulates certain thoughts and ideas concerning the proper way to lead. You should now be eager to put those ideas to the test of practice as a commanding officer. Your officers and sailors are waiting to find out what your policies are and how you will communicate your ideas to them.

This can be done in several ways. Some simply allow the passage of time and events to reveal their philosophies and expectations. They never openly define them. Many successful commanders have taken this path, particularly those not skilled in communications, either written or verbal. Most COs, however, have found it better to establish a quick rapport with their officers and sailors by addressing them directly and as soon as practicable. This initial address need not be long, formal, or all-inclusive, but it should be carefully prepared, and it should include the most important elements of command.

What are these elements? Our first source is Title 10 of the U.S. Code—the basic law governing the U.S. military. In it, the basic elements of American command philosophy are clearly stated: "Commanding officers and others in authority in the naval service are required to show in themselves a good example of virtue, honor, patriotism, and subordination. They will be vigilant in inspecting the conduct of all persons, they will guard against and suppress dissolute and immoral practices according to regulations. They will take all necessary and proper measures under the laws, regulations, and customs to promote and safeguard the morale, physical well being, and general welfare of the officers and enlisted personnel under their command."

These requirements are law. You must meet them all. Additional guidance is spelled out in greater detail in *Navy Regulations*, chapter 8 in particular. The articles in this chapter delve into specific requirements: Commanding Officers in General (section 1); Commanding Officers Afloat (section 2); and Special Circumstances (section 3). These articles are a must-read, in that they bring great clarity to what is expected of a CO. They should help to *inform* your command philosophy.

There are also several keys to command philosophy that have stood the test of time quite well and should be considered as you assume your command. They are drawn from a wide range of leaders at sea, from Admiral Lord Nelson to Admiral Arleigh Burke. Not all may fit your command style, but you should think about each idea and consider how it might fit into your individual philosophy of command.

The first key is the simplest: you must take care of your people. Every crew will very quickly sense the difference between a commanding officer who doesn't put the welfare of the crew at the top of the command's priorities and one who does. Mission accomplishment is the reason your command exists, but the best way of ensuring that you accomplish the mission—from a command perspective—is by taking care of your people. If you take care of your people, you will accomplish the mission. It really is that simple.

Taking care of your people involves a wide variety of actions on the part of a CO, including taking an active interest in every aspect of professional development, training, safety, advancements, messing, berthing, and recreation. Admiral Lord Nelson was the first and strongest proponent of this approach. His crews—in a time of brutality, squalor, and constant deprivation—were trained, advanced, well cared for, and properly fed. His concern for the sailors was famous throughout the fleet. And his ships, although tautly run, were happy and invariably triumphed in battle. Admiral Ernest King—one of the toughest and most demanding officers in U.S. naval history—was likewise well known for helping his officers and crew members in every way, even years after they had left his command. Take a similar and sincere approach to your crew, and your command will be similarly successful.

The second great key to command is likewise a simple one: you must know your command. This is an increasingly important requirement, reflecting the increased complexity inherent in command of a modern Aegis destroyer, a large amphibious or littoral combat ship, a *Seawolf-* or *Virginia*-class submarine, or a squadron of F/A-18E/F or Joint Strike Fighter aircraft. Fifty years ago, an entire warship was less complicated than today's propulsion plant, airborne radar, or sonar suite.

In order to most fully understand your command, you will build on the general principles of science and engineering you studied in school. Throughout the long Navy pipeline of schools leading to command, you will have had ample opportunity to learn about the details of your command. Take full advantage of that education. Even after you arrive on your ship, you should have a program in place that educates you (and other officers and chiefs) in the technical aspects of the command. Some COs ask to look at a technical manual each week; others arrange lectures in the wardroom; and some spend a week focusing on each department, learning week by week the complexities of their ship, submarine, or aircraft. If you are to be the best warfighter in your command, you must be the systems expert as well. Whatever your leadership style, don't slight this requirement. Some of the Navy's greatest innovators have also been great leaders—Admiral Bradley Fiske, Assistant Secretary of the Navy Theodore Roosevelt—who understood the importance of knowledge in command. Roosevelt, in an address before the 1892 graduating class of the Naval Academy, reminded the new officers, "It cannot be too often repeated that in modern war, the chief factor in achieving triumph is what has been done in the way of thorough organization and training before the beginning of war."

Related to this is the importance of ensuring that others in the ship are also knowledgeable of the command's systems. If you have shown your own interest in a thorough knowledge of the command and have made it plain to your officers and sailors that you expect the same from them, you will find that they will respond eagerly. This means hard work:

arranging classes, making time available, and providing paths of advancement and qualification for all officers and sailors. But the rewards will be great—both for them and for you.

The third key is embedded in your own character. You must be loyal, honest, and ethical in all your dealings, both private and public. Let it be known that you expect honesty at all times, both up and down the chain of command. Never tolerate the covering up of unsavory facts—of trying to "fog one by," as one CNO used to say. Require that all reports be honest and thorough.

A good model to follow can be found in the words attributed to John Paul Jones and memorized by generations of midshipmen:

> It is by no means enough that an officer of the Navy be a capable mariner. He must be that, of course, but also a great deal more. He should be as well a gentleman of liberal education, refined manners, punctilious courtesy, and the nicest sense of personal honor.
>
> He should be the soul of tact, patience, justice, firmness, and charity. No meritorious act of a subordinate should escape his attention or be left to pass without its reward, even if the reward is only a word of approval. Conversely, he should not be blind to a single fault in any subordinate, though at the same time, he should be quick and unfailing to distinguish error from malice, thoughtlessness from incompetency, and well meant shortcoming from heedless or stupid blunder.
>
> In one word, every commander should keep constantly before him the great truth, that to be well obeyed, he must be perfectly esteemed.

All who observe you in command should draw the conclusion that you are a patient leader. Set the highest of standards, but recognize that not everyone will be able to attain perfection, especially on the first try. Virtually everyone in your crew will want to work hard and perform well; it is up to you and your chain of command to give them the opportunity and motive for doing so. Swearing and outbursts of temper are not acceptable methods of correcting behavior. Giving in to the temptation to throw a fit will simply add more confusion to a situation that is already unacceptable. Your job is to bring order out of chaos, not to create more disorder. Firm direction with continuous follow-up will solve almost any problem.

A good commanding officer must understand human nature and the motivation of sailors. You must be able to reconcile the differences between subordinates of strong character so that they cooperate rather than collide. Your personal demeanor must radiate energy; you must appear to be strongly determined to achieve the goals you set for your command. You must electrify your subordinates, yet remain personally cool while doing so.

The fourth key to command philosophy is the tone of the command. Even the smallest ship or squadron undergoing the most demanding employment can maintain an excellent tone. The first thing contributing to a good tone is appearance. Let your crew know that you want a combat-ready command, clean at all times, and you will get it. Frequent and thorough sweep-downs will do more to keep up everyday appearances than excessive painting and scrubbing and will generate pride in those doing the work. Again, most sailors understand that you learn a great deal about a ship from the appearance of the ship's boats and their crews. Additionally, a ship's or squadron's quarterdeck speaks volumes about attitude at a command. Finally, a ship is also known by the personal appearance of its officers and crew.

Admiral Raymond Spruance was a master at setting the tone of a ship. He inspired quiet confidence in his officers by showing them he trusted them. When a potentially dangerous situation began to develop under way, Captain Spruance would quietly ask what the officer of the deck intended to do, rather than giving specific orders to solve the problem. His officers soon learned that he trusted them, that he would let them take the initiative when danger threatened, right up until the last minute, when he would take charge if necessary. The tone of this bridge and quarterdeck was one of assurance and professional ability. The attitude below decks was the same, for Spruance insisted that his officers foster the same relationships with their juniors that he had with them. His ships were superbly commanded, and they had superb tone.

Communications with the crew is the fifth key element in command philosophy that is well worth considering before you take command. Any sailor will do the job better knowing what is to be done and when it has to be finished. This can and will be communicated by your XO and is primarily the job of the chain of command. What is important for you as commanding officer is to articulate to your crew *why* a given task must be accomplished. Your crew should know and understand how each challenge undertaken by your ship, squadron, or submarine fits into the larger picture of combat readiness and the U.S. Navy. You can do this in a variety of ways.

Some commanding officers have a brief "captain's corner" in the plan of the day. This gives them an opportunity to think about and write—in just a few short phrases—what is currently "on the plate" of the command and how it fits together. It is also a place where you as commanding officer can give a short burst of philosophy, comment on safety, pass along a compliment, make a general warning, or communicate anything you consider important to the crew on a daily basis. You should also—on a ship or submarine—use the general announcing system to communicate ideas. Don't overdo it, but jumping on the 1MC at least once a day—particularly while under way—is a great boost for the crew. Additionally, most ships and submarines today have internal television systems. This is an ideal medium—if you're a good speaker, you come across well on camera, and you don't overuse it. Perhaps once a week, try to appear on TV for your crew members, speaking honestly, naturally, and sincerely, preferably without notes. Prior to addressing the crew, gather your thoughts and think about your message. The crew will listen to what you have to say, so these are opportunities to reinforce your philosophy. Your consistency will be noticed.

Boldness is another quality worth considering in forming your command philosophy. Many of the tactical evolutions routinely performed by small, fast warships or high-performance aircraft place them in what a merchant marine officer or an airline pilot would consider extremely dangerous circumstances. The considered yet bold acceptance of this continual hazard must be an integral trait of a commanding officer. You must train yourself to make quick decisions with the conn, the engineering plant, the section of aircraft, and the weapons system; and your reactions must be based on knowledge so that they are sound and correct. Recklessness has no place at sea, but without boldness, our ships and aircraft cannot realize their full potential for combat. Boldness is not the characteristic of a ship or squadron as a whole; it is an attitude of the commanding officer and the officers serving in the command, and it must be fostered, tempered, and encouraged.

Two of the Navy's boldest leaders at sea in the twentieth century were Admiral William "Bull" Halsey and Admiral Arleigh Burke. Admiral Halsey once commented on his reputation as an aggressive warfighter by saying, "Most of the strategists think I was a poor strategist, and maybe they were right, but I had to execute a lot of their strategic plans that wouldn't have worked if I hadn't pushed them boldly and aggressively." And perhaps the best comment on boldness was made by Admiral Burke, who, in the days after World War II, said, "Decide how you want to make your attack, and be sure you have a sound and simple plan. Then you hit him with everything you have. Do it fast. If your ship can't make 31 knots, crank it up as fast as it will go. Then pound! Pound! Pound! You may think the enemy isn't yielding, but if you keep it up, he'll weaken, and suddenly you'll break through."

There are different ways of approaching your command philosophy depending on how expansive you desire it to be and how you choose to promulgate it. The size and experience level of your crew should be weighed in determining how much or how little detail you delve into. In the end, the process of gathering your thoughts to define your command philosophy is a positive process for you, your officers, and crew. Your philosophy will be as good as the time you put into it.

Lastly, in putting together your thoughts on a command philosophy, don't take yourself too seriously. A sense of humor goes a long way in the demanding business of going to sea, and you could do a great deal worse than to remember the words of baseball great Satchel Paige: "Don't look back. Someone might be overtaking you."

Look ahead, don't take yourself too seriously and resolve, above all, to enjoy every minute of your command tour. The day of your relief will come all too soon.

2

Commissioning a Ship or Submarine

And see! She stirs!
She starts—she moves—she seems to feel
The thrill of life along her keel,
And, spurning with her foot the ground,
With one exulting, joyous bound,
She leaps into the ocean's arms.

—Henry Wadsworth Longfellow, *The Building of the Ship*

Placing a new ship (or a recommissioned older one) in commission is one of the most challenging tasks a naval officer can undertake. As prospective commanding officer (PCO), you are the on-site representative for the type commander and shipbuilding program manager and must coordinate the myriad of issues associated with both building the ship and putting together a cohesive fighting team. The job is made more challenging by the way the precommissioning crew is assembled; generally only about one-third will have ever been to sea before, and many of your veterans will be returning to sea after years of disassociated shore duty. Additionally, every program, every policy, and every instruction must be scripted from scratch and implemented for the first time. It is a fascinating and rewarding tour, but it will no doubt be one of the most difficult. At its essence, however, training the crew to operate safely at sea is the PCO's most important task.

Your Role in Ship Construction

Each major shipyard in the United States has a supervisor of shipbuilding, conversion, and repair (SUPSHIP) assigned to monitor the day-to-day progress of ship construction. The SUPSHIP normally reports to Naval Sea Systems Command and is the overall program manager, who is responsible for your ship from cradle to grave. The SUPSHIP is an engineering duty officer who is well versed in the ins and outs of the process and is the best source of information on how to interface with the shipbuilder. It is in your best interest to meet with the shipbuilder as quickly as possible after you are notified that you will be the PCO of one of the vessels under construction in the yard. For the most part, the SUPSHIP controls the funding and quality assurance process that is critical to getting your ship built correctly.

The SUPSHIP will assign a ship superintendent to serve as your single point of contact and spearhead the construction of your ship on the waterfront. The ship superintendent will also be an engineering duty officer, or a government employee with years of shipbuilding experience, and will be the government's "go-to" person to get things done. Your relationship with your ship superintendent will be one of the most important factors in getting the ship built the way you want it. The shipbuilder will assign a hull manager as the waterfront director for your ship. One of the most important things you can do is to establish a close, personal working relationship with your hull manager and his or her team of craftsmen.

The reality of the process is, however, that the shipbuilder is generally working from a fixed-price contract on a vessel similar to dozens of others the yard has already built. Your role is not to critique the substance of how your hull manager assembles the product; he or she knows how to build ships, and you are probably not in a position to offer much in the way of helpful advice. You *can*, however, help to set a positive tone between the shipbuilder, the SUPSHIP, and the precommissioning crew that encourages teamwork and emphasizes training, quality assurance, and ship cleanliness. Additionally, you play an important role by bringing an operator's perspective to the production and review process.

U.S. Navy Regulations, chapter 8, section 3, addresses specific duties required of a prospective commanding officer and is a must-read, as are the various type commander instructions addressing the role of the PCO.

But none of these sources capture the inherent nature or challenges of the process. You are essentially on independent duty, and although the type commander for the coast where the ship will be homeported will sign your fitness report, he or she will expect you to report regularly until the ship is delivered (when ship custody transfers to the Navy). Each type commander and program manager has different reporting requirements, but many of the traditional weekly progress reports have been canceled or assumed by the SUPSHIP.

It is important to quickly develop an understanding of the basic design and layout of the ship and of the upcoming changes that will affect her later in life. The contract from which the vessel is built is years old and does not incorporate the variety of ship alterations that will be installed within weeks of ship custody transfer. It is imperative to also develop a close working relationship with the program manager's representatives; they have the information on what the future holds, and they need your input to do their work correctly. Personal visits, frequent phone calls, and regular emails are important tools in continuing to build this relationship.

One of the most important things you provide to the shipbuilding process is feedback. The SUPSHIP is often too close to the problem to see what you see, and the program manager is too far away to know what sailors need to do their jobs better. Regular, high-quality, detailed correspondence can have a direct, positive influence on how your ship and others are built. It is important for you and your crew to have access to and understand the ship specifications that govern construction. You have a vested interest in the quality of the product that the SUPSHIP and his or her staff do not. An intimate knowledge of the specs will allow you to be a force for positive change and corrective action. Finally, and perhaps most significantly, you bring the operator's perspective to the process. You are the only one who does, and part of your job is to represent all the sailors who will sail in your ship.

The Precommissioning Unit

The precommissioning unit (PCU) is the organization that will eventually become your command. Each shipyard has a building to support the PCU, assemble the crew, and continue the training and integration process. The focus of effort during this phase should be to complete the administrative requirements so that you can focus on training as the ship gets closer to completion. The personality and reputation of the crew are built first and foremost at the PCU; it is a critically important rung on the ladder.

Although you are designated as the prospective commanding officer in your orders, you will formally assume command via letter to your type command upon reporting on board. From that day on, you will wear the command at sea pin and exercise the full responsibilities of a commanding officer, including administering nonjudicial punishment. This represents a relatively recent and welcome policy change from the days when PCOs were technically the officer in charge of the PCU until delivery. More broadly, the PCU begins the vessel and crew's transition to a United States ship at ship custody transfer, and the designation "USS" is officially designated at the commissioning ceremony. It is interesting to note that a new ship is placed "in service—special" when custody for the vessel shifts to the government, and the DD-250 form is signed by the SUPSHIP and the PCO. It is placed "in commission without ceremony" months before the actual ceremony.

The PCU exists to assemble and provide a structure for the crew. Your emphasis in the first days of the PCU should be on setting up the administrative procedures that will govern the ship after you move aboard and then, more importantly, on training the crew. The sailors generally arrive in phases—technical experts and leadership first, and the balance of the crew later. The manning process is cumbersome at best and demands the dedicated effort of your XO and command master chief as well as close liaison with the Bureau of Naval Personnel (BUPERS) to make it work.

In many cases, the building yard is a long way from the primary Navy training sites in Norfolk and San Diego. To accommodate the large influx of sailors destined for a new ship, the Fleet Training Centers have created precommissioning detachments (PCDs) to support integration, administration, and training schedules. This structure allows for the precommissioning crew to be assembled in a common area, develop team dynamics, work together, train, and prepare to transition to the building yard. Management of individual training pipelines is the most important function for the PCD.

In most building yards, there will be either a Navy Fleet Introduction Team or a team of private contractors hired by the program manager to help with the integration and training process. These are usually very strong groups with vast experience with precommissioning crews. Heeding their advice on how to do it better can make the difference between a good precommissioning experience and a bad one.

The Precommissioning Crew

Building a warfighting team from the disparate group of individuals assigned to the PCU may be the biggest challenge you face as PCO. The crew will come from a variety of backgrounds, few of them with significant experience in your class of ship and many with no seagoing experience at all. *Training the crew to operate safely at sea is your most important task.*

Although there is a nominal precommissioning screening process for sailors who receive orders to a PCU, there will still be those who arrive unprepared for the rigors of precommissioning duty. They may have significant personal or family problems or not be physically qualified. There is no such thing as a "hand-picked precom crew," and the leadership challenges are in many cases greater than on a normal fleet ship because of the lack of structure in the early days of the PCU.

BUPERS will assign a single point of contact for officer and enlisted detailing and will look to you to do the same. The detailer will work two or three ships at a time and is your best advocate in the bureau. He or she will write orders to route prospective crew members from their previous command, through the PCD to the PCU and, eventually, to the ship. Because this process is so complicated and so closely tied to the well-being of the crew, your point of contact must understand the subtleties of the detailing process and the associated issues related to household goods moves, family separation, and training requirements. Many sailors do not understand the accounting codes in their orders and make bad decisions for themselves and their families because they do not know the rules. Crew members are required to fulfill a two-year minimum activity tour after ship custody transfer.

It is important to have well-run "welcome aboard" and "sponsor" programs in place for the new crew. Many will be coming from remote areas, and the information provided in a welcome aboard package will help ease the transition and stress associated with what may be three permanent change of station moves in less than two years. Publish a newsletter, write letters to the families, set up an aggressive family support group—each of which will provide you a vehicle to discuss the ship's schedule and the importance of long-range planning for each family.

Launching

The launching ceremony has changed a great deal over the past few years. Rarely does a ship "slide down the ways;" more often today she is moved into a drydock and floated out or is pushed in sideways off of the construction platform. The official ceremony is still notable for the designation and presence of a ship's sponsor, who breaks the traditional bottle of champagne across the bow.

Launching is completely the responsibility of those who built the ship. It is *their* ceremony, and you and your crew will be invited to participate as much as your schedules and travel requirements support. You will have an opportunity to meet and socialize with the significant players in the building of your ship, but you will have little to do with the ceremonial aspects of this event.

In most cases, the PCO is not involved with the designation of the sponsor. Sponsor candidates are screened and eventually selected by the Secretary of the Navy. Sponsors will, whenever possible, have some association with the ship's namesake and may sometimes be the spouse of a senior political or military leader. Liaising with the sponsor at the christening is an important part of the process. You will have a lifelong association with them, and this is the first opportunity for the two of you to meet and discuss plans for the ship and its commissioning ceremony.

Sea Trials

Sea trials (or builder's trials) are the best training opportunity your crew will have before moving aboard, but they are completely the responsibility of the shipbuilder, who will hire a civilian master who is responsible for the safety and navigation of the ship and will use shipyard operating engineers to work the equipment and stand watches. You and your crew will have the opportunity to inspect the ship as she operates, participate in the quality assurance effort, and write trial cards on the discrepancies. You will be given a limited number of seats on each trial and will be able to bring some of the crew to sea. It is a training opportunity not to be missed.

The specifics of sea trials vary by ship class and program manager. For Aegis ships, the PCO will be temporarily assigned to the SUPSHIP in order to be in a position to accept custody for and fire the missiles and guns. You will execute a demanding training regimen prior to going to sea for builder's trials and will be the sole point of coordination for all evolutions that involve live ammunition.

The last trial, frequently called an acceptance trial, is customarily sponsored by the SUPSHIP, who presents the ship to the Board of Inspection and Survey (INSURV) for final acceptance. If INSURV accepts the vessel, it will authorize the SUPSHIP to accept the ship on behalf of the government, and the ship will be placed "in service—special."

Ship Custody Transfer to Sail Away

The period of time between ship custody transfer and sail away may be the busiest of your entire life. The ship must be loaded with the consumables, repair parts, equipment, computers, and paperwork that will allow her to operate smoothly when the crew moves aboard. The load-out process itself is an arduous task that demands a well-polished plan and the commitment of senior leaders and crew alike. This period is made significantly more difficult by the arrival of the balance crew at the PCU just prior to move aboard; many of these sailors are new accessions and are unsure of their roles and what to do, let alone how to take custody of a new ship. In just a few weeks, this group has to be indoctrinated to you, your XO, the organization, the shipyard, and the precom process.

After load out, the crew will move out of the PCU and embark the ship. It is a difficult transition because you are now responsible for the safety and operation of the ship and crew while no one is yet qualified to operate the equipment or stand the watches. The degree of pain suffered at move aboard is a direct reflection of the quality of the training program implemented during the earliest PCU days.

The months between move aboard and sail away are dedicated to learning the ship and preparing for operations at sea. The emphasis should necessarily be on firefighting, damage control, safe steaming, and safe navigation. A comprehensive program of certifications and fast cruises will help this process along. Your immediate superior in command (ISIC) will be intimately involved in the light-off certification, crew certification, and final fast cruise.

Commissioning

Commissioning is the highlight of the ship construction process. The ceremony is rich in tradition and is an opportunity to reaffirm the role of the Navy, acknowledge its heritage, recognize the crew members and their families, and thank the SUPSHIP and shipbuilder for their support and expertise. Commissioning ceremonies are high-interest media events and are often attended by thousands of people. You play the key role in the commissioning process; the success of your commissioning ceremony will depend on the amount of quality personal attention you offer.

Over the years, the choice of location of the commissioning ceremony has evolved from one that is largely the decision of the PCO to one that is more centrally managed by the Secretary of the Navy; it is useful to ask very recent PCOs how the process worked for them. Of late, PCOs submit a letter via Naval Sea Systems Command to the Secretary of the Navy recommending an order of preference for several candidate sites, although in some cases the commissioning site may have been already determined by the Secretary. Although it is generally easier to hold the ceremony in the builder's yard prior to sail away, most commissioning sites are chosen for historical or political reasons, such as a tie to the ship's namesake or a desire to positively connect a city or region to the Navy through the experience of a ship commissioning. Aim to select a site as early in the process as possible, and work with the program manager and the Secretary of the Navy's office to secure the official site designation. As soon as the site is chosen, it is imperative that you contact local political organizations, Navy League chapters, and other interested parties to designate a commissioning committee and assign its chairperson. You should have a site and a committee formally designated at least a year prior to the commissioning ceremony.

Commissioning preparations will take up an inordinate amount of your time as the date of the ceremony approaches. The formerly bimonthly

Fig. 2-1. A ship's commissioning day is her official "birthday" as a U.S. Navy warship and should always be attended by pomp and circumstance. Here, USS *James E. Williams* (DDG 95) is dressed for the occasion.

meetings will occur nearly every week, and you (and your XO and commissioning coordinator) will spend many hours on the phone arranging details. You will need to travel to the commissioning site frequently and be prepared to respond to emergent taskings and crises. An aggressive, creative public affairs program will ease the burden and help make your ceremony memorable.

It is your responsibility to liaise with the commissioning committee and keep them headed fair as they help plan the ceremony. Since the Navy will pick up the bill for only a portion of the festivities, the committee will by necessity be involved in large-scale fundraising on your behalf. It is important for you to review the ethics regulations on what you can and cannot do and be involved with as the committee raises funds. In most cases, there is a CO's reception the night before the commissioning, a VIP breakfast the morning of the ceremony, and a reception after the ceremony; these are paid for directly and solely by the commissioning committee. The government will pay to set up the dais, chairs, public address system, and decorative bunting. There will likely be experienced contractor support from the program manager.

You are responsible for nominating principal speaker candidates and forwarding the recommendations to the Secretary of the Navy for final selection. In some cases, the speaker may change only days prior to the actual ceremony, so it is important to be flexible. Likewise, the composition of your platform guests can—and usually does—change right up to the last minute. Your commissioning coordinator has to be prepared to implement changes as they occur.

Post-Commissioning

After commissioning, your ship will begin an extensive post-delivery test and trial period during which you will run the new ship through its paces, fire missiles, shoot the guns, learn underway replenishment, and sail to the new homeport. Despite being primarily an engineering evaluation of your ship, the post-trial period provides some of the finest training opportunities available in the Navy today.

In most cases, the shipbuilder will assign a warranty engineer, who will ride the ship and take care of emergent issues during the one-year warranty/guarantee period. Except in cases involving specific government-furnished equipment, the warranty engineer will be the shipbuilder's single point of contact for repairs and documentation of discrepancies for correction during post-shakedown availability (PSA). This individual, normally an experienced ship engineer, will be able to access the building yard for repair parts, technical information, and support of any kind. He or she should be treated as an integral member of your wardroom, with appropriate messing and berthing. In most cases, the warranty engineer will fit extremely well into a close-knit and productive wardroom and will provide you with invaluable assistance through the first year of commissioned service, while your ship is still under warranty. During this period, it is absolutely essential that your crew develop material self-assessment skills and learn to accurately document material history discrepancies. These are the fundamental skills that will keep your complex engineering and combat systems running as designed long after the ship's warranty period expires.

During PSA, your ship will return to a shipyard for completion of items left unfinished during construction, correction of those items discovered during shakedown and covered by warranty, and installation of new items that were not ready while the ship was still in the builder's yard. PSAs run from one to four months, depending on ship class, and they may or may not be executed in the parent builder's yard. The challenge during PSA is to maintain the sharp edge the crew will have developed while operating the ship at sea during shakedown.

Precommissioning Philosophy

Building a ship is a special experience, and from the moment you assemble your team you should strive to instill a sense of teamwork, loyalty to the ship, dedication to the very challenging task at hand, and, above all, a culture of excellence, insisting on the highest standards. Think about developing a philosophy for your precommissioning experience, perhaps including some of the ideas below from previously successful PCOs:

- Ensure that each new sailor receives, upon assignment to the ship, a letter from you explaining the precommissioning process, including its special rewards and challenges.
- Work closely and continuously with BUPERS to ensure that all assigned crew members are qualified; remember, you will have *everyone* as a team together for at least three years, which is remarkable in today's Navy. Assemble a team that you want to work with for a prolonged period.
- Instruct your XO to focus on the training, manning, and personnel side of the precommissioning process while you are involved in the construction side. This will mean an initial separation, with

your XO in the prospective homeport and you in the building yard. Work hard to maintain connectivity and consistency between the two detachments.

- Spend plenty of time talking to other PCOs, especially those who are taking ships through the process just ahead of you. There is never a need to reinvent the wheel; don't place excessive burdens on your team simply because you want to be "different." Evaluate what those ahead of you have accomplished, and if it works, take it on board.
- Fuse your entire crew as quickly as possible and get them to the building yard. Next, work hard to get them into the ship at the very first opportunity.
- Take every opportunity to get the crew to sea on other ships of the class while your ship is being built. One day at sea on a similar ship is worth a month in a school or a week walking around the building yard.

Final Thoughts on New Construction

The construction of a new ship is an ongoing leadership challenge, but one that comes with great rewards. Perhaps no commanding officer will have the impact that the first one does. Certainly, no single crew will ever play as important a role in establishing the standards, reputation, and legacy that will follow the ship throughout her life. The first crew will forever be a tight-knit group because they are the plank owners and collectively shared in the challenging process—and rare privilege—of bringing a ship to life.

Now that the commissioning ceremony is over, however, your time in command has really just begun. If you have trained your crew well, put in place an effective organization, and stayed abreast of the construction issues during the long process, your ship and crew will be ready to make the transition to a team of warfighters prepared to join the fleet as an operational asset.

3

Organization and Administration of the Command

The Captain, in the first place, is lord paramount.
He stands no watch, comes and goes when he pleases,
is accountable to no one and must be obeyed in everything,
without a question even from his chief officers.

—Richard Henry Dana, *Two Years before the Mast* (1840)

The wooden sailing vessels that composed the great navies of the nineteenth century were small, simple ships when compared with their modern counterparts. Most of the crew's efforts were put into manning the sails. Roughly half the men stood watch at all times when under way, ready to change or trim a huge area of canvas. Potential enemies came into sight slowly, giving the ship time to shift to its battle organization, which provided for manning the guns with approximately half the crew while the remainder tended the wheel and sails. The ship either sailed or fought or did both at once. The ship's organization could therefore be simple. There was essentially a single watch, quarter, and station bill; a simple battle organization; no administrative boards except for an occasional court-martial; and only a few other bills, such as fire, collision, and prize crew. The administrative needs of the crew were tended to by a select and small group of specialized workers: cook, sailmaker, carpenter, and so forth. A handful of officers stood watch and administered the ship, all under the eye of the captain.

Modern navies, of course, are quite different. A smaller percentage of the crew is directly involved in propulsion, and this number continues to decline as automation further reduces manning requirements in gas turbine (and eventually, electric drive) main engineering spaces. Guns, missiles, torpedoes, electronics, and communications equipment are extremely complex, requiring a large complement of well-trained men and women to operate. During wartime, instant attack can be expected from the air, the surface, and the depths of the sea. There are higher numbers of specialized administrators—culinary specialists, yeomen, retail specialists, and personnel specialists—to tend to the needs of the crew, in addition to entirely new (and sometimes merged) ratings, such as information technology specialists (ITs). More officers are embarked to manage and oversee the complex system that is today's warship.

Reflecting these technological changes, the ship's organization has ballooned. The modern warship still has a watch, quarter, and station bill and a battle organization, but there are other bills and boards as well, many of them quite complicated. Besides general quarters (condition I) and normal steaming (condition IV), there are at least two other principal watch conditions and several minor ones.

As ships became more complex, the trend throughout the twentieth century was for their organization to follow suit. Yet today, three decades into the twenty-first century, many new technologies are emerging that may move us back toward the more streamlined manning arrangements of the nineteenth century. Fleet design concepts, including distributed maritime operations—with emphasis on high-technology distributed systems, stealth, precision engagement, unmanned vehicles, and network-centered warfare—permit a reassessment of the ways in which we man, organize, and administer our modern warships. Beginning with the littoral combat ships (LCSs) *Freedom* and *Independence* and continuing with *Zumwalt*-class destroyers, there has been a decline in the overall manning on new classes of warships, which has consequently led to changes in every aspect of administrative and battle bills. The LCS class employs multiple crews rotating through individual hulls, each tailored for specific shipboard missions, such as surface warfare and mine warfare. The Navy continues to advance unmanned concepts and unmanned ships, which also require new thinking with respect to administrative and battle bills. While this chapter will focus on both "traditional" twentieth-century approaches to manning and our newest trends, it is important for every commanding officer to work toward streamlining and improving the overall efficiency and effectiveness of his or her command.

General Principles of Organization

The *Standard Organization and Regulations of the U.S. Navy (SORM)*, OPNAVINST 3120.32 series, describes some of the principles of organization in chapters 3, 4, and 6. You should read these chapters carefully. We will cover most of the basic principles here.

The dictionary definition of the word *organize* is "to bring into systematic relation the parts of a whole." Sound organization is essential for good administration. Organizations must be designed to carry out the objectives of command, and they should be based on the division of activities and on the assignment of responsibilities and authority to individuals within the organization. Further, to ensure optimum efficiency, every essential function must be identified as the specific responsibility of a given unit or person. There must be a clear definition of individual duties, responsibilities, and authority.

PLANNING AN ORGANIZATION

To assist you in planning, it is helpful to define several basic terms. We will list them here as well, since they will be used repeatedly throughout this chapter. *Accountability* refers to the obligation of the individual to render an accounting of the proper discharge of his or her responsibilities. *Authority* is the right to make a decision in order to fulfill a responsibility, the right to require action of others, or the right to discharge particular obligations placed upon the individual. *Delegation* is the right of a person in authority to send another to act or transact business. Authority may be delegated, but accountability may never be. There is nothing new about these definitions; they have been used and understood since the inception of the Navy.

Fig. 3-1. The captain's touch is felt everywhere and by everybody on board and sets the tone for the entire ship.

SETTING UP AN ORGANIZATION

Your ship, when you relieve, will already have an operating organization; if you commission a new unit, you will be required to develop one. You should occasionally review the validity of your organization by doing the following:

1. Prepare a statement of objectives, missions, and tasks.
2. Familiarize your key planners with the principles of organization.
3. Group the ship's functions logically so that they can be assigned to appropriate segments of the organization.
4. Prepare/update manuals, charts, functional guides, and ship's instructions.
5. Establish policies and procedures.
6. Indoctrinate all personnel concerning their individual and group responsibilities.
7. Set up control measures to ensure the achievement of your objectives—that is, a feedback and assessment loop.

In a smooth-running organization, every individual is aware of the unit's mission and his or her role in executing it. This gives purpose and clarity to your crew's daily work effort while synchronizing their energies toward a common command goal. A wellspring of talent lies in your crew and wardroom, and clear, overarching guidance sets the conditions to tap into this reservoir of creativity and innovation without stifling it. Additionally, organizations remain relevant—and effective—by adapting. Consider this when your leadership team presents you with recommendations for change; it's how organizations remain current.

The *SORM*, chapter 1, sets forth four principles of unit administration to serve as guidelines:

Hierarchy: In order to operate efficiently, each member must understand where they fit within the organization and the duties and responsibilities associated with that billet. Therefore, every unit is defined by an organization chart that clearly delineates where each sailor fits within the organization and the chain of command.

Unity of command: Establishes the commanding officer as ultimately responsible for the unit and the personnel assigned.

Span of control: Refers to the ideal number of people that one person can supervise effectively, but also recognizes the scope of the assigned functional responsibilities and the time available to the supervisor. Ordinarily, a supervisor should be immediately responsible for not fewer than three or more than seven subordinates.

Specialization: Each sailor with the organization who holds a billet within that chain of command should be uniquely qualified to execute the duties and responsibilities required by that position.

While these principles provide sound guidance, variations will play out as you adapt your organization for optimal battle effectiveness. The virtues of flat organizations and the agility they bring to decision-making should be valued. Speed of action and visibility across the organization in the interest of synchronization are increasingly valued in today's information-intensive environment. Additionally, intrinsic in any organizational framework is the manner in which information flows and decisions are made. The study of this—captured in the evolving discipline of "knowledge management"—is increasingly important in today's information age.

ORGANIZATIONAL AUTHORITY

Chapter 3 of the *SORM* describes in some detail the derivation of the authority of officers. Petty officers also derive that authority that comes from position in an organization. *U.S. Navy Regulations*, articles 1021 and 1037, is the source of authority for both. The exact kinds and limits of authority exercised by each individual will be defined by ship, department, division, and other direction specific to the organization.

ORGANIZATIONAL DIRECTIVES

All ship organization is ultimately derived from *Navy Regulations*. Article 0804 provides that all commands will be organized and administered in accordance with law, *Navy Regulations*, and the orders of a competent authority, and that all orders and instructions issued by a commanding officer will be in accordance with these directives. Article 0805 goes on to state that the CO should never leave the ship without an organized force sufficient to meet emergencies and, consistent with requirements, capable of conducting operations.

Article 0843 sets forth relations with military units and personnel embarked for passage but not part of ship's company. Briefly, this article provides that such units will be subject to the orders of the ship's commanding officer, will comply with the CO's uniform and other regulations, and will perform their share of mess and other common duties, but that they will otherwise be administered through their own organization. When a unit is embarked for transportation only, its officer in command retains authority, subject only to the overriding authority of the CO.

After *Navy Regulations*, the next level of guidance is the *SORM*. We have already covered some of its content relating to organizational and administrative philosophy. Most of the *SORM*, however, is devoted to covering shipboard organization in detail. Chapter 1 covers basic administration; chapter 2, standard unit organization; chapter 3, the roles and responsibilities of departments, divisions, boards, and committees; chapter 4, watch organizations; chapter 5, general guidance and regulations; and chapter 6, unit bills. The development of each subject is so complete that many sections can be adopted almost verbatim by any ship.

The next input to your organizational efforts will be your type commander. Many type commanders promulgate a standard organization and regulations manual for each type under their command. Some use the *SORM* as their basic organization, with modifying addenda at the back of the book. Others have kept their old standard organizations, modifying them to correspond to the standard. A few have written completely new standard organizations. In any event, each type organization directive must conform to the standard directive.

The final level of detail is your own ship's organization. You may make it as simple or as complicated as you desire, but bear in mind that it must still conform to the standard organization set forth in the *SORM*. Note again that the italicized sections of the standard cannot be modified. Other sections may be changed in detail as you see fit, but not in principle.

After reviewing these directives, you are now ready, if commanding a new ship, to promulgate your own organizational instructions and standing orders. These will include a battle bill (with a condition watch system); a watch, quarter, and station bill; administrative, operational, and emergency bills; a safety program; a training program; and the necessary boards and committees. The *SORM* includes some fifty bills and more than twenty boards and committees. We can be thankful not all of them are necessary on most ships.

If you are taking command of a ship already in commission, you will be spared the time-consuming task of organizing your ship. You will, however, want to spend some time determining what changes you want to make, and this will cover much of the same ground, though at a faster pace.

We will now cover briefly the major components of the task of organizing a ship. Again, most of the required reference material is in the *SORM* and in your type commander's addenda or standard manual.

Organization for Battle

A warship is built to fight, and your ship's allowance of officers and sailors has been tailored to that task. Anyone without a battle station is therefore not essential on board. A sailor's place in the battle bill should be a source of pride. Many a ship's cook or barber has fought as a gun or mount captain or as a vital member of a missile or torpedo crew. This feeling of pride should be encouraged, particularly since the technical requirements of today's weapons systems have made such qualification by nontechnical personnel more difficult.

Chief directives contributing to the formulation of your battle bill are *Surface Ship Survivability* (NTTP 3-20.21), *Required Operational Capabilities (ROC) and Projected Operational Environment (POE)* (OPNAVINST F3501.311 series), and the *Repair Party Manual* (COMNAVSURFORINST 3541.10 series). These publications (some confidential) describe shipboard battle organization and conditions of readiness and should be used as your guide. They will be supplemented by a type commander's standard battle bill. You will probably have to adapt the standardized guidance and tailor it somewhat for your ship, since today's rapid changes in weaponry and equipment are resulting in a variety of subclasses within each ship class.

The battle bill assigns sailors to stations according to (a) their qualifications and (b) the requirements of the various weapons, equipment, and machinery of the ship. Where possible, divisions or parts of divisions should be assigned to related battle stations as a group; for example, main propulsion division, to the engine and auxiliary spaces; first division, to a forward repair locker. When this is impracticable, you should make every effort to assign sailors who work together administratively to battle stations where they can continue to work as a team.

Condition watch teams will be formed from the battle organization (condition I). They will man selected ship control, communications, weapons, and engineering stations. A few non-watchstanders should be left over to man commissary stations, key administrative posts, and a few other billets.

If combat action occurs on your watch, you will initially be tempted to keep the crew at general quarters (GQ) for long periods of time. Soon, however, you will have to reconcile the fact that your officers and crew still need rest and food, that a minimum of personal and ship cleanliness is still required, and, in general, that the work of the ship must continue even under conditions of high readiness for combat. You should anticipate the need, over long periods at GQ, for easements in certain aspects of readiness—this must be controlled and methodical in execution. At a minimum, plan to have your cooks and mess personnel so distributed in the battle bill that they can be spared for food preparation and service even during GQ—that is, battle messing. While they are otherwise occupied, the ship will still be able to conduct engagements and perform defensive actions, and they can quickly be summoned back to battle stations. Setting condition I (GQ) brings the ship to maximum operational readiness, both offensively and defensively. In addition to manning all combat systems, it also brings the ship to its highest material condition of readiness for damage control.

To maintain combat endurance over extended periods, ships can also be prepared to fight from condition II or III, after having initially set the highest damage control condition at GQ. To sustain high conditions of readiness longer, specific condition II levels of readiness have evolved (for example, IIAS—anti-submarine warfare; IISurface—anti-surface warfare; IIAir—anti-aircraft warfare; IIDC—Localized Damage Control; and IIStrike). These conditions allow the crew to take care of necessities while still retaining the required offensive and defensive capabilities of condition I for specific threats. This flexibility offers extended warfighting readiness for protracted periods, with sufficient personnel on watch and ready for instantaneous action. In today's high-speed world, when operating in a threatening environment, offensive and defensive action—at a moment's notice—will be required.

Another factor to plan for, either before the initiation of action or soon thereafter, is the rotation of those personnel whose duties require close and continuous concentration. Examples of these are lookouts, radar system operators, air and surface trackers, electronic warfare operators, sonar operators, and key supervisory watch personnel. They are your eyes and ears, and the safety of the ship will depend on their alertness; ensure that they stay fresh by providing reliefs.

Condition Watch Organization

Some condition watches to consider when making up your condition watch bill include the following:

Condition I: General quarters

Condition II: Halfway between general quarters and normal watch (often warfare area–specific)

Condition III: Wartime cruising. Approximately one-third of the crew will be on watch. Armament will be manned to match threat conditions.

Condition IV: Normal peacetime cruising

Condition V: Peacetime watch in port. Enough personnel aboard to man emergency bills and to get under way.

Condition IA: Amphibious battle stations. Reduced armament readiness; boat launching and control stations fully manned.

Condition IIAW: Variation of condition I to meet anti-air warfare threat

Condition IIAS: Variation of condition I to meet anti-submarine warfare threat

Condition IIMH: Variation of condition I to meet mine threat for mine countermeasures units.

In preparing bills for the above conditions, bear in mind that in wartime (and that is what we are preparing for), condition watches, continued for hours on end, will soon "get old." Even in peacetime, after eight hours of daily watch, not much is left of a person's productive time. With today's automated systems, during protracted periods of hostilities, you should find yourself able to modify some condition watches to allow some personnel to work or train in the vicinity of their stations. This is dependent, of course, on the specific type of watch they are standing and the demands of the individual task. The *SORM*, chapter 4, also discusses shipboard conditions of readiness in general terms.

Watch Organization

The *SORM*, chapter 4, covers in detail the watch organization of ships in general, both in port and under way. In making up your own watch bills, remember that those portions of the *SORM* in italics must be included as they are. The other parts of the chapter may be modified as you desire.

DEVELOPMENT OF A WATCH ORGANIZATION

You should, in developing your watch organization, start with the requirements of the *SORM*. Figure 3-2 shows standard arrangements that should fit any type or size ship. Review them and the *SORM* and deliberate on what would make you feel comfortable. Delete those functions that do not apply to your own ship, add your own ideas, and the result should constitute your watch bill in chart form. You should then refine this, using the ideas of your department heads and modifying your draft as necessary to suit the qualifications of your personnel. The last step is the writing and printing of directives for your organization book. These should fully delineate the responsibilities and duties of each watchstander.

This would also be a good time to set up a training system, to make sure the personnel who will stand these watches will be properly qualified and will in turn pass on their skills to others.

ESTABLISHMENT OF WATCHES

Once your watch organization is in print and a training system is in place, you are ready to implement the watch system. The *SORM* requires that watches of the officer of the deck (OOD) and the engineering officer of the watch be continuous. Marine officers below the grade of major may stand OOD watches in port and junior OOD watches at sea. Petty officers and noncommissioned officers may be used as OODs in port in addition to your officers. Additionally, depending on the size of the ship, it is not uncommon to see chiefs and first-class petty officers qualify as underway OODs. This can be the case if there is still opportunity remaining in the watch bill amid the pool of junior officers who must qualify and stand watch as a matter of fundamental professional development.

The general duties of watch officers are set forth in the *SORM*, chapter 4, which covers orders of the sentries, watchstanding principles, use of deadly force, length of watches, performance of duty while on watch, setting and relieving the watch, and special watches. Your instructions, with the italicized portions of the *SORM* included, should be all your watchstanders need to read to stand a taut and knowledgeable watch. Additional information is available to them in the *Watch Officer's Guide*, published by Naval Institute Press.

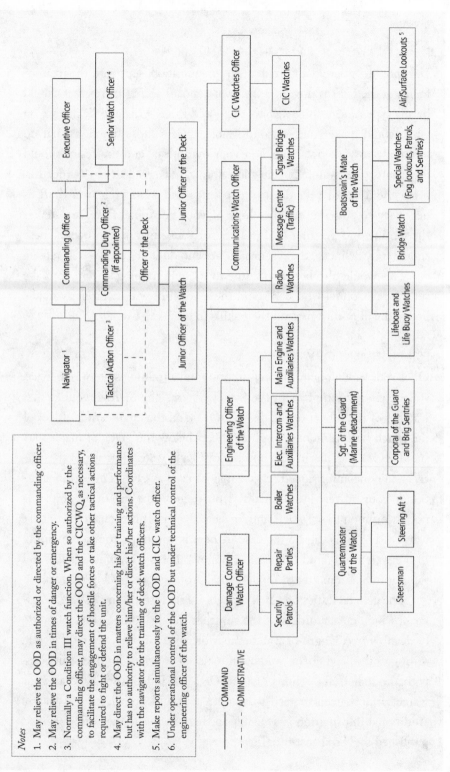

Notes

1. May relieve the OOD as authorized or directed by the commanding officer.

2. May relieve the OOD in times of danger or emergency.

3. Normally a Condition III watch function. When so authorized by the commanding officer, may direct the OOD and the CICWQ, as necessary, to facilitate the engagement of hostile forces or take other tactical actions required to fight or defend the unit.

4. May direct the OOD in matters concerning his/her training and performance but has no authority to relieve him/her or direct his/her actions. Coordinates with the navigator for the training of deck watch officers.

5. Make reports simultaneously to the OOD and CIC watch officer.

6. Under operational control of the OOD but under technical control of the engineering officer of the watch.

COMMAND ——————

ADMINISTRATIVE − − − − −

Commanding Officer

Executive Officer

Senior Watch Officer [4]

Navigator [1]

Commanding Duty Officer [2] (if appointed)

Tactical Action Officer [3]

Officer of the Deck

Junior Officer of the Deck

Junior Officer of the Watch

CIC Watches Officer

CIC Watches

Communications Watch Officer

Radio Watches

Message Center (Traffic)

Signal Bridge Watches

Engineering Officer of the Watch

Boiler Watches

Elec. Intercom and Auxiliaries Watches

Main Engine and Auxiliaries Watches

Damage Control Watch Officer

Security Patrols

Repair Parties

Quartermaster of the Watch

Steersman

Steering Aft [6]

Sgt. of the Guard (Marine detachment)

Corporal of the Guard and Brig Sentries

Boatswain's Mate of the Watch

Lifeboat and Life Buoy Watches

Bridge Watch

Special Watches (Fog lookouts, Patrols, and Sentries)

Air/Surface Lookouts [5]

Fig. 3-2. Conventional watch organization under way, Condition IV watch.

LOGS

The two main logs to be kept by your watches are the Deck Log and the Engineering Log. Other important records are the Magnetic Compass Record, the Bearing Book, the Engineer's Bell Book or "bell logger" (now automated on nearly all ships), the Combat Information Center Log, and the Combat Systems Officer of the Watch Log. Give your personal attention to the keeping of these documents. They are both important historical records and legal documents; they might be referred to in years to come for a number of reasons.

Submarine Watch Organization

The *Submarine Operations and Regulations Manual* (submarine *SORM*), chapter 2, provides specific direction with regard to the submarine watch organization. Some of the more important highlights are noted here. First and foremost, the submarine *SORM* echoes the shipboard version in that "the Commanding Officer shall establish such watches as necessary for the safety and proper operation of the command"—in other words, safety first. A nuclear-powered submarine operates in three dimensions—the X, Y, and Z planes. A submarine watch organization is like an anchor chain—only as strong as its weakest link. Consequently, each watch-stander must be properly qualified and fully aware of his or her responsibilities as they are essential to the safe and proper operation of the ship.

Officers are assigned watches both in port and at sea according to the watch bill prepared by the senior watch officer—typically the department head with the most experience or time on board the ship. Officer watch bills are prepared by the senior watch officer and approved by the CO, as are any changes to the officer watch bill.

Enlisted watch bills are prepared by the chief of the boat (COB), who is the senior enlisted adviser to the CO and typically the most experienced chief petty officer aboard ship. The COB prepares the regular underway and in-port watch bills for approval by the XO. Any changes must also be approved by the XO.

Because of the highly complex nature of the systems aboard a submarine, no officer or enlisted person shall be assigned to stand watch unless specifically qualified by the CO or ship's specific directives. Accordingly, the XO and the engineer officer are responsible for establishing

and maintaining a watch qualification book. The engineer's watch qualification book is specific to watches in the ship's nuclear propulsion plant.
No member of ship's company, officer or enlisted, will stand watch unless
he or she is qualified and proficient, as noted in the nonnuclear and nuclear watch qualification books.

While under way, the three key watchstanders on a submarine are
the officer of the deck, the diving officer of the watch, and the engineering officer of the watch. It is required that each of these three key watchstanders *not* assume the watch until every person in the watch section
has relieved and is fully integrated on watch. This allows for a seamless
integration between watch sections and a smooth turnover process.

Finally, it is important that supervisors take into account the readiness of their watchstanders to assume the watch. Crew rest can become
a problem when you have only a limited number of qualified watchstanders. Supervisors cannot assume that each individual watchstander
is ready to stand the watch. Maintenance and training can take its toll in
hours off watch, especially when in a three-section or port and starboard
rotation. Consequently, underway watches are normally not longer than
six hours in duration, and circadian watch rotations that offer rest periods
on or around the same time each twenty-four-hour day are preferred.
With the CO's permission, propulsion and non-propulsion plant watches
may be extended as needed to meet operational requirements.

Unit Bills

A unit bill sets forth the commanding officer's policy and directions for
assigning personnel to duties or stations for specific purposes or functions.
The *SORM* states that unit bills will include the following elements:

- a preface, stating the purpose of the bill
- assignment of responsibility for the bill's maintenance
- information of a background, or guidance, nature
- procedure, containing the information and policies necessary to
  interpret the material
- the special responsibilities of each person with regard to planning, organizing, directing, and controlling the functions and
  evolution of the bill.

Chapter 6 of the *SORM* contains sample bills for every conceivable type of ship for every possible contingency or evolution. They are intended as a guide for type commanders and commanding officers. Your type commander will probably have modified the bills in the *SORM* to suit his or her desires and the types of ships he or she commands. You, in turn, may modify further the bills that concern your particular ship.

Watch, Quarter, and Station Bill

The watch, quarter, and station bill is the commanding officer's summary of assignments of the personnel to duties and stations specified within each of the unit's bills. As its title states, it lists the watches, berthing assignments, and bill assignments for each officer and sailor. It is an important working document for department heads and division officers. It should reflect this importance by being kept up to date and should be posted for ready reference by all personnel. Ships maintain these bills on computers, but posting copies in common areas is still a good practice as they are central organizing documents with which everyone must be familiar.

Command Organization

While the primary organization for a ship (and the reason for its existence) is the battle organization, it remains a fact that 95 percent of a ship's time, even in war, is spent on administration. This requires an organization of its own, the ship's organization plan. Figure 3-4 shows a typical administrative organization of a large ship; yours might be much smaller. The normal progression of organization is from the CO through the XO, heads of departments, division officers, and so on, down to the section leaders and nonrated sailors. We will now discuss each level of organization in greater detail.

HEADS OF DEPARTMENT

In addition to the specific duties and responsibilities assigned to a department head (DH) by his or her billet, each one also has certain general duties. First of all, the DH is the representative of the CO in all matters pertaining to the department and must conform to policies and orders. All persons in the department are subordinate. The DH may confer directly with the captain concerning matters relating to the department whenever

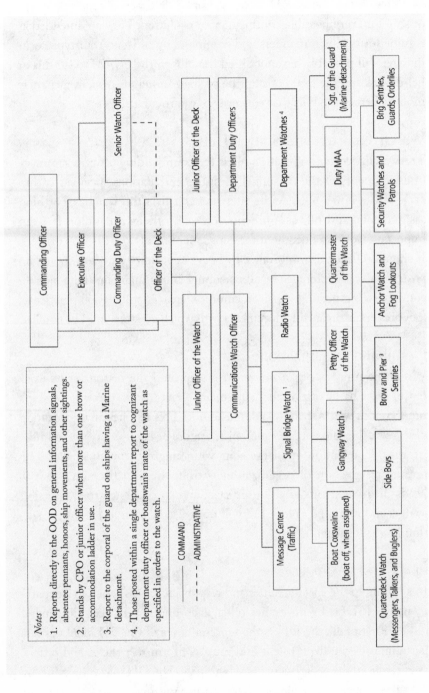

Fig. 3-3. Conventional watch organization in port.

Notes

1. Reports directly to the OOD on general information signals, absentee pennants, honors, ship movements, and other sightings.

2. Stands by CPO or junior officer when more than one brow or accommodation ladder in use.

3. Report to the corporal of the guard on ships having a Marine detachment.

4. Those posted within a single department report to cognizant department duty officer or boatswain's mate of the watch as specified in orders to the watch.

—————— COMMAND

- - - - - - ADMINISTRATIVE

he or she believes such action necessary for the good of the department or the ship. (Of course, the DH should use this right judiciously and should inform the XO as soon as possible.) The DH must keep the CO informed as to the general condition of machinery and equipment, particularly in cases that might affect safety or operational readiness, and must not disable machinery or equipment without permission. Each CO will articulate his or her expectations regarding the degree of direct communication desired with department heads. Whatever that level is, it is incumbent on the department head to keep the XO informed of developments as nearly in parallel as possible and practicable.

The more specific responsibilities of each head of department are set forth in the *SORM*, chapter 3. You should read them carefully and insist that your heads of departments do likewise. Aside from normal duties, additional specific requirements are laid on a department head during the precommissioning period, during fitting out, and during the period prior to detachment. For example, before being relieved, the DH is required to inspect the department, submitting a joint report with the relieving officer to the commanding officer. You should read this portion of the *SORM* carefully and insist that your department heads do likewise.

DIVISION OFFICERS

Officers are assigned to command major divisions of each department. They are assigned junior division officers, enlisted section leaders, and other leading petty officers.

The division officer (DIVO) occupies an essential place in the ship and is the final officer link between you and your crew. The DIVO's performance of duty is essential since the enlisted sailors see the DIVO daily; they will react strongly to his or her leadership, good or bad. The *SORM* lists the DIVO's specific duties, but a more detailed reference is the *Division Officer's Guide*, published by Naval Institute Press.

BOARDS AND COMMITTEES

A board or committee is a group organized under a president, chairperson, or senior member to evaluate problems in depth and to make recommendations to higher authorities for action. Many organizational functions in the Navy lend themselves to administration by these groups. Chapter 3

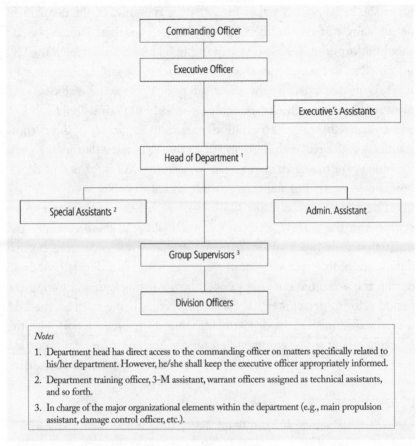

Fig. 3-4. A sample command/departmental organization.

of the *SORM* describes the composition and purpose of the most common ones aboard ship. You will probably not need them all, but some will prove useful by undertaking long or detailed analysis of matters that do not require your immediate attention or decision. They are generally policy-setting groups, though you may choose to delegate executive functions to a few.

Littoral Combat Ship: Evolving Twenty-First-Century Concepts

The future will see a continuous press to improve the efficiency of our warships in all aspects of their operations—from combat systems to engineering and deck watchstanding to maintenance and crew-training concepts. Manning, in particular, is the single largest cost driver for the Navy, and the littoral combat ship (LCS) class takes a dramatic step in reducing the number of crew members assigned to a ship. Leveraging improved technology and automation, the LCS takes smaller crews to sea and, with them, evolved methods in fighting, watchstanding, and administrative organization. The foregoing sections in this chapter reflect the details of twentieth-century shipboard organizational structures, tried and proven. They will adapt, though, as the fleet sees increasing numbers of newer, more modern combatants and the efficiencies they bring. What remains timeless is the imperative of a shipboard organization to clearly provide for *accountability, authority, delegation,* and, ultimately, reliable *execution.* In this sense, the general guidance addressed in the *SORM* has enduring relevance. The streamlined watch organization aboard the LCS pairs technology with multi-crewing concepts. This direction in manning places a premium on high-quality training as individuals take on multiple responsibilities. The details of this organization will be refined and evolve as the LCS operates in the fleet in greater numbers.

Fig. 3-5. LCS 7 *Detroit*

Fig. 3-6. LCS 10 *Gabrielle Giffords*

LCS ORGANIZATION

The LCS reflects significant changes in both ship design and manning. LCS units are organized into divisions, which are groups of individual ships with similar warfare capabilities and embarked mission modules that correspond to surface warfare and mine countermeasures. Through the use of advanced systems and automation, the core crew size for the LCS has been reduced to approximately fifty personnel, which is augmented with about twenty mission module personnel and, if equipped, twenty-four aviation detachment personnel. LCS sea frames employ multirole watches for officers and enlisted personnel in both in-port and underway watch sections. New watch stations and functions—hybrid positions—have evolved to reflect the manpower savings brought about by technology and increasingly automated ship control, engineering, and combat systems capabilities. While the CO, XO, tactical action officer, and OOD endure, new terms such as defensive systems operator, combat system manager, force net supervisor, tactical action coordinator, total ship computing environment supervisor, readiness control officer, engineering propulsion technician, and in-port engineering monitor describe new underway and in-port watch stations. Detailed reviews conducted in 2016 and 2020 resulted in adjustments to LCS operational and manning constructs. As LCS presence grows in fleet operations, it will be important to be familiar with the evolving capabilities and limitations of this unique platform.

Ship's Regulations

Ship's regulations have traditionally been one of the most important elements in a ship's organization. Here, at least, is one thing that retains the flavor of tradition, with many of its rules dating back to the days of wooden ships—though, of course, they have been thoroughly updated where necessary.

Chapter 5 of the *SORM* contains a useful set of ship's regulations. You may be of the opinion, after a quick review, that they are too lengthy or too excessively detailed. Bear in mind, however, that they have evolved over many years, the product of the experiences of thousands of COs facing the same problems you will be facing. Most of them, in fact, started as *Navy Regulations* and were gradually downgraded to ship's regs.

Granted, the range of subjects covered is peculiar. They start, alphabetically, with topics such as "Address and Telephone Number Requirement" and "Alarm Bells" and end with "Unauthorized Entry" and "Wartime Information Security Programs." They cover diverse subjects, from petitions, protest, and dissident and related activities to swimming, grooming, hitchhiking, and a host of other specific topics. But before you decide to cut some out, remember that if some of your sailors conduct themselves as you would not want them to, the court-martial or nonjudicial punishment hearing you convene will have to prove that they violated a law or regulation of some kind. The ship's regulations should, therefore, cover those rules of conduct that you want observed; and they must be *duly promulgated* to be legal. This means they must be *approved* by competent authority and *posted* in a place where the crew can be expected to see them. Ship's regulations signed by you and posted on the division bulletin board in the sailors' living compartment constitute legal promulgation.

Bearing these considerations in mind, you will probably want to use the standard regulations as a *minimum* rather than as a *maximum*. Past COs have found each one to be necessary or it wouldn't be there.

Organization for Embarked Staff

The chances are good that you will carry either a permanently or temporarily embarked flag or a major commander at some time. Your organization should take both possibilities into account.

The basic guidance for relations with an embarked commander and accompanying staff is contained in *Navy Regulations*, chapter 7. Articles 0710 and 0711 outline the organization of a staff and the authority and responsibilities of officers assigned to it. Article 0720 describes its administration and discipline. This article states that the staff of an embarked commander, along with the enlisted persons serving with them, are subject to the internal regulations and discipline of the ship. The specifics for assignments of regular stations for battle, emergencies, administration, and discipline are coordinated between the ship's executive officer and the senior staff officer of the embarking commander.

Additional details on accommodating an embarked staff are covered by the *SORM*. The organizational changes to take aboard a flag are not complex, but they are important. Billeting, office, and command spaces amount to a clear articulation and understanding of support requirements, the commander's standing orders, and requirements for information flow.

Ship's Routine

Establishment of a formal routine is essential to the smooth operations of any large organization—including a ship. If a daily routine is lacking, vital functions such as training and qualification, maintenance, and even watchstanding will suffer as surely as night follows day. This is especially true of periods spent under way and deployed. Officers and sailors must then attend to their departmental and divisional duties as well as stand watches, but it is hard for even the most organized, motivated person to stand watch on a one-in-three basis if the daily routine is disorganized.

The plan of the day (POD) is the document that formalizes the ship's routine. The *SORM* addresses the plan of the day in detail in chapter 5. It provides that a plan of the day, published daily by the XO or an authorized representative, will constitute the primary medium for the promulgation of such orders and directives as the XO, or the duty officer when the XO is absent, may issue. The POD will be posted on all department and division bulletin boards and will be read at quarters when the ship is in port. Each member of the crew is then responsible for obeying the orders it contains.

Your POD will prove most effective in administering the daily routine of the ship if it

- is complete and addresses all ship-wide major events;
- is published early (preferably the day before its execution) to allow departments to adjust to key events;
- is used to assist the ship's training program with training and qualification notes;
- is used to honor those awarded recognition for superior performance, recent promotion, or reenlistment;
- includes topics of general interest to the crew, such as upcoming port calls and mail deliveries.

Correspondence

CORRESPONDENCE ACCOUNTING SYSTEM

It is essential that you have an absolutely reliable correspondence system. All incoming matter must be opened and logged as soon as received, then routed promptly through the XO and you to action and information personnel. The routing sheets can be filled out by anyone of your choosing, depending upon the size of the ship. Large ships usually use the ship's secretary for the captain's correspondence and the XO's yeoman for routine correspondence. Small ships usually task a yeoman with all correspondence. In any event, make sure that all correspondence is promptly put in the hands of the person designated to take action and that a deadline for providing a reply is established.

Part of this system should be a tickler file, preferably kept by the XO's yeoman. Many commanding officers keep a small personal tickler file on selected important correspondence. Having ensured that each piece of correspondence will reach a person who will present a proposed answer to you within the required time, you can now turn your attention to the content of the letters.

COMMAND COMMUNICATIONS CONTENT

As CO, you should be conscious of your choice of words in all conversation and writing. Poor communications skills will handicap you in whatever you attempt. Your success is improved by the use of plain, forceful words, correctly chosen and arranged into well-composed sentences and paragraphs so as to convey your meaning directly, clearly, and unequivocally.

In addition to care in conversation and writing, you should always think at least one level above yourself. Try to imagine yourself as the senior officer who is receiving your request, answer, or statement. Is your case stated clearly? Will the problem be understood from what you have written, and have you made it easy for the senior officer to approve your request? Have you answered the simple questions of *how, when, what, where,* and *why?* Finally, if the written work is directed to an organization that may not understand shipboard terminology, have you completely explained or described the situation so that they can understand it? This last point is particularly important in communications involving investigations and fitness reports.

TONE

As commanding officer, you set the *tone* in which your command will speak. Your right to do so is obvious. Confusion and misunderstanding will occur, however, when you are unsure about the tone you desire or when your subordinates do not understand what you want. There are many examples of this. On one ship, officers had letters constantly returned for rewriting until they learned that their captain did not like to see the word "however" in the middle of a sentence. On another, the XO would not sign letters of fewer than two paragraphs. Misunderstandings such as these waste time and are hardly good for morale. If you seem to be returning a lot of correspondence for rewrite, a solution is to *make a list* of your pet words and expressions and circulate it for the wardroom to see. Such a list of fifteen or twenty desired and "forbidden" items can save much writing and rewriting.

GUIDANCE

A substantial part of your job as CO is the training of your officers. This training should include showing individual subordinates how to express themselves on paper. Many otherwise excellent young officers have failed to learn this aspect of their profession along the way and have as a result been less effective at the XO level than they might have been.

If the "list" approach mentioned above does not result in acceptable correspondence, then you will have to devote more attention to this aspect of officers' training. Bear in mind, however, that harsh actions and words are rarely of value in teaching the art of corresponding and communicating. Stern discipline and quick censure may keep a person alert on a bridge or engine room watch, but they are ineffective in stimulating someone to think and write with enthusiasm and imagination.

Another approach to training young officers to write is the "sigh and sign it" system. It is best understood by reading one destroyer commanding officer's description of it: "Sure, the junior officers on my ship write some clumsy letters, but unless they are in error or could cause a misunderstanding, I let them go as written. The young officer gets a feeling of accomplishment out of seeing his letter go off the ship to carry out the ship's business. Next time he does it better because he has had more experience. However, if his work shows no improvement, then the executive officer or I talk to him and give him a few hints about what a good Navy letter should look like." You might keep this advice and this system in mind the next time you are tempted to "nitpick" a letter. Who will read it? What harm can it do if it is less than perfect? Is it really written badly, or is it just written differently from your style?

You will now have established a workable system for receiving, routing, and processing correspondence and for producing satisfactory answers. You can afford to pass on solving some of the administrative problems that correspondence will bring you.

Make sure you have a copy of *The Naval Institute Guide to Naval Writing*, by Robert Shenk, handy. It is published by Naval Institute Press.

Investigations
From time to time, even in the best-run ships, incidents will occur that require investigation. These may range from minor injuries to personnel or damage to equipment up to more serious matters. As CO, you should familiarize yourself with the investigation process and be prepared to

carry it out properly. A carefully conducted investigation is not to be feared and in most cases will be to your advantage.

The *Manual of the Judge Advocate General* (*JAGMAN*) explains the three types of fact-finding bodies in the Navy: courts of inquiry, boards of investigation, and one-officer investigations. While investigations conducted by a court of inquiry are always "formal," those conducted by the other two fact-finding bodies may be either "formal" or "informal." The difference is that the "formal" investigation is convened by a written appointing order, testimony is taken under oath, and the proceedings are recorded verbatim.

Only an officer authorized under the Uniform Code of Military Justice (UCMJ) to convene a general court-martial (or other person designated by the Secretary of the Navy for the purpose) may convene a court of inquiry. You, as a commanding officer, may convene either a board or a one-officer investigation. The informal one-officer investigation, convened either orally or in writing, is the type most frequently used in small ships.

Whenever you have reason to believe that you may become a "party" (defined as a person whose conduct or performance of duty is "subject to inquiry" or who has a "direct interest" in the inquiry), ask your superior in command to order the investigation. This ensures objectivity and reduces the possibility of reinvestigation. Where reference to a superior is impracticable, however, or where the incident is of such a minor nature that objectivity can be maintained in spite of an apparent personal interest by the convening authority, the *JAGMAN* states that the matter need not be referred to a superior in command, since one investigation does not preclude a subsequent investigation of the same subject by order of either the same or a superior commander.

Informal investigations are discussed in detail in the *JAGMAN*, which also includes required guides, forms, and checklists. You should be familiar with these provisions, since most of your investigations will be of this type.

Classified Information

Some of your correspondence will be classified, and your handling of it will have to conform closely to the classified information handling regulations. Violations can lead to serious consequences, both for the violator and his or her commanding officer. *Don't let this happen in your ship.* Understand the appropriate regulations, school your administrative personnel, and give the subject command attention.

Navy Regulations, article 1121, states in part that no person in the Department of the Navy shall convey or disclose, by oral or written communications, publication, graphic (including photographic), or other means, any classified information.

Security of classified information should be an integral part of your command philosophy. It is wrong to assume that mere promulgation of the regulations will guarantee protection. Such regulations cannot meet every situation and cannot possibly cover all ship's equipment and the many classified details of operations and performance capabilities.

One of your primary concerns, then, is to ensure that classified information is not revealed to those without a need to know. This subject is also part of the larger subject of ship's security, which we will now discuss in detail.

Ship's Security

The security of the ship is another twenty-four-hour administrative concern of the CO. In this case, we are not talking about security in the sense of fire or flood prevention, but rather the protection of classified correspondence, materials, and equipment; unclassified but vital areas, such as the engineering spaces; and other ship functions that might be the target of sabotage. This subject is so intermeshed with that of the preceding section that much of the information discussed will apply equally to both. Definitions of various levels of classification and some of the bills are the same for correspondence as for physical security.

Under the security program, your primary concern will be to develop several subprograms, which will

- control access to the ship and to specific areas within it by means of rules, alarm systems, locks, and guards;
- ensure that classified correspondence and objects are clearly marked, strictly accounted for, used only by authorized personnel, and securely stowed when not in use;

- ensure that all personnel are screened, instructed, and monitored to ensure their integrity, reliability, and understanding of the techniques for safeguarding classified information and nuclear weapons (OPNAVINST 5510.1 series).

To accomplish the foregoing, you will need to establish certain regulations and bills.

SECURITY REGULATIONS

The *SORM* contains most of the information you will need to establish a strong security program. It prescribes the following bills for use afloat:

- *Security Bill,* which describes and assigns responsibilities for the handling and safeguarding of classified material and information
- *Ship's Official Correspondence and Classified Material Control Bill,* which details procedures to be followed in handling classified correspondence
- *Ship's Visitors' Bill,* which specifies procedures and restrictions for control of visitors
- *Ship's Anti-Sneak/Anti-Swimmer Attack Bill,* which specifies procedures for defending the ship from external or internal attack
- *Ship's Security from Unauthorized Visitors Bill,* which promulgates instructions for dealing with unauthorized visitors when "repel boarders" action is not required
- *Security Watch and Antiterrorism Bill,* which outlines tactics, techniques, and procedures to deter, detect, defend against, mitigate, and recover from terrorist attacks

Chapter 3 of the *SORM* prescribes that a security manager be appointed to assist the commanding officer. This officer can legally be appointed only by the CO or by a legally convened court-martial acting to safeguard security within the command.

An effective security manager is vital to the success of the command security program. The officer you assign to this post should be well versed in all aspects of classified material control and security regulations. In the information age, computer and automatic data processing security is increasingly critical, and command attention and consistency in this area are vital. The security of our networks (unclassified and classified) is a matter of warfighting effectiveness and survival. The most recent stand-up of several cyber-related commands addressing these threats is an indication of how serious this new and evolving challenge is. As a commanding officer in charge of numerous networked systems, it is your responsibility to actively exercise and enforce security procedures.

CLASSIFICATION CATEGORIES

OPNAVINST 5510.1 and the *SORM* describe the various categories of classifications and define terms used in security programs. All crew members should be instructed in the different classification categories and should understand how they are handled. This means indoctrinating them in the meanings of the following terms:

Need to Know: the need for certain information by an individual in order to fulfill his or her duties. A security clearance does not in itself establish a "need to know."

Personal Security Clearance: an administrative determination by competent authority that an individual is eligible, from a security standpoint, for access to classified information up to and including the designated category

Top Secret: information the unauthorized disclosure of which could result in exceptionally grave damage to the nation

Secret: information the unauthorized disclosure of which could result in serious damage to the nation

Confidential: information the unauthorized disclosure of which could reasonably be expected to cause damage to the national security

Restricted Data: all information concerning the design, manufacture, or utilization of atomic weapons, the production of special nuclear material, and the use of nuclear material in the production of energy

For Official Use Only: information not requiring safeguarding in the interest of national defense but still not considered releasable to the general public

Access: the ability and opportunity to obtain knowledge or possession of classified information

Security Areas: in certain ships, equipment and material of different classifications create the need for defining security areas on a graduated basis concerning the necessary restrictions on access, control of movement within the area, and type of protection required. Security areas are categorized in OPNAVINST 5510.1 as follows:

Exclusion Area: an area containing classified information of such nature that access to it means, for all practical purposes, access to such information

Limited Area: an area containing classified information such that uncontrolled movement by a visitor would permit access to it, but such that while within it access may be prevented by escort and other internal restrictions and controls

Controlled Area: an area adjacent to or encompassing limited or exclusion areas, but such that uncontrolled movement by a visitor does not permit access to classified information.

Public Relations

Public relations is an important responsibility and enduring concern. You must be ready to take advantage of every opportunity to make a contribution to the Navy's overall public affairs program and strategic communication messages. While you will be assisted by your public affairs officer (PAO), you must personally oversee the administration of the public affairs program. The PAO needs your command interest, and you, in turn, cannot afford a major error in administration.

Much of your contact with the press and public will occur when you are on independent operations. On independent duty, while you will be executing public relations on your own, significant assistance is available via reach-back through your chain of command, up to the fleet commander level and beyond. When operating as part of a fleet or when within the continental limits of the United States, even more assistance is available from staff public affairs officers, larger ships, and shore commanders.

The following discussion of the administration of public affairs includes those aspects that apply both to independent operations and to periods when you are under another commander.

Shipboard public relations is essentially the advancement of the proper interests of the Navy—and the nation—by putting forward the ship's "best foot," with due regard for the requirements of good taste, honesty, and security. As a commanding officer, you are entrusted as an ambassador (as is each member of your crew) in delivering strategic messages both in your presence and in your actions. This is part of your mission.

VISITORS

In a small ship, most of the CO's "public relations" has to do with visitors. Visitors cannot be casually invited or lightly treated. Article 0714 of *Navy Regulations* makes you responsible for the control of visitors to your command. You must comply with the relevant provisions of the *Department of the Navy Security Manual for Classified Information* and other pertinent directives. *Navy Regulations* further requires that commanding officers take such measures and impose such restrictions on visitors as are necessary to safeguard the classified material under their jurisdiction. Finally, it requires that COs and other officially concerned personnel exercise reasonable care to safeguard the persons and property of visitors, as well as to take precautions to safeguard the property and persons within the command. The general visiting bill in the *SORM* describes visiting procedures in detail and should be reviewed carefully prior to each "open house" or other visiting occasion.

When general visiting and tours are permitted, encourage your officers and crew to entertain visitors with such general information about the ship and the Navy as they can without disclosing classified data. In addition to security provisions, warn your sailors to be alert for pilferage, theft, and sabotage. Always maintain positive control of tour groups—deciding in advance how many guides will be assigned to a given group of visitors. Set up clearly marked routes so as to avoid crowding, confusion, and possible injury. Limit the number of people in any one space at a given time, and have medical personnel available. Create a festive and welcoming air by arranging unclassified displays or exhibits with descriptive posters and by rehearsing escorts in the briefs they can give while conducting groups around the ship. Courtesy, patience, and tact are the keys to success during these tours.

Unclassified, controlled visits of foreign nationals, within the capacity of the ship to handle them, may be authorized by the commanding officer, subject to local restrictions. Classified visits must be authorized by the CNO in accordance with the *Security Manual*.

DEALERS, TRADESMEN, AND AGENTS

Navy Regulations, article 0811, prescribes that, in general, dealers or tradesmen or their agents shall not be admitted within a command. You may grant exceptions to this to conduct public business, to transact private business with individuals at the request of the latter, or to furnish services and supplies that would otherwise not be sufficiently available to the ship's personnel. Personal commercial solicitation and the conduct of commercial transactions are governed by separately promulgated policies of the Department of Defense. The acceptance of gifts or "special favors" from tradesmen are strictly governed by Department of Defense and Department of the Navy ethics regulations.

Although you should encourage your crew to make financial and insurance provisions for their dependents, you should never allow solicitation of them by a specific company. The purchase of insurance, mutual funds, and financial plans is the private business of the individual and must be dealt with as such. Unfortunately, salespeople are inclined to take advantage of various service connections and demand the crew's time for a "presentation" that sooner or later becomes a sales pitch. You have firm grounds for refusing any such request. Regulations prohibit commercial companies from soliciting participation in life insurance, mutual funds, and other investment plans, commodities, or services at any naval installation, with or without compensation. It also prohibits personal commercial solicitation and sale to military personnel who are junior in grade and rank. The intent is to eliminate any and all instances where it would appear that coercion, intimidation, or pressure was used because of rank, grade, or position.

PRESS RELATIONS

Press personnel and correspondents occupy a unique and important place in our society. They are quite conscious of this position and of what they hold to be their prerogatives. Their need to produce interesting news and your requirements regarding security can conflict on occasion. This makes relations with the press an important business for the CO.

Generally, press releases are not made directly to the press by ships, but there may be emergencies or special occasions where you will be authorized or even directed to make a press release locally. Ask for help from your squadron or group commander if you need it. If not, be sure you comply with the provisions of the *Public Affairs Manual*. You may originate hometown news releases, but these should be sent to the Home Town News Release Center for screening and release.

When direct contact with the press is authorized or directed by higher authority, you should review with your PAO the questions the press might ask and the areas of possible inquiry. Write down the details of the situation you are preparing to discuss and be sure of your numbers. Rehearse your answers if time permits. If your ship does not have a PAO of sufficient experience, ask for help from your chain of command.

When you meet the press, be honest and forthright. If you feel you cannot furnish an answer for some reason, tell the press why. If you do not know the answer, say so and offer to provide it as soon as possible. Most journalists are professionals. They are required by their editors to ask probing questions, and they don't always expect an answer.

Command Interest

There are many details in administering a ship, and this chapter has touched on most key matters. The organization and administration of your ship, in execution, are primarily the executive officer's functions, but never delude yourself that you can afford to neglect either. As in all areas of command, as soon as you fail to manifest interest in organization or administration, they will become of less interest to your officers and crew. Show an appropriate interest, and your officers and crew will do the rest, while you can concentrate on training the men and women under your command to beat any force they oppose.

4

Executive Officer, Department Heads, and Wardroom

You will face—as you search that hidden terrain at the very
heart of yourself—what your heart is all about. You will find
yourself at the heart of an officer, and I truly hope you will
like what you discover about yourself in that moment.

—Former Secretary of the Navy Sean O'Keefe

Developing the Wardroom

Very little that you do as a captain personally is more important than
the personal and professional development of the officers assigned to
your command. Each of the men and women in the wardroom, from the
executive officer to the most junior ensign, is a responsibility entrusted
to you by the Navy and our nation. Your job is to train, lead, evaluate,
and—perhaps most importantly—inspire them in the execution of their
responsibilities. If you wake up every morning and ask yourself "How
can I best train and lead the wardroom today?," you will be well on your
way to a successful command tour. Let's talk about the executive officer,
the department heads, and the wardroom one at a time.

Executive Officer: Status, Authority, and Responsibilities

The executive officer is senior to all the department heads and is the direct
representative of the commanding officer. While executing the orders of the
CO, the XO takes precedence over all other officers attached or assigned,
and the orders given are to be considered as coming from the CO.

U.S. Navy Regulations states that the XO shall be an officer eligible to succeed to command, and who, when practicable, will be next in rank to the CO. When the officer so assigned is absent or incapable of performing duties, the commanding officer shall detail the senior line officer in the command to succeed the XO. *Navy Regulations* goes on to say that the XO, while in the execution of duties as such, will take precedence over all other persons under the command of the CO.

In the *SORM*, we can find details—lots of them. According to this reference, the XO is the direct representative of the CO. All orders issued by the XO will have the same force and effect as though uttered by the captain and must be obeyed accordingly by all persons within the command. The XO will be primarily responsible to the CO for the organization, performance of duty, training, maintenance, and good order and discipline of the entire command. The XO will recognize the right of a department head to confer directly with the CO on matters relating specifically to the department. It is clear, however, that the most important duties of the XO lie in the conforming to and carrying out of the policies of the commander and in keeping the CO informed of all significant matters relating to the ship and crew.

SPECIFIC DUTIES OF THE EXECUTIVE OFFICER

Under current regulations, the duties of the executive officer are, simply, such duties as the commanding officer assigns. However, the executive officer cannot literally "do everything." Like the commanding officer, the XO must delegate to subordinates—in this case, the department heads. The wise commander will insist on this delegation and will support the results, good or bad. Further, the CO should encourage the XO to use the ship's organization, requiring that heads of departments delegate their authority downward in turn. An XO must use the abilities of all, coordinating their activities and correlating their purposes. If XOs do not delegate and try to run the whole ship centrally and solely, they doom themselves, their commanding officer, and their ship to failure.

One example should suffice. XOs must be the ship's planners, but they must subordinate to this function the larger everyday role of administrator and expediter. Administration and planning are important, but only when they implement larger goals. Delegation operates here when the XO originates the overall plan and requires subordinates to make dependent plans.

Remember at all times that being executive officer is no piece of cake. The XO must resolve conflicts, establish unity of purpose, and mold the spirit of the ship in accordance with your guidance; the XO must ensure that these duties are carried out within the policies set forth, and everything must reflect your personality rather than the XO's. This is a tall order, particularly for a relatively senior officer, one who has formed his or her own opinions and is preparing for eventual command, or who may have already had the experience of a command tour previously.

RELATIONSHIP WITH THE COMMANDING OFFICER

Official directives make plain what the relationship should be. *Navy Regulations* provides that the commanding officer shall keep the executive officer informed of all policies and normally shall issue all orders relative to the duties of that command through the XO. Accordingly, the CO will normally require that all communications of an official nature from subordinates be forwarded through the XO. The two exceptions to this, already mentioned, are the department heads, when necessary, and those senior to the executive officer (sometimes the medical or dental officers). Even these officers, however, must keep the XO informed on matters related to the functions of the command.

Obviously, the executive officer must use the proper sense of judgment in carrying out your policies. Equally obvious is that you, as the commanding officer, must preside wisely. While you must require that your XO carry out the spirit and letter of the regulations, there will be times when you can learn, if you encourage initiative and ask for opinions and advice. This is particularly true if the XO has served in your ship type before and when you may not have.

There are ways you can help the XO to function more effectively. For instance, with regard to those provisions of the regulations that use the word "normally" when discussing communications "around" the XO, many senior officers counsel against permitting department heads excessive latitude. You will strike a balance based on your style, factoring speed of information flow with strict centralization via the XO.

Again, it is unwise to take upon yourself the executive officer's duties. This will be an especially inviting pitfall for you as a new commanding officer if you were XO in your last sea tour. In fact, it is doubly wrong. It occupies your attention uselessly and at the same time deprives you of your executive officer's best efforts.

Finally, keep your executive officer informed at all times of your thoughts and intentions about changes of policy and schedule. XOs are only as good as the last information made available to them. Remember that the XO is in many different meetings and conversations that you may not be in and sometimes may have information that is different from yours.

The commanding officer must ask throughout their tour, *How do I use my executive officer, and how does my executive officer use me?* Is the XO an administrator, a policy-setter, or both? Is the XO really the second-in-command? Do I have to lean on the XO for performance? Does the XO follow me or go another way? How is our rapport? How much do we talk each day, and where? Is the XO strong or weak? Does the XO's skill-set complement mine or create friction? What is my evaluation of the XO's potential for command? The answers to these questions provide a basis for judging whether your relationship is healthy and providing the results you want as far as proper administration of your ship is concerned, as well as whether you are giving the XO an adequate opportunity to demonstrate and extend individual abilities.

In the last analysis, the XO's performance will depend on yours. Successful commanding officers will develop in their executive officers the ability to manage their own and the crew's time and effort to do the most for the ship. The CO will instill in the executive officer the most efficient methods of keeping the CO informed of the required aspects of the ship's administration and operation. The CO will delve into details when necessary to ensure that correct action is being taken but will not preempt responsibility or seem to run a one-man show. It is imperative that a commanding officer grant sufficient authority to the XO in order to ensure execution of his or her responsibilities. The CO must set and make known priorities. There is never enough time or money to do everything; the XO must know what you want done first. A continuous appraisal of "What have we accomplished? What do we intend to do next?" with the XO will ensure that you are both running on the same track. All these are things you must do to make the command more effective.

One exception to this principle is punishment—which is the prerogative and duty of the commanding officer and cannot be delegated. Establish early on with your executive officer what you consider punishment and what is only "completing a prescribed duty satisfactorily." Never tolerate unofficial extra duty, but do support the XO's judgment of when required work has been completed so that liberty can begin. Avoid like the plague any form of mass punishment. Either find the culprit or make known your displeasure in some other manner.

Try to find ways to break free time for your XO to work. As soon as you can establish the XO's competence in ship- and linehandling, shift your training effort in these fields to more junior officers.

You will have a large amount of correspondence that your XO has to read, route, and designate for action or reply. Having it all routed to you first is a well-established practice, but unless you like being bogged down, let it pass through you with minimal or no comment on the routing slip. Let your young action addressees develop their initiative. If you have idiosyncrasies about writing style that you feel strongly about, produce a list of dos and don'ts (as suggested in the previous chapter) as soon as possible, but in any event, don't accept poor grammar. A good tickler system run by your executive officer is essential. Keep a selective tickler file for very important items for your own use as well.

Finally, even though your executive officer's primary function is to be your alter ego, make the most of their contributions. Make the XO an integral part of your team, soliciting and employing their suggestions. Use the XO's input when you're able, providing it supports your general philosophy and guidance (even though you may not be thrilled with all the ideas). This makes for a strong leadership team. See that the XO has a share in the success of your command.

TRAINING FOR COMMAND

Most XOs are already screened for command and "fleet up" to commander command following their XO tour. Your role as trainer and mentor is critical. You are training your relief. *Navy Regulations* states that the commanding officer shall afford frequent opportunities to the executive officer, and to other officers of the ship as practicable, to improve their skill in shiphandling, an essential fundamental aspect for command. There are many good books on the subject. The best is *Naval Shiphandling*, published by Naval Institute Press. Over the course of a career, your XO has benefited from specific ship-type simulator training and assessments. Regardless, require that your executive officer demonstrate theoretical knowledge of the kind contained in *Naval Shiphandling*. The next step (if the XO is, in fact, new to your ship type) is to have them observe your shiphandling under a wide variety of conditions and maneuvers. Then allow the XO to take the conn, with corrections given by you only to avoid damage.

The second important requirement for training of your executive officer for command is preparation for battle. Every general quarters drill, every emergency drill, and all exercises involving the ship's armament, engines, and equipment are opportunities to impart to XOs (and, of course, to the rest of your crew) your philosophy of fighting a ship. The XO's role as damage control training team leader is pivotal in reinforcing these skills.

With these two essentials in hand, what remains is your assessment of the XO's overall character and command ability and your efforts to improve their attributes in these areas. This task can be simplified by asking yourself, "What (in addition to professional competence) are the characteristics of a good commanding officer?" Here are several: physical and moral courage, tenacity, endurance, common sense, integrity, enthusiasm, command presence, composure, and managerial ability.

A similar list made a century ago might have focused exclusively on physical courage, tenacity, and endurance. These qualities are clearly needed today, but emphasis has shifted over the years to also include the mental side. Very few of us are born with all the attributes of an outstanding naval officer, and just like you, your executive officer will probably lack some of them. You should constantly try to learn and build together. You must collaboratively explore, critique, and then take advantage of capabilities and compensate for deficiencies.

The qualities of common sense and integrity are among the most important of those listed. If an officer is to take actions that can affect the entire Navy or even the country, one must realize that help is available if one asks for it, but officers must also be prepared to stand on their own. Similarly, when a problem arises, it must not be covered up. An officer of integrity will bring it out in the open, try to solve it, and, if unable to, report to higher authority without fear of the consequences.

Command presence may be one quality an officer is born with, but it can be enhanced by careful attention to personal detail. Uniforms should be kept clean and neat and be worn with pride. The appearance, conduct, and language of the commanding and executive officers should be the standard for the ship. Your XO will have many occasions throughout the day to address small groups of officers and sailors. Encourage the XO to take a few minutes before each one to organize their thoughts so that communications will be coherent and firmly and clearly delivered. The industry, enthusiasm, and dedication that you demonstrate throughout the day, as well as in your contacts with your executive officer, will encourage the XO to display the same qualities he or she sees in you. If you are unenthusiastic and unprofessional, you will hardly convince your XO that command is the best job in the Navy.

Composure is generally defined as a state of mind in which an individual remains calm, efficient, and effective in spite of adversity. Most executive officers have many opportunities during an average day to show composure, or lack of it. When the 0730 boat is late returning with the liberty party, when the OOD drops binoculars over the side while leaning over to reprimand the coxswain, and when the commodore wants to know why the colors were hoisted five minutes late, the XO's composure will be severely tested. If they can hear the stories of the individuals involved, resolve differences, and take appropriate disciplinary action, all without raising their voice or showing undue dissatisfaction, they will have sufficient composure to meet almost any situation. A healthy sense of humor is an enormous plus.

The executive officer must have managerial ability. The technical complexities of machinery and equipment, the large amounts of funds required for maintenance, supplies, and the general running of ships, and the massive quantity of administrative matters generated by higher command need a firm managerial hand. Make sure your XO demonstrates the ability to manage those assigned to solve these problems and does not attempt to take them on personally.

An impatient or intolerant commanding officer will often have such an uneasy and uncomfortable relationship with an executive officer that it detracts not only from the CO's daily performance of duty but also from efforts to prepare the XO for command. The wise commanding officer corrects and critiques their executive officer in private and commends them in public, and requires, of course, the same behavior from them in relation to their own juniors.

If you can train your executive officer in this careful way, and end their tour by giving them good marks, you will have helped produce a fine prospective commanding officer—and your relief. You will likely have improved your own style of command, too. The instruction and qualification of future commanding officers is, next to command itself, the most important task a senior naval officer has.

The Executive Staff

The function of the executive staff is to assist the executive officer in the discharge of administrative responsibilities. The duties of staff members are set forth in the *SORM*, chapter 3. It is important, however, to work for a good spirit in the staff, as well as toward professional competence.

The size of your XO's staff will depend on the size of your ship. In a large vessel, you will have officers assigned to each billet in the standard organization illustrated in figure 4-1. In smaller ships, a single officer may fill more than one of them. In very small ships, either some of them will be left vacant completely, or they will be filled by petty officers. Your own desires will also determine how many of your personnel can be assigned full or part time. In general, the XO's office will include an administrative assistant (usually a junior officer or chief yeoman), the ship's secretary (an ensign or rated yeoman), and a personnel officer (an ensign or rated personnel specialist). Exact ranks and rates will depend on the size of the ship.

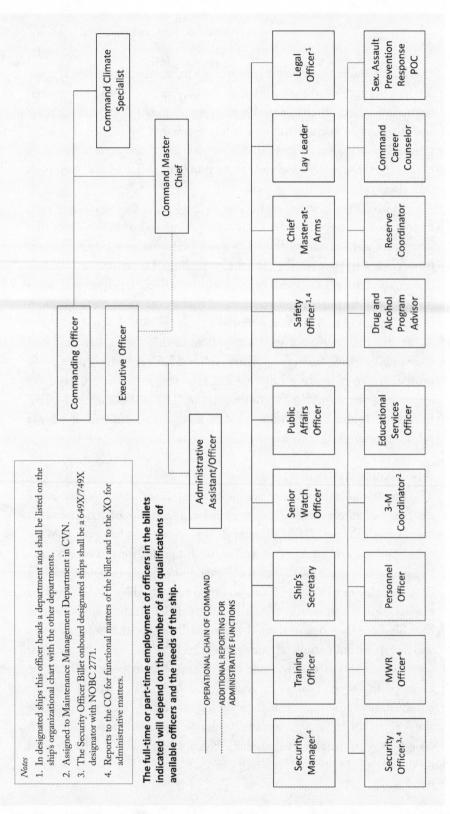

Notes

1. In designated ships this officer heads a department and shall be listed on the ship's organizational chart with the other departments.

2. Assigned to Maintenance Management Department in CVN.

3. The Security Officer Billet onboard designated ships shall be a 649X/749X designator with NOBC 2771.

4. Reports to the CO for functional matters of the billet and to the XO for administrative matters.

The full-time or part-time employment of officers in the billets indicated will depend on the number of and qualifications of available officers and the needs of the ship.

——— OPERATIONAL CHAIN OF COMMAND

------- ADDITIONAL REPORTING FOR ADMINISTRATIVE FUNCTIONS

Fig. 4-1. The executive assistants. These officers serve under the executive officer and carry out many of the ship's administrative functions.

Other officers shown on the organization chart, if assigned, will usually have small offices or will operate from their staterooms. The master-at-arms (MAA) force is also part of the XO's staff. In a large ship, it can be quite extensive, including a chief MAA, a mate in each division, and brig guards. In smaller ships, the force will be reduced accordingly; in a submarine, it may consist of only the chief of the boat. In all vessels, the chief MAA (or chief of the boat) should be a leader of impeccable record and outstanding capabilities.

Figure 4-1 shows the public affairs officer as being directly under the executive officer. You should make sure, however, that it is understood between you, the XO, and the PAO that they have *direct* access to you on public affairs matters. (The PAO should, of course, fill in the executive officer as soon as possible after finding it necessary to contact you directly.) If you do *not* make this arrangement, your PAO, with a request to answer an important question and a deadline, will not be first with the truth, which then often requires additional work to correct. If an impatient reporter goes without an answer to a question, an unnecessarily adverse story may appear in the paper the next morning. *Public affairs will not wait on protocol.* It is your *personal* responsibility, and *no one* in your organization should be allowed to slow down the process, even inadvertently.

Chaplains, when assigned, are placed directly under the executive officer, as are combat cargo officers on amphibious ships. When no medical officer is assigned, enlisted medical personnel are part of the executive staff.

The senior watch officer on large ships is sometimes assigned under the navigator but usually is assigned under the executive officer. The senior watch officer is the senior person standing deck watches. His or her job is to make up the watch list for officers at sea and the duty list in port. In large ships, the command duty list is handled by the XO or senior head of department. You should make the senior watch officer responsible for instruction of watch officers and recording of qualifications and practical factors for watchstanders. This arrangement not only reduces the executive officer's workload but also gives the senior watch officer good experience in conducting and administering.

In submarines, the chief of the boat is the command senior enlisted leader on board. As such, they are your principal enlisted adviser and are responsible for keeping you aware of existing or potential situations, procedures, or practices that could affect the welfare, morale, job satisfaction, and efficiency of enlisted personnel. The *Submarine Organization and Regulations Manual* addresses their duties in detail. In dealing with the chief of the boat, you and your XO must ensure that they are looked upon with respect and given the latitude, authority, and responsibility needed to perform effectively. A good rapport will go a long way toward improving the effectiveness of your chain of command.

The Maintenance and Material Management (3-M) coordinator, an officer or senior enlisted performing collateral duty, is the XO's assistant for matters pertaining to the Planned Maintenance System and the Maintenance Data Collection System. On a submarine, however, they will work more closely with and for the department heads.

The leading yeoman is also uniquely important in the submarine force. They assist the XO in all clerical and personnel matters, though they must also be available to other officers. Exact duties are set forth in the *Submarine Operations and Readiness Manual*.

Temporary Succession to Command

Navy Regulations provides that in the event of the incapacity, death, relief from duty, or absence of the commanding officer, the executive officer shall succeed to command until relieved by competent authority or until the regular CO returns. If the XO is unable to take over, others then succeed to command by rank if attached to the ship and eligible for command at sea.

An officer who succeeds to command as a result of incapacity, death, departure on leave, detachment without relief, or absence owing to orders from competent authority of the officer detailed to command has the same authority and responsibility as the officer they succeeded.

Relieving Commanding Officer in Extenuating Circumstances

On rare occasions, an executive officer may have to relieve the commanding officer in extenuating circumstances. This should be done only after extremely careful consideration. *Navy Regulations* covers the subject completely and should be studied thoroughly before contemplating such a step. It is rare these days that a ship is not in radio or Internet protocol (IP) communication with the chain of command to seek guidance. In any event, the provisions of *Navy Regulations* must be strictly followed. The executive officer who relieves under this article must make sure that the case is documented and witnessed in such a fashion that it will stand up in a military court.

A good executive officer makes your job easy by getting the most out of your officers. They will indeed work them to their limit, but if the XO assigns work fairly, supervises well, and praises appropriately, your officers will produce beyond their expected capabilities.

The Ship's Officers

The officers of a ship are the driveshaft between the commanding officer, who holds authority and responsibility, and the enlisted sailors, who man the watches, the weapons, and the equipment that give life, mobility, and power to the ship. Without officers, a ship would be a static piece of machinery without a transmission; with them, she can become a smoothly functioning weapon of war, capable of accomplishing as much as the captain can command and inspire. The ship is a composite that must come together and come to life—hull and fittings, officers and crew, metal, weapons, habits, temperaments, mutual confidence, loyalty, pride, courage, brains, muscle, judgment, initiative, discipline, reliability, trust, respect—and the captain can bring it to life, keep it alive, or let it go dead. A fusion of technology, talent, and focus is essential to the success of your warfighting mission.

Unfortunately, you don't get to pick all of your officers, and sometimes they do not come completely trained and ready to fit into the organization. You will have to take those ordered to your command and lead them so that you get the maximum benefit from their abilities. Analyzing their potential is not an easy task, but you should work hard at it. When you have finished studying your officers' professional and physical qualifications, remember also the less apparent qualities of leadership every good officer must have. Sometimes character and intensity can overcome a lack of qualification. It is important to look for confidence-inspiring qualities in your officers. Such men and women will *avert* disaster. In this section we will review and examine the command authority given to your officers by *Navy Regulations* and other directives; the limits on their authority; their ordering and assignment; career patterns and broadening; the responsibilities and qualifications of officers for various positions in the ship's organization; additional responsibilities of department heads, division officers, and watchstanders; leadership training; social usage; and fitness reports (FITREPs).

Basic Authority and Responsibilities of Officers

The authority and responsibility of a naval officer begin the day he or she accepts a commission or warrant, whose very wording—"Know ye that, reposing special trust and confidence in the patriotism, fidelity, and abilities" of the person commissioned—is an inspiration to the new officer. This is followed by an equally moving occasion—when the officer takes the oath of office, swearing to support and defend the Constitution of the United States against all enemies, foreign and domestic; to bear true faith and allegiance to the same; to take this obligation freely and without any mental reservation or purpose of evasion; and to "well and faithfully" discharge the duties of the office into which the officer is about to enter. This is indeed an oath not entered into lightly.

Thus, the day he or she accepts a commission or warrant and takes the oath, an officer takes on certain basic responsibilities by virtue of these actions. At this time, and later, other responsibilities and the authority to carry them out are given by *Navy Regulations* and other directives. These sources should be examined carefully by all of your officers, so that they will know the extent and limits of their authority, and by you as a commanding officer, so that you can instruct and guide them.

Authority and Responsibilities under *Navy Regulations*
GENERAL AUTHORITY

Navy Regulations is quite general concerning officers. Every officer in the naval service shall be acquainted with, obey, and, so far as his or her authority extends, enforce the laws, regulations, and orders relating to the Department of the Navy. The officer must faithfully and truthfully discharge the duties of the office to the best of his or her ability, in conformance with existing orders and regulations and oath of office. In the absence of instructions, the officer shall act in conformity with the policies and customs of the service to protect the public interest. This requirement is very broad and covers a multitude of possible circumstances where an officer can, and should, take action. Every officer, then, upon acceptance of his or her commission or warrant, and upon taking the oath, accepts these general duties of all officers.

REQUIRED CONDUCT

Navy Regulations goes on to require all persons (including officers) in the naval service to show in themselves good examples of virtue, honor, patriotism, and subordination. All persons are to act to the utmost of their ability and the extent of their authority in maintaining good order and discipline as well as in other matters concerned with the efficiency of the command. All persons in the naval service must obey readily and strictly, and execute promptly, the lawful orders of superiors.

Amplifying Directives Concerning Authority and Responsibilities

AUTHORITY FROM ORGANIZATIONAL POSITION

While the basic authority for all officers stems from *Navy Regulations*, as discussed above, additional authority and responsibility come from the officer's organizational position.

The final fixing of responsibility has been a topic of interest in the military profession for thousands of years. One of the best discourses on the subject is by Admiral Hyman G. Rickover. Responsibility, he said, is

> a unique concept. It can only reside and inhere in a single individual. You may share it with others, but your portion is not diminished. You may delegate it, but it is still with you. You may disdain it, but you cannot divest yourself of it. Even if you do not recognize it or admit its presence, you cannot escape it. If responsibility is rightfully yours, no evasion, or ignorance, no passing the blame, can shift the burden to some one else. Unless you can point your finger at the man who is responsible when something goes wrong, then you never really had anyone responsible.

These are strong but true words. The concept is an almost sacred one in our Navy.

ORGANIZATIONAL AUTHORITY

Organizational authority of an officer comes from their assigned billet within an organization. The command structure to which the officer is assigned is based upon guidance from this instruction as promulgated by command, department, division, and other instructions. The organizational structure sets forth the positions, duties, and responsibilities of all persons in the structure, and invests authority accordingly.

Limits on Authority: Lawful Orders

INJURIOUS OR CAPRICIOUS CONDUCT

Notwithstanding the almost unlimited authority and responsibility of a naval officer, there are limits. They must be well known by you and your officers and carefully observed. *Only lawful orders must be given and obeyed.*

Most naval officers are familiar with the semi-fictitious examples of Captain Queeg of *The Caine Mutiny* and Lieutenant Roberts of *Mister Roberts*. These stories drew upon true events. Other examples from history are difficult to bring to the attention of the reader and do not illustrate the point as well as the semi-fictional examples. Read both books, or at least watch the movies; they will illustrate the points in question better than fact.

Navy Regulations, article 1023, Abuse of Authority, prohibits persons in authority from injuring their subordinates by tyrannical or capricious conduct or by abusive language.

AUTHORITY

The *SORM*, article 1.2.1, in discussing authority, points out that it includes the right to require actions of others by oral or written orders. It should be delegated to the lowest level of competence commensurate with the subordinate's assigned responsibility and capabilities.

RESPONSIBILITY

The *SORM*, article 1.2.1, goes on to describe that unit administration is responsible for providing an environment that motivates the crew to effectively and efficiently execute their duties free from harassment.

CONTRADICTORY ORDERS

Navy Regulations, article 1024, covers contradictory and conflicting orders. If an officer contradicts orders given to another by a common superior, he must immediately report that fact to the superior whose orders he contravened, preferably in writing.

If an officer receives such a contradictory order he shall immediately exhibit his previous orders, unless instructed not to do so, and present the facts in writing to the officer who has given him the latest order. If that officer insists upon the execution of his own order, it shall be obeyed and the circumstances reported to the officer issuing the original order.

Article 1032, Authority to Place Self on Duty, prohibits an officer from placing himself on duty by virtue of his commission or warrant alone.

PUNISHMENT

The *SORM*, article 1.4.3, notes that each commander may dispose of offenses by members of that command under the *Manual for Courts-Martial* and should address them in a timely manner.

EXTRA MILITARY INSTRUCTION

In an effort to clear up any uncertainty, you should clearly understand the effective use of extra military instruction (EMI). Your primary resource for EMI should be the *Manual of the Judge Advocate General*. More letters have been written to COs by parents, congressional representatives, and concerned citizens on this subject than on all others put together. Making sure your officers, leading petty officers, and enlisted personnel understand this subject will cut your administrative and letter-writing load drastically.

The *JAGMAN*, article 0103, defines "extra military instruction" as instruction in a phase of military duty in which an individual is deficient, and is intended for and directed toward the correction of that deficiency. It therefore must be used for this purpose and not as a substitute for punitive actions that should have been taken under the UCMJ. The *JAGMAN* further describes how to implement this form of instruction and states that it will not be assigned for more than two hours a day, may be assigned at a reasonable time outside of working hours, will be no longer than necessary to correct the deficiency, and will not be assigned on the sailor's

Sabbath. Further, an individual who is otherwise entitled to liberty may commence liberty upon completion of EMI.

EMI assignment during normal working hours may be made by any officer or petty officer as part of their inherent authority. EMI after working hours should be assigned by the commanding officer but may be delegated to officers and petty officers. If it is so delegated, the CO must monitor the process.

WITHHOLDING OF PRIVILEGES

Certain privileges may be withheld temporarily, as sanctioned by the *JAGMAN*, article 0104. This procedure may be used to correct infractions of military regulations or performance deficiencies of a minor nature where stronger action is not required. Examples of privileges that may be withheld are special liberty, exchange of duty, special pay, special command programs, movies, libraries, and off-ship events on base. The authority to use this procedure rests with the individual empowered to grant the privileges.

ADDITIONAL WORK ASSIGNMENTS

The *JAGMAN*, article 0104, is an important article and is usually the cause of misunderstanding as to lawful or unlawful deprivation of liberty. It states that deprivation of liberty as punishment, except under the UCMJ, is illegal, and therefore no officer or petty officer may deny liberty as a punishment for any offense or malperformance of duty. This is clear enough. The article then goes on to state that since it is necessary to the efficiency of the naval service that certain functions be performed and that certain work be accomplished in a timely manner, it is therefore not a punishment when certain persons are required to remain on board and perform work assignments *that should have been completed during normal working hours*, for the accomplishment of *additional essential work*, or *for the achievement of the currently required level of operational readiness*. This is the crux of the problem. Good leadership and management practices will cure any resultant problems. This means extending working hours for all hands or for certain selected persons *only when absolutely necessary*. When you do, or when your officers recommend that you do, you should make every effort to ensure that your crew understands the necessity for such action. If they understand it, they will carry it out readily and well; if not, you can expect some additional mail.

If these areas of authority are clear in your mind, they will give you little trouble. If your officers understand the limits of *your* and *their* authority, they will perform more efficiently and with greater confidence, and your ship will benefit accordingly.

Assuming that you are prepared to evaluate and assign your officers to their proper billets when they arrive and are ready to supervise their use of their authority, it is now time to discuss their ordering and assignment.

Ordering and Assignment of Officers

OFFICER DISTRIBUTION

The commander, Navy Personnel Command, has the responsibility for assigning qualified officers to authorized billets. The commander also has the parallel responsibility of assigning each officer opportunities for the development of their professional and personal capabilities. The officer distribution system, in implementing these twin responsibilities, assigns officers according to the requirements of the service and the individuals' professional needs, their record and qualifications, and, where possible, their preference as to billet, ship type, and location.

THE OFFICER DISTRIBUTION SYSTEM

The officer distribution system is organized under the commander, Navy Personnel Command, as follows. A group of placement officers monitors ships and other organizations by types. Another group of officers monitors ranks or stage of career progression (division officers, department heads, etc.). These officers are called detailers. The placement officer posts the requirements for billets with the appropriate detailers, giving dates of expected rotation and qualifications. The detailer tries to fill the billet with an officer of appropriate rank and qualifications who is due to rotate at the proper time. The two officers then get together to work out details of orders to be issued. The placement officer usually informs the ship XO and CO of the results, and the detailer contacts the officer to be ordered, giving advance notice.

The greatest help you can give the officer distribution system (other than patience and understanding) is to keep submitting up-to-date inputs for your Long-Range Officer Rotation, Training, and Readiness Plan. The placement officer uses this document to monitor your present status and future needs. The most important entries on it are those indicating the billets for which each officer is in training and their qualifications to fill them. Back up your input with monthly phone calls.

COMMUNICATIONS WITH DETAILERS

Encourage your officers to take care in submitting their preferences. The detailer will generally follow their wishes if at all possible.

As commanding officer, your input to your officers' detailers can play a large part in retaining them in the Navy and furthering their professional development. For one thing, your involvement in the detailing process clearly displays your concern for your officers. It also tends to ameliorate the detailer-constituent disagreements that sometimes occur.

Career Patterns and Broadening

If you can do so without decreasing readiness, you should do all within your power to increase the professional competence of your officers by giving them opportunities to broaden their assignments and experience.

CAREER PATTERNS

Before you take any specific action, analyze the career patterns to date of each of your officers. Study their officer qualification records and past assignments, and then call them in individually and find out where each thinks they are heading professionally. They may not know. If so, you will have to be a counselor. There are various books, documents, and directives bearing on the subject; unfortunately, they relate to the past, while you need to predict the future.

You may know more about career counseling than anyone else aboard, simply by virtue of your experience. If you have someone recently assigned to Navy Personnel Command, it is worth your time to discuss their recent experience as a detailer or placement officer. Additionally, read the directives concerning the subspecialist programs and career specialty areas. These are constantly evolving to meet the needs of the force. Read the Secretary of the Navy's latest letters of instruction to the presidents of the flag and other selection boards. These documents will indicate trends that will probably be valid for many years. This information is of value to all of your officers. A wealth of up-to-date information is available online via the Navy Personnel Command's website (https://www.mynavyhr.navy.mil /Navy-Personnel-Command/), which also has links to myriad additional personnel-related resources.

IMPORTANCE OF COMMAND AT SEA

Notwithstanding the pace of progress, there are certain essentials that will never change. Command at sea will always be vital for promotion to senior ranks. An officer may reach senior rank by other paths, but command at sea will always be the route for the majority of officers. Any officer aspiring to command at sea should begin by learning all they can about their command. This is best accomplished by serving in the three basic departments—operations, weapons, and engineering. In aviation squadrons, rotation will occur naturally, as it will in submarines.

COUNSELING

With the above factors in mind, you can counsel your officers easily. You do not need to be an expert about the details of specific subspecialist programs or specialty career paths; this data is easily found via the personnel command website. However, if you do have expertise, experience, or opinions in these areas, it will be of help to your officers in making their preferences known for future shore assignments.

Your most important role in their career advancement will be to encourage them into as broad a span of billets as possible. Advise them to qualify in a second or third major departmental area. They may resist, since obviously they may not perform as well in an unfamiliar billet. It will take a good officer with a long-range outlook to agree if they think they will have to accept lesser FITREP marks in exchange for a "broadening experience."

SELF-IMPROVEMENT

Even if not assigned to a "broadening" billet, your officers can broaden themselves, especially with your encouragement. A selection board looks for these efforts, and you should make them more visible by including them in your FITREP remarks. More than one aviation captain has been selected as a carrier commanding officer because he or she took the trouble to qualify as an officer of the deck under way when serving in an embarked squadron. Give all of your officers a chance to handle your ship, including radical maneuvers.

With these comments concerning billet assignments in mind, let us now review the qualifications required to fill various billets. Since we are talking about all kinds and sizes of ships, you will find many positions described that do not apply to the ship you are commanding at the present time. We will discuss them by major departments.

The Executive Officer's Assistants

CHAPLAIN

The chaplain is responsible for all religious activities as well as such other appropriate duties as may be assigned to them. They may conduct worship according to the manner and form of their own church but must do everything possible to provide for the other denominations, either by presiding personally, by using lay leaders, or by arranging for visiting chaplains. They should make themselves available for counsel on all matters and should be your liaison with the Navy Relief Society and the American Red Cross.

COMMAND CAREER COUNSELOR

The command career counselor is responsible for establishing a program to disseminate career information and furnish career counseling. The specific rating dedicated to this counseling function signals its importance. Large ships will usually have more senior personnel assigned to this billet. Whomever is assigned must be positively motivated, thought of highly by the crew, and a good administrator.

DRUG AND ALCOHOL PROGRAM ADVISER

This officer's responsibility is to advise you on the establishment of a drug and alcohol abuse prevention program and then to establish and administer it. Large ships may have a junior line officer assigned to this program full time. This is a line and not a medical function, but the medical department should be called upon for expertise and lecturing. Small ships will have to make this a collateral function. Junior officers from the Naval Academy, Naval Reserve Officers Training Corps, and Officer Candidate School will have had some grounding in this area but may need further instruction if they are to do a satisfactory job.

EDUCATIONAL SERVICES OFFICER

The educational services officer administers educational programs and also acts as a member of the training board and assists the training officer. They may be assigned other duties in the educational and training area, and they usually administer examining boards and examinations. Only very large ships can afford to fill this billet on a full-time basis. An officer from any source can be used but will require instruction.

LEGAL OFFICER

The legal officer is the staff assistant to the commanding officer and executive officer on all matters concerning the interpretation and application of the UCMJ and other laws and regulations in the maintenance of discipline and the administration of justice. They should also make themselves available to the personnel of the command for rendering legal advice.

On large ships, a member of the Judge Advocate General's Corps is usually assigned to this billet. If one is not available, a graduate of the Military Justice School should be assigned or a junior officer sent to this school prior to reporting. On small ships, the XO may assume these responsibilities, unless the ship can spare an officer to attend school.

PERSONNEL OFFICER

The personnel officer is responsible for the placement of enlisted personnel in accordance with the personnel assignment bill and for the administration and custody of enlisted records. As with officer personnel, you will not receive enlisted personnel in the exact number of rates your ship's allowance calls for. Your personnel officer will have the same task you face with officers in fitting those personnel actually received into the listed billets. On large ships, a personnel officer is usually full time. On smaller ships, a personnel specialist performs the job. You will be fortunate if you have a limited duty officer who was a personnel specialist previously or otherwise has personnel experience.

PLANS AND TACTICS OFFICER

This officer is responsible for leading, directing, and synchronizing warship plans; planning for the long-range employment of a task unit and the tactical training of all watchstanders; and serving as the lead tactical trainer for the unit. This officer reports to the commanding officer concerning operations, intelligence, and tactical employment of the unit and assigned aircraft and to the executive officer for the administration of the plans and tactics department, which usually includes the training officer and independent duty intelligence specialist, with the warfare tactics instructors reporting as required for tactical and training purposes.

POSTAL OFFICER

This officer supervises the postal functions of the command. It is an important billet in that accountability for postal funds is a sensitive matter. Obviously, receipt of mail is important to the morale of your command. However, these duties cannot occupy an officer full time, and even on a large ship this duty is usually assigned collaterally. No particular schooling or qualification is required.

PUBLIC AFFAIRS OFFICER

The PAO is charged with carrying out the public affairs program of the command. This billet may seem to be a sleeper to some, but it is more important than you may think when first considering it. As noted in the previous chapter, *you*, as commanding officer, are responsible for the public affairs program of your ship, and you cannot afford to delegate the function so completely that you lose control of it. You must employ the talents and capabilities of the PAO to the utmost, but they cannot assume your final responsibility, nor can the executive officer, under whom they nominally operate. It is important that you establish the fact that you are available to the PAO at all times. Large ships may have a full-time PAO, but small ships assign the duty collaterally. Naval Academy graduates will have had a short course in public affairs and can fill the billet, but the important factor is that the officer should be able to write and speak well. Common sense and social ease are also important qualifications.

SAFETY OFFICER

On ships other than aircraft carriers, a safety officer is assigned the responsibility for the ship's safety program. They distribute safety information, maintain safety records, and carry out and monitor the safety program. On large ships other than aircraft carriers, this is usually a full-time billet. On small ships, it is a collateral duty. In aircraft carriers and aircraft squadrons, it is a head-of-department billet. Any officer, preferably engineering-oriented, can be assigned.

SHIP'S SECRETARY

The ship's secretary is responsible for the administration of ship's correspondence and directives, the administration and custody of officer personnel records, the preparation of the commanding officer's personal correspondence, the supervision of preparation of officers' FITREPs, and the ship's nonclassified reference library. In large ships, the ship's secretary is an officer assigned full time. On small ships, a rated yeoman performs the job. An outstanding junior officer is usually assigned as ship's admin officer. No specific qualifications are necessary, though the ability to handle English well is desirable.

SPECIAL SERVICES OFFICER

The special services officer carries out the ship's special services program, which includes athletics, recreational activities, and entertainment. The officer is the custodian of the recreation fund and all special services equipment. Large ships have a full-time special services officer, while others assign it as a collateral duty. No special qualifications are required, but a former athlete usually gets the job.

TRAINING OFFICER

The training officer is an adviser and assistant to the executive officer for training matters. This officer is a member of the training planning board and prepares and monitors training plans and schedules. This position has received increased prominence in recent years and is now a full-time position owing to the pivotal importance of maintaining readiness. On large ships, a senior officer is assigned to this billet. On small ships, a junior officer is typically assigned the duty.

3-M COORDINATOR

This officer is responsible for administering the ship's Maintenance and Material Management system. On large ships, a fairly senior officer will be assigned to this billet. On small ships, a junior officer or senior enlisted person will be assigned, usually full time. Whomever is assigned should have completed formal schooling in administration and operation of the shipboard 3-M system or have had appropriate personnel qualification standards in the 3-M system.

SECURITY MANAGER

The security manager is responsible for all matters concerning security of classified information. They prepare destruction bills, security procedures, clearance requests, and declassification plans. No specific qualification is required.

COLLATERAL DUTIES

There are several other duties assigned as collateral duties to officers and sometimes to leading petty officers. These will vary from ship to ship. Some representative examples include the following:

- athletics officer
- communications security material custodian
- crypto-security officer
- library officer
- mess caterer
- mess treasurer
- movie officer
- naval warfare publications control officer

- nuclear handling supervisor
- nuclear safety officer
- photographic officer
- radiation health officer
- secret control officer
- security officer
- senior watch officer
- sexual assault prevention and response victim advocate
- top secret control officer.

Officers of the Operations Department

In addition to carrying out the duties of a head of department, the operations officer is responsible for the collection, evaluation, and dissemination of the combat and operational information required by the missions of the ship. This includes air, surface, and subsurface search; control of aircraft; collection, display, analysis, and dissemination of intelligence; preparation of operating plans and schedules; meteorological information; and repair of electronics equipment.

The operations officer on all ships is a relatively senior officer and should be well qualified both by previous duties and by having completed as many applicable schools as possible. You will be assigned a qualified or nearly qualified officer of appropriate rank to fill this billet unless your roster shows a person now assigned to you who is about to be declared qualified.

The following officers generally report to the operations officer. (On large ships, they may, where indicated, be separate department heads.) On small ships, unless indicated otherwise, they will be part of the operations department:

- administration and training assistant
- air intelligence officer (supplied by the appropriate type commander)
- carrier air traffic control officer (supplied by the appropriate type commander)
- combat information center (CIC) officer

- computer programmer
- cryptologic officer (when the ship has a special intelligence capability)
- electronic warfare officer
- first lieutenant (when the ship has a combat systems department but not a deck department)
- intelligence officer
- meteorological officer
- photographic officer

You will do well to review the responsibilities and duties of your operations officer and their relations with you. The officer will be close to you many hours of the day.

Officers of the Navigation Department

The navigator is the head of the navigation department and is responsible under the commanding officer for the safe navigation and piloting of the ship. The assistant navigator, if assigned, reports to the navigator. The engineering officer reports to the navigator concerning steering matters.

The navigator's relationship with the commanding officer is, like that of the executive officer, a close one. The navigator should be an officer whom you trust personally, one who will tell you promptly and honestly when he or she doesn't know where the ship is, one who will make accurate and frank recommendations.

Require the navigator to check all chart corrections entered by the quartermasters, to keep clean and neat navigation workbooks and bearing books, and to make necessary software updates to installed electronic navigation charting systems. These are official and important records, and if they are ever needed at an investigation, their neatness and correctness will pay dividends. He or she should in turn require the watch officers to write proper logs. Knowledge of electronic navigation systems includes complete familiarity with all operating modes, input sources, and specific data in use as well as the ability to recognize when these systems are operating in a degraded manner.

Officers of the Communications Department

In ships with a communications department, the communications officer acts as its head. He or she is responsible for visual and electronic exterior communications systems and the administration of the interior systems supporting them. Assistants to the communications officer include the radio officer, the signal officer, the custodian of the electronic key management system, the crypto-security officer, and the communication watch officers. You will have to train your own communications officer. You will be fortunate if you have an officer of appropriate rank with some communications experience.

Communications, like navigation, is very much a part of your everyday affairs. You should make every effort to master it. It is just as important in port as under way. The success of all your efforts depends upon knowing *what* your ship is to do and *when* it is to do it; thus, you can succeed only if communications with your seniors are fast and reliable. There is nothing that makes an officer in tactical command (OTC) unhappier than a ship with bumbling communications. You may have the best ship in the unit, but if the OTC can't get the word to you, you are useless to them.

Efficient communications can be achieved. Success starts with knowing your equipment. Both you and your communications officer should know the location, characteristics, capabilities, and limitations of every transmitter, receiver, and transceiver on your ship. Know the effective range, frequency range, power, tuning capabilities, and frequency-shifting speeds of your equipment. Send for the manuals and study them. Ask questions. You will find out what your subordinates know about the equipment and what they *don't* know; this will surprise you sometimes. Require frequent and accurate tuning and the use of the most efficient internal transmission and switching setups. If you display such interest and knowledge, your communications officer will try to equal or exceed you, and your sailors will love it. When you go to a pre-sail conference for an exercise or deployment, be prepared to make sensible and informed decisions about the communications plan to be used. If you know your equipment, you won't be trapped into agreeing to guard more circuits than you have equipment or watchstanders.

When your equipment is working at maximum efficiency, you can turn your attention to other matters. The "word" is no good if it arrives on your ship and you never hear it. Consequently, you must ensure that the communications department has a rapid and accurate system of routing incoming messages and filing them for future use. The same is true for the outgoing system. Note that this communications flow is conducted electronically today. Good drafting is a matter of knowledge ingrained by habit. Make sure your messages are concise, clear, and free from "overkill." Obviously, precedence, classification, and necessity should be considered.

A ship's most obvious interfaces with higher authorities (and other ships) are its voice radio circuits, its visual communications, and IP-based modes (including chat rooms). Visual communications require practice to set in order. Sharp lookouts for incoming calls, willingness to relay, and prompt two-blocking of flag hoists all contribute to your ship's reputation. The more difficult task is to excel at voice communications. This is the single most critical indication of the success of your communications department and numerous watch teams, and even of the overall competence of your ship. *You and your communications officer must work at it continuously.* We have already emphasized the careful and frequent tuning of your equipment. Next, be sure that you, as commanding officer, know and observe circuit discipline, proper procedure, correct vocabulary, and authentication and numeral coding procedures. If you demonstrate expertise and concern, your watch officers and enlisted operators will rise to your level. Insist on clear diction, prompt responses, correct phraseology, confident tones of voice, and avoidance of slang or redundancy. Monitor your ship's air control circuits from time to time; they are the most frequent sources of violations.

In essence, after safe navigation and maneuver, communications is probably the most important area for your personal concern. The communications officer and other officers of this department should be carefully chosen and schooled.

Officers of the Combat Systems and Weapons Department

Ships having a combat systems department will have a combat systems officer serving as its head. They will be responsible for the supervision and direction of the ship's combat systems, including ordnance equipment. On some ships, the combat systems and weapons departments are merged. If they are separated, the weapons department normally includes the anti-submarine warfare (ASW) officer, gunnery officer, and ordnance officer. Under the combat systems officer, if assigned, are the following assistants:

- ASW officer
- communications officer
- department administrative assistant
- electronics material officer
- fire control officer
- ordnance officer or gunnery officer
- strike officer
- system test officer
- weapons officer

Most of these officers will be partially qualified. Ask your detailer to order them to additional schools en route, or send them yourself at the next opportunity.

Officers of the Air Department

On ships with an air department, the air officer is assigned as its head. He or she is responsible for the supervision and direction of launching and landing operations and for the servicing and handling of aircraft. The air officer is also responsible for salvage, firefighting, aviation fuels, aviation lubricants, and safety precautions. There will usually be only one such qualified officer sent to your ship.

The air officer's assistants will include the assistant air officer, the catapult officer, the arresting gear officer, the aviation fuels officer, and the training assistant (air). Most of these officers will be qualified by schooling or previous experience before their arrival aboard.

In ships without air departments, where a Navy helicopter detachment is embarked, an aviation department should be organized with an aviation officer as its head. The officer should have under them a qualified helicopter control officer.

Officers of the Embarked Air Wing

The commander of an embarked squadron has the status of a department head. On an aircraft carrier, the air wing commander is a major commander of equal status to the carrier's CO. They are responsible for the tactical training and indoctrination of the air wing and for the coordination and supervision of its various squadrons and detachments. The air wing commander will be ordered to this billet by name.

Officers of the Deck Department

In ships with a deck department, the first lieutenant will be the department head. He or she is responsible for the supervision and direction of the employment of the equipment associated with deck seamanship and, in ships not having a weapons or combat systems department, of the ordnance equipment. Most likely, there will be a senior officer ordered to your ship with previous experience in your type whom you can assign. The following are the first lieutenant's assistants if billets exist: combat systems or gunnery officer, cargo officer, ship's boatswain, and boat group commander.

Officers of the Repair Department

In ships with a repair department, the repair officer will be its head. He or she is responsible for the accomplishment of repairs and alterations in those ships and aircraft assigned to the repair ship. There will be an officer ordered to your ship whose experience will indicate they are meant to be your repair officer. The repair officer will have as assistants the assistant repair officer, the electrical assistant, the hull assistant, and the machinery assistant, as well as other assistants, depending upon the class of repair ship or tender.

Officers of the Engineering Department

The engineering officer or chief engineer heads the engineering department. He or she is responsible for the operation, care, and maintenance of all propulsion and auxiliary machinery, the control of damage, and, upon request of the head of department concerned, those repairs beyond the capacity of other departments.

The chief engineer is a very important officer in your organization. He or she will have great influence over the other officers in the department in building their approach toward good engineering practices and procedures. In small ships, this influence is at a maximum, since the officers under them usually will have had no other exposure to engineering. Other officers not in their department will also be influenced. You should do everything possible to encourage officers in other departments to learn all they can about engineering. Have your executive officer and chief engineer set up tours of the plant, lectures, and opportunities to examine machinery when open for inspection or overhaul. In small ships, and even in large ones, officers who really want to broaden themselves can do so by volunteering to stand instruction watches in engineering spaces, taking qualifying courses, and otherwise trying to qualify for engineering. Make notes in the FITREPs of such officers, including their attitudes, accomplishments, and status of qualification. It will help them later. Such entries have been significant in selection for promotion in the past. In the end, qualification as engineering officer of the watch is a significant determining factor in screening for department head positions in the surface warfare community.

Keep abreast of proceedings in the engineering department through your engineering officer. You will do well to require an engineering night order book and to approve it personally. *Engineering Administration* has samples of engineering night orders. This is a sound practice from an administrative point of view and provides for continuity of control in the absence of the engineering officer. Having such a night order book also helps in indoctrinating young officers in proper engineering procedures.

The advent of nuclear power has required many changes in ship organization. If a nuclear-powered warship does not have a separate reactor department, the chief engineer will be detailed as the reactor officer. Under this arrangement, the duties of the reactor and mechanical assistants devolve upon the main propulsion assistant, and an additional billet for reactor control officer is provided. The *SORM* for nuclear submarines/ballistic missile submarines amplifies this organization.

The following are assistants to the engineering officer where billets are assigned: main propulsion assistant, reactor control assistant, damage control assistant, electrical officer, and other assistants as provided in nuclear-powered ships.

SUBMARINE SHIP'S DIVING OFFICER

The position of ship's diving officer is normally performed as a collateral duty assigned to the damage control assistant (DCA) or another warfare qualified junior officer. The responsibility affiliated with the position of submarine ship's diving officer is significant. First and foremost, it is the ship's diving officer's responsibility to ensure the watertight integrity of the submarine prior to conducting a dive. In order to do so, the ship's diving officer takes reports from all spaces on the "rig for dive." Rig for dive is a time-honored tradition and skill on board a submarine. Literally every valve or system on board the ship that is subject to submerged pressure is checked by a qualified enlisted "first checker" and verified by an officer "second checker" before the ship is submerged. Personnel conducting first and second checks in spaces throughout the submarine must be qualified "rig for dive" in that space or warfare qualified in submarines in order to take on the burden of responsibility for verifying the watertight integrity of that space prior to a dive. The ship's diving officer is responsible for the training and qualification of these individuals.

Prior to executing a dive, the ship's diving officer will report to the officer of the deck and the CO on the status of the rig for dive. Each exception or anomaly to the rig for dive will be reported to the CO for assessment and consideration. Once a report of a satisfactory rig for dive is complete, the CO will make a determination on the readiness of the submarine to conduct the dive and transition to submerged operations. It makes perfect sense to assign this responsibility to the ship's DCA, who, by nature of the position, is responsible for all nonnuclear mechanical systems on board the ship, many of which are regularly exposed to sea pressure. Next to the engineer and the commanding officer, the DCA is often the most familiar with the material condition of all systems and equipment on the rig-for-dive checklist.

Additionally, the ship's diving officer will maintain an accounting of all supplies, foodstuffs, weapons, and other consumables that come aboard the ship during refit and load out prior to deployment. The addition and subtraction of tons of weight aboard ship during a refit or upkeep must be accounted for and compensated for prior to the initial dive after an in-port period. Using modern accounting techniques, a spreadsheet, and sharp mathematical skills, the ship's diving officer will determine how to compensate the ship for the addition or subtraction of weight. This results in the movement of ballast (water) throughout the ship prior to the initial dive. The CO will approve the compensation, which amounts to a worksheet that specifies a fulcrum of water to shift fore to aft or side to side in variable ballast tanks, to ensure that the ship maintains an even trim and equilibrium after the dive. For the duration of submerged operations, the ship's diving officer will oversee a "running compensation" that tracks changes of weight in the ship, with each ensuring that a sufficient trim is in place when the submarine operates near the surface at periscope depth. The watch-to-watch running compensation is maintained by a senior enlisted petty officer, the chief of the watch on *Los Angeles*–, *Seawolf*–, and *Ohio*-class submarines, and the co-pilot on the *Virginia*-class submarines.

The responsibility of the ship's diving officer is essential to the safe operation of the submarine and her ability to complete assigned missions. This should be bestowed upon the most competent and conscientious of junior officers.

Officers of the Reactor Department

In ships with a reactor department, the reactor officer is the head of the department. A post-O-5 commanding officer, they will be ordered by name and in almost all cases will be senior to all engineering and reactor department officers. They will be responsible for the operation, care, maintenance, and safety of the reactor plants and their auxiliaries. They will receive all orders concerning these responsibilities directly from you and will make all corresponding reports directly to you. They report to you for reactor matters and act as your technical assistant. They report to the XO for administrative matters.

The special nature of a nuclear plant requires that the reactor officer and the engineering officer cooperate very closely. The reactor officer and their assistants are responsible for some specific duties normally prescribed for the engineering officer and their assistants on nonnuclear-powered ships not having separate departments.

The reactor officer will be aided by an assistant reactor officer and six principal assistants: a reactor electrical assistant, a reactor mechanical assistant, a main propulsion assistant, a reactor training assistant, a reactor maintenance officer, and a chemistry-radiological assistant. The reactor officer and their assistants will all have had significant previous experience in reactor operations.

Specific responsibilities of the reactor officer and their principal assistants are described in the *Engineering Department Manual for Naval Nuclear Propulsion Plants (EDM)*, promulgated by the director, Naval Reactors (NAVSEA 08).

Officers of the Research and Deep Submergence Departments

In ships having research as their mission, a research officer is assigned as head of department and carries out responsibilities regarding research. In ships having deep submergence as their mission, a deep submergence officer serves as head of department and carries out appropriate responsibilities.

Officers of the Supply Department

In ships having a supply department, its head is designated as the supply officer. He or she is responsible for procuring, receiving, storing, issuing, transferring, selling, accounting for, and, while in their custody, maintaining all stores and equipment of the unit. On large ships and most medium-sized ships, an officer of the Supply Corps is ordered as supply officer. On very small ships, the CO must designate a line officer as supply officer. The supply officer of a large ship will have as assistants a food service officer and a disbursing officer.

Officers of the Medical and Dental Departments
MEDICAL OFFICER

The senior medical officer is the head of the medical department and is responsible for maintaining the health of all personnel, making appropriate inspections, and advising the commanding officer on hygiene and sanitation. Almost all large ships will have a medical officer ordered. Smaller ships without them will have a hospital corpsman qualified for independent duty, who will function under the executive officer. First aid instruction is an important duty of medical officers. In battle, damage control requirements for closed doors and hatches and restricted access will result in many isolated areas. Prompt first aid until the wounded can be moved to battle dressing stations will save many lives.

DENTAL OFFICER

The dental officer is the head of the dental department and is responsible for preventing and controlling dental disease and for supervising dental hygiene. Small ships without a dental officer have their dental affairs overseen by the leading hospitalman, who arranges periodic dental checkups and other care at nearby facilities. Ship-wide "dental readiness" is a metric tracked by the chain of command prior to ship deployments.

Department Heads

The duties of officers assigned as heads of departments in various ship organizations have been outlined in previous pages. Those who are so designated have certain other duties by virtue of that designation.

As stated before, heads of departments may confer directly with you concerning matters within their department if they believe such action to be necessary for the good of their department or the naval service. This right should be used carefully, and in any event the executive officer should be brought up to date as soon as possible.

The head of department is responsible for organizing and training the department for battle, preparing and writing bills and orders for the department, and for assigning and administering all of its personnel. A detailed description of all responsibilities and duties is contained in the *SORM*.

The head of department on a large ship may have an assistant department head and an administrative assistant. On almost all ships, he or she will have a department training officer and division officers.

Division Officers

Division officers are assigned to major groups of personnel within each ship's organization. They train, supervise, and administer all personnel assigned to their division and are responsible for their total performance.

They assign division personnel to watches, battle bills, other bills, and nonrecurring assignments. Their detailed responsibilities are outlined in the *SORM*, article 3.34. Division officers usually have other duties assigned collaterally and have assignments in the battle and other bills.

Division officer billets are filled by junior officers ordered to you often without specific qualifications or schooling. BUPERS does provide pipeline training for selected billets, but if you want additional training, you will have to make arrangements with the placement officer for them to be ordered to specific schools en route. This is often a negotiation. Alternatively, you may send them on temporary additional duty at first opportunity after they have reported, when you can spare them.

Division officers are your direct contact with the sailors of your command. Time spent in observing, training, and encouraging them—in concert with their department head, of course—is a good investment.

The detailed duties of the division officer are outlined in the *SORM*. The *Division Officer's Guide*, published by Naval Institute Press, is a bookshelf must for all division officers. It merits your reading also. It translates the listing of duties into chapters and paragraphs that tell the division officer how to carry them out.

Watchstanding

The preceding paragraphs have set forth the duties of officers with regard to specific billet assignments and the administering organization. However, your ship won't move far or accomplish much without a watch organization. Your watch organization is the point of execution for *all* that you do. It is your *nervous system* in every mission area. Your ship's effectiveness and reputation are a direct reflection of your watch team's performance. Its smooth operation, manning by competent personnel, and vigilance cannot be overemphasized.

SENIOR WATCH OFFICER

A watch organization begins with a senior watch officer. The senior watch officer, under the XO, is responsible for the assignment and general supervision of all deck watch officers and enlisted watchstanders in port and under way. He or she maintains records concerning the qualifications of all deck watchstanders, coordinates their training, and prepares appropriate bills.

DECK WATCHSTANDING

The *Watch Officer's Guide*, published by Naval Institute Press, is a good source of information on deck watchstanding. It covers the deck watch in general, log writing, shiphandling, rules of the road, and other safety-at-sea problems. It also covers the duties of the OOD in port.

CIC WATCHSTANDING

The duties, responsibilities, and requirements of the CIC watch officer and his or her subordinates are set forth in the *Operations Officer's Manual*, also published by Naval Institute Press. The CIC is a vital part of a ship's operations. You must delve deeply into the details of the CIC and its watches. It is integral to fighting your ship effectively.

ENGINEERING WATCH

The chief engineer is responsible to you for preparing and administering the engineering watch bill and for qualifying all watchstanders. Ensure that the engineer is strict in qualifying procedures and maintains adequate records of those qualified.

Cooperation between your OODs and your engineer officers of the watch is essential. In order to be sure that your OODs understand the problems below decks, insist that they be familiar with *Engineering for the Officer of the Deck*, published by Naval Institute Press. This publication describes, in easily readable form, "what happens below" and why.

COMMUNICATIONS WATCH

As stated above, you should keep a close eye on your communications watch across all mediums: visual, voice, record traffic, and IP chat rooms. With alert watchstanders, you will be informed rapidly of the requirements of your superiors and can make correspondingly rapid responses and reports. You will be synchronized. Without a competent watch, you will run scared, never sure you're up to speed and always playing catch-up. Work with your communications officer, his or her communications watch officers, your topside signal officer, and your CIC officer. It will pay dividends.

Leadership Training

After your officers are placed in their proper billets, qualified and trained for their primary responsibilities, and integrated into a viable watch bill, your ship should be properly officered.

It is time now to turn to improving your officers as individuals. This starts with leadership training. You, as commanding officer, must lead in this effort. You can get help from your XO and your heads of departments in organizing and carrying out a leadership training program, but you need to spark this effort with your own personal interest and drive. Even if you are blessed with these personal qualities, you will need external help. There are many fine texts that you can use. One good one is *Naval Leadership*, compiled by a group of officers at the Naval Academy and published by Naval Institute Press.

The discussion of leadership training for officers falls into six easily identifiable categories: personal characteristics, moral and ethical leadership, personal relations with seniors, personal relations with juniors, techniques of counseling and communication, and the role of the officer in training. Let us examine each of these aspects of leadership in more detail.

PERSONAL CHARACTERISTICS

First, an officer must *want* to be a naval officer. A person who doesn't want to go to sea, command, fight, and lead ought to seek another profession. This does not mean being overly aggressive personally. Some of our greatest naval officers have been quiet individuals who preferred peaceful solutions if possible, but who fought hard and aggressively when necessary.

MORAL AND ETHICAL LEADERSHIP

Moral and ethical leadership has always been important in our Navy. Americans have long felt that the first essential for a leader is self-confidence, a strong moral position, and a sense of self-worth. In this area, "moral" means what is *right*, considering integrity, sense of duty, and obligation to one's country. Morals and ethics must also be constantly discussed and practiced in order to develop. Flowing from a sense of self-worth is the attribution of equal worth to others. Any person with this attitude cannot be bigoted, partial, or unfair toward other people. Integrity and honesty are paramount.

PERSONAL RELATIONS WITH SENIORS

No officer can be an effective leader if he or she cannot first be a good follower. Simply put, this means being loyal to seniors, but not blindly loyal. Encourage your juniors to question in their own minds your decisions and the decisions of all seniors. They need not be outspoken, contentious, or overly aggressive about their disagreement. In some cases, only the mental process needs to be followed, and no expression of it is necessary. In those cases where there is definite disagreement, juniors are duty-bound to express their honest opinion to their seniors. Explain carefully to your officers the classic procedure of military dissent: if one disagrees with an order or decision of a senior, one should say so, privately if possible, but promptly, frankly, and fully. Once the decision is explained or reaffirmed, one must then immediately and loyally proceed to carry it out. If you find young officers who are inept in their relations with seniors, counsel, instruct, and correct them.

PERSONAL RELATIONS WITH JUNIORS

Once junior officers learn to follow, they are ready to learn to lead. Their own personal characteristics are the basis of this ability. They must also learn to communicate, for no one can know what their leader wants them to do if they do not receive a lucid and correct order. Communication means the ability to speak (and write) clearly, logically, plainly, and promptly. It means giving orders impersonally, yet leaving no doubt that they are to be obeyed. It means talking before small and large groups, both extemporaneously or from a prepared text, using proper, simple language, free from slang, idiom, and obscenity. Always remember that communications is in the eye of the receiver, not the communicator. You should constantly seek to determine if your orders, detailed or broad, are understood in the way you intended.

Other characteristics will help a senior lead well. Seniors must learn to not tolerate small deficiencies, but to correct them patiently, and to not accept large deficiencies at all. They must plan ahead to ensure that their juniors do not do useless work that foresight could have avoided. They should know all of their sailors but should avoid using first names or nicknames or taking other familiarities. They must be considerate, fair, and tactful, but firm and exacting. Above all, if they know their job, their machinery and equipment, and tactics, they will be respected by their juniors, who will probably forgive or tolerate any deficiencies.

TECHNIQUES OF COUNSELING

A leader must gain the confidence of subordinates to be able to counsel them. This means finding out as much as possible about their families and relationships in order to analyze their problems and provide help. The leader can begin this by examining their service records. After this grounding, discreet questioning can add to knowledge without invading privacy. If each division officer has a basic knowledge of the record and personal situation of each sailor, they will recognize when someone appears to be troubled and will be able to help with problems the sailor cannot handle alone. The Navy Relief Society, the American Red Cross, and various legal aid societies can be called upon for assistance. After learning as much as they can about their subordinates, an officer will find, however, that most problems can be solved by cultivating the art of listening and by learning to analyze character. Building skill as an "active listener" improves a leader's effectiveness in counseling situations at all levels.

THE ROLE OF THE OFFICER IN TRAINING

Most of an officer's career is spent in training. No sooner is a sailor, a gun crew, or a CIC team trained adequately than ends of enlistments or transfers start the training cycle all over again. An officer must recognize that training is both never-ending and important. Sailors must first be trained to fill the ship's billets. Next, they must learn the administrative duties of their rates, and then they must know the duties of their battle stations, emergency and other bills, and their watchstanding duties. In addition, they must be trained for advancement in rating and to further their general education.

For the officer, this means formulating a plan, procuring manuals, training aids, course books, and other materials, and then preparing lectures, on-the-job training sessions, discussions, and examinations. This is an endless task, but a satisfying one if done well. Make sure your officers do it well, and encourage them by your example.

OTHER CHARACTERISTICS

There are many other necessary personal characteristics of a leader than those we have discussed above, including loyalty to country, command, and associates, both senior and junior; courage, both physical and moral; honesty; sense of humor; modesty of mind and demeanor; self-confidence; common sense; judgment; enthusiasm and a cheerful demeanor; tact; self-control; and consideration of others. You can't teach these qualities, nor any of the others; but you can recognize them, provide an example of them, encourage them, and create a climate in which they can flourish.

Professional Competence

In the context in which we are using it, professional competence starts with general education and includes qualifications to fill billets, other technical qualifications (such as air controller), watchstanding qualifications, and general professional capabilities.

When officers report for duty, their general education may be well advanced, but it is *never* completed. Officers should be encouraged to take university extension courses, to read in disciplines other than their educational majors, to read widely in the liberal arts, and to prepare for future postgraduate formal education. You can help by encouraging them and by making time available. The Navy Leader Development Framework provides a guide for officers to follow throughout their career that is meant to build character, competence, and connections.

All officers must be required to master their billets. This can be done by reading manuals and publications, taking on- and off-ship qualification courses, asking questions, and receiving instruction from seniors. When their services can be spared, officers should be sent to shore-based schools to increase their knowledge and prepare them for more important and demanding billets.

Cross-training should be accomplished whenever the ship can afford it. In most cases, junior officers can be rotated without impairing the efficiency of the ship excessively. Where this cannot be done, encourage your officers to complete courses of instruction in other departments, to stand qualification watches, and to examine equipment and machinery when it is opened for overhaul or repairs. Follow up with entries in FITREPs to reflect the initiative of the officers and the status of their progress.

Qualification in such specialties as air control, catapult operation, and other areas that are not primary duties should be encouraged. When possible, officers should be sent to school in excess of the numbers you require. This gives you flexibility in future assignments and broadens the professional competence of the officers involved.

Watchstanding should be made to seem a privilege rather than an onerous chore. To do so, you will have to set the tone. Good watchstanders should receive your approbation in public and your private acknowledgment in the form of good FITREP entries. Encourage junior officers to qualify in other areas, such as deck watchstanders qualifying in engineering, and vice versa. This broadens professional competence.

Finally, encourage your officers to prepare for eventual attendance at war college and for their joint professional military education requirements by taking correspondence courses in strategy and tactics.

Your involvement, example, and encouragement will help your officers to enlarge their areas of professional competence and personal character. If you find officers who are not interested in doing so, counsel them, for otherwise they have little future in the Navy. We fight and operate as part of a joint force. To be effective, we must continually grow professionally and personally.

Social Customs

As commanding officer, you also have the responsibility of guiding the social development and conduct of your officers and, by example and advice, of influencing the involvement of their spouses.

The first essential of an officer's social presence is being considerate and respectful of others. This single, simple quality is the basis for correct social conduct. With this quality in hand, the mechanics of proper social behavior can be learned; they are not difficult.

GENERAL SOCIAL CONDUCT
Naval Ceremonies, Customs, and Traditions, published by Naval Institute Press, covers the general conduct expected of officers in the wardroom, ashore, and in the messes of other navies. Some of the history behind

these customs is included, and the explanations of their origin help the young officer to understand them. *Social Usage and Protocol* (OPNAV-INST 1710.7) is the Navy's official and very adequate guide for invitations, seating, dining, receptions, calls, ceremonies, and almost any social event that would involve your ship or any of your officers. Any officer, armed with a sense of consideration for others and having reviewed the contents of these two publications, can move in any social circle in the world with confidence and success.

WARDROOM

Your wardroom (and other messes on a larger ship) is the center of social usage for your ship and should receive your personal attention. If you command a large ship and have your own mess, you will have to depend on your XO to set the tone of the wardroom mess. Correct social usage begins here. Make sure that it is clean, well run, correct in all respects but not stuffy, and a place where your officers will be proud to bring their guests.

Fig. 4-2. A sharp and welcoming wardroom is the first requirement for a satisfactory onboard social life for the officers of a ship, but making it a home requires the courtesy, hospitality, and friendliness of all the members of the wardroom. Equally important is the wardroom's value in hosting international gatherings, such as this multilateral meeting on USS *Sterett* hosted by Destroyer Squadron 7 in Singapore.

Help the wardroom to extend its social presence ashore by making it easy to have wardroom-sponsored social affairs. The subject of social calls and visits is fully covered in *Naval Ceremonies, Customs, and Traditions.*

The Captain's Role with the Wardroom

Your role and activity as a CO are *full-contact* undertakings; make the most of it while in command. As commanding officer of a ship or submarine or as skipper of an aircraft squadron, you have several important roles you must execute with regard to your wardroom or ready room.

First, you are the leading planner, tactician, and mariner/airman of your command. Take every opportunity to share your experience and knowledge. This can be done formally through classroom sessions and discussions; during extended planning sessions and briefings for upcoming events; and, most effectively, "on the deckplates" during the execution of actual operations. Step up to the plate! Your team expects to see you take the lead and orchestrate events running the gamut from a simple anchoring to a complex anti-air warfare exercise. Ask yourself, "What have I taught the wardroom today?" And remember, you're their senior mentor.

Second, you are the "voice of experience" in terms of your officers' career patterns. Shortly after taking command, you should have a detailed conversation with each of your officers concerning their goals, aspirations, and current levels of qualification. Work out with them a career plan, and try to provide a focused set of alternatives that covers the next five years. Find out what your officers want to do, and try to guide them into the kind of assignments that will be best for both them and the Navy.

Third, when it comes time for them to shift assignments within the command, you should work with the XO, the appropriate department heads, and the officers themselves to make sure they move to good new jobs. For example, you may want to shift your younger division officers between engineering and combat systems/operations jobs. In an aircraft squadron, you must orchestrate the movement among your department heads. This is critical to their career development and part of your job.

Lastly, when your officers approach the end of their tour with your command, you must work with both them and BUPERS to find them the right job. This is not always the job they want, and you must help your officers understand that any new assignment is a balance between the needs of the Navy and the desires of the individual. But you should always work hard on behalf of your officers, calling the detailers if you believe it warranted to try to adjust assignments to best balance the requirements of the situation.

As a flip side to working for your current officers, you must also work with the bureau—this time with the placement side instead of the detailers—to ensure that you get the right kind of officers assigned to your command. This does not mean you should attempt to manipulate the system to obtain a handpicked group of officers. Rather, you should work with the placement officer to make sure the bureau understands the unique needs of your command, the implication of your particular schedule, where your command is in the training cycle, and the many other variables that go into assignment of officers to your ship, submarine, or squadron—in sum, the right "fit" for officers inbound to your wardroom. Timing is essential in this aspect of your responsibilities, and forehandedness is paramount to ensure results.

Fitness Reports

There is no magic answer here. Writing good, accurate FITREPs is challenging; and above all, making decisions that rank your officers is hard work. Start by reviewing the well-written FITREP instructions before you work on individual fitness reports. Require your XO to carefully review the entire package of drafts by your department heads. Make sure no one in your command is ever asked to "write up their own FITREP," but make sure that the officer about whom the report is being written has the opportunity to provide comprehensive input to the process.

When it comes to ranking, there is no easy answer. The bottom line is that you, as commanding officer, must make the tough calls. You should make those calls on the basis of performance, long-term potential for naval service, and the specific qualities described in the FITREP itself: professional expertise, equal opportunity, military bearing/character, teamwork, mission accomplishment/initiative, leadership, and tactical performance. Avoid a system that is based on seniority, length of time in the command, or any other artificial discriminator. And it goes without saying that personal favoritism has no place in a fair system of evaluation. In the end, you must remember that you were placed in command because of your judgment, fairness, and balance. Rely on those traits, and make the best call you can on ranking. Don't ever try to rig the system.

When you are relatively new in command, you may want to discuss in general terms the subjects of FITREPs, rankings, and wording with your immediate superior or other COs "on the waterfront or flight line" who have been around a little longer. They can give you a steer on any particular nuances in your community, but don't rely too much on any individual's opinion or view—except your own, Captain.

Conclusion

As Secretary of the Navy Sean O'Keefe correctly said in 1992, what matters in the end is what your officers carry in their hearts. As their captain, you will have the opportunity to influence every aspect of their lives during their assignment to your command. You will be an endless source of information, inspiration, and leadership to each of the young men and women with whom you serve. It is the highest responsibility you will execute in command, and you should cherish it.

Be honest, friendly, and interested in your wardroom—from the seasoned executive officer, who should be your closest counselor, to the most junior ensign, who spends most of each day learning his or her new trade. Take care of them. Help them. Correct them when you must; praise them whenever you can. Above all, Captain, listen to *your* heart in all of your dealings with your officers; it will not fail you.

5

Master Chief of the Command, Chief Petty Officers, and Crew

Men mean more than guns in the rating of a ship.

—Captain John Paul Jones

Leading the Crew

It is really very simple. Your job as commanding officer will be to instill pride and professionalism in each and every crew member. Success in this endeavor will depend in large measure on the personal attributes you bring to command and the degree to which you give your subordinates responsibility and require that they perform. You must ensure that the entire crew—from the command master chief to the newest seaman recruit—seeks success, that they desire to be part of a winning team. No sailor in the Navy would leave a demanding winning command to serve in a permissive loser. Remember: your crew will perform and serve at the level you demand.

The command atmosphere you set will determine the nature of your crew's efforts. In particular, integrity is a quality that you must demonstrate. The crew has opportunities each day to measure it, and they will set their standards by those you show in your own behavior. Your impartiality, a component of integrity, is a necessity in building a good crew. The old expression "a taut ship is a happy ship" is true largely because in such a ship, there is impartiality of treatment, fairness, and thus justice; crew members know where they stand and what is expected of them.

Another factor involving command integrity is loyalty. The commanding officer has every right to expect the crew to be loyal to the ship—and to the CO personally, who represents the ship. Loyalty, however, must be worked for; it does not come automatically. Along with being mindful of the well-being of the officers and crew, the captain inspires their loyalty by exhibiting their own, not in words, but in deeds. The officers and crew expect the CO to be loyal to the chain of command, to "make the best of what you have," as Admiral Ernest King phrased it in his famous order to the Atlantic Fleet of 24 March 1941. When—as sometimes happens—the "best you have" is not good enough for readiness, or where the process of achieving readiness works real hardship on your sailors, you must do what you can to alleviate their problems while making suggestions up the chain of command for bettering the situation.

A crew considers a captain who stands up for them to be loyal. Sailors who brag about their ship are beyond price, but they do not come to think of their ship as a "good ship" simply by being told it is. Integrity, impartiality, and loyalty of command bind the captain, wardroom, and the crew into an effective fighting unit.

The Command Senior Enlisted Leader
FUNCTION
At the unit level, command senior enlisted leaders (CSELs) include command master chiefs (CMCs), chiefs of the boat (COBs) on submarines, or command senior chiefs. The CSEL, the principal enlisted adviser to the commanding officer, keeps the CO aware of existing or potential situations, procedures, and practices that affect the welfare, morale, job satisfaction, and effective employment of crew members. The CSEL reports directly to the commanding officer.

DUTIES, RESPONSIBILITIES, AND AUTHORITY
The command senior enlisted leader will take precedence over all other members of equal or subordinate pay grades within the command during the tenure of their assignment. The *Command Senior Enlisted Leader Program* as outlined in OPNAVINST 1306.2 series assigns command senior enlisted leaders the following duties and responsibilities:

- to establish and maintain the conditions that provide all of their people with the opportunity to be successful, and to do so while treating each other with dignity and respect
- to provide advice and recommendations to the chain of command as well as to their respective ISIC CSEL
- to demonstrate institutional and technical expertise and hold the chief petty officer (CPO) mess to the highest possible standards of professional excellence
- to actively teach, uphold, and enforce standards
- to provide leadership to enlisted sailors and assist in the growth and development of junior officers
- to promote and instill the Navy ethos and Navy core values in all sailors
- to educate and inspire CPO messes to embrace the master chief petty officer of the Navy's mission, vision, and guiding principles
- to assist commanders and COs in all matters pertaining to welfare, health, job satisfaction, morale, utilization, and training of sailors in order to promote standards of good order and discipline
- to advise commanders and COs on formulation and implementation of changes in policy affecting the command(s)
- to promote and ensure official ceremonies honoring sailors are embraced and executed
- to ensure heritage and tradition are key components of sailor development
- to lead the CPO mess on the development of character, pride, and professionalism in all sailors
- to provide oversight on the delivery of proper, accurate, and timely communications throughout the command(s)
- to communicate with and support Navy families
- to chair, coordinate, monitor, and participate with the following boards, committees, programs, and other groups:
  › command sponsor program
  › command indoctrination
  › career development boards
  › Navy family ombudsman, fleet and family support center liaison

> mentorship program
> sailor recognition and awards boards
> CPO 365
> CPO and petty officer leadership courses
> chief's mess training
> president of CPO mess
> command development team
> sailor of the month, quarter, and year programs
> enlisted warfare qualification programs
> family advocacy program
> bachelor enlisted quarters program
> commissary and Navy Exchange advisory board (if required)
> general mess and ship's store advisory board
> humanitarian reassignment and hardship discharge screening boards
> command physical readiness program
> morale, welfare, and recreation committee and advisory board
> command managed equal opportunity program
> command assessment team
> command training team
> command advancement program
> command delivered leadership development training
> single sailor program
> liberty risk program
> sailor housing advisory committee
> safety and operational risk management committee
> sexual assault prevention and response
> personal financial management
> suicide awareness and prevention
> operational stress control

IMPORTANCE OF THE COMMAND SENIOR ENLISTED LEADER

To a large degree, the morale of your crew and therefore the success of your command will depend on the effectiveness of the CSEL. As the *key* link between you and the crew, CSELs expedite the execution of command policy and advise you when that policy requires redirection. If they don't carry out these important functions, command communication will be slowed, resulting in a ship less able to fulfill its assigned missions. The CSEL does *not*, however, take the place of the normal command system; they assist its functioning, as we will point out later.

A good command senior enlisted leader will make it his or her responsibility to know what is going on in the command. On smaller ships, the CSEL should be aware of all personnel problems and should ensure that proper action is being taken to correct them. For example, if your drug prevention program fails to the point that the ship experiences a major "drug bust," you should consider carefully the effectiveness of your CSEL. It is his or her responsibility to sense and ferret out those indicators that normally precede such personnel problems.

Your relationship with the CSEL must be one of total openness and frankness. It does little good for morale for him or her to become a "rubber stamp" for all command policy. Yet when policy is set, he or she must support it thoroughly and ensure that subordinates do so as well. The CSEL must carefully consider the comments of the crew regarding policy and forward them up to you when appropriate.

COMMAND SENIOR ENLISTED LEADER AND THE CHAIN OF COMMAND

CSEL positions were created to strengthen the chain of command, *not* to replace it. As CO, you must therefore ensure that the role is used as a command strengthening mechanism. It is not a vehicle for bypassing the chain of command with petty gripes and complaints. You must ensure that all hands understand the CSEL's role as that of principal enlisted adviser to the commanding officer.

Chief of the Boat

The chief of the boat is a time-honored Navy tradition on board submarines whereby a senior chief or a master chief petty officer serves as the senior enlisted adviser to the commanding officer. This position is the equivalent of the command master chief or command senior chief aboard a surface vessel. Occupying a post of special trust and confidence, the COB assists the commanding officer with morale, good order, and discipline in the crew. There is only one COB aboard a submarine. The COB's responsibilities are enormous, and his or her performance and personal demeanor will have a tremendous impact on the crew. Typically, the COB will be the first person to greet and interview a new sailor arriving on board the command; for those fresh from submarine school, who have heard all about the COB, it may be one of the most memorable experiences of their career.

Being a COB is not a "given" in the Submarine Force. You cannot simply pass a test and become a COB; the selection process for all CSEL positions is thorough, intrusive, and detailed in OPNAVINST 1306.2 series. Personnel records are examined with an eye toward stellar on-the-job performance, unmatched qualifications and experience, and time at sea. In some cases, when the COB is a senior chief petty officer, he or she may not be the highest-ranking CPO in the chief's quarters. Regardless, he or she should assert themselves as the leader of the chief's quarters and the crew by demonstrating the utmost professionalism in the flawless performance of their duties. The COB should be the most experienced diving officer of the watch on the submarine. The COB should set the standard for other diving officers and chiefs of the watch. Accordingly, many commanding officers prefer to have their COB as "battlestations dive," where top performance under pressure and "maintaining the bubble" under the most stressful conditions is of paramount importance to survival and the successful completion of the mission.

The COB's responsibilities are considerable and expansive, and that is why only the very finest of Submarine Force E-8s and E-9s are chosen to occupy this position. The COB is responsible for the grooming and uniform standards of the crew. The COB is also responsible for cleanliness (fore *and* aft) aboard ship and typically will recommend to the executive officer a cleanliness routine for underway and in-port watch sections and "field days," when necessary. There is truth to the old adage "You get what you inspect," and the most effective COB will always have an eye for the cleanliness of the spaces. A good COB will never walk by a discrepancy without taking action to correct it, otherwise he or she has just lowered the standard in the eyes of the crew. Furthermore, each space on the ship should have a chief petty officer's name assigned to it. In the event that standards in a space start to slip, the COB should hold that CPO accountable.

The COB plays a key role in good order and discipline. Use of the UCMJ and captain's mast should be a last resort. Good COBs are highly effective counselors and should provide counsel for both good and bad performance by crew members. In the event that counseling fails and captain's mast is inevitable, the COB should be present and should provide the commanding officer with an honest and forthright assessment of a crew member's performance and recommendation for punishment and/or retention in the naval service.

COBs are also, by design, the senior enlisted career counselors aboard ship. The COB should be a graduate of the Senior Enlisted Academy and therefore be well trained for myriad collateral duties. All in the chain of command have a responsibility for career development, but sailors will look to their COB and the chief's quarters, which is a direct reflection of the COB, for advice and important career and retention or reenlistment decisions.

The COB is also the administrative assistant to the executive officer. He or she prepares the enlisted watch bills for approval by the executive officer and provides oversight of the Watch Qualification Book. A good COB can make a huge difference in the success of any command. Commanding officers should maintain a continuous and open dialog with the COB and ensure that there is synergy and continuity in messaging from the pinnacle of command to the crew.

Chief Petty Officers

The Navy chief petty officer continues to occupy a position of general respect unmatched by comparable ratings in the other services. This distinction is fundamental to the way our ships operate at sea. It is your business to recognize the importance of the chiefs, to protect and enhance their prestige, and to use all your authority to ensure that their ranks include only well-qualified officers.

The importance of the CPO has never been greater than today. Under the division officer, the CPO is responsible for young, inexperienced personnel who must operate equipment of increasing complexity. The pivotal point of the chain of command is the individual chief, who must be made a *participating* member of your chain of command and must clearly understand their authority as well as their responsibilities to you.

You should quickly put to rest any chief's concern regarding authority. This concern often appears as complaints about the "diminishing authority" of senior petty officers. For example, a brainstorming session between the chief petty officers of a frigate and their commanding officer resulted in a three-page list of those authority areas in which they considered their present involvement inadequate. Among them were for following:

- scheduling of maintenance activity for their divisions
- assignment of enlisted evaluation grades
- issuance of EMI
- scheduling of divisional training
- preparation and approval of personnel for advancement in rate
- use of the nonjudicial punishment system
- award recommendations
- supervision of maintenance
- supervision of cleanliness and preservation
- senior supervisory watchstanding

At the end of the meeting, after the CO had made it clear that the CPOs would participate more fully in these activities in the future, he stated, "Now you all know more regarding your *authority*. It is your *responsibility* to see that each item is carried out to the best of your ability. It is *my responsibility* to see that you do."

CAREER DEVELOPMENT TEAM

It is widely recognized that sailors' ability to achieve professional career goals positively influences their desire to stay on active duty. Thus, career development, with an emphasis on retention, will be one of your prime responsibilities in command. The career development team concept as outlined in the *Navy Enlisted Retention and Career Development Program*

(OPNAVINST 1040.11 series) was initiated to foster a career "satisfaction environment" within all commands and to develop a means of strengthening policy and programs designed to increase retention and career development. The command career development team on each ship is organized as follows:

- Commanding officer: serves as the senior career counselor aboard
- Executive officer: serves as career development team coordinator
- Command career counselor: works directly for the commanding officer, serving as the principal adviser on policies and regulations related to Navy career planning matters. The command career counselor serves as a primary technical assistant in support of the command's retention team and maintains an awareness of revisions and innovations in career development programs through access to directives, reference materials, experience, and training.
- Command senior enlisted leader: works in close association with the career counselor to support the command's career development team efforts. Works with senior petty officers to enhance the retention and counseling effort and to motivate the Navy's number one asset—the senior petty officer
- Department head: serves as career development team coordinator for their department
- Division officer: serves as career development team coordinator for their division
- Service-oriented divisions/departments: personnel, disbursing, medical, and dental departments support the career development team as required and provide personalized services to enhance the climate in support of retention

As the senior counselor, your specific responsibilities are to

- establish and maintain an aggressive and proactive career development program (CDP);
- frequently measure command CDP effectiveness;
- ensure that the command career counselor is properly trained and supported within the command;

- involve every level of the command structure in the CDP, including CO, XO, CMC, COB, senior enlisted leaders, command career counselor, departmental career counselors and department-leading chief petty officers, and additional stakeholders as desired (chaplain, educational services officer, personnel officer, etc.);
- ensure that the proficiency and motivation of the team members are maintained at a high level;
- accord appropriate ceremony and attention to reenlistments, advancements, awards, and other ceremonies and special occasions.

The overall Navy Enlisted Retention and Career Development Program was designed to give latitude to each command in formulating its own program. Each ship will face a unique situation because of its own homeport, deployment schedule, facilities available, and other factors. Your initial objective should be to identify those areas that adversely affect career development so that you can deal with them. Each person counseled will reveal problem areas. Once these are identified, you can begin to eliminate them. For example, the command's first-term retention may be excellent, but the second- and third-term reenlistments can be down. In this case, your program should place increased emphasis on issues facing second- and third-term personnel.

Keep in mind always that *all* retention areas must be considered. It's easy for one facet of the program to absorb your attention when other problem areas may be as bad or worse. To meet the needs of the command as a whole, the system you establish must "police" itself through appropriate control or feedback designed to ensure that *all* elements of the problem receive the necessary attention.

Specific Aids to Retention

ADVANCEMENT

Advancement is one of the primary reasons enlisted personnel stay in the service. Professionally developing, moving up the ladder, making more money, having more responsibility, and having more benefits are things that everyone seeks as measures of a successful career. Without the command's use of available service schools and correspondence courses, however, advancement becomes difficult for your crew. Approval of travel to service schools and provision of assisted study hours and on-the-job training will assist an individual's quest for advancement and thus improve their dedication to a career. It will also help those of your crew who desire specific training for striker designation and change of rating. Another useful technique is the publication of lists of personnel who are eligible and ineligible for advancement-in-rate examinations. This can help motivate both groups.

After advancement results are published, hold individual or group ceremonies with the entire department or crew attending, depending on the size of the group and the desires of the individual. Such ceremonies will not only give recognition to those advanced but also may "light off" those who have previously lacked motivation.

EDUCATION

It is a sound assumption that higher education will provide better career opportunities. Although benefits change with the years, there will always be *some* educational programs available to your enlisted personnel. Those available today provide the greatest opportunities ever for personal enrichment. The *Retention Team Manual* and online resources describe the current programs in detail. By providing flexible hours and command recognition of the importance of the various educational programs available, you will generate interest and involvement—and enhance your retention climate.

DEPENDENTS' ORGANIZATIONS

The welfare and happiness of your crew's dependents are an important element of morale. You can reach dependents in many ways, but one of the best is through dependents' organizations. The following programs and ideas can be presented to the ship's spouses' club and other dependents' organizations for consideration:

- welcome aboard packages
- designated sponsor
- spouses' club president and ombudsman contacting all newly reporting families
- luncheons for new families and departing families

- organization during deployments of potluck suppers, picnics, card games, bazaars, swimming parties, sightseeing tours, bowling leagues, and other recreational activities
- welcome home parties for the command, using Navy clubs and facilities
- a list of educational institutions available in the area with points of contact so dependents can continue their education (The GI Bill may provide unique opportunities in this area.)

REENLISTMENT

There is no guarantee that your command career development efforts will produce Golden Anchor Award retention results. However, by having an effective career development program, by providing an atmosphere of genuine interest in each individual's desires, and by showing command concern for the family unit, you can strengthen your reenlistment program significantly.

Fig. 5-1. Dependents help the morale of your officers and crew. You must always be concerned with their welfare.

At set intervals, have personnel office staff provide the career development team members with a list of personnel who do not meet the professional growth requirements for reenlistment. They can then contact the ineligible members and encourage and help them to meet the requirements.

Finally, if the reenlistee is agreeable, hold a reenlistment ceremony with all hands present. This serves a fourfold purpose: it provides recognition to the reenlistee; it displays the results of the command career development program; it may encourage others to reenlist or to work on eligibility; and it reemphasizes the solemnity of the Oath of Enlistment to all hands.

Though not all-inclusive, the following is a list of additional benefits you may want to provide the reenlistee:

- photograph of the ceremony
- letter of congratulation to spouse or parents
- reenlistment day liberty
- reenlistment leave
- command plaque with name and date of reenlistment
- head of line privileges for a given period of time
- reenlistment benefit book

REQUEST MAST
When an individual submits a special request form (chit) through the chain of command, *it will be the most important thing on their mind until an answer is returned.* Resentment sets in rapidly if the chit is slowly or sloppily handled or if it disappears in someone's pocket or in-basket. Few things say so clearly to a person that they aren't very important as a badly handled request chit. Remember, that chits are a personal, *formal* test of your personnel management standards. It isn't a "yes" answer that is important; it is that the command cares enough to give *a thoughtful answer quickly.* It is not uncommon for COs to stipulate processing time requirements for special request chits. This is a pulse point for morale.

WELCOME ABOARD/SPONSORS
This is an area where many commands fail in their retention efforts. Some years ago, a young second-class petty officer assigned to a fast attack submarine stopped to chat with the CO prior to his discharge. The captain

asked him if there was anything he personally would recommend to improve the retention climate on board. The petty officer replied, "I'm grateful for the education and I liked my shipmates, but I knew the day I reported that I'd leave at the completion of my obligated service." When questioned further, he said, "When I reported aboard I got absolutely no assistance in settling into my new job. When I asked the chief of the boat about a place to sleep, he assigned me to a temporary bunk in the torpedo room next to a torpedo, and I was never assigned a personal locker. From that first day I knew that if the system cared that little for me I did not want to be part of it." The CO learned from this unfortunate episode, but the Navy lost a fine young petty officer. Ensure that your welcome aboard practices are formalized and always carried out. Sponsors should be intelligently chosen and must contact the new personnel before their arrival in the area. Send spouse-to-spouse notes when this is possible. Publishing a "welcome aboard" note in the plan of the day, introducing the crew to each newly reporting individual, can also prove highly beneficial. First impressions go a long way.

THE FAMILY

Family happiness is vital to continued career satisfaction. There is no way a command can solve all family problems, but concern for them can go far in easing the difficulties of service life and can certainly improve your retention program. Some thoughts in improving your practices in this area are to encourage spouses to come aboard often, both for ceremonies and formal counseling and presentations on Navy career benefits. Make the spouse a "co-star" in award, advancement, and reenlistment ceremonies. Scheduling a few minutes for coffee with the CO can often turn a spouse into a real booster of the command and its programs.

PROFESSIONAL APPRENTICESHIP CAREER TRACKS

The Professional Apprenticeship Career Tracks (PACT) program allows undesignated personnel to enlist and explore different ratings before moving into a job they are interested in. Recognition for professional achievements and initiative through designation as a PACT sailor can be decisive in a further reenlistment decision. This is not to imply that all undesignated personnel should be designated through this process. Only those who have shown a sincere desire and personal initiative in preparing for a particular rating should be designated.

RECOGNITION

Recognition is the most important ingredient in a successful retention program. It is a measure of the command's care, concern, and appreciation for the efforts of an individual. The use of "all hands" quarters to recognize individual and group achievements is very important. "Positive strokes," when deserved, are a proven method of improving the morale of a crew. There are other levels in the command, such as in work centers or divisions, where recognition ceremonies can also be carried out. The act of recognition is more important than the level of recognition.

Discipline

Aboard ship, discipline means prompt, willing responsiveness to commands. The best discipline is self-discipline—individuals doing the right thing because they *want* to do it. You can create it in your command by building willingness, enthusiasm, and cooperation. It will then exist not only while sailors are under the eyes of their superiors, but while they are off duty as well.

Admiral Arleigh Burke wrote, "A well disciplined organization is one whose members work with enthusiasm, willingness, and zest as individuals and as a group to fulfill the mission of the organization with expectation of success. Lack of discipline results in loss of smooth, determined operating action and combat efficiency."

In striving for a high level of discipline, remember that sailors admire an individual who lives in accordance with the code he or she enforces. Sailors will resent a CO who demands behavior from followers that he or she doesn't personally exhibit. The captain who expects steadfast obedience and cooperation from the crew will do well to give the same obedience and cooperation to his or her own seniors. This example, when combined with ability and a genuine interest in sailors' well-being, will eliminate many disciplinary problems.

POSITIVE DISCIPLINE

Naval Leadership, published by Naval Institute Press, describes positive discipline as follows:

> Positive discipline is the development of that state of mind in which individuals endeavor to do the right thing, with or without specific instructions. In order for positive discipline to operate most effectively, it is necessary that personnel *know* their jobs thoroughly. Training, therefore, is one of the basic factors involved in this type of discipline. The commanding officer must strive constantly to train his men to perform their duties in such a way as not to break regulations. In this way he is disciplining them just as surely as by punishing them after an infraction, but in a much more productive manner.

The following actions on your part will assist in the achievement of positive discipline:

- Maintain a general attitude of approval of the crew. A feeling of distrust on your part is soon transmitted to the crew and causes a general sense of insecurity.
- Let your crew know what is expected of them. This can be done by formal written directives and by clear verbal instructions.
- Keep the crew informed of their mission. Sailors work better when they fully understand the relationship of what they do and how they do it to the whole task of the ship.
- Let your crew know that their officers are behind them as long as they perform their duties to the best of their abilities.
- Keep your crew informed of their progress. This is equally important whether their work is good or bad.
- Keep your crew informed, within security restrictions, of any changes that will affect their future.
- Assure the crew by your actions that each will receive fair and impartial treatment.

- Improve your own professional ability. Enlisted personnel have been asked what they think makes a good leader. They say they like and respect professional competence more than any other single attribute.
- Delegate authority, with corresponding responsibility, as far down in the organization as competence exists.

PUNISHMENT

Punishment—like the positive discipline it is intended to uphold—is your personal responsibility. It cannot be delegated, since it can legally be awarded only by you or by a legally convened court-martial acting in accordance with the UCMJ. No officer except the commanding officer has any authority to inflict punishment on any person they are assigned to control. Your subordinates must be careful not to assume this authority under the assumption that they will save time for you, that the accused will get a fairer deal from them than from you, or for any other reason. You must ensure that your officers and chiefs understand they can exercise only *positive* discipline in guiding the offender's future actions. That failing, they must place the offender on report for you to deal with. Insist that all infractions are fully investigated before this is done. The mast process aboard ship should be a tribunal feared and respected by all crew members.

MILITARY JUSTICE

Present-day command qualification requires training and examination in military justice. It is essential that you review the *Manual for Court-Martial* and the *JAGMAN* frequently, especially prior to any legal proceeding. The captain who relies on past experience to conduct mast is being unfair to the crew and may land on the wrong side of the military justice system.

The American military justice system is designed as the last resort in enforcing standards of behavior and discipline in the services. It is governed by the Uniform Code of Military Justice, which came into effect in 1951. The UCMJ is a compromise between the necessities of military discipline and the need to guarantee that this discipline does not rest simply on the wishes of the commanding officer. As an added safeguard, an all-civilian Court of Appeals for the Armed Forces, insulated from military control, reviews records of military trials to ensure due process and correct application of the law. The following constitutes a brief overview of the system, as an aid to you in explaining it to the crew.

The military justice system provides for three kinds of courts-martial. The most formal is the *general* court-martial. This court can impose any punishment up to and including death, subject to the limitations described in the UCMJ's Table of Maximum Punishments.

The second type is the *special* court-martial. There are two options of special court-martial, both convened for less serious offenses. A limited forum special court-martial may convene for certain minor offenses without the accused's consent but is limited in maximum punishment to six months confinement and forfeiture of pay and may not impose a bad conduct discharge. A full special court-martial can impose up to one year of confinement and a bad conduct discharge.

The *summary* court-martial is the third kind of court-martial. It requires no trained lawyer to serve as the "judge" and is less formal than either a general or special court-martial. It is a one-person court, composed of a commissioned officer, generally not below the grade of O-3, on active duty. Punishment at summary court-martial does not constitute a criminal conviction. The maximum sentence it can impose, depending on the accused's rank, is no more than one month confinement, hard labor for forty-five days, restriction of sixty days, or forfeiture of two-thirds of one month's pay.

Procedures of general or special courts-martial are somewhat different from civilian courts. For instance, the number of jury members usually is smaller: four in a special and eight in a general court-martial. The members will be officers, unless the accused is enlisted and requests that enlisted members be detailed to the court-martial. In that case, at least one-third of the members' panel must be enlisted personnel.

After an evidence-gathering investigation, the first step in the general court-martial process is a preliminary hearing, called an Article 32 hearing. This is similar to a civilian preliminary hearing or grand jury hearing. However, in contrast to civilian criminal procedure, a defendant must be present, must have a military attorney present, and may question witnesses or present evidence.

The results of the Article 32 hearing are then submitted to the "convening authority"—that is, the officer in the chain of command with the power to convene the court. The convening authority determines what the next step is in the court-martial case. In another departure from civil law, the convening authority then appoints the court's members.

As the judge does in civilian criminal courts, the military judge of a general court-martial gives detailed instructions of law for the members to apply to the evidence before them. This "jury," in addition to determining guilt or innocence, may impose a sentence if the accused elects members for sentencing.

The accused has the right to request that the military judge act as a jury—a "judge alone" trial. The accused may also request that the government produce witnesses the accused thinks essential, but the defense has no subpoena power to compel witnesses to testify.

The conduct of the court-martial is similar to that of a civilian criminal court, with the prosecution presenting evidence first, followed by the defense. If a guilty verdict is reached, the trial goes to the presentencing phase, during which evidence is presented concerning aggravating and mitigating factors of the crime, potential for rehabilitation, the crime victim's statement, and the accused's general military record. The accused may give other evidence in extenuation and mitigation—for instance, proof of good character. If sentencing is by the members, the military judge will then advise them as to the maximum penalty permitted.

When an accused elects jury members, three-fourths of them must concur to determine a sentence. If three-fourths of the members do not agree on a sentence, the military judge may declare a mistrial. A sentence of death must be affirmed by unanimous decision.

Decisions by a court-martial are then forwarded to the convening authority for action. The convening authority may reject a conviction, order a rehearing, or disapprove, reduce, commute, or suspend a sentence, but it cannot impose a harsher punishment. The military justice system also has an automatic appellate review for all general courts-martial cases and all special courts-martial resulting in a bad conduct discharge.

In more serious cases, a court of criminal appeal reviews the case. After this, the accused may appeal a case to the Court of Appeals for the Armed Forces, the five-person court comprised of civilian judges. Final appeal of a court-martial case is to the U.S. Supreme Court.

In addition to the three kinds of courts-martial, service members may be subject to nonjudicial punishments called Article 15s, after the article of the UCMJ that governs nonjudicial punishment. All service members may be subject to Article 15 actions, but some types of punishments are applicable only to certain ranks.

Article 15 permits the commanding officer to impose such punishments as follows:

- restriction to specified limits
- extra duty
- reduction to the next lower grade, if the grade from which the accused would be reduced is within the promotion authority of the commanding officer
- forfeiture of pay
- correctional custody

The accused may submit matters in extenuation and mitigation to the commander and may have counsel present when appealing. Further, the officer who imposes the punishment, or his or her superior, can suspend the punishment, set it aside, or remit any part of it. Any suspension of punishment does not affect the question of guilt or innocence, however.

Passing and Getting the Word

It is worth your attention to determine how well the word is passed in your ship. It is often a shock for a commanding officer in talking to one of the younger sailors to find out that the individual does not know what the ship's operating schedule is, what exercises the ship is engaged in, or, for that matter, the name of their division officer, the executive officer, or the captain!

Making a habit of "passing the word" on policy and future expectations and inculcating the same habit in officers and petty officers is one of the most important contributions a captain can make toward a successful command tour and a well-integrated synchronized crew. Various ways and means of communicating have been discussed in this chapter and elsewhere. Nothing is more destructive to a person's morale than not knowing what is going on.

A corollary to passing the word is the commanding officer's getting the word about the policies and objectives of his or her superior in command. Getting the word in a timely manner allows you to efficiently implement policy from above. Failure to promulgate current policy changes and directives can result in a disorderly implementation, which displays to the crew that the commanding officer is not running the ship efficiently.

Use of the 1MC

One of the best tools at your disposal in command for communicating with the crew is the 1MC. It is a "real time" means to let everyone in the ship know about events. While at sea, you should strive to get on the 1MC once or twice a day, providing the crew with a general update of the day's events and any late-breaking changes. Remember: this is not an opportunity to impart long ideas about philosophy or to direct traffic around the ship; you have other vehicles for such communications. The 1MC is all about short bursts of interesting information, ranging from port visit schedule changes to operational achievements. It is a good place to give out the occasional "BZ" to exceptional performers, and a little humor can go a long way. When you first take command, let the crew hear your voice a bit, then pulse the XO and the command master chief for an honest appraisal of your style; encourage them to be brutally honest.

Some ships use a "morning report" format, which can be done by either you or the officer of the deck: a quick summary of major events, weather, and operational status. Keep it short. Another thing to consider is a late-evening "roundup" from you as captain, giving your quick impressions of the day's work and passing along a little encouragement. Be sure in both cases to consider timing: don't interrupt movies in the evening or start transmitting too early in the morning.

Fig. 5-2. Never forget that the hard work of any ship is performed by young sailors. A good captain will find ways to acknowledge and reward their contributions.

Equal Opportunity

U.S. Navy Regulations states that equal opportunity and treatment shall be accorded all persons in the Department of the Navy irrespective of their race, color, religion, sex (including gender identity), national origin, or sexual orientation.

The subject is covered in greater detail in the *Navy Equal Opportunity Program Manual* (OPNAVINST 5354.1 series) and should be well understood by all officers in command. The policy of equal opportunity has its roots in the Constitution, which all service personnel are sworn "to support and defend," and in the moral concept of human dignity. As commanding officer, it is your responsibility to maintain a work environment that is free from discrimination and harassment. You must instruct all those under your supervision in the concept of equal opportunity, and you must implement the equal opportunity program on your ship, and do so leading from the front.

As commanding officer, you must ensure that every person meets the same standards of performance for advancement. Similarly, each person appearing before you at mast must be judged solely on the merits of the case. Ethnic background, religious belief, gender identity, sexual orientation, and political persuasion must be separated from qualification and performance standards. By the same token, never think that you are obligated to compensate for previous racial injustices by using reverse discrimination. Rather, strive for *real* equality in all aspects of your command.

Sexual Harassment Prevention and Response

Sexual harassment erodes good order and discipline and prevents your unit from achieving a high state of operational readiness. In order for a command to be effective, the entire crew must be able to work together in an environment free from sexual harassment. The *Navy Sexual Harassment Prevention and Response Program* (OPNAVINST 5300.13 series) governs policy and guidelines to ensure sailors understand their roles in preventing sexual harassment as well as the actions to take in response to potential harassment situations.

Sexual harassment can be overt or subtle and can encompass a wide range of behaviors, such as unwelcome sexual advances, requests for sexual favors, and deliberate or repeated offensive comments or gestures of a sexual nature. Other examples include the display of inappropriate sexually oriented material in common areas or persistent and unwanted requests for dates, inappropriate email, text messages, or photos. While not an exhaustive list, the key point is that all levels of the chain of command must understand what constitutes sexual harassment and make clear that it will not be tolerated. Key command responsibilities outlined in the *Navy Sexual Harassment Prevention and Response Program* include the following:

- develop, disseminate, and enforce a sexual harassment policy statement, which must include expectations regarding sexual harassment prevention and response and procedural compliance
- ensure that a comprehensive visual inspection throughout the command is conducted on a regular basis, not less than annually, to

ensure all workplaces and common access spaces are free from materials that create a degrading, hostile, or offensive work environment

- ensure an annual assessment of your unit sexual harassment prevention and response program is conducted
- ensure Department of the Navy procedures for processing sexual harassment reports are prominently displayed to include the name and telephone number of the command's points of contact (command climate specialist [CCS], command-managed equal opportunity program manager, and the appropriate servicing equal employment opportunity office) for sexual harassment issues
- ensure all individuals are familiar with their right to submit an informal, formal, or anonymous sexual harassment report and the methods for submission
- ensure personnel are aware of the policies and procedures for filing a report of retaliation
- promote the chain of command as the primary and preferred channel to identify, process, and resolve reports of sexual harassment
- consult a CCS to provide analysis and recommendations regarding all informal, formal, and anonymous sexual harassment reports as well as any other issues that affect the command climate of a unit
- track and monitor the reporting and status of the command and subordinate command's sexual harassment reports
- ensure fitness report or performance evaluation entries are made for all service members found guilty at courts-martial or other courts of competent jurisdiction or who receive nonjudicial punishment
- ensure all formal report command investigations, and all documents pertinent to the formal report, are retained for a period of two years
- provide, upon turnover, the incoming commander with a written report of all command and subordinate commands open sexual harassment report investigations
- provide annual equal opportunity, sexual harassment, and grievance procedures general military training for all assigned command members. Ensure senior leadership is personally involved in the training.

Families and Dependents

The welfare of dependents has been partially treated in our discussion of retention. However, there are other aspects of this challenge that you should consider.

The importance of the family as a unit of the Navy team has been well established over the years. Morale, job performance, retention, and unit readiness are directly linked to the well-being of the families of those you command. The key to success here is *concern*. You must display your concern in your daily actions involving personal problems and hardships and by your command's earnest efforts to inform dependents of their privileges and the services available to them.

Common Navy programs and dependent privileges and services are described online in numerous official websites and at local fleet and Family Service Centers aboard naval installations (described below). These sources should be made available to spouses of your crew members by means of seminars, welcome aboard packages, and individual counselor interviews.

Family Service Centers and Ombudsmen

Two of the best resources you have in the endless challenge of taking care of your command's families are the Navy's Family Service Centers and your own command ombudsman.

The Family Service Centers are located at major Navy bases all around the world. They provide an enormous array of services, information, and assistance to your command's families. Staffed by trained counselors, the centers provide classes in everything from parenting to financial planning; assist in spousal job hunting; give advice on moving and finding a place to live; provide welcome aboard packages describing the area; and refer your families to other services they may require. As a new commanding officer in an area, you should take the time to drop by the Family Service Center, perhaps with your CMC and ombudsman, to see for yourself all they can provide.

The Navy's outstanding ombudsman program has been steadily improving over the past several decades. Today's ombudsmen are well-trained, motivated, and informed volunteers who provide a bridge between you and your families. They serve as communicators, facilitators, and referral experts to your command's families. You will receive the pro forma resignation of the incumbent ombudsman when you take command; normally you will ask them to remain in the post until you decide on a new ombudsman. After consultation with your XO and CMC, you may want to ask the incumbent to remain indefinitely, or you may choose to appoint a new ombudsman.

If you are going to change ombudsmen, you should work closely with the XO and CMC on the selection process. Volunteers can be solicited in the plan of the day, but often a better approach is for the CMC to ask several spouses to apply. You should personally interview each of them, seeking to determine if they have the character, temperament, and time to do the job properly.

Being an ombudsman is a demanding and challenging task. After a week of formal Navy schooling, the new ombudsman is expected to field phone calls ranging from requests for information on the ship's schedule to advice on how to set up a move. The ombudsman should set up a "care line," which is a prerecorded message available to your command's families providing the latest information on the command. The ombudsman must be able to refer your command family members to appropriate resources and keep you informed of any problems that arise.

Your relationship with the command ombudsman should be friendly and close. Invite him or her to a meeting, perhaps at breakfast, every couple of months, taking the time to talk about the situation in the command. You will be amazed at what you learn. You may want to invite the XO and CMC to the meetings. Make sure your ombudsman has all the resources necessary to do the job. These include a complete social roster of the entire ship, updated monthly; a cellular phone for official calls; expenses for babysitting, travel, and administrative overhead; and anything else he or she needs. The ombudsman should be encouraged to be in touch with the command's social side, generally through meetings with the chairperson or president of the command's support group.

In general, as in so many things, you will get out of the ombudsman program about what you put into it. Properly executed, this program is a superb resource for you in taking care of your command's families. Good ombudsmen are worth their weight in gold to your command; treat them accordingly.

The Enlisted Performance Evaluation

Enlisted evaluations are vitally important for a person's promotion and for selection for special billets. You are responsible for ensuring that they are submitted on time and that they give a fair assessment of an individual's performance. In preparing these important documents, keep your comments succinct, objective, and consistent with the marks assigned. Outstanding crew members should receive marks and written evaluations that reflect their contribution to the command. Special accomplishments should be highlighted. Unique or difficult watch qualifications, performance as leading petty officer, assignment as command chief, contribution to a Ney Award, and so forth are accomplishments that each leading petty officer and division officer should include in evaluations. You must insist that your chain of command fully understands the importance of the enlisted evaluation system as defined in BUPERSINST 1610.10 series, including the use of evaluations as described below:

- to determine eligibility of a member for reenlistment, for honorable discharge, and for good conduct awards
- to permit the commanding officer to accelerate the advancement of outstanding members and to reduce it for those who show themselves incompetent
- to inform the various selection boards that select members for advancement, appointment to commissioned status, assignment to special duties, and special education programs.

Adequate performance evaluations are essential for all the above reasons. Failure to objectively appraise a person's performance is a grave failure to meet a public trust and can constitute an injustice not only to the individual but to his or her peers as well.

As commanding officer, you must ensure that the preparation of enlisted evaluations is not lost in the flood of other required reports, inspections, and special projects that occur from time to time. It is no understatement to say that fitness reports and evaluations are the most important documents processed on your ship.

PERFORMANCE EVALUATION HINTS

The comments and hints that follow, taken from senior and master chief petty officer selection board remarks regarding evaluation preparation and wording, are applicable to all evaluation reports. Study them and pass them along. They can help upgrade your enlisted evaluation system.

- Once an individual is selected as a senior enlisted petty officer (E-6 through E-10), department heads and commanding officers should endeavor to give him or her a variety of assignments to evaluate potential for further advancement. These can be made in such a way that they do not prevent the individual from demonstrating their ability to carry out their primary responsibility. Too many CPOs are content to remain within the confines of their work centers. In this capacity, however, they cannot be judged on their ability to function satisfactorily on department and command levels, which they will have to do as E-8 and E-9 leaders.
- The detailers sometimes have to fill the more difficult (less desirable) assignments with qualified personnel. This possibility should be considered and commented upon.
- Don't waste narrative comments on describing how well the ship did on deployment, inspection, and so forth. Tell exactly *what* jobs the individual had and *how well* they were performed.
- Eliminate flowery adjectives and get to the point in plain English.
- Place your emphasis on the individual's ability, potential, and willingness to accept positions of leadership and management. Indicate *why* he or she should be advanced.
- Take care to list all collateral duties, awards, education, and qualifications. If an individual is marked higher or lower than peers, explain the reason clearly in the narrative.
- Don't recommend an individual for advancement just for meeting the time in service requirements.
- School commands should not mark students. Their evaluations should read simply, "student under instruction."
- Proofread the evaluation to ensure that no blocks are left blank. Don't leave the selection board to reconstruct the record.

- Write succinctly, in organized paragraphs.
- Don't say your command is composed of "highly selected" or "specially chosen" individuals if it is not. The board will know better, and your efforts will be discounted accordingly.
- Fill in blocks on duties completely and specifically. Don't assume that board members know what duties specific billets in your unit entail.
- Establish an evaluation review board or some other method of ensuring that correct evaluations are submitted.
- Don't shortchange your enlisted personnel. They make your ship!

The Captain's Role with the Crew

The best way to take the measure of your crew is simply to spend time with them. There is a great deal to be said for being the kind of captain who is well known for turning up at unexpected times. One way to look at this is that you are perpetually walking around your command trying to catch people doing something good.

Try to schedule at least one activity each day that will draw you to a part of the ship, submarine, or squadron where you do not normally go. A great choice on a surface ship, for example, is to do a planned maintenance spot check every day. Make it a surprise to the division concerned, take the 3-M coordinator with you, and enjoy the exchange with your people on the deckplates. You will demonstrate how important you think maintenance is to the command, have a chance to interact with your hardest workers, and get the opportunity to spot-check an important function.

Spend as little time as possible in your stateroom. Nothing happens there! As a default position if nothing else is going on, head up to the bridge. Talk to everyone on the bridge team. Then walk around the decks. And don't forget to tour one of your main engineering spaces each day. If you "take a spin around" at least once in the morning and once in the afternoon, you'll be amazed how much you pick up about what is happening in your world.

Bear in mind that you cannot walk past something that isn't right. The minute you do, you've accepted that standard—be it something as mundane as a dirty ladder back or as complicated as an improperly conducted signal processor check on the SPY 1D radar. Be especially vigilant for safety violations of any kind.

Sailors will work the hardest for commanding officers they like and respect. Know your job, interact with your people in positive ways, and keep everyone focused on safety and the mission at hand. You'll enjoy every day you spend with your sailors.

6

Maintenance
and Logistics

If the equipment doesn't work in battle, it doesn't make
much difference how much else the officers know,
the battle is lost—and so are the people in it.
So—it can be right handy to be a good engineer first—
and a brilliant theorist after.

—Admiral Arleigh Burke, *Winning Naval Battles*

A Philosophy of Maintenance and Logistics

U.S. Navy Regulations, under the heading "Care of Ships, Aircraft, Vehicles, and Their Equipment," states that the commanding officer shall cause such inspections and tests to be made and procedures carried out as are prescribed by competent authority, together with such others as he or she deems necessary, to ensure the proper preservation, repair, maintenance, and operations of any ship, aircraft, vehicle, and equipment assigned to the command. Philosophically speaking, such a policy is certainly not unique to the Navy. Civilian engineers and industrial managers have emphasized such maintenance procedures for years. What is unique about the challenges you will face in the areas of maintenance and logistics is the requirement to take your systems into the unpredictable world of combat. Thus, as Admiral Burke said after World War II, "All that equipment has to work the way it ought to or it is simply excess baggage." Today, the Navy sends extraordinarily complex systems to sea as we prepare for potential combat operations. Your challenge is to maintain them in a condition to fight. That additional level of responsibility must form the basis of your command philosophy as it applies to maintenance and logistics. You should work hard to communicate that aspect to your crew.

Because your systems must go into combat, and because your people's lives will depend on your equipment, your maintenance and logistics team must approach the challenges they face with an "attention to detail" philosophy—aimed at reducing all possible defects, improving reliability, demanding required performance, and creating a culture of self-sufficiency.

Many senior engineering officers feel that mistakes are caused by a lack of knowledge on the part of maintenance personnel and by a lack of attention to the task at hand. The first condition can be corrected by testing all personnel to determine that they have the necessary knowledge to perform their tasks and stand their watches. The second condition, lack of attention, is a state of mind that can be changed. The supervisor must observe the sailor's mental habits. Are they mentally lazy? Uninterested? Overqualified, and thus bored? Your maintenance and logistics team must be reminded to watch each detail and maintain an orderly "scan" or examination of each indicator of success or failure of that responsibility. With focus and energy, they can reach the goal described above in all things and at all times. You, as commanding officer, may have to accept some slowing down as your sailors get used to more thorough performance, but attainment of habit and development of confidence will soon bring them back to near their previous speed. Lack of defects will more than improve the overall performance.

Your insistence on accountability for maintenance performed and strict adherence to maintenance and operating procedures forms an essential part of the ship's general philosophy concerning the safe and proper operation of all equipment and the logistic support of the entire ship.

Emphasis on Maintenance and Repair Afloat

Realize this from the first: you will have to stress material readiness throughout your tour; it will be a never-ending requirement. Today's fleet consists of complex and highly capable ships. Any single casualty or material failure, if quickly corrected, will seldom detract from the ship's readiness for war. Those that are not quickly corrected, however, will usually precipitate an avalanche of problems that, once started, is very difficult to reverse. This snowball effect can result in a significant degradation of the ship's readiness, as well as an extraordinary amount of work. Careful attention to detail on the part of all hands is a necessity for all ships, large or small. Demand uniform *formality* with respect to the definition, reporting, logging, and clearing of material deficiencies, whether large or small. Insist that identified deficiencies be pursued aggressively in accordance with the priorities you have established, and train your personnel not to learn to "live with" deficiencies. Similarly, you must attack your ship's established corrective and preventive maintenance routines with vigor and care. An unenthusiastic or careless attitude toward scheduled preventive maintenance will result in the certain degradation and failure of mechanical, electrical, and electronic equipment. These failures will affect operating time and cause the expenditure of large amounts of effort and money to repair.

The fleet can ill afford expenditures of time, money, and manpower to correct damage from improperly performed maintenance. Keep in mind that the improper maintenance your sailors perform today may—in some cases—take years to catch up with your ship. You won't be there to see the result, but the Navy will suffer. More commonly, the effects can be immediate and catastrophic. In this era of highly complex threats and high-tech combat systems afloat, your gear must perform precisely as designed.

TRAINING JUNIOR OFFICERS

Most maintenance errors can be prevented by conscientious planning and supervision by officers and senior petty officers. Personnel reporting to a ship for the first time generally have little practical training in maintenance and test procedures. They can gain competence only through conscientious training aboard ship—by supervised on-the-job experience. It is false economy to assign inexperienced personnel to independent maintenance jobs without at least spot supervision.

To ensure that this supervision is effective, you must provide your junior officers with proper training in maintenance management and the need for material readiness afloat. Among the many duties of a commanding officer, there are few that have more lasting importance than the responsibility for the proper employment and development of junior officers. One of your most crucial responsibilities is direct training of these young men and women. The influence and impact of your policies on their eventual development cannot be overemphasized.

Your division officers should not be confined solely to routine administrative functions and repetitive training tasks. They must be taught how to perform their divisional responsibilities, and then they must be *used* as division officers. They must know that they are held directly responsible for the repairs, maintenance, and equipment assigned to their division. All too frequently, when a problem occurs, the department head will bypass the division officers or usurp their authority. You should prevent this. Division officers must be required to work on these problems alone, at least initially. They will be consulted concerning, and held accountable for, all the material matters of the division.

In an effort to increase this awareness among their junior officers, some COs have instituted a policy of having a junior officer accompany them on at least one of their daily tours through the ship. They then discuss each of the discrepancies noted on the tour. As a result of these tours, these COs have noted a significant increase in awareness of conditions and responsibility for material readiness.

Material Readiness

GOOD ENGINEERING PRACTICE

"Good engineering practice" means the safe and proper operation of engineering plants. It is a philosophy based on a respect for, and an understanding of, the equipment being operated. It applies not only to shipboard propulsion plant operation but to everyday operations and maintenance routines on all other shipboard systems as well. Good engineering practice begins with each watchstander. It means such things as feeling pipes and equipment for abnormal temperatures, listening to equipment for unusual noises, fixing minor discrepancies such as drips, packing leaks before they become more serious, keeping the bilges pumped down, and double-checking logs and records.

Good engineering practice recognizes that there is a "right way" and a "wrong way" to perform maintenance. Although written instructions and procedures usually specify the right way to maintain a piece of equipment, there are many instances for which specific guidance is not given. It is then necessary for the operator to use his or her judgment, experience, and knowledge of equipment to determine the action to take—in short, to exercise good engineering practice.

The exercise of good engineering practice is the essence of material readiness. The commanding officer will improve the engineering practice of the command by insisting on the involvement of subordinates (in particular, officers) in the material management of the command.

OFFICER INVOLVEMENT

Obviously, officers are not trained as technicians, nor should they be so employed. As managers and trainers, however, junior officers must learn the practical aspects of their division's responsibilities. This includes the ability to recognize when proper tools and instruments are being utilized and when and how various tasks are performed by the division. This may require an officer to perform certain tasks personally to learn the required knowledge. It definitely requires officers' periodic, routine verification that their division is properly performing assigned maintenance functions, by their thorough review of required documentation.

Proper officer involvement in the technical supervision of a division requires a thorough theoretical and practical technical knowledge of appropriate operating and maintenance procedures. The officer acquires this by study of applicable documentation and by sufficient on-the-job practice and observation to understand the correct methods of operating and conducting maintenance procedures. For example, division officers responsible for a diesel engine should understand thoroughly each step in the diesel lineup and operating procedure. They must have the practical knowledge to recognize whether the procedure is being conducted properly when they monitor the personnel actually performing the lineup and operation. They should know what inspections are required and how they are conducted.

They must actively direct the planning of division work to ensure that required maintenance is completed at necessary frequencies and in the required sequences, as set forth by Planned Maintenance System instructions.

They must review maintenance, alignment, and operational data to ensure that they are within allowed specifications, that trends are analyzed, and that they correctly reflect the readiness of the systems and equipment under their charge.

They must have a thorough enough knowledge of the correct specifications to readily recognize abnormalities.

They must examine completed work and maintenance records and other data to ensure that they are maintained in accordance with applicable directives, that the operation or maintenance action has achieved the desired goal, and that the records reflect this.

They must establish and use checkpoints to ensure that complicated or lengthy work proceeds satisfactorily. Checkpoints are a technique of requiring periodic reports to determine that work is proceeding as planned. Prudent choice of checkpoints in a procedure or maintenance task keeps an officer informed about what is going on without the close degree of supervision implied by monitoring.

They must insist that their senior subordinates actively involve themselves in the planning, supervision, and execution of all divisional maintenance, training, and operational responsibilities.

Application of good engineering practices will enhance the professional development of the officer, improve the performance of the division, and result in increased material readiness of the entire ship.

Preventive Maintenance
THE 3-M SYSTEM
The Navy ships' Maintenance and Material Management system was created to help manage required maintenance in an atmosphere of growing complexity of equipment, increased tempo of operations, and decline in available resources in order to ensure maximum readiness. The 3-M system is an integrated system to improve the management of maintenance and provide for the collection and dissemination of maintenance-related information for use in developing better management, engineering analysis, and techniques of equipment maintenance.

The ships' 3-M system, when properly used, provides for the orderly scheduling and accomplishment of maintenance and for reporting and disseminating maintenance-related information. It comprises two subsystems—the Planned Maintenance System (PMS) and the Maintenance Data System (MDS).

The PMS pertains to the planning, management of resources (personnel, material, and time), and scheduling to keep equipment running within its design characteristics. It defines uniform maintenance standards (based on engineering experience) and prescribes simplified procedures and techniques for the accomplishment of maintenance. The procedures and tools of the PMS are described in detail in *Ship's Maintenance and Material Management System Policy* (OPNAVINST 4790.4).

When used properly, PMS improves maintenance practices and significantly upgrades equipment readiness. One of your most difficult challenges in command will be to utilize this vital system effectively. Over the years, type commanders have investigated the way PMS is used in the fleet. They found considerable differences between procedures on maintenance requirement cards (MRCs) and those in equipment technical manuals, and between the procedures on the MRCs and the actual performance of maintenance. In particular, they found that equipment guide lists were not always prepared properly, and that in several cases, the preventive maintenance item they asked about had never been accomplished. This was evident from the failure to refer to technical manuals, the finding of errors in manuals and on MRCs, the use of improper tools, the identification of improper equipment wiring, the identification of long-term equipment misoperation, and the general unfamiliarity of personnel with maintenance procedures. In some cases, the type commander and Board of Inspection and Survey inspections showed that no preventive maintenance procedures at all were in effect and that no one had even requested the MRCs and manuals that would have been needed to institute them.

TESTING EFFECTIVENESS

The simplest test to use to measure your preventive maintenance effectiveness is to select a single maintenance action and audit its performance from start to finish. The commanding officer can do this by checking the following:

- the preventive maintenance requirement card against the technical manual and feedback reports
- the use of correct tools
- the identification and use of proper repair parts
- the use of correct safety procedures, tag-outs, and internal ship command control procedures
- the use of proper work procedures

Corrective Maintenance

In the area of material management, you must strive to get deficiencies identified early and to develop a positive plan to correct them. The wise commanding officer will not tolerate the "it's always been that way" syndrome and will insist upon a strong corrective maintenance program. You must expect the sailors to attack every minor deficiency before it becomes a major problem and results in a last-minute crisis before a deployment or other operational requirement.

Maintenance Training

In the area of maintenance training, you must ensure that ship's force personnel understand what is expected of them and of repair or maintenance activities. Furthermore, you must build in each of your sailors a desire to determine and correct the "fundamental or root cause" of equipment malfunctions rather than merely treating its symptoms.

Training on individual equipment must include formal presentations on maintenance procedures, hands-on training sessions, and formal examinations to determine the effectiveness of the program.

SHIPBOARD TRAINING PROGRAM

In a more general sense, the program should ensure that all personnel understand the following rules:

- For each work item to be accomplished, specific procedures that define the system and component to be worked on, the work to be accomplished, and the desired results must be formulated and approved by proper authority. This is generally what has been done by the 3-M system.

- Proper permission will be requested from higher authority prior to commencing maintenance work.
- Systems will be tagged out properly prior to maintenance.
- Watchstanders are responsible for monitoring work being performed by outside maintenance activities.
- Watchstanders should report to duty officers any discrepancies they notice—for example, missing danger tags or tags attached to the wrong components.
- Safety precautions as outlined in the *SORM* will be strictly enforced.

Maintenance Records

CURRENT SHIP'S MAINTENANCE PROJECT

The Current Ship's Maintenance Project (CSMP) is a meaningful maintenance control document that provides the depth of information necessary to evaluate and quantify the backlog and scope of work for ship's force, intermediate maintenance activity (IMA), and depot accomplishment, as well as to plan, schedule, and fund upkeeps, availabilities, and overhauls. The CSMP is increasingly important as a controlling record at all levels of supervision. Unfortunately, observations by type commanders indicate that the CSMP is not always maintained properly on all ships. They identified specific problems and issued the following solutions:

- Junior officer and work center supervisors must develop a working knowledge of the CSMP.
- The CSMP should be cleared promptly of deferred maintenance that is no longer required or has been completed.
- Ships must identify deferred maintenance as it occurs and enter it into the CSMP.
- Deferred maintenance documents must be prepared thoroughly to generate complete work requests.
- Maintenance documents must be delivered to the designated CSMP maintenance activity on time.

CSMP accuracy, completeness, and management are important. If the ship's CSMP is not a valid assessment of material condition and maintenance requirements, you should examine internal handling of MDS documents, internal CSMP distribution and use, and junior officer/work center supervisor knowledge and understanding of the CSMP. Upkeep and availability work packages can be significantly improved through advanced planning from an improved CSMP.

Testing

After most repair and maintenance work, equipment must be tested to see that it is working properly. Where these tests are not properly organized and supervised, the expression "give her the smoke test" may be much more than a joke—and unacceptably costly in wasted time and resources.

The basic assumption in the testing of equipment should be that it will not respond as expected (or else why the test?) and that the personnel involved are unfamiliar with the procedures to be followed (as testing is seldom a routine operation). Where a series of large, expensive, or inherently dangerous components are involved in a system test of one sort or another, poor procedures may have very serious consequences indeed.

TESTING GUIDELINES

For such systems, it is good engineering practice to follow, as applicable, the following guidelines:

- The test must be properly authorized. For many components or systems, this involves the approval of higher authority and perhaps the material command concerned.
- The test procedures must be approved by an authorized source and reviewed for accuracy on board by the head of department concerned (and in some cases, the commanding officer). In most cases it is mandatory to commit procedures to writing and quality assurance procedures.
- Brief all personnel involved about the purpose of the test, prerequisites (i.e., steps to be taken before the test begins), step-by-step procedures in sequence, communications, precautions, out-of-commission indications, expected readings and results of the various test stages, and possible casualties.

- A test station bill, separate from the normal watch bill, should be drawn up, with specific assignments of qualified personnel by name where tests of any complexity are involved. This bill should provide for personnel relief if the test is to be of appreciable duration. The relief personnel should be given the same briefing as the original test gang.
- The station bill should include the communications circuits to be manned.
- Make up proper data forms, where applicable, before the briefing. Operating personnel should not normally be assigned data-collecting duties. Data-gathering communications circuits should be separate from operating circuits.
- Valve and switch lineups following the written test procedures should be made independently by two persons prior to the test. Double-check any changes made during the test as well.
- Plan for a rehearsal, or dry run, before complicated or potentially dangerous tests. The officer in charge should check each station and each communications channel before the rehearsal and the actual test.
- Testing is not comparable in urgency to operating. If anything "goes sour," the test should come to "all stop" and the equipment put in the safest condition possible while the difficulty is resolved.

Quality Assurance

All type commanders have issued detailed instructions regarding quality assurance. It is good engineering practice for the ship to have a strong quality assurance program in order to check maintenance and recertify repaired systems.

IMPORTANCE OF INSPECTION

When outside activities conduct repair work, a ship's ability to inspect the quality of that work takes on even greater importance. One of the challenges of our Navy repair and overhaul system is that the quality assurance system within the repair organization generally reports to the repair or production officer rather than directly to the commanding officer of the repair facility. This means that even with the best inspectors available, originally objective reports on quality can often be considered subjectively if they influence completion dates. Needless to say, it is up to you to look long and hard at the thoroughness and quality of the work completed by repair or maintenance activities. An inquisitive, involved CO will help impose objectivity in the system.

Material Inspections

One of the characteristics of a good commanding officer is the ability to inspect and know what "*right*" looks like." Whether material, personnel, or administrative, no inspection can be properly performed unless the inspector knows what to look for. This ability is not inborn, but comes through years of experience spent mostly on the receiving end of inspections.

If a captain really knows how to inspect, good things will happen in short order. A sense of pride will develop within the ship when previously unnoticed discrepancies are now noticed and quickly corrected. The commanding officer who knows how to conduct a material inspection will soon discover fewer items to comment upon unfavorably, as material readiness improves. This ability to inspect must be something that you pass on to your crew through both example and training. It is tied directly to your mission success.

USE OF INSPECTION FORMS

In preparing yourself to conduct effective material inspections, you would be well advised to review the annual summaries of shipboard deficiencies noted by the Board of Inspection and Survey, the type commander assessments, and the Fleet Operational Reactor Safeguards Examinations. These summaries are provided to applicable ships and form a useful general index of where trouble can be anticipated.

Your Ship as Others See Her

The captain who serves the ship well is one who can stand back occasionally and see her as others do. This is not easy.

To start with, take physical appearance. The conduct of morning quarters on deck is the business of the executive officer, but you are in unfortunate straits if you are the only officer in the squadron who does not know that quarters on your ship is referred to in the flag mess as the "0800 mob scene." The military appearance of your formations, the smartness of your deck watches, the proper handling of colors, anchor lights, and absentee pennants, the cleanliness of your quarterdeck, topside areas, and paint applications—all these are taken by the rest of the fleet as outward signs of your ship's inward state, and more than likely, they are right.

Without deluding yourself that dressy show can long conceal less pleasant realities below decks, you will do well to make firsthand, periodic checks on how these outward symbols look from the flag bridge as well as to check on the details of watchkeeping and maintenance below decks.

Since this chapter deals primarily with the subject of maintenance, it is also appropriate to consider at this point how a maintenance activity views your ship.

In the eyes of any maintenance activity, the best customers are those who solve problems during availabilities at the lowest possible level. You can do this by encouraging communications at every level in both chains of command. This occurs naturally once good relations have been established and ship's force and maintenance activity people know each other.

Fig. 6-1. Little things mean a lot—and nowhere more so than on a modern warship. Proper maintenance of small boats can mean the difference between accomplishing your mission and failing to do so.

Maintenance activity COs appreciate the ship captain who keeps them informed. They will work closely to improve this type of relationship. The other end of the spectrum is the commanding officer who cries "wolf" at every difficulty to the next senior in command (i.e., the commodore).

Ships that perform well during availabilities make use of the ship superintendent. They keep this individual informed on what they need and cut in on ship conditions that might preclude specific maintenance or testing.

Maintenance activities appreciate ships that react quickly to emergent work by timely submittal of necessary work requests. Delay in this will only cause problems downstream, when many work items are simultaneously scheduled for completion. In this regard, maintenance activities also feel positively about the ship that conducts required testing when possible right after repairs rather than waiting until the end of the maintenance period.

Maintenance activity COs feel secure when they work with a ship CO who is safety-conscious. They are particularly sensitive to diver safety and the fact that refit poses many hazards to personnel and machinery. The alert CO will concentrate efforts on general safety, with particular emphasis on hull integrity and personnel safety.

Finally, maintenance activity personnel (uniformed, civilian, and contractor) appreciate praise and feedback. This praise, where warranted, can inspire them to increase the quality of the refit or upkeep period.

By keeping this advice in mind, you can better the chances that your ship will receive a good maintenance availability.

Availability Planning

An "availability" is the period assigned a ship for the uninterrupted accomplishment of work that requires services of a repair activity ashore or afloat. Availabilities can range from five-day preventive maintenance availabilities for LCS to multiyear CNO availabilities. The latter are normally planned well in advance and usually follow the timelines provided in the *Integrated Project Team Development (IPTD) Program* (CNRMCINST 4790.4), which provides teams with a foundation for the successful execution of a major availability.

The key to success in availability or upkeep/refit planning is early and complete preparation. This starts by educating all work center supervisors in the proper preparation of work requests. This training must include the mechanics of filling out work requests but also must ensure that the following items will be clear to the maintenance activity when you submit the work package:

- accurate identification of the problem, including just what assistance is required
- inclusion of all necessary equipment nameplate data, reference publications, drawings, and repair procedures
- inclusion of equipment location
- identification of knowledgeable shipboard contact personnel
- assignment of correct level of maintenance assistance: IMA, depot, or drydock
- identity of key events
- special controls identified, if applicable
- commanding officer or designated representative signature

Once the work center supervisors are well versed in work request preparation, you must ensure that your departments identify all work necessary prior to submission of the work package to the repair activity. Late submittal of known work items will degrade the effectiveness of the availability and also create ill will between the maintenance activity and the ship.

At present, most maintenance activities also perform certain routine work items during an availability. These include lagging, sail loft work, "powder coating" to improve material preservation against the elements (saving precious labor hours for the crew), and fuel and lubricant analysis, as examples. The well-prepared ship will ensure that work requiring lists, such as lagging, are properly prepared, indicating the problem and exact location.

Another significant input to availability planning is the CSMP. The end product of the CSMP is a listing of all ship's work items yet to be accomplished, including responsibility, status, and complete description. Ships with good maintenance programs work to keep the CSMP updated at all times. This provides the maintenance activity with a complete status of current work and allows them to plan most of the availability well before your work package arrives. The results are obvious. The better the planning input, the better the resulting work period. The work packages are normally developed and discussed during 50 percent and 75 percent "lock" conferences or meetings.

Once the work package is complete, the next milestone in a successful availability is the arrival conference. This permits the ship, the immediate superior in command, and the maintenance activity to discuss the work package in detail and to factor in controlling work items.

You can help your ship and your reputation by being prepared to discuss all work items in detail. You must have the facts regarding all work items in order to be able to make recommendations on management decisions. Furthermore, you must leave the conference with a clear understanding of the various actions taken on work requests, and you must get this information to the crew. Since the arrival conference sets the tone for availability, you and your availability coordinator (usually the engineering officer) must attend. If possible, division officers and leading petty officers should be invited as well. They can learn from the experience and will be able to transfer firsthand information on the conference to their subordinates.

Most maintenance activities conduct periodic management or work review meetings throughout the availability. Generally, only you and your availability coordinator are invited. These meetings track work items with a view toward maximizing maintenance activity effectiveness. It is during these meetings that supply effectiveness is measured, emergent work is reviewed, and the critical flow points are checked for validity.

To be effective at management meetings, you must be well briefed on the status of all work items on the ship. You must do your homework and have the facts prior to the meeting. Some successful COs have used a process whereby they discuss each pertinent work item with the respective department head in the presence of the ship's superintendent just prior to the meeting. This gives them the up-to-date job status as seen by the ship and the maintenance activity. You may also develop other methods that provide you a more consistent understanding of the status of the availability.

During the management meeting, try hard to avoid placing others in an adversary position, particularly if you don't have all the facts. Likewise, if you feel it necessary to introduce a big issue at the meeting, it is wise to "grease the skids" with the maintenance activity and administrative seniors prior to it.

In summary, the success or lack of success that attends upkeep, availabilities, and overhauls depends greatly upon the relations established between the ship and the maintenance activity, whether afloat or ashore. Sources of friction often encountered are a lack of understanding on the part of the ship's officers and crew of the organization of the repair activity and a lack of knowledge about the differing responsibilities of the ship and the maintenance activity.

When going alongside a tender for upkeep or into a yard for availability, it is good practice to obtain an organizational chart of the activity. Study it and promulgate its contents to the leading personnel in your ship. It can usually be assumed that the tender or yard knows which gear comes under which shipboard department, but a good many stumbles, fumbles, and grumbles come about from the ship's company thinking that one shop or office in the yard or on board the tender is taking care of something when actually it is the concern of another. Availability or refit period success is enhanced when ship managers know who in the maintenance activity hierarchy they interface with on repair management issues.

The communications network set up by the ship is all-important in establishing the proper rapport with the maintenance activity.

Repairs and Maintenance Advice

New concepts continue to reshape the shoreside repair structure in an effort to ensure ships receive effective and on-time maintenance. As CO, you need to understand how they work in your homeport. As an example, in San Diego there is a large supervisory organization working for the surface type commander called Southwest Regional Maintenance Center. Headed by a senior Navy captain from the engineering duty officer community, this organization directs all maintenance activity in the homeport and for the surface force. They control maintenance dollars for all repair efforts, and the various intermediate maintenance activities report to them. The centralization of this in-port maintenance promises to create efficiencies in the process that will make your job as CO easier. In essence, it creates "one-stop shopping" for waterfront maintenance customers. Pay a call on the CO of the regional maintenance organization and his or her subordinate commands early. You should also meet the repair officer (essentially the "operations officer" of the regional maintenance organization) as early as you can.

Your ship will have a port engineer assigned by the type commander. These well-qualified civilians represent a long-term, shore-based adjunct to your own engineering officer. The port engineer works for the type commander and provides day-to-day support for all repair work in the ship. Your chief engineer should be working on a daily basis with the port engineer, and you should get to know that individual very well too. When your port engineer is doing a good job, be sure to let their boss know. Likewise, when you experience a problem or frustration in the world of maintenance, if your port engineer cannot solve the problem, ensure that their chain of command knows the situation as well.

Another factor at work on the waterfront in the world of maintenance is the increasing privatization of repair efforts. You can still affect the quality of work being done for you, but now you must work through the contracting agency (generally the regional maintenance organization) to do so.

Drydocking

Normal drydocking is scheduled during the regular overhaul period. Drydocking may also be accomplished between regular overhauls (interim drydocking) for routine maintenance or to repair or replace propellers, repair shafting, sonar, or other underwater damage, or examine the bottom for possible damage or deterioration.

Drydocking is accomplished in a Navy yard or naval repair facility or at a commercial yard under contract to the Navy. When docking at a commercial yard, arrangements will be made for the proceedings by an industrial manager.

Prior to docking, the commanding officer and the docking officer or commercial dockmaster should hold a conference to discuss the time of docking, tugs and pilots, the condition of the ship when entering, and the housekeeping arrangements for the visit. These consist of the brows to be furnished, utility services to be provided, sanitary services needed, garbage and waste removal arrangements, and other necessary services. Reactor safety provisions should be discussed for nuclear-powered ships.

At this same conference, provide the yard with any information about the last docking and the ship's docking plan, if not already held, and make arrangements regarding working and linehandling parties.

A similar conference is held near the end of work to set the time and date of undocking and other events leading to it, such as flooding of the dock. Weight shifts must be reported and arrangements made for berthing.

RESPONSIBILITY FOR SHIP DURING DRYDOCKING

Article 0871-4 of *Navy Regulations* prescribes that when a ship operating under her own power is being drydocked, the CO shall be fully responsible until the extremity of the ship first to enter the dock reaches the sill and the ship is pointed fair. The docking officer then assumes responsibility and retains it until the dock is pumped dry. In undocking, the docking officer assumes responsibility when flooding commences and returns it to the CO when the last extremity of the ship crosses the sill and the ship is pointed fair. In a commercial drydock, the responsibilities are the same, with the supervisor of shipbuilding being responsible for ensuring that the contractor performs satisfactorily.

SAFETY IN DRYDOCK

In drydock, the CO of the ship is responsible for ensuring the closure, when unattended, of all valves and openings in the ship's bottom on which no work is being done by the repair facility. At the end of working hours, the CO of the repair facility is responsible for closing all valves and openings in the ship's bottom being worked on. Prior to undocking, the CO of the ship shall report to the docking officer any material changes in the amount and location of weights on board made by the ship's force and confirm that all sea valves and other openings in the ship's bottom are closed. Flooding will not commence until the CO has made this report.

Preparation for Regular Overhaul

Experience with ship overhauls indicates that their success depends in large measure on the preparations made by the ship's CO during the pre-overhaul period. During the overhaul, heavy demands are placed on the crew for auxiliary and propulsion plant operations, preventive maintenance, ship's force overhaul work, monitoring of shipyard work, and training. Ships that have prepared for these demands during the pre-overhaul period have more time during the overhaul to meet them. In order to assist you in preparing for your next overhaul, we will now discuss the areas requiring special attention before overhaul begins.

PRE-OVERHAUL TESTING

Since the results of pre-overhaul tests are used in determining the scope of work required, accurate recording of data and expeditious completion of these tests are important.

OVERHAUL WORK PACKAGE PLANNING

One of the key elements in the successful accomplishment of shipyard overhaul is planning. Years before the overhaul or conversion starts, representatives of the fleet, shipyards, and technical commands work together to define the desired work package. As a result of approved alterations, deferred maintenance actions, and improved repair techniques, this package is periodically refined. Ideally, as the shipyard period begins, overhaul planning is complete and a workable schedule exists for the accomplishment of the required package. Realistically, this is not a totally achievable goal. Additional work will result from arrival inspections, open and inspect deficiencies, and equipment breakdowns during the overhaul. Aside from this, though, any other major deviations from the initial work package will confuse orderly planning and can eventually destroy even the best schedule. In this case, much shipyard effort is wasted and delays become inevitable, with a resultant rise in total costs.

Ship's force can significantly affect the impact of "new work" on planning efforts. It is your responsibility to prepare thoroughly for the shipyard overhaul. This is accomplished by reviewing the proposed work package and by submitting work requests for *all* necessary items not included.

The earlier you identify this work, the more easily it can be assimilated into the package and thus minimize disruption. Recent reviews of supplemental work packages submitted after overhaul commencement have shown that pre-overhaul preparation was inadequate. In addition, a shipyard can refuse to do new work identified after the overhaul starts, based on its total workload. This rejection leaves only two options for the ship's type commander: designation of the work as mandatory and acceptance of a schedule slip, or disapproval of the work.

REVIEW OF OPERATING PROCEDURES AND INSTRUCTIONS

While the ship's force is doing pre-overhaul and overhaul tests, they will be exposed to infrequently used operating procedures and instructions. Ships must utilize the period prior to overhaul to familiarize themselves with these procedures and instructions.

PREVENTIVE MAINTENANCE

Preventive maintenance must be kept current before and during the overhaul. Numerous delays in post-overhaul test programs can be avoided if equipment is properly maintained during the overhaul.

WATCHSTANDING AND SURVEILLANCE OF SHIPYARD WORK

During overhaul, the combination of abnormal shipboard conditions and the presence of shipyard workers not familiar with the ship makes it imperative that ship's force maintain close surveillance to ensure safety. The crew must be indoctrinated well before the overhaul in the following areas:

- the necessity to tag out systems in accordance with shipyard procedures prior to the commencement of work
- the need for and procedures involved in providing adequate support for fire protection and keeping the number of fire hazards to a minimum
- maintenance of proper standards of system and component cleanliness

CONTACTS WITH THE OVERHAUL SHIPYARD PRIOR TO OVERHAUL

During upkeeps prior to overhaul, shipyard personnel may visit the ship to check alteration plans to verify that all interferences have been identified. This can save a great deal of potentially wasted time. The yard may also ask to review shipboard records to aid their planning and material procurement. You can use these contacts with the shipyard to obtain documents to familiarize the crew with shipyard administrative procedures, such as rip-out control, tag-out of systems, and verification of valve lineups prior to the start of overhaul.

In summary, know your job, work hard, and conduct good follow-up inspections, and you can get as effective and efficient an overhaul in these days of complex equipment as was common years ago. The conduct of proper overhaul preparation and the overhaul itself are not new to the Navy.

Joint Fleet Maintenance Manual

In 1996 CINCPACFLT and CINCLANTFLT (now COMPACFLT and COM Fleet Forces Command) jointly issued a new multivolume maintenance manual, CPF/CLF Instruction 4790.3. This *Joint Fleet Maintenance Manual* (*JFMM*) is the best single source of information on maintenance issues and should be readily available to every ship, submarine, and aircraft squadron commanding officer in the U.S. Navy. (The latest *JFMM* version is COMFLTFORCOMINST 4790.3 Rev D and can be found at http://www.navsea.navy.mil/Home/SUBMEPP/Products /JFMM/.) As soon as you take command, ensure that all your officers and sailors involved in maintenance are fully conversant with the *JFMM* and that copies are available in every departmental office for quick reference.

In broadest terms, the manual serves as a standardized, basic set of minimum requirements to be used by all type commanders and subordinate commands; provides clear and concise technical instructions to ensure that maintenance is planned, executed, completed, and documented within all fleet commands; acts as a vehicle for implementing regional maintenance policies across all platforms; and includes a comprehensive set of process descriptions for use by Navy schools engaged in training officers and sailors involved in maintenance. Let's take a closer look at what is contained in this excellent "one-stop shopping" guide to maintenance.

Volume 1, *New Construction*, covers everything a commanding officer needs for the overall program of new construction, including detailed discussions of responsibilities for NAVSEA, the building yard, the design/planning yard, the CO, and various support activities. It also includes specifics on pre-delivery activities, such as shipbuilder's test program, equipment load-out, logistic support, and the various trials (dock, fast cruise, and sea). The volume also has information on post-delivery deficiencies and the post-shakedown availability.

Volume 2, *Integrated Fleet Maintenance*, is the "heart of the matter" and covers the fundamentals of executing both CNO-scheduled and type commander–driven availabilities. This section of the *JFMM* contains superb information on the planning, execution, and documentation of repair periods as well as day-to-day maintenance activity.

Volume 3, *Deployed Maintenance*, focuses on the execution of maintenance during forward deployment and includes a remarkably well-produced section of information on maintenance support in each of the forward deployed areas—the Mediterranean, the Arabian Gulf, and the western Pacific. There is also a specific section for maintenance activity involving Military Sealift Command and U.S. Coast Guard vessels.

Volume 4, *Test and Inspections*, offers detailed information on technical specifics for a wide variety of programs, including boilers, diesels, industrial plant equipment, marine sanitation devices, shipboard electromagnetic systems, INSURV issues, small boats, oxygen and nitrogen systems, degaussing, corrosion control, elevators, and maintenance of technical libraries. There is also a section specific to naval air issues, including carrier systems such as catapults and aircraft launch/recovery. A final section looks in detail at submarine systems, including submarine salvage, submarine batteries, Trident system issues, noise reduction, and operating depth policy.

Volume 5, *Quality Maintenance*, includes wide-ranging discussions of personnel qualification systems, welder requirements, work procedures for specific systems, departures from specification requests, audits and surveillance, testing requirements, material control, and quality assurance records. There is also a set of blank reproducible forms and form instructions in this volume.

Volume 6, *Maintenance Programs*, was not included in the initial drafting of the *JFMM* but was later added to provide guidance in the execution and management of maintenance programs (underwater hull cleaning, fleet technical assistance, painting and preservation guidelines, corrosion control, etc.) applicable to units of the Navy. The forty-two chapters are not meant to be all-encompassing but to cover most maintenance-related programs you may find on board; type commanders may have additional, more detailed guidance for some of these same programs.

Volume 7, *Contracted Ship Maintenance*, is a must-read for most COs, since you will most likely be impacted by contractor-provided maintenance during your tour. It provides information relative to the procurement, oversight, and execution of ship maintenance and modernization work performed in the private sector. Though most of this will fall under the Supervisor of Shipbuilding, it is wise to understand how it will impact the maintenance a ship receives.

Frankly, it is difficult to envision a question that could not be answered by a quick perusal of this superbly organized work. It should be a familiar reference to your department heads, and you may find yourself dipping into it from time to time as you work on your command's maintenance program.

Afloat Logistics

The science of logistics has for many years been an important part of our mobility-conscious armed forces. Ashore, at headquarters, it means determining the needs of all elements of our Navy and then procuring and supplying these requirements worldwide. Solving these complicated problems requires the best talent the Navy has. Logistics is no longer good enough if it only responds to requests; it has to constantly adapt to be predictive in nature in order to supply the fleet with what it needs, when it needs it, and where it needs it.

Afloat, logistics is the determination of what individual ships need to carry out their projected tasks plus the supply of these items and services both before they leave port and on a continuing basis by replenishment under way.

Afloat logistics is carried out on the individual ship level by the commanding officer and supply department. In large ships, the commanding officer will be assisted by a well-qualified Supply Corps officer. In small ships, you may have either a newly commissioned and schooled officer of the Supply Corps or a line officer. This section is intended to help the CO with the demanding task of running a small ship with an inexperienced supply or junior line officer. It will also be of assistance to the captain of a large ship in monitoring the performance of the supply system.

The supply officer of a small ship has one of the most difficult jobs the Navy can offer. This officer is responsible, often singlehandedly, for administering all ship's supplies and equipage, coordinating a budget of millions of dollars, and providing food and personal services for the entire wardroom and crew. The billet appears even more difficult when one considers that the average supply officer assigned to such a ship has had little or no prior experience in supply matters and that his or her seniors, the commanding officer and executive officer, can often provide only cursory direction in the daily management of the department.

Ship Supply Officer's Responsibilities

OPNAVINST 3120.32D Change 1 (the *SORM*) states that in addition to his or her duties as head of department, the supply officer is responsible for procuring, receiving, storing, issuing, shipping, transferring, selling, accounting for, and, while in their custody, maintaining all stores and equipment of the command.

Specifically, depending on the size and organization of the ship, the supply officer is responsible for the following:

- the operation of the general mess, including preparation and service of food
- the wardroom mess on ships with an established billet for a supply corps officer as wardroom mess officer
- the ship's store and stores for sale and issue of clothes and small stores
- disbursing, including the responsibility for procurement, custody, transfer, issue of, and accounting for funds (In cases where an assistant for disbursing is assigned, the supply officer exercises general supervision over and inspection of the accounts of the assistant for disbursing.)

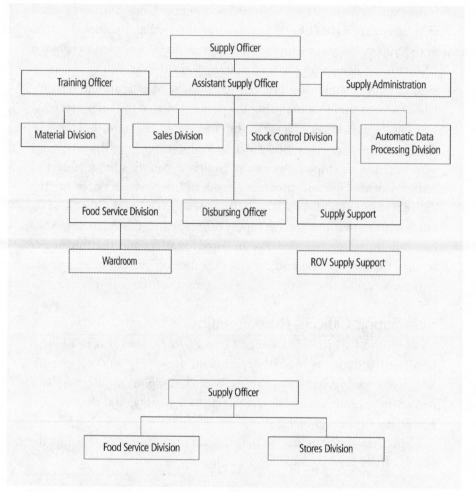

Fig. 6-2. Typical supply department organization.

When there is an assistant for food service afloat or for the ship's store, that officer may relieve the supply officer from personal financial accountability and responsibility for food service or ship's store material. The supply officer must request such relief in writing, and it must be approved by the CO. It is terminated upon relief or detachment of the supply officer or his or her assistant. In any case, the supply officer will continue to be responsible to the commanding officer for the overall administration of the supply department.

Supply Department Personnel
THE SUPPLY OFFICER

On a large ship, the supply officer will undoubtedly be an officer of many years' experience in all aspects of logistics. On a destroyer or smaller amphibious ship, it is usually a lieutenant with prior afloat supply experience. On the other hand, the supply officer on a submarine is likely to be a young ensign directly out of the Naval Supply Corps School. This discussion, as we stated earlier, is directed *specifically* to the small ship with a first tour or junior supply officer.

Your young supply officer was specifically chosen for assignment as an independent duty department head as a result of their outstanding performance at supply school or in a division officer tour. These officers report aboard technically qualified as supply department head and will need strong support and counseling from you and your executive officer. They may also require some help in establishing themselves in the wardroom with their contemporaries, who often tend to be overly critical of the "chop" and their apparent inability to meet their divisional supply needs and culinary desires. Challenges such as these can make life uncomfortable for your supply officer, reduce their effectiveness, and, left unaddressed, can dim their enthusiasm for continued service.

SUPPLY DEPARTMENT ENLISTED PERSONNEL

Your young supply officer will normally be supported by subordinates who are well qualified. It is not uncommon, however, for the Navy to experience shortages of senior logistics specialists and mid-grade culinary specialists. These shortages can complicate problems. In order to adjust for this, should you experience shortages in qualified personnel, you will have to ensure that an adequate training program is established. This is difficult to accomplish aboard a small ship, and it behooves you to take advantage of the excellent tender and shore establishment training programs established for logistics specialist and culinary specialist personnel. The monthly training schedule is usually published in advance, and ship personnel are always invited to participate. Use of this convenient formal training will help not only the ship but also your enlisted personnel in their advancement.

Repair Parts and Material Management

COORDINATED SHIPBOARD ALLOWANCE LIST

The Coordinated Shipboard Allowance List (COSAL) shows the repair parts, special tools, and other material required on board to support installed equipment. All of your onboard parts are based on the COSAL.

Your ship's COSAL is complete at initial outfitting and is checked at every supply overhaul, but an active COSAL maintenance program is necessary to maintain supply efficiency while the ship is operating. Maintenance actions regarding the COSAL occur when equipment is added to or deleted from the ship. Parts for most new equipment changes are funded by the Naval Sea Systems Command COSAL allotment, so the ship is not charged. Failure to update the COSAL can result in out-of-commission time for critical equipment, failure of your ship to meet its commitments, and unhappy unit and type commanders.

INVENTORY MAINTENANCE

Your onboard repair parts are determined by your allowance (COSAL) and are adjusted by demand (usage). When discussing usage, the term "selected item" (SIM) is often used. A selected item is one that is required twice or more within a six-month period. The idea here is to spotlight material in regard to its inventory, control, and need to be reordered. A SIM is an item inventoried semiannually, and it is also recommended before deployment. Stock items that are not designated as SIM will be completely inventoried only at the time of the ship's supply overhaul.

You can upgrade your inventory control system by tasking the supply department to spot-inventory a designated number of parts each week. However, many ships have been lulled into a false sense of security by spot-inventorying from stock records rather than actually locating the parts. A more effective method is to insist on actual location using stock record inventories. In addition, this is a good way to find and identify parts your crew may have hidden in lockers without stock records.

On the other hand, your inventory control system will lose effectiveness if you permit or are perceived to condone "deployment" spares. The use of "deployment" spares breaks the system's feedback link, hides the need for greater repair part support for certain equipment, and will frustrate your efforts to improve inventory control. Your attitude toward deployment spares should be: if we really need it, submit an allowance change request.

REPAIR PARTS MAINTENANCE

Many a ship has been forced to interrupt scheduled operations because a normally carried critical spare was not on board. This tale becomes tragic when investigation shows that ship's force realized the problem but failed to take proper action to correct it. There are different versions to the story, but in almost every case, the error was a lack of management of repair parts.

Each head of department is responsible for maintaining a full allowance of repair parts and for requesting that the supply officer replace damaged, worn out, or missing items. Depending on ship size, the CO can require either the heads of departments or the supply officer to maintain stock records. In either case, repair part petty officers must be assigned from each division to assist in the work. Repair part availability is directly proportional to the degree of strictness of accounting for each part.

To make things simpler, logistics specialists on small ships should be required, except in genuine emergencies, to make *all* issues of onboard repair parts at sea, and while in port to make *all* issues during normal working hours. Time and time again, supply inspection teams report that generally those ships that allow division repair parts petty officers to draw parts from the individual repair parts lockers are those ships with poor stock record validity. Ships without a full allowance of logistics specialists should leave the assigned sailors off the underway watch bill. In addition, specific procedures requiring the command duty officer's approval should be adopted for issues of repair parts in port after normal working hours. On larger ships, where it would be difficult for a logistics specialist to make each and every issue, the command must ensure that the repair parts petty officers are thoroughly trained in stock record keeping, allowance lists, and location of material, and that *they alone* have access to the lockers for their divisional parts.

Regardless of whether the ship is large or small, you must train supply personnel to take rapid replacement action on every repair part issued from stock. The supply officer should take follow-up action on all requisitions more than three months old.

CANNIBALIZATIONS

There will be times when the ship will need to "cannibalize," or take a critical part or component directly from, the physical plant of another vessel. (Note here that stock transfers from one ship to another are not cannibalizations.) You must submit requests through your commodore for both inter- and intra-squadron cannibalizations. When considering whether cannibalization is warranted, keep in mind that only mission-essential transfers will be approved and that if your request is not backed up by a casualty report (CASREP), you are probably overreacting. In any case, review your type commander's directives to understand fully the policy on cannibalization.

CONSUMABLES

In small ships, consumable material is not controlled by detailed stock records but rather in a running account. Most smaller ships have found that the "commodity manager" concept for consumables is sound. Under this concept, one division or department is responsible for providing a particular commodity to the entire ship. This system precludes wholesale duplication of stock where space is in short supply and also improves consumable financial management. Where the commodity manager concept is used, it is essential that the ship devise consumable load lists from actual usage. These load lists should be refined often to support actual usage of an item through a deployment. Periodic informal reports from commodity managers to the CO or XO may prevent a minor disaster during independent operations. There have been several classic consumable problems over the years—the ship on independent operations that reaches the "low level alarm" on toilet paper, for example, or the ship that runs out of machinery-wiping rags with six weeks of independent steaming to go. These are problems you don't need, and you won't have them if your system is set up properly.

CONTROLLED EQUIPAGE

Controlled equipage is given extra management control afloat because of high unit cost, vulnerability to pilferage, and importance to the ship's mission. Over the years, the number of required controlled equipage items has been reduced to make management simpler. You should review additions carefully so as not to dilute the system's effectiveness. Modern power tools and portable test equipment are two categories that should definitely be included, though. In maintaining your controlled equipage inventory, require that all *signature required* material be accounted for. Most ships have found that the use of custody cards is the best way to maintain the system. Remember that if culpability is suspected for a controlled equipage item, you must require a formal survey.

REQUISITION MANAGEMENT

You must imbue your officers with a strong sense of responsibility regarding requisition prioritization. The priority of any requisition must be carefully determined, for the shore supply system can act only on the priorities ships assign it. Improper priorities are like false fire alarms; abuses only erode prompt and proper operation of the system.

Many operational commanders use "hot" or critical list systems to highlight command concern for certain items. These lists, if used efficiently by minimizing their length, can guide the supply officer's efforts to obtain critical spares. This is made easier by keeping onboard status records up-to-date through a reconciliation process with the IMA. The supply officer should reconcile outstanding requisitions and financial status at least weekly. Deployed ships should forward error lists so that support personnel have a proper picture of their requisition and financial accounting status for spare parts. This reconciliation process, plus constant monitoring of requisitions, will also identify overage requisitions. This is important since some old, unfilled requisitions are probably no longer needed and should be cancelled. The present fleet commander Material Obligation Validation program strives for a goal of 98 percent validity of all outstanding requisitions. One hundred percent is a reasonable goal; less than 80 percent is UNSATISFACTORY on an annual supply inspection.

FINANCIAL MANAGEMENT

Budget planning for spare parts and supplies is a valuable tool for all ships and promotes foresight among the different shipboard departments. Your financial account for spare parts and supplies is termed your operating target (OPTAR). On a small ship, your commodore may maintain the account, and you do the spending. On a large ship, you will maintain your own. You can avert embarrassing situations if you observe your budget, make your personnel aware of constraints, and insist upon frequent reconciliation of your account with the squadron. You will find that your parent squadron or type commander will invite input on your needs, but be ready to back up your requests with facts. Most COs have maintained control of OPTARs by personally reviewing requisitions above a particular threshold value.

Supply Readiness Monitoring and Supply Assistance

There are several methods for you to monitor your ship's supply readiness. The most obvious is to learn the details of the supply system and ask your supply officer the *right* questions. All too often, line officers take on a supply system problem without adequate knowledge of basic inventory control, financing, and prioritization. Several years ago, a young supply officer in the process of being relieved for his displayed inability to operate his department described his problems to his commodore. He said that he couldn't dine in the wardroom for fear of being ridiculed by his peers and the commanding officer. He described how his critical list of needed repair parts had grown to well over one hundred and that he had not had time to perform COSAL maintenance in over six months. The lesson here is obvious. Your young supply officer needs the same support (and probably more) that you give your other junior officers. Their responsibilities must be clearly defined and given priorities. You can never accept substandard performance, but you must be alert to see that your supply officer is not placed in "reaction mode" and does not overreact to every comment, request, and gripe from the wardroom and crew. A proven way to build your young supply officer's confidence and performance is to ensure that the executive officer supports them, much like a mentor would help a young enlisted sailor, until they are clearly capable of taking charge.

Supply inspections also provide an excellent assessment of the ship's internal supply management. These inspections, normally conducted at eighteen- to twenty-month intervals, will bring out any major deficiencies. The wise commanding officer will review the inspection report with a critical eye toward *trends*, as well as absolute grades, and will set up a continuing program to solve identified deficiencies.

Supply Overhaul

Supply overhauls are designed to upgrade supply effectiveness by establishing proper repair parts support for the ship's current configuration. A successful supply overhaul requires the combined efforts of shore-based support activities, fleet staffs, and ship's force. Normally, supply overhauls are conducted in conjunction with shipyard overhauls. In view of the number of activities involved, they are generally not conducted without prior approval and planning of your type commander. Supply overhauls are called integrated logistics overhauls because they encompass a complete audit and update of not only the ship's supply package, but also the preventive maintenance support system and all technical manuals; they also provide training to all hands in COSAL maintenance. This system has proven worthwhile, improving the coordination of preventive maintenance requirements, technical manual support, and the COSAL.

SUPPLY OVERHAUL EVENTS

A schedule of milestones for your supply overhaul is generally promulgated about a year prior to the scheduled start. To establish an accurate configuration baseline and effective COSAL, a validation baseline of all shipboard equipment must be completed well before the overhaul starts.

During your overhaul, the initial allowance of onboard repair parts for newly installed equipment and components and new items appearing in the COSAL as a result of Allowance Parts List revisions will be provided, using Commander Naval Sea Systems Command funds. Funding for deficiencies other than these is the responsibility of your type commander. As you can see, failure to record consumed spare parts prior to overhaul to conserve OPTAR funds will catch up later, when the type commander has to pick up the tab for needed spares.

During your overhaul, numerous configuration changes will be made to the ship. The Naval Supervising Activity (NSA) has responsibility for all COSAL changes during overhaul. You and the Supply Operations Assistance Program team are responsible for forwarding COSAL change data to the NSA for all configuration changes made by the ship's force and by special assistance teams outside the shipyard overhaul effort. Your supply officer must be alert to identify these and to provide the information to the allowance section of the shipyard. Continuous liaison with the allowance section and careful review of alterations conducted by your crew are required throughout the overhaul to ensure that your COSAL reflects the final configuration of the ship.

In conclusion, then, to ensure that complete equipment support is achieved during your supply overhaul, you must carry out the following responsibilities:

- Sufficient enlisted personnel must be assigned to support the supply overhaul.
- Applicable instructions and procedures must be fully understood by ship's supply support personnel.
- Written procedures must be established to coordinate the issue, control, accounting, and replacement of allowance list material withdrawn during the course of overhaul work. Issue of material from your ship should be made only in cases of urgent need and where the material is not readily available from other sources. Such issues should require the approval of the supply officer as a minimum.
- You must ensure that prompt follow-up action is taken for all shortages. Prior to departing the shipyard, you must ensure that your current status is provided to the parent tender for continued monitoring and expediting.

Alterations and Improvements

Each type commander administers an alteration and improvement program. Your type commander's program is based on the Surface Ship Modernization Program (SSMP), an integrated program that combines ship alterations of a technical and military improvement nature and integrates them into scheduled ship overhauls. The Navy's SSMP consists of all alterations applicable to specific ships on a yearly basis within a five-year period.

The current year program then becomes the schedule for implementing presently funded ship alterations. Future year programs form the basis for annual Navy budget submissions. Based on the SSMP, material managers budget and procure supporting material and identify COSAL support as needed.

In support of the shipboard alteration program, you must ensure that your department heads keep abreast of information on package alteration kits that are, or will become, available for the ship. You must ensure that package alterations are installed expeditiously after receipt and that proper COSAL maintenance is conducted to support the change. Finally, you must ensure that completed installations are reported in a timely manner and that feedback is provided to Navy technical agencies when difficulty is experienced in completing any alteration.

Food Service
FOOD SERVICE OFFICER

Although you may assign a separate food service officer, the more common practice in smaller ships is to have the supply officer carry out this function. In most ships, the wardroom eats from the general mess, and no provision is necessary for a separate wardroom mess. The young supply officer will probably have little or no experience in the management of messes. Thus, it behooves you to keep a close eye on their operation of both the general and wardroom messes. You should review the menu review board minutes carefully and should insist that actionable input from the board is taken on by the supply department. This process is now simplified with standardized cycle menus as the norm in the fleet. Make it clear to the food service officer that you expect a high level of performance from each person assigned food service responsibilities. If a meal is not palatable, find out why. You should not sit in the wardroom and eat poorly prepared food. If it doesn't taste good to you, it doesn't to the crew. As commanding officer, you should strive for the reputation of being the best feeder in the Navy. Getting this reputation does not take as much money as it does attention.

An important corollary to rejecting substandard performance in the food service area is to recognize outstanding work. On the mess decks, the junior mess cook is of equal importance to the leading culinary specialist. These personnel and those who work with them should be publicly recognized for superior work. This type of recognition pays dividends. Recognition is directly related to morale, job satisfaction, and retention. Additionally, it sets the tone for all food service operations and will result in improved relations between the culinary specialists and the rest of the crew.

FOOD SERVICE PERSONNEL AND SERVICE

You should strive to improve the skills of food service personnel. In doing so, you must work to improve both management and the personal desire for excellence of your subordinates.

An example of improved food service management is in the area of menu planning. Few, if any, ships continue to require the leading culinary specialist to write a menu from scratch each week rather than using the cycle menu. Significant time has been saved on this job with the adoption of a cycle menu. Each week, the cycle menu is reviewed to reflect

Fig. 6-3. Recognizing outstanding food service management is directly related to improved morale.

special events and seasonal fruits and vegetables, but the basic foods are fixed. A cycle menu will not hurt quality or variety if properly managed.

In the area of motivation, you must use technical training and your own support to strengthen the food service organization's morale. Your food service division will respond in a positive manner to frequent sanitation inspections and insistence on attention to detail. Obviously, these rules apply to wardroom service as well as to the enlisted dining facility. The key to success in food service throughout your tour will be consistent *attention to detail* and *prevention of deterioration of service* afforded your officers and crew.

ACCOUNTABILITY

NAVSUP publications set forth stringent requirements regarding financial accountability files. Improper accounting and procedural control in the food service area can ruin a career. As commanding officer, you must involve yourself in food service accounting to the degree necessary to ensure *its* effectiveness and *your* peace of mind.

It is not necessary that you become a *full-time* food service or commissary officer to monitor properly the food service operation of your ship. It does take some knowledge, however, to ask the proper questions and conduct necessary audits. More importantly, it takes some of your time and interest to get the point across to food service personnel that you will accept nothing less than strict adherence to food service accounting.

Replenishment at Sea

Each ship should leave its base, tender, or port as fully provisioned and supplied as possible. Normal fleet operations provide for further replenishment, when needed, at sea. Each fleet unit must be ready to use the U.S. Navy's outstanding system of extending almost indefinitely the time and range of operations.

First, each ship must know how to communicate its requirements to replenishing ships. *Operational Reports* (NWP 1-03.1) stipulates that underway replenishment requirements be submitted twelve to twenty-four hours in advance of the rendezvous. Complete instructions for submission of these reports are contained in *Replenishment at Sea* (NWP 14).

Fig. 6-4. Personnel assigned to the supply department
are poised to collect a vertical replenishment delivery.

Second, each ship commander must be skilled at bringing the ship
alongside promptly and accurately, and maintaining it there. The crew
must be skilled in rigging replenishment systems and receiving and strik-
ing below provisions, ammunition, and fuel received by all means, including helicopters.

Submarines replenish at sea only in emergencies and must be particularly careful to set out on patrol or on operations fully supplied.

The Captain's Role in Maintenance and Logistics

You must take some time as you approach the assumption of command and outline for yourself what you think your appropriate role should be in the interrelated challenges of maintenance and logistics. The first consideration is your own background. Whether you are about to take command of a ship, submarine, or aircraft squadron, you will have had at least some grounding in both maintenance and logistics. Take some time and think through your own skills and how applicable they will be to the challenges at hand. Were you the chief engineer of a nuclear attack submarine? In your squadron XO role, were you heavily involved in the supervision of the maintenance officer and the maintenance department? When you were in your department head tour on a destroyer, were you the operations officer, with very little interaction with either maintenance or logistics? Start by setting out your own experiences in these two areas.

Next, shortly before taking command, you will be afforded an opportunity to visit with the applicable type commander's staff as well as the ISIC staff. Pay particular attention to what you hear from the staff personnel in the logistics and maintenance shops. Hopefully you will hear a candid assessment of the strengths and weaknesses of your command from an outside and relatively dispassionate source. Key indicators—"gauges"— you should focus on are readiness statistics, operational availability percentages, length of time between CASREPs, budget trends, cannibalization requests, inspection results, food service reviews and participation in the Ney Award competition for food service, and general reputation. Normally you will be provided with hard-copy printouts of your command's situation in both maintenance and logistics.

Armed with a review of your own strengths and weaknesses and the status of your command, you are ready for turnover. During the turnover, take a hard and thorough look at all of the indicators discussed in this chapter. Bring to bear the information you've obtained from your staff visits as well as your personal experience and expectations. Naturally, during the turnover week, you should refrain from making any policy statements or giving any orders; a command has only one skipper, of course!

Once you have relieved, you should be in a reasonably good position to discuss your philosophy on both maintenance and logistics with your wardroom and your chief's mess. You may want to consider drafting a short one- or two-page statement of your approach in these areas, or your thoughts could be included in a broader command philosophy. You could also choose to include your thoughts in another document. Whichever approach you take, it is wise to provide your team with something in writing that lays out the basics of your feelings on maintenance. Some good things to address include standards for notification of department head, executive officer, and commanding officer; policies on CASREPs; expectations for supplies (e.g., "never out" lists, goals for restocking); desire to compete for the Ney Award; mess deck standards; relationships with outside repair activities (e.g., times when only the CO will speak for the ship, guidelines for peer relationships with staffs); and general repair philosophy and adherence to good engineering practices. An excellent source of thoughts for the maintenance portion of your statement is the *Naval Engineer's Guide*, published by Naval Institute Press. From a logistics perspective, you may want to rely on a discussion with your type commander's assistant chief of staff for supply matters, a very senior and experienced supply officer. Naturally, the key source of information is your personal experience and philosophy.

A central element of your philosophy will be an understanding, shared by everyone in the ship, of the CO's role in maintenance and logistics. In general, you will want to be very involved in maintenance and logistics issues that directly affect the maneuverability and combat capability of your ship at a command level—essentially everything that warrants a CASREP or has immediate impact. You will also probably choose to be closely involved in the PMS, undertaking two or three checks a week where you actually watch the maintenance personnel work. On some ships and submarines, the CO does one every day! Most captains find it helpful to be involved in the mess decks in some way each day, at least dropping by between meals, walking through the galley, or joining the food service staff on the serving line. You will be amazed how the crew appreciates your interest in their well-being as reflected in time spent in the galley. Plus, you may walk in just as the chocolate chip cookies come out of the oven!

Conclusion

Maintenance and logistics: they are truly the twin pillars upon which the day-to-day capability of your ship rests. Admiral Burke, as usual, had it exactly right; all the brilliant tactical thoughts in the world won't matter if you don't have working equipment. This is an area in which experience will help, but the real determinant is command attention. Walk your decks, talk to your maintainers and logisticians, and never, ever take them for granted; your command will prosper. It is surprising how a ship that is a good "feeder" always seems to score well on the gunfire range; how a squadron with high maintenance results drops ordnance on target time after time; and how the submarine with the best engineering practice is always the one launching green flares signifying a hit in the joint task force exercise. A coincidence? Hardly. General Dwight Eisenhower said about logistics, "You will not find it difficult to prove that battles, campaigns and even wars have been won or lost primarily because of logistics." You should strive to be the commander "who gets there first with the most"—by building a winning team in the world of maintenance and logistics, a foundation intrinsic to your operational success.

7

Safety

The mark of a great shiphandler is never getting
into situations that require great shiphandling.

—Fleet Admiral Ernest King

Prior to World War II, safety at sea was a relatively simple matter. All of shipboard safety could be treated under three major categories. First, the ship had to sail safely, which meant avoiding grounding and collision through good navigation and proper shiphandling. Second, fireroom casualties, mainly boiler explosions and fires, had to be avoided by the observance of traditional precautions and the careful use of checklists. Third, ammunition had to be received, stored, moved, and fired safely. This task was the subject of elaborate, almost sacred safety precautions, which were observed to the letter. As for additional hazards, most ships had a paint locker, which occasionally produced a rousing fire (and a resultant flurry of corrective instruction), and a five-inch gun mount loading machine, which amputated at least one finger a year. Other than these, the safety program, then not yet dignified by a name, was simple, straightforward, and, for the most part, effective.

Today, safety is a much more complex subject. Nuclear power, nuclear weapons, high-pressure steam plants, exotic missile propellants, more powerful conventional explosives, aviation fuels, automatic gun- and missile-loading machinery, complex replenishment systems, the threat of biological and chemical warfare, the possibility of shipboard illness outbreak, nuclear contamination, toxic chemical concerns, and a host of other developments make a far-ranging, integrated, formal safety program necessary. The safety program now covers almost every function of your ship, from the location of your brow to the storage of special weapons.

Many of the areas that require safety bills and programs are unique to each type of ship. Many are relatively simple and require no discussion. These programs will be found in OPNAVINST 3120.32 (the *SORM*) series. Those general programs of the greatest importance, however, will be discussed in the following pages.

Accident Prevention Education
RESPONSIBILITY

The *SORM* assigns the commanding officer the ultimate responsibility for all safety matters within their unit. To help carry out their responsibilities in this area, the CO may appoint a safety officer to provide day-to-day staff assistance. The *SORM* also requires that a command safety program be built on policies and goals established by the captain. A typical safety organization is shown in figure 7-1.

A good safety program must imbue the crew with the understanding that *safety is an all-hands responsibility*. All crew members must develop an attitude that makes them stop and think before they make, or allow another person to make, that one wrong move that can bring disaster. Regardless of your shipboard manning level or the degree of supervisory experience on board, you must aim for this attitude in every sailor, down to the rawest seaman recruit. This is even more critical today as we move toward manning our ships with smaller crews.

SAFETY OFFICER

You will have to use insight and judgment in appointing your safety officer. Assigning this program to the "boot ensign" will guarantee its failure. This officer will serve as your principal adviser on all internal safety matters, and their relationship with you, the executive officer, and the crew is the key to success.

A successful safety program does not have to mean extra work for the crew. The most successful programs, in fact, are those that have been

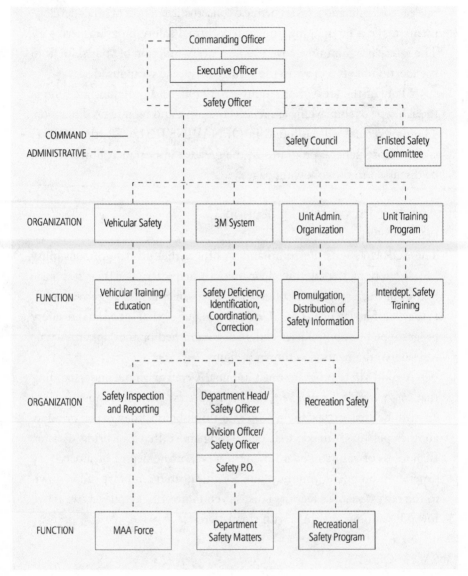

Fig. 7-1. Safety organization.

incorporated into the ship's normal training and qualification procedures and routinely factor operational risk management (ORM) in all significant operations and activities. This can be done by concentrating safety training efforts in areas that complement shipboard operational and administrative training.

As an example, accident prevention education can be presented as part of the ship's general military training. This can be done in a painless way by proper dissemination of pertinent safety bulletins. The Navy spends thousands of dollars annually cataloguing and publishing journals, magazines, defective material reports, lessons learned, and many other items focusing on safety. The wise will learn from the mistakes of others; the foolish are destined to learn by their own bad experiences. Needless to say, these products should also be routed and reviewed by all supervisory personnel.

ROUTINE INSPECTIONS

Another safety-related training vehicle is the use of routine inspections to highlight safety hazard awareness as well as material conditions. Daily inspections of spaces by division officers and leading petty officers should be directed to instill hazard awareness in their personnel. Your periodic inspections as part of your zone inspection program, and those by your other senior officers assigned—XO and department heads—will emphasize the same points. In addition, selected monitoring of hazardous evolutions will tell you much about your ship's safety awareness.

OPERATIONAL RISK MANAGEMENT

The use of ORM is a part of normal everyday procedure. Applicable both in port and at sea, it is a systematic method of identifying and assessing hazards, evaluating options to help control those hazards, then supervising the execution of required tasks to the appropriate degree to minimize the assessed risk. Two items of note: First, ORM is not a mechanism to completely avoid risk; it is a tool to help manage it. Much of what we do at sea is inherently dangerous and requires great skill; landing aircraft, replenishment at sea, and safely navigating in fog are prime examples. We must perform these tasks and excel in them. They are a part of our core professional competencies. ORM helps us execute these challenges smartly. Second, we must guard against ORM becoming so routine in our planning that we pay it only lip service by going through the motions without thinking. There is no added value in that. ORM is discussed in detail in OPNAVINST 3120.32 series and in a separate instruction,

OPNAVINST 3500.39 series. It is also outlined in the *Watch Officers Guide* and on the Naval Safety Center website (https://navalsafetycenter .navy.mil).

NAVAL SAFETY CENTER

Your command accident prevention program can get off to a good start by inviting the Naval Safety Center inspection team aboard to perform a safety survey. Safety Center surveys are completely informal. They are designed to provide the ship with the latest safety information and to discuss hazard identification and safety management techniques with your key personnel. No preparation is required other than making time and personnel available.

Most surveys consist of several elements. First, an all-hands accident briefing is generally presented, detailing current accident prevention methods. A wardroom briefing is conducted simultaneously with the all-hands briefing. Next, the survey team conducts a hazard review. This passes the latest safety programs and accident prevention methods to each division. The team will, if you desire, also conduct a hazard identification walk-through with key personnel. This is carried out using a checklist derived from hazardous items identified by INSURV inspections and through the ALSAFE messages provided from the Naval Safety Center.

Your ship's safety program should also be reflected in the watch station qualification program and in the formal certification of watchstanders. This can readily be done by promulgating standard procedures to cover all operational, maintenance, and repair evolutions and by making use of these procedures mandatory. Abundant information is available online via the Naval Safety Center website noted above, including magazine and news articles, videos, posters, podcasts, plan of the day notes, presentations, success stories, and statistics—everything you need for a successful safety program.

SAFETY INVESTIGATIONS

Finally, your safety program should provide a way to analyze accidents afloat and to report them properly when necessary. Ensure that your safety officer is thoroughly versed in the conduct of investigations. Particularly, direct him or her to place emphasis on determining why the accident happened. Your safety officer should also be familiar with material damage and injury reports, the use of accident reports for accident analysis, and hazard reporting.

All this might seem like a large load for one junior officer. However, familiarity with the references below will provide all the information necessary to do the job properly:

- OPNAVINST 3120.32 series, *Standard Organization and Regulations of the U.S. Navy*, chapter 7
- OPNAVINST 5100.21 series, *Afloat Mishap Investigation and Reporting*
- OPNAVINST 5102.1 series, *Investigating and Reporting*
- OPNAVINST 5100.19 series, *NAVOSH Program Manual for Forces Afloat*
- *Watch Officer's Guide*, published by Naval Institute Press

You can give your program another boost by sending your safety officer to the unit safety supervisor's course, taught at the fleet training centers on both coasts.

Shipboard Outbreak Prevention and Mitigation
POLICY

Close-quarters living and working environments on ships make public health measures an important safety issue, a lesson driven home once again for both the U.S. Navy and the nation writ large during the COVID-19 global pandemic that began in 2019. Infectious disease prevention and mitigation encompass a wide range of measures to stop the spread of infectious disease. Increasing crew education on disease transmission modes, increasing the frequency of hand washing, aggressive disinfection and cleaning protocols, social distancing, and use of personal protective equipment are but a few examples. The basic idea is that vigorous prevention, early detection, and swift mitigation measures will limit impacts to operational readiness and keep your crew safe. Key references for shipboard illness prevention and mitigation include Navy Tactical Reference Publication (NTRP) 4-02.10, *Shipboard Quarantine and Isolation*, and Department of Defense Instruction 6200.03, *Public Health Emergency*

Management (PHEM) within the DOD. The five-level PHEM framework provides a graduated response to illness prevention:

1. ROUTINE: Normal operations—no community transmission
2. ALPHA: Limited community transmission beginning—limited health alert
3. BRAVO: Increased community transmission—strict hygiene required
4. CHARLIE: Substantial and sustained community transmission—social distancing required
5. DELTA: Severe and widespread community transmission—restriction of movement required

When linked to the health protection condition framework, shipboard illness prevention, mitigation, and recovery measures provide a scalable protocol for prevention and containment of infectious disease.

Your crew should be familiar with the specific tactics, techniques, and procedures required to contain a shipboard illness outbreak. Conducting shipboard illness outbreak drills is one way of increasing the odds of success. While NTRP 4-02.10 provides general information on quarantine and isolation actions, you must fully understand how those measures are applied within the lifelines of your specific ship. A shipboard instruction can be a helpful resource in this regard.

Watch Officers and Safety
WATCH OFFICER RESPONSIBILITIES

A ship is administered departmentally, but her operation at sea is directed on a watch basis. Watch officers assigned directly assist the captain with the safe navigation and operation of the ship. The *SORM*, chapter 4, authorizes you to establish such watches as are necessary for the safe and proper operation of the command. In addition, it directs that the watch of the officer of the deck and of the engineering officer of the watch be regular and continuous while under way.

The remarks below amplify those watch officer responsibilities and relations provided by *U.S. Navy Regulations* and the *SORM*, especially as they relate to safety under way.

HPCON	IN PORT	PRE-UNDER WAY	UNDER WAY
A	• Increase sanitation, disinfection, and other public health measures as needed • Wear PPE as instructed • Practice social distancing • Adjust schedules to maximize social distancing • Conduct refresher training on illness awareness • Inventory personal protective equipment (PPE) and cleaning supplies • Restrict/prohibit visitors; screen any essential visitors for symptoms, contact with a known case, and travel history	• Increase sanitation, disinfection, and other public health measures as needed • Wear PPE as instructed • Practice social distancing • Adjust schedules to maximize social distancing • Conduct refresher training on illness awareness • Inventory PPE and cleaning supplies • Restrict/prohibit visitors; screen any essential visitors for symptoms, contact with a known case, and travel history	• Increase sanitation, disinfection, and other public health measures as needed • Wear PPE as instructed • Practice social distancing • Adjust schedules to maximize social distancing • Conduct refresher training on illness awareness • Inventory PPE and cleaning supplies • Execute modified minimal personnel watch bill
B	• Maximize social distancing • Limit access to work centers and watch floors • Prohibit group gatherings (MWR, group PT, etc.) • Only key personnel attend briefs • Secure or limit gyms, ship store, barbershops • Eliminate self-service on the food lines • Open doors and hatches to reduce touching of handles	• Maximize social distancing • Limit access to work centers and watch floors • Prohibit group gatherings (MWR, group PT, etc.) • Only key personnel attend briefs • Secure or limit gyms, ship store, barbershops • Eliminate self-service on the food lines • Open doors and hatches to reduce touching of handles • Implement restriction of movement (ROM) prior to under way	• Maximize social distancing • Limit access to work centers and watch floors • Prohibit group gatherings (MWR, group PT, etc.) • Only key personnel attend briefs • Secure or limit gyms, ship store, barbershops • Eliminate self-service on the food lines • Open doors and hatches to reduce touching of handles
C	• Limit access to work centers/watch floors • Implement minimal manning allowable • Limit meetings to virtual or teleconference only • Electronically disseminate all briefs and products • Limit close contacts to >6 feet and <15 minutes over a 24-hour period • Duty section only	• Limit access to work centers/watch floors • Implement minimal manning allowable • Limit meetings to virtual or teleconference only • Electronically disseminate all briefs and products • Limit close contacts to >6 feet and <15 minutes over a 24-hour period • Eliminate food service while pier side • Utilize only essential personnel required to conduct pre-under way checks and maintenance	• Limit access to work centers/watch floors • Implement minimal manning allowable • Limit meetings to virtual or teleconference only • Electronically disseminate all briefs and products • Limit close contacts to >6 feet and <15 minutes over a 24-hour period
D	• Eliminate food service and issue meals ready to eat (MRE) and other self-service options • Disperse berthing to separate personnel • Personnel not on watch or conducting official business remain in stateroom or in rack with curtains drawn • Berthing lounges secured • Implement minimal watchstanding personnel	• Eliminate food service and issue MREs and other self-service options • Disperse berthing to separate personnel • Personnel not on watch or conducting official business remain in stateroom or in rack with curtains drawn • Berthing lounges secured • Implement minimal watchstanding personnel	• Eliminate food service and issue MREs and other self-service options • Disperse berthing to separate personnel • Personnel not on watch or conducting official business remain in stateroom or in rack with curtains drawn • Berthing lounges secured • Implement minimal watchstanding personnel

Fig 7-2. Prevention Framework Linked to Health Protection Condition (HPCON) Actions

OFFICER OF THE DECK

The officer of the deck under way is that officer on watch designated by the commanding officer to be in charge of the ship. They are primarily responsible, under the captain, for the safe and proper operation of the ship and for the safety and performance of her personnel. The OOD must keep continually informed concerning the tactical situation and geographic factors that may affect the safe navigation of the ship and must take appropriate action to avoid grounding or collision in accordance with tactical doctrine, the rules of the road, and the orders of the commanding officer or other proper authority.

The OOD reports directly to the CO for the safe navigation and general operation of the ship, to the XO for carrying out the ship's routine, and to the navigator for sightings of navigation landmarks and course and speed changes.

ENGINEERING OFFICER OF THE WATCH

The engineering officer of the watch (EOOW) is the officer or petty officer designated by the engineering officer to be in charge of the engineering department watch. The EOOW is responsible for the safe and proper performance of the engineering department watch in accordance with the orders of the engineer, the commanding officer, and higher authority. The EOOW reports to the OOD for status of the propulsion plant and for direction as to standby power requirements and other services anticipated or ordered; the EOOW also reports to the engineering officer for technical control and on matters affecting the administration of the watch.

COMMAND DUTY OFFICER

The *SORM* also provides for an in-port watch organization, led by a command duty officer (CDO), to ensure the security and safety of the ship. The CDO is responsible for security, for the conduct of routine, and, in the absence of the regularly responsible officer, for the supervision of all ship's activities. He or she succeeds to the responsibilities and authority of command when all eligible ship's officers senior to him or her are absent or incapacitated.

As head of the in-port watch organization, the CDO must ensure that all hands are continuously alert to their responsibilities while in a duty status. Fire, flooding, sabotage, and enemy attack are always possibilities. Early detection will prevent or minimize damage. The CDO is your direct representative. Since the suicide attack by an explosive-laden small boat on USS *Cole* while it was moored in Yemen, our attention to force protection has grown significantly. The CDO's role in maintaining a vigilant in-port duty section cannot be overstated. The CDO's intensity and, with it, the effectiveness of your ship's security will be reflected in each watchstander.

THE SUBSAFE CERTIFICATION PROGRAM

The following is an excerpt from the testimony of Rear Admiral Paul Sullivan, deputy commander for Ship Design, Integration, and Engineering, Naval Sea Systems Command, before the House Science Committee on the SUBSAFE Program, on 29 October 2003. As a bottom line, he states, "Let me reiterate that since the inception of the SUBSAFE Program in 1963, the Navy has had a disciplined process that provides MAXIMUM reasonable assurance that our submarines are safe from flooding and can recover from a flooding incident." He further testified,

> On April 10, 1963, while engaged in a deep test dive, approximately 200 miles off the northeastern coast of the United States, the USS *Thresher* (SSN-593) was lost at sea with all persons aboard—112 naval personnel and 17 civilians. Launched in 1960 and the first ship of her class, the *Thresher* was the leading edge of U.S. submarine technology, combining nuclear power with a modern hull design. She was fast, quiet, and deep diving. The loss of *Thresher* and her crew was a devastating event for the submarine community, the Navy, and the nation.
>
> The Navy immediately restricted all submarines in depth until an understanding of the circumstances surrounding the loss of the *Thresher* could be gained. A Judge Advocate General (JAG) Court of Inquiry was conducted, a *Thresher* Design Appraisal Board was established, and the Navy testified before the Joint Committee on Atomic Energy of the 88th Congress.
>
> While the exact cause of the *Thresher* loss is not known, from the facts gathered during the investigations, we do know that

there were deficient specifications, deficient shipbuilding practices, deficient maintenance practices, and deficient operational procedures. Here's what we think happened:

- *Thresher* had about 3,000 silver-brazed piping joints exposed to full submergence pressure. During her last shipyard maintenance period 145 of these joints were inspected on a not-to-delay vessel basis using a new technique called Ultrasonic Testing. Fourteen percent of the joints tested showed substandard joint integrity. Extrapolating these test results to the entire population of 3,000 silver-brazed joints indicates that possibly more than 400 joints on *Thresher* could have been substandard. One or more of these joints is believed to have failed, resulting in flooding in the engine room.
- The crew was unable to access vital equipment to stop the flooding.
- Saltwater spray on electrical components caused short circuits, reactor shutdown, and loss of propulsion power.
- The main ballast tank blow system failed to operate properly at test depth. We believe that various restrictions in the air system coupled with excessive moisture in the system led to ice formation in the blow system piping. The resulting blockage caused an inadequate blow rate. Consequently, the submarine was unable to overcome the increasing weight of water rushing into the engine room.

The loss of *Thresher* was the genesis of the SUBSAFE Program. In June 1963, not quite two months after *Thresher* sank, the SUBSAFE Program was created.

The SUBSAFE Program has been very successful. Between 1915 and 1963, sixteen submarines were lost due to non-combat causes, an average of one every three years. Since the inception of the SUBSAFE Program in 1963, only one submarine has been lost. USS *Scorpion* (SSN 589) was lost in May 1968 with 99 officers and sailors aboard. She was not a SUBSAFE certified submarine, and the evidence indicates that she was lost for reasons that would not have been mitigated by the SUBSAFE Program. We have never lost a SUBSAFE certified submarine.

The purpose of the SUBSAFE Program is to provide maximum reasonable assurance of watertight integrity and recovery capability. It is important to recognize that the SUBSAFE Program does not spread or dilute its focus beyond this purpose. Mission assurance is not a concern of the SUBSAFE Program, it is simply a side benefit of the program.

SUBSAFE requirements apply to the SUBSAFE Certification Boundary—those structures, systems, and components critical to the watertight integrity and recovery capability of the submarine. The SUBSAFE boundary is defined in the *SUBSAFE Manual* and depicted diagrammatically in what we call SUBSAFE Certification Boundary Books.

SUBSAFE certification is applied in four areas:

- design
- material
- fabrication
- testing

Certification in these areas applies both to new construction and to maintenance throughout the life of the submarine. The heart of the SUBSAFE Program and its certification processes is a combination of Work Discipline, Material Control, and Documentation:

- Work discipline demands knowledge of the requirements and compliance with those requirements, for everyone who performs any kind of work associated with submarines.
- Material Control is everything involved in ensuring that correct material is installed correctly, beginning with contracts that purchase material, all the way through receipt inspection, storage, handling, and finally installation in the submarine.
- Documentation important to SUBSAFE certification falls into two categories—Selected Record Drawings and Objective Quality Evidence (OQE). Drawings associated with SUBSAFE boundaries must be maintained current throughout the life of the submarine

to enable us to maintain SUBSAFE certification. OQE are created when work is performed and consist of documents such as weld forms, Non-Destructive Testing forms, mechanical assembly and hydrostatic test records, etc. These records document the work performed and the worker's signature certifying it was done per the requirements. Without objective quality evidence, there is no basis for SUBSAFE certification.

Once a submarine is certified for unrestricted operation, there are two elements, in addition to audits, that are employed to maintain the submarine in a certified condition. They are the Re-Entry Control Process and the Unrestricted Operation/Maintenance Requirement Card (URO/MRC) Program.

Re-entry Control is used to control work within the SUBSAFE Certification Boundary. It is the backbone of certification maintenance and continuity. It provides an identifiable, accountable, and auditable record of work performed within the SUBSAFE boundary. It is the process we use to collect the OQE that supports certification.

The URO/MRC Program facilitates planned periodic inspections and tests of critical equipment, systems, and structures to ensure that they have not degraded to an unacceptable level due to use, age, or environment. NAVSEA manages the program by tracking performance to ensure that periodicity requirements are not violated, inspections are not missed, and results meet invoked technical requirements.

A key element of certification and certification maintenance is the audit program, established in 1963. During testimony before Congress Admiral Charles Curtze stated, "To ensure the adequacy of the application of the quality assurance programs in shipyards a system of audits has been established." This system of audits is still in place today. There are two primary types of audits: Certification Audits (performed at the completion of new construction and at the end of major depot maintenance periods) and Functional Audits (to periodically review the policies, procedures, and practices used by each organization, including contractors, that performs SUBSAFE work).

In 1988, at a ceremony commemorating the twenty-fifth anniversary of the loss of *Thresher*, the Navy's ranking submarine officer, Admiral Bruce Demars, said, "The loss of *Thresher* initiated fundamental changes in the way we do business, changes in design, construction, inspections, safety checks, tests and more. We have not forgotten the lesson learned. It's a much safer submarine force today."

Shipboard Operating Principles

The standard shipboard operating principles of *integrity, formality, level of knowledge, questioning attitude, procedural compliance,* and *forceful back-up* provide a foundation for safe operations on board ship. These principles are well documented in Navy publications as well as in the latest edition of the *Watch Officer's Guide*, published by Naval Institute Press.

Watchstanding Principles

Procedures for safety at sea and in port are clearly defined in the *SORM*. In addition to providing the formal organizational requirements of this instruction, you must stress proven watchstanding principles to your subordinates as prerequisites to the safe and efficient operation of the ship and for its security from all hazards.

Watchstanders must clearly understand that their effectiveness is a function not only of their basic understanding of operations and equipment, but also of their watchstanding habits and regard for safety. Even the best operational and safety training program will be only as effective as the standards they keep. The following paragraphs briefly describe those attributes required by the members of a watch section to enable them to maintain the ship in a safe manner.

Attention to Duty: Watchstanders must be vigilant and attentive to all details. The appearance of normal, steady state conditions should never be an excuse for relaxing attention. Watchstanders should never conduct business except as required by the duties of the watch.

Conduct While on Watch: Each individual must stand watch in a smart military manner. In doing so, loud conversation and unnecessary noise are never appropriate. Reading of any material not directly pertinent to the watch should never be allowed.

Physical Condition of Watchstanders: No individual should be allowed to relieve the watch unless physically and mentally able to stand an alert, effective watch. Watchstanders whose abilities are impaired by sickness or exhaustion should inform their supervisors and request a relief.

Congestion: The conduct of any watch requires proper access to equipment and clearly defined duties and responsibilities. Spectators should never be permitted at any station or in any space where they might obstruct or distract the watch.

Communications: All watchstanders must conduct communications in strict accordance with the ship's interior communications bill.

Casualty Action: Watchstanders should read and understand all casualty procedures pertinent to the watch station. They should review these procedures periodically as necessary to ensure complete familiarity. While on watch, they should be encouraged to review mentally the actions they would take under various casualty conditions.

Log Keeping: Keeping logs and data sheets, while important, must never be allowed to interfere with the effective and safe operation of the ship and its equipment. If it does, the watchstander should report it immediately to the next senior in the watch organization.

All watchstanders must understand the significance of log entries and trends evident therefrom. A review for trends at the time of recording hourly readings may indicate a system change that can be diagnosed and rectified before the situation deteriorates into a casualty.

Instrumentation: Experience with naval machinery and equipment has emphasized the importance of instrumentation and records. In general, it is best to proceed by either assuming that all instruments are reading correctly or operating on the safe side of the worst indication of the instrument. Never blame the instrument until investigation has proven it defective.

Relieving the Watch: Relieving the watch should be a controlled and precise procedure. The ability to handle casualties and tactical decisions is significantly reduced during the transition period between watches. Accordingly, observe the following procedures during watch relief:

1. The relieving watch should be on station sufficiently early to become familiar with equipment conditions and the overall situation and still relieve on time.

2. The relieving watch must make a thorough and complete inspection of all spaces and equipment under his or her cognizance *before* relieving the watch. This is particularly applicable to engineering and weapons areas but is not limited to them.

3. Both the relieved and the relieving watch are responsible for ensuring that the relieving watch is completely aware of all unusual conditions that exist. These include the tactical situation, equipment out of commission or being worked on, outstanding orders, deviations from normal "lineup," forthcoming evolutions, and any other matters pertinent to the watch.

Underway Operational Safety
UNDERWAY SAFETY DIRECTIVES

Navy Regulations and the *SORM* both state that the commanding officer is responsible for the safe navigation of the ship or aircraft, except as prescribed otherwise for ships at a naval shipyard or station, in drydock, or in the Panama Canal. The Surface Ship Navigation Department Organization Regulations Manual (NAVDORM) also provides detailed guidance on policies, procedures, and organizational standards for the conduct of operations at sea. In time of war, or during exercises simulating war, the provisions of these references pertaining to the use of lights and electronic devices may be modified by competent authority.

The commanding officer of a ship and, as appropriate, of an aircraft, shall

- keep informed of the error of all compasses and other devices available as aids to navigation
- ensure that efficient devices for fixing the ship's position and for ascertaining the depth of water are employed when under way on soundings, when entering or leaving port, or upon approaching an anchorage, shore, or rock, whether or not a pilot is aboard; circumstances warranting, speed must be reduced to the extent necessary to permit these devices to be operated efficiently and accurately
- observe every precaution prescribed by law to prevent collisions and other accidents on the high seas, inland waters, or in the air;

when under way in restricted waters or close inshore, and unless unusual circumstances prevent, steam at a speed that will not endanger other ships or craft or property close to the shore
- take special care that the lights required by law to prevent collisions at sea, in port, or in the air are kept in order and lighted in all weather from sunset to sunrise and ensure that means for promptly relighting or replacing such lights are available

Failure to heed these regulations has resulted in disaster at sea as a result of grounding, allision, or collision.

GROUNDINGS, ALLISIONS, AND COLLISIONS

The U.S. Navy conducted a comprehensive review of incidents involving groundings, allisions, and collisions that occurred between 2007 and 2017, most notably collisions involving USS *Fitzgerald* and USS *John S. McCain* in June and August 2017, respectively. The analysis revealed numerous causal and contributing factors and underscored the importance of five broad themes:

Fundamentals: maintaining basic skills in seamanship and navigation as well as rigor in individual qualification processes, proficiency, and adherence to existing standards

Teamwork: the extent to which the surface force deliberately builds and sustains teams, and whether they are tested with realistic and challenging scenarios

Operational safety: the processes and tools by which ships are made ready for tasking and are employed, and by which technology is used to safely operate at sea

Assessment: the extent to which ships and headquarters plan, critically self-assess, generate actionable lessons learned, and share knowledge across the force

Culture: the sum of the values, goals, attitudes, customs, and beliefs that define identity and influence the conduct of work

Analysis of collisions, allisions, and groundings shows that one or more of thirteen causal and contributing factors were involved:

1. Noncompliance with safe navigational practices (fundamentals)
   a. Failure of the OOD to notify the captain and the navigator as soon as he or she doubted safety or position
   b. Improper application of known gyro error
   c. Failure to use dead reckoning plot effectively
   d. Failure to take fixes frequently enough
   e. Failure to fix position by distance run between successive bearings when only one landmark was identified
   f. Failure to use Fathometer and line of soundings
   g. Failure to adjust course to remain on the dead reckoning track
   h. Poor judgment in evaluating the effects of wind and tide
   i. Failure to account for set and drift and to apply the proper course correction
   j. Making a radical change in course (deliberate or accidental) without informing ships in the vicinity
   k. Too much reliance on nonfixed aids to navigation, such as buoys
2. Incorrect action in extremis (fundamentals)
   a. Failure of crews and commanders to quickly recognize and respond to unfolding risks of collision
   b. Failure to stop and assess the situation or take emergency action when doubt of safe position first arose
   c. Failure to respond deliberately and effectively when in extremis
   d. Injudicious use of the ship's power
   e. Failure to understand the tactical characteristics of the ship
3. Substandard proficiency of bridge and CIC watchstanders (fundamentals)
   a. Failure to adequately train personnel for the task
   b. Failure of watchstanders to perform a specific required action or protocol that they had been trained, qualified, and certified to perform
4. Substandard risk management and planning (operational safety, assessment)
   a. Failure to plan for safety and recognize the risks associated with operations in demanding environments
   b. Laying down the ship's intended track too close to known shoal water or over water too shallow for the ship's draft

      c. Failure to plot danger and turn bearings on the chart ahead of time

      d. Failure to have available the latest Notice to Mariners concerning temporary dislocation of aids to navigation

5. Substandard bridge and CIC coordination (teamwork)

      a. Failure to realize in time that there was a risk of collision

      b. Reliance on the CIC and consequent failure to make a sound evaluation of the situation on the bridge

      c. Failure of the CIC and the bridge to ensure that the conning officer understood tactical signals

6. Substandard CIC performance (fundamentals)

      a. Reliance on the CIC and consequent failure to make a sound evaluation of the situation on the bridge

7. Inadequate use and understanding of technology (fundamentals)

      a. Insufficient level of knowledge and failure to use navigation tools

      b. Reliance on radar navigation alone

      c. Failure to adjust radar settings for environmental conditions

      d. Failure to use installed automatic radar plotting aids effectively

8. Practice of not using Automatic Identification System (operational safety, assessment)

      a. Failure to activate Automatic Identification System in congested waterways as a means to share position, course, and speed information with ships operating in close vicinity

9. Substandard use of lookouts (fundamentals, operational safety)

      a. Failure of bridge personnel to keep a sharp visual lookout

      b. Failure to use visible aids to navigation properly

      c. Failure to check for steady bearing (visually or electronically) in a closing situation until too late

      d. Failure to use maneuvering boards, alidades, or bearing circles

      e. Misidentification of lights and other fixed aids to navigation

10. Watch bill execution (culture)

      a. Failure to comply with approved watch bills

      b. Inadequate watchstanding procedures for accommodating temporary reliefs, resulting in key personnel not being on station or unapproved personnel on watch

11. Poor log keeping (fundamentals)
    a. Nonstandard use of terminology, indicative of poor watch-standing formality and the erosion of discipline
    b. Failure of leadership to conduct formal reviews of log keeping information that could have prevented issues before they emerged
12. Ineffective shipboard training programs (operational safety, assessment)
    a. Failure to maintain a rigorous training regimen that establishes and maintains high standards
    b. Failure to maintain adequate level of knowledge among watchstanders
    c. Failure to train individuals on unique equipment configurations on the bridge and CIC
    d. Inadequate oversight and approval of training
    e. The absence of documentation of training conducted
13. Inadequate fatigue management (culture)
    a. Failure to manage fatigue when transitioning from ashore to at-sea watch rotations
    b. Failure to implement circadian watch bills or to align shipboard routines when implementing circadian watch rotations

In addition to identifying broad areas for improvement and causal and contributing factors, six traits were identified as common among each of the mishap ships:

1. Someone decided not to or did not perform a specific required action or protocol that they had been trained, qualified, and certified to perform.
2. The ship, crew, or watch team had a previous near miss, often in similar circumstances, but no explicit action was taken to correct potential causes.
3. Poor log keeping was observed for the entire duration of the period examined by investigators.
4. Ineffective risk identification and mitigation in operational and daily planning was found.

5. Lack of watch team coordination was evident.
6. Mishap ships were generally regarded as above average performers prior to the mishap.

These errors still occur far too often. The wise commanding officer will review the below list often, asking, *Does my organization suffer in any of these areas?*

- failure to obtain or evaluate soundings
- failure to identify aids to navigation
- failure to use available navigational aids effectively
- failure to correct charts
- failure to adjust a magnetic compass or maintain an accurate table of corrections
- failure to apply deviation or error committed in its application
- failure to apply variation or to allow for change in variation
- failure to check gyro against magnetic compass readings at frequent and regular intervals
- failure to keep a dead reckoning plot
- failure to plot information received
- failure to properly evaluate information received
- poor judgment
- failure to do own navigating (following another vessel)
- failure to obtain and use information available on charts and in various publications
- poor ship organization
- failure to "keep ahead of the vessel"

In addition to reviewing your organization for these errors, you should ask yourself the following questions each time you review the navigation picture with the navigator or the OOD:

- What is the reliability of the present indicated position? How was it obtained?
- Does the OOD clearly understand his or her responsibility under *Navy Regulations* to positively establish the ship's position and track as being safe?

- Where do the greatest hazards lie on the track ahead?
- What is the bottom contour along the track?
- Will there be adequate warning of approaching danger?
- What would the worst conditions of set, drift, and position mean?
- Am I rushing the ship at the expense of safety?

TRAINING OODS

"A collision at sea can ruin your entire day." This witticism, apocryphally attributed to Thucydides, has been repeated in some form by many mariners over the years, but the toll associated with collisions at sea remains deadly. The effective commanding officer will train officers to ask themselves these same questions prior to relieving and while on watch as OOD or JOOD.

All too often, grounding investigations determine that the OOD did not clearly understand the burden on them regarding the safe navigation of the ship. The *NAVDORM* clearly describes the OOD's obligations in regard to navigational safety. *The officer of the deck under way must be aware of the tactical situation and geographical factors that may affect safe navigation and take action to avoid the danger of grounding or collision following tactical doctrine, the U.S. Coast Guard Navigation Rules of the Road, and the orders of the CO or other proper authority.*

Investigations have also shown the tendency for the OOD to take insufficient interest in navigation simply because the navigator or an assistant was on the bridge. Each OOD must understand that the navigator's position as the authoritative adviser on the safe navigation of the ship does not relieve the OOD of any responsibilities. The OOD should constantly seek validation of where the ship is. Do the visual cues match the plot and the radar picture? If not, why not?

NAVIGATIONAL READINESS

Procedures for checking your ship's navigational readiness are important, and proper use of them will pay dividends. An excellent resource is the conduct of frequent (at least semiannual) navigation check rides. These one-day events can be performed by your ISIC or the Afloat Training Group in your homeport. Your own experience and attention are, of course, the key here.

Most of the errors cited above are elementary, but still they are made all too often. In addition to training your officers in the academics of watchstanding, you must imbue them with a general attitude of vigilance, a highly developed sense of responsibility, and the faculty of good judgment. They should be engaged in a continuous loop of observation, assessment, and validation based on all the "gauges" surrounding them—technical and natural. You must stress the value of mental review of casualty actions while the watch is slow and insist upon formal communications by watchstanders. Failure to use proper phraseology and to preserve strict formality of address among members of the watch is asking for trouble.

Fig. 7-3. Even in the calmest weather, anchoring is a potentially dangerous evolution. Here, the guided-missile destroyer USS *Mustin* (DDG 89) is at anchor off the coast of Shimoda, Japan, during the 78th Black Ship Festival.

UNDERWAY OPERATIONAL SAFETY

Safety at sea is enhanced by emphasis on all of the areas mentioned above. By such emphasis, safety becomes command philosophy and policy. You must avoid letting the routine performance of safety measures deteriorate into carelessness.

Many COs tend to standardize the procedures they use to approach channel entrance ranges and make turns and speed changes in proceeding to or from their berth. This standardization can help the captain in the development of his or her supervisory ability on the bridge by allowing a shift of concentration from decision-making to supervisory observation.

Supervisory ability is distinct from the ability to conn the ship or, specifically, to conduct any evolution personally. It involves keeping in mind what the OOD is doing, where the navigator wants to go, what lookouts are reporting, what signals are in the air, what is happening on the forecastle, who is at quarters aft, whose barge is passing down the side, and whether or not the ship ahead is turning early—*but without you being directly involved.*

Cultivation of this faculty permits overall observation of the ship's performance, avoidance of dangers that more preoccupied personnel may miss, and, finally, the ability to handle the ship successfully in combat. When the captain's personal skill must be applied to the conn, or when attention must be focused on any other one facet of operations, something vital may be missed. In contrast, the captain who insists on navigational and piloting briefs before entering restricted waters, who ensures that subordinates plan and brief supervisory personnel prior to any nonstandard or complicated evolution (and debrief afterward, to review lessons and reinforce good practice), will be better prepared to practice overall supervision. This is particularly true when the risk of overlooking something important is increased by several days of strain, lack of sleep, and physical "pounding" from elevated sea states.

A Pacific Fleet letter by Fleet Admiral Nimitz has bearing on this:

> There are certain psychological factors which have fully as much to do with safety at sea as any of the more strictly technical ones. A large proportion of the disasters in tactics and maneuvers comes from concentrating too much on one objective or urgency,

at the cost of not being sufficiently alert for others. Thus, absorption with enemy craft already under fire has led to being torpedoed by others not looked for or not given attention; while preoccupation with navigation, with carrying out the particular job in hand, or with avoiding some particular vessel or hazard, has resulted in collision with ships to whose presence we were temporarily oblivious. There is no rule that can cover this except the ancient one that eternal vigilance is the price of safety, no matter what the immediate distractions.

No officer, whatever their rank and experience, should flatter themselves that they are immune to the inexplicable lapses in judgment, calculation and memory, or to the slips of the tongue in giving orders, which throughout seagoing history have often brought disaster to men of the highest reputation and ability. Where a mistake in maneuvering or navigating can spell calamity, an officer shows rashness and conceit, rather than admirable self-confidence, in not checking his plan with someone else before starting it, *if time permits*. This is not yielding to another's judgment; it is merely making sure that one's own has not "blown a fuse" somewhere, as the best mental and mechanical equipment in the world has sometimes done.

Who Has the Conn?

DISTINCTION BETWEEN CONN AND DECK

When under way, you must ensure that the OOD is thoroughly aware of the distinction between the conn, which is the actual control of the movements of the ship, and the deck, which is the supervisory authority of the watch as outlined in the *SORM*. A conning officer who is also OOD has all the responsibilities imposed by the *SORM* as well as those imposed by the directives of the commanding officer.

CHANGING THE CONN

In order to ensure that no confusion exists over who has the conn, a definite routine of taking it over and relinquishing it must be followed. The status of the conn must be clearly understood by the OOD, verbally acknowledged, and, most importantly, loudly brought to the attention of all personnel who perform manually the orders given by the officer who has the conn. A considerable measure of responsibility for the ship's safety remains with the OOD even when he or she is relieved of the conn by the CO or other qualified officer.

Although there is no official set of rules about the conn, the following principles have been evolved through the experience of seamen. You may relieve the OOD of the conn at any time. In addition, you may instruct the OOD how to proceed without previously assuming the conn. Any direct order to the wheel or engine order telegraph will, however, in itself constitute assumption of the responsibility for direction of the ship's movements—the *conn*. Under these conditions, in order to ensure efficient response and eliminate the possibility of conflicting orders, the OOD should announce to the bridge watch, "The captain [or other officer as appropriate] has the conn," and immediately thereafter report to that officer, "Sir/Ma'am, I have relinquished the conn."

INVOLUNTARY RELIEF OF THE OFFICER OF THE DECK

In the previous section, it was pointed out that you can relieve the OOD of the conn at any time. Over the years, the authority of the XO and the navigator with regard to involuntary relief of the OOD has changed. Prior to 1973, the XO and the navigator could relieve at any time. At present, chapter 3 in the *SORM* states that the navigator may relieve the OOD as authorized or directed by the CO in writing.

The authority of the XO is less clear. The general authority of the executive officer delegated by the commanding officer would seem to cover the matter, but it is advisable, in order to avoid misunderstanding, to give the same authorization in writing to the XO to relieve the OOD. Both officers should be instructed to inform the CO as soon as practicable after relieving.

Good Sea Manners and Shiphandling Tips

Naval Shiphandling, by Captain R. S. Crenshaw, USN (Ret.), published by Naval Institute Press, should be read by every officer who goes to sea. In addition to providing a comprehensive explanation of the principles of shiphandling, this excellent book includes most of the information and advice that makes up our body of shiphandling "thumb rules." These are the rules that are picked up as one's experience broadens at sea and that in total are the wisdom that prevents one from repeating mistakes. They might be called the safety precautions or "good manners" of shiphandling.

In listing these tips, Captain Crenshaw made no attempt to record them in order of their importance. We reproduce them here to provoke thought for safety at sea.

Keep your ship's stern away from danger. If the propellers and rudders become damaged, you are crippled. If the stern is free to maneuver, though, you can usually work your ship out of trouble.

Don't take a chance. If you recognize it as a chance, it is probably too risky.

When ordering rudder, look in the direction you intend to turn. This is as wise at sea as in a vehicle ashore.

Check to make sure that the rudder moved in the direction you ordered. Watch the helmsman move the wheel if you can. Check the rudder position indicator to see what the rudder actually did. Check the compass for direction. On a surfaced submarine, check the rudder.

When ordering rudder, tell the helmsman your intended final course. You may be distracted during the turn, and the ship will continue to swing.

When swinging to a new course, bring the rudder amidships a number of degrees before reaching the new course equal to one-half the rudder angle being used. When using thirty degrees of rudder, order the rudder amidships when you have fifteen degrees yet to go. This works remarkably well for coming smartly to a new course.

Beware of a ship lying to. She is often moving imperceptibly.

Don't trust your sense of distance in a flat calm. This sense is undependable under any conditions but is at its worst across a glassy sea.

Don't attempt precise maneuvers when going astern. Ships handle awkwardly when backing and occasionally veer erratically.

Give buoys a wide berth. You can't see the cable to the buoy anchor from the surface. Many a screw has been damaged on a buoy that had been "cleared."

If you are confused, consider that the other ships in the formation are, too. When the situation seems confused, a normal maneuver by another ship may catch you by surprise.

When uncertain what to do, come to formation course and speed. This will give you time to clarify the situation.

During a complex formation maneuver, remember the direction toward open water. This is the avenue to safety; you may need it.

When collision is imminent and a safe course of action is not apparent, start backing immediately and turn toward the danger. The backing will delay the collision and reduce the impact. The turn toward the danger will reduce the target you present, and a ship can withstand impact better forward. A head-on collision will crumple the bow, but the ship can be cut in two if hit from the beam.

Never trust a compass or a chart. Keep checking the ship's heading by landmarks and auxiliary compass. A compass doesn't announce its departure when it goes out. And all charts have minor inaccuracies; some have major ones.

If blown against a ship or pier when going alongside, stay there until you have made complete preparations to get clear. The ship is normally quite safe resting there but can sustain major damage trying to pull clear without assistance.

Never trust a mooring; check it. Anchor chains part, mooring shackles break, buoys break adrift, even bollards pull out of piers. Check the position regularly.

In low visibility, keep the radar tuned for short range. The power setting and tuning of the main control console should be selected for best coverage of the band 0–5,000 yards. Though you can expand the presentation by changing the scale setting on the remote scope on the bridge, you can't get optimum results unless the main console is properly adjusted. Remember: it is the contact at short range that presents the danger!

When sounding fog signals, shorten the interval once every few minutes. You may be synchronized with another ship and not hear her signal because of your own.

Sound the danger signal early. This is legal, and it declares that you do not understand the other ship's intentions. It will prompt her to commit herself and thus clarify the situation.

A ship on a steady bearing is on a collision course. Take precise bearings on approaching ships, and check the trend.

Avoid passing starboard-to-starboard close aboard. The other ship may evaluate the situation as being nearly head-on and cause a collision situation by altering her course for a port-to-port passage. It's safer to alter course to starboard at an early stage and pass port-to-port.

Join other ships by coming up from astern. Relative speeds will be lower, and the whole maneuver will be more comfortable for yourself and your formation mates.

The faster the ship is moving through the water, the better control you will have. Both rudder force and hull stability improve with speed, and wind and current are felt less.

When adjusting position alongside with the lines over, don't wait for the ship to begin moving before stopping the engines. The time lags are too long for this.

Steer your ship as you would a boat. Look ahead and steer where good sense indicates. Orient to the real world of landmarks, channels, buoys, ships, and obstructions. Keep your head up and your eyes open. Charts, maneuvering boards, and compasses are aids, not substitutes. If the navigator's recommended course doesn't look right, stop your ship and "let her soak" until you are sure that the course you are taking corresponds both with the indications of the chart and the physical situation you see.

When following a tortuous channel, or the movements of another ship, steer with rudder angles instead of ordering successive courses. You are fitting curves to curves, and you must adjust as you move along the curved part.

When entering a narrow channel, try to adjust your heading to compensate for cross wind and cross current before getting into the narrow part. This can be deceptive visually and very tricky.

When required to maneuver by the rules of the road, turn early and turn plenty. Make your intention completely clear to the other vessel; you can refine your course later.

When the bow goes to port, the stern goes to starboard; make sure to allow room for it. In a tight place, where even a small drift in the wrong direction spells trouble, leave a spring line secured to check a faulty movement until the ship is actually moving in the right direction.

If your ship loses power or steering, notify any other ships in the vicinity immediately so they can stand clear. Be prepared to drop anchor immediately and indicate your change of status with appropriate day shapes.

Keep the jackstaff up when maneuvering in port. It is a valuable aid in verifying the ship's head with respect to other ships and land-marks and in judging the rate of swing of the bow in a turn.

Shiphandling in Heavy Weather

Crenshaw's *Naval Shiphandling* provides excellent information on han-dling a ship in heavy weather. All members of your wardroom should be familiar with it.

It is one thing to pass the word "secure ship for heavy weather," but another to have it done effectively. You would be wise to order a thorough inspection each time the ship is preparing for a storm. Hatches, lifelines, storerooms, holds, and engineering spaces should get special attention. The more effort spent in preparing for heavy weather, the less damage the storm can cause.

As opportunity permits during bad (but not dangerous) weather, experiment to determine the best courses and speeds for the ship during rough seas. The average and extreme rolls of the ship on courses into and with the seas should be compared, and any tendency to pitch severely or to pound noted. Prove to yourself and to your crew the capabilities and limitations of your ship so that when actually faced with a hurricane or typhoon, you can have confidence in your ability to cope with it. Decide firmly the best method of handling the ship in a hurricane or typhoon and make sure that all conning officers are acquainted with this decision. Know your ship—and its capabilities—intimately.

The Commanding Officer's Role in Safety

As you begin a command tour, whether of a ship, submarine, or aircraft squadron, you should outline a few very basic goals. Whether you commit these to paper and keep them to yourself, incorporate them into a written command philosophy to share with your shipmates, or merely think them through in a quiet moment is completely up to you. It is the process of focusing on your ultimate goals that matters most.

Certainly at the very top of your list of command goals should be a commitment to do all within your power to minimize risk to personnel and equipment. *In peacetime, there is no higher goal.* As you prepare for command, and indeed every day you spend as captain or skipper, you should think about your specific role in accomplishing this worthy goal.

Perhaps the first thing to consider is the old standard of personal example. Ensure that every aspect of your personal behavior in the command sets the standard, including safety checks on personal electronics, safe equipment in your stateroom, safety glasses and earplugs worn whenever necessary, fire-retardant uniforms, steel-toed shoes; if you "drop by" the engine room in a pair of docksiders and don't bother to put in earplugs because you're "just sticking your head in," a very bad signal is sent to your sailors. Your stateroom on the carrier, for example, should have strict adherence to safety checks for all electronics, from an electric razor up through the television set. When you walk by a rig during an evolution, you should be the first one wearing a safety helmet properly. Rank does have some privileges, even in today's Navy, but safety violations are definitely not among them.

A second place you can have a positive impact with your crew from a safety perspective is in the area of command communications. You have all the tools: 1MC, plan of the day, perhaps a monthly command plan. Part of your daily message to your team should focus on safety. Occasionally sport a "safety button" with the green cross on your uniform or ball cap. Make sure you personally attend all the safety council meetings, and come up with at least one good idea to throw on the table. You may want to consider having the safety officer start up a monthly "safety newsletter" for your command. There are dozens of easy-to-use desktop publishing products that can make this a fun and enjoyable publication for the crew, complete with a monthly message from the CO, an XO's focus "issue," a few words from the ship's safety officer, a "dumb move of the month" (with names changed to protect the not-so-innocent), and so forth. Encourage your safety team to share their good ideas by submitting articles on safety to one of the numerous Naval Safety Center publications, *Proceedings*, or *Surface Warfare*.

A third high-impact area for you as CO in the safety world is driving the command toward appropriate recognition and awards. This should be as important in your command goal focus as the Ney Award for food service, the Battle E, or any of the Combat Systems Awards. Appoint a smart, articulate officer to the program—normally the operations officer in a ship and, of course, the designated safety officer department head in a squadron. Make him or her outline a plan to establish, improve, and maintain the highest level of safety. Use the type commander's annual safety award program as a specific goal, and insist on regular reports on how your command is improving in all areas of safety management. Insist that you review the list of safety petty officers, and ensure they are well respected, articulate, and good examples. You can't do it yourself, but you can ensure you have a top-flight team moving toward a specific goal.

Recognize that shiphandling and flight safety are your special province. As the leading mariner or aviator in your ship, submarine, or squadron, take every opportunity to inculcate an attitude of safe shiphandling and airmanship in your subordinates. In this day of billion-dollar warships—many with deep and sensitive sonar domes—and multimillion-dollar aircraft, there is no excuse for putting your ego ahead of the safety of your ship, submarine, or aircraft. Never hazard your ship, submarine, or aircraft for the sake of showy shiphandling or flashy airmanship. Take the assistance of professional pilots in shiphandling, listen to experienced controllers in the air, utilize tugs when available (or have them in standby as necessary), and always select the safest way to handle the expensive asset the Navy has placed in your care. Any other approach is simply wrong. In this regard, you may want to call upon the expertise of the pilots in your homeport for coming to your ship or submarine and discussing shiphandling with your wardroom. They will make more landings over a few months than you will likely make in a career, so use them as a resource to help train and educate your wardroom. Senior aviators from outside the squadron can also be used in this regard.

Finally, you should be the leader in making use of outside resources. In addition to taking advantage of the excellent support from the Naval Safety Center, think about how you can use other waterfront assets to help you out. You may want to consider setting up a mutual "safety check" with a sister ship, submarine, or aircraft squadron; outside eyes are always the best in seeing the safety issues you may be walking by day after day. Additionally, your ISIC staffs will all have designated safety personnel who can help by doing informal "walk arounds." You can bring in organizations from outside the Navy as well, perhaps a police or fire department to assist in educating your crew. Don't forget that part of your safety responsibilities extends to your crew's home life and time away from the command as well as within the lifelines or on the flight line. Set up programs that reflect safety in the home, both for your sailors and their families.

Conclusion

In the end, safety is the area where you, as commanding officer, must find the time—always—to rise above the day-to-day fray that absorbs your XO and department heads. In their press to get everything done expeditiously and "just right," they will be highly tempted to cut corners from time to time. You are the safety conscience of your command. Remember that the minute your immediate subordinates get the impression that you are willing to cut a few corners, stand by: a true disaster is just over the horizon.

Admiral King, in the quotation at the head of this chapter, had it exactly right—and not only for shiphandling. In the world of safety, you avoid trouble by looking downrange for potential problems and avoiding them altogether. In concert with your mission, you have no role more important than protecting your crew and your command.

8

Training and Inspections

We don't rise to the level of our expectations,
we fall to the level of our training.

—Archilochus

The true end of all training is efficiency in war.

—Admiral Sir Cyprian Bridge, *The Art of Naval Warfare*

Building Your Team—A *Winning* Team

As the leader of a combat organization, you are the captain of not only a ship but also a team of individuals who must be prepared to undertake the Navy's fundamental mission: to conduct prompt and sustained combat operations at sea and to *prevail* while executing this mission.

Building that winning team is the heart of your command responsibility, and everything you say and do is in furtherance of that overarching mission. To help you accomplish the building of a first-rate fighting team, you will have the tools you developed in the years leading up to your command—judgment, professional skill, knowledge, common sense. You will also find that the Navy provides a myriad of helpful assessments and inspections that will test your team in demanding conditions short of combat. At times, the seemingly endless march of requirements that stem from training will stress you and your team to an extraordinary degree. Yet you must always remember that what you undergo in the training cycle is only a small percentage of the true stress of combat operations. You must exhibit an attitude of excitement and anticipation during training and inspections. All those serving in your command will take their cue from you, and if you appear apprehensive, nervous, and unprepared, so will your entire team. If, on the other hand, you take the attitude that training evolutions and inspections are your command's chance to shine, your enthusiasm will communicate itself quickly to every corner of your ship, submarine, or squadron.

The same things you learned in sports about how teams succeed apply to building a combat team. You will be as strong as the weakest link; superstars help, but they cannot carry the day alone; the sharing of credit is a crucial element in promoting team unity; pulling together in unison, your team is far stronger than the sum of its individual elements; teams need good leaders at every level; and it is a combination of heart and head that wins in the end. Remember to play with courage, and don't overestimate the views of those who endlessly take counsel of their own fears. Fortune usually does favor the bold. And while the race is not always to the swift, that's usually a good way to bet. If both intensity and focus truly characterize you and your crew, you're sure to be leading a winning team.

Fig. 8-1. Taking part in multi-ship maneuvers and operations is an exciting moment in the life of any CO.

The Training Cycle

Admiral Chester Nimitz, in addition to being a superb wartime commander, was an expert on training. He once made the following observation in describing the fundamentals of training: "First you *instruct* men, then you *drill* them repeatedly to make the use of this knowledge automatic, then you *exercise* them, singly and in teams, to extend their individual abilities ship-wide; then the authority one level above the person who trained them *inspects* to ensure that the desired results have been achieved."

In a broad sense, this is what you must do. On a continual basis, you must maintain a *training organization*, prepare a *training program*, and, under this program and using this organization, instruct your individuals and teams, while following up with critiques and debriefs. When instruction is completed, *drills* are used to ensure the thoroughness and quality of instruction and to instill automatic reactions. *Ship exercises* then extend the drilling of individuals to the drilling of ship's teams. These intra-ship (unit-level) exercises then progress to inter-ship (intermediate-level) exercises to bring the unit up to fleet standards. Finally, administrative seniors make *inspections* to determine the state of training of each ship. Inspections can cover a wide range of administrative and operational areas. All of these areas of preparation will be described in subsequent sections, but before getting too involved in them, you should be in touch with your type commanders and your ISIC. This will be a part of your training pipeline en route to command as well.

The Optimized Fleet Response Plan

While there is naturally a great deal of variability between the training cycle of different ships, submarines, and squadrons, it is still useful to look at a typical cycle for a surface combatant. Doing so will provide a frame of reference that will be roughly applicable for every type of Navy command at sea. All of this is referred to as the Optimized Fleet Response Plan (OFRP), and the *Surface Force Training and Readiness Manual* (SFTRM), COMNAVSURFPAC/COMNAVSURFLANTINST 3502.7, describes it as follows:

OFRP is a balanced, sustainable, and predictable approach to maximize employability. The OFRP aligns Navy capabilities and missions in support of combatant commander and Navy requirements. Defined in the joint COMNAVSURFPAC/COMNAV-SURFLANT (CNSP/CNSL) instruction 3502.7, the OFRP consists of four phases: maintenance, basic, advanced/integrated, and sustainment. The transition from one phase to the next is driven by material readiness and demonstrated proficiency with each phase consisting of training, evaluations, and assessments of the ship. Each phase supports all subsequent phases with the goal to build proficiency across the OFRP through progressively complex individual, unit, and group level training events based on standardized and repeatable measures of performance. Ships will attain Basic Phase completion when all applicable certification exercises are met by achieving a grade of 80% or higher and TORIS [Training and Operational Readiness Information Services] Mission Area Figure of Merit (FOM) score of 80% or higher.

The *SFTRM* is the definitive reference for executing the training cycle. As stated in its executive summary,

The *SFTRM* provides overarching strategy and policy required to generate and sustain surface ship material and operational readiness. *SFTRM* execution depends on the integration of manning, maintenance, training, and sustainment throughout all OFRP phases. It begins with meticulous maintenance planning to generate the material readiness required to support unencumbered, effective training and operational readiness that ultimately leads to a self-sufficient ship.

This detailed and excellent publication provides a superb summary of overall training requirements as well as a wide variety of broad training information. It includes extensive sections on the training cycle, unit training and qualification programs, the establishment of shipboard training teams, team training, unit competitions, training reporting, and readiness reporting. Of note, there are equivalent manuals and instructions available from the aviation and submarine type commanders (TYCOMs) for submarines and aircraft carriers and squadrons as well.

Having reviewed the applicable type commander training manual (in our example, the surface force version), a more complete picture of the OFRP phases is presented in the following extracts.

MAINTENANCE PHASE

The maintenance phase begins at the start of a CNO availability or other availability as designated by the TYCOM. During the maintenance phase, the ship will improve personnel, equipment, supply, training, ordnance (PESTO) pillar readiness to be able to perform in the basic phase. The ship should strive to complete all required schoolhouse training, ensure installed systems are operational, verify training and qualification programs are fully established and maintained, complete administrative checks with Afloat Training Groups, and complete all classroom training for post-maintenance operations. The maintenance phase normally ends when shakedown is completed, which verifies the ship's material condition is able to support basic phase training.

BASIC PHASE (UNIT-LEVEL TRAINING)

The basic phase normally follows the maintenance phase and focuses on ensuring the ship conducts unit-level training and improves PESTO pillar readiness to be able to perform in the advanced and integrated phases. Basic phase completion does not mean a ship is fully trained or proficient in group or other composite unit operations.

ADVANCED/INTEGRATED PHASE

The goal of advanced/integrated phase training is to progress individual unit warfare skill sets through multi-unit tactical warfare training and then further into a single, cohesive strike group, amphibious ready group, or mission-oriented deployable unit capable of operating within a challenging multi-warfare, joint, multinational, and interagency environment, and to assume tactical leadership roles as a task force commander, task unit commander, or warfare commander. At the conclusion of the integrated phase, the numbered fleet commander with CNSP/CNSL recommendation will grant deployment certification.

SUSTAINMENT PHASE

The sustainment phase begins upon completion of the integrated phase, and the numbered fleet commander deployment certification continues through any deployments and ends with the commencement of the subsequent maintenance phase. Ships will maintain readiness to conduct prompt and sustained combat operations during sustainment phase. Ships will use this time to conduct both internal and external material assessments to support Availability Work Package development for the next maintenance phase. Ships will use their training teams to maintain proficiency in all mission areas through the accomplishment of repetitive exercises while in sustainment and may be required to conduct a sustainment exercise by the numbered fleet commander.

It's worth noting that though identical ship types undergo identical training continuums, variations in performance will always occur. Leadership makes the biggest difference in this process—especially in training and ultimately the professional performance of your unit. It's what builds *winning teams*.

Shipboard Training Program
THE IMPORTANCE OF TRAINING

The basic directive for shipboard training is chapter 8 of the *Standard Organization and Regulations of the U.S. Navy*, OPNAVINST 3120.32D Change 1. The *SORM* points out that the training of personnel to operate and maintain shipboard equipment and systems is one of the prime factors contributing to operational readiness, combat effectiveness, and performance of the command. This training requires instruction of operator and maintenance personnel in the requirements of their rates as well as the additional requirements of their Navy Enlisted Classifications (NECs).

The *SORM* further states that developing and maintaining proficiency is done through the following:

1. In-rate shore-based operator/maintenance training, a prerequisite to fleet unit assignment for certain individuals
2. In-rate operator basic training, traditionally accomplished ashore
3. Individual watch station qualification, completed at the fleet unit and facilitated through shore-based training
4. Systems training for operators/teams that includes subsystem training (undersea warfare, air warfare, repair party, etc.) and total integrated systems training (combat systems, damage control, etc.). While subsystem basic training is normally provided ashore, proficiency training should be accomplished in the fleet unit. Integrated systems training is conducted in the fleet unit.
5. General military training conducted both ashore and in fleet units
6. Ship-wide training accomplished through drills such as general quarters, etc. It incorporates the skills achieved in the above categories and hones the unit's overall combat effectiveness

REQUIREMENTS FOR EFFECTIVE TRAINING

The *SORM* identifies the following requirements for effective training:

1. Dynamic instruction: Instructor preparation and presentation must be professional and reflect a thorough knowledge of the subject matter.
2. Positive leadership: The chain of command, from the most junior personnel to the commanding officer, must actively participate in the training sessions/evolutions.
3. Self-study: A major component of training is self-study. Self-study materials are available in correspondence courses, onboard training packages, computer aided instruction, and other forms of individualized forms of training. Although these materials are designed for self-training, tutoring should be provided by supervisors when necessary.

The second requirement above is aimed directly at you as commanding officer. If you show interest and concern, all those under you in the training organization will follow your lead.

Formulating a Training Program

Training without a firm, sound program is wasted. Thucydides, around 404 BCE, recognized this when he wrote, "The Persians' want of practice will make them unskillful, and their want of skill timid. Maritime skill, like skills of other kinds, is not to be cultivated by the way or at chance times." This is just as true today as it was 2,400 years ago. Put your strongest efforts into the development of a training program.

Your shipboard training program should be created while your ship is still under construction or early in its yard overhaul. It must be based on chapter 8 of the *SORM*. This publication and the parallel supplements promulgated by each type commander should become your "bibles" for training.

The *SORM* covers training in detail. It gives general guidance for the establishment of a training program and examples of the products/plans and milestones that should be included.

Your training program must include the formation of a shipboard training organization, the carefully considered appointment of a training officer, the constitution of a planning board for training, the formulation of a set of detailed training plans, and the creation of a comprehensive set of training records, and then, with these preliminary organizational steps accomplished, the use of these tools to instruct, drill, exercise, and inspect your crew. We will take up each of these steps in turn.

FORMING A TRAINING ORGANIZATION

The backbone of your training program must be a strong and effective training organization. A typical organization is shown in figure 8-2. Yours will vary somewhat according to your ideas and the numbers and qualifications of personnel assigned. *No* organization will work, however, unless those assigned to it are instructed as to what is wanted and how you want them to carry out their missions. This means instructing the instructors, making sure adequate teaching materials are on hand, and ensuring that lesson plans are prepared and made available.

TRAINING OFFICER

Acknowledging the pivotal importance of effective training aboard all ships, large and small, a training officer billet (typically a second-tour

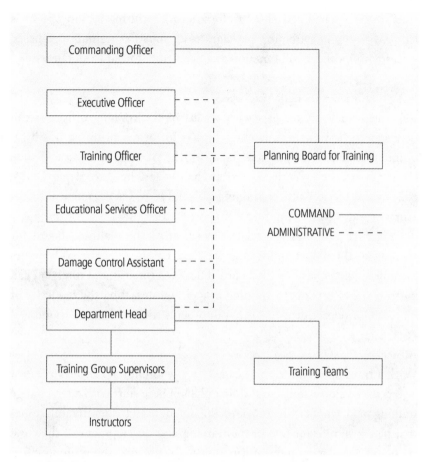

Fig. 8-2. Shipboard training organization showing composition of the planning board for training.

division officer) is now established for all ship types. This was formerly a collateral duty, often shared between the ship's XO, the operations officer, and a designated junior officer. Specific training officer requirements are detailed in the *SFTRM* (chapter 2, section 212), as are responsibilities of CNSP/CNSL (section 200), Administrative Control Chain of Command (section 204), Afloat Training Groups (section 205), and Commanding Officer (section 211).

You'll find that your training officer will be your right hand when it comes to the success of your ship's training program. From getting the right specialized training and skills in your ship's company (NECs) to tailoring your training schedules (short to long term), ensuring required rigor is factored into ship's training packages, and updating training databases, your training officer will function as a department head in all but name.

PLANNING BOARD FOR TRAINING

Regardless of your decision with regard to the training officer, it can be retrieved by your next action, which is to form a planning board for training, as required by article 3.3.13 of the *SORM*. You must include on this board the executive officer as chairperson, heads of departments, educational services officer, training officer, DCA, CMC, medical representative, safety officer, and reserve coordinator.

Figure 8-2 shows the relative position of the planning board for training in the ship training organization. Ensure that the XO applies firm direction as head of the board. The XO's interest and direction can buttress the efforts of the training officer, counteracting the tendency of more senior department heads to put other activities ahead of training.

TRAINING PLANS

With a training organization headed by a well-chosen officer, your next step is to develop a series of training plans. These start with a long-range training plan, which is the top-level document used to identify milestones that play a significant role in the training and development of the crew. It should contain enough information to ensure that the training effort can be made effective. The annual employment schedule, a list including frequency of all required examinations/inspections/certifications/assist visits, and a list of all TYCOM-required exercises should normally be included. The short-range, quarterly, and monthly/weekly training plans, which should go into more detail, can be formed from it. Minor details should not be included in the long-range training plan. This plan should cover the battle efficiency competition cycle (if in effect) or other training cycles, such as between deployments.

The short-range training plan is the mechanism for detailed planning and scheduling of training. It is normally broken down into quarterly, monthly, and weekly segments, which promotes effective scheduling of resources and allows the early identification of conflicts, when resolution is easier to develop.

The quarterly training plan's purpose is to identify unit plans that may affect the scheduling or conduct of training, either group training or formal schools. The planning board for training uses this schedule as a guide to coordinate unit-wide training evolutions required to meet identified milestones.

The monthly training plan sets the daily schedule of training, evolutions, and operations for each month. It should be prepared by the training board and should show all unit training, evolutions, and operations scheduled in the quarterly plan, expanded with necessary detail to include instructors and training locations. Figure 8-3 shows a representative monthly training plan.

Each division officer should prepare a division officer's plan and keep records of all operational drills, team training periods, and instructional periods in the division. Your training officer should require that all division officers keep these records. Proper instruction on the division level is the final payoff for your program. Without it, all the plans are just pieces of paper.

You must also plan for the training and indoctrination opportunities that do not occur as part of your planned program. This includes a variety of presentations for all hands, such as career benefits, equal opportunity, drug and alcohol abuse prevention, and sexual assault prevention and response.

Newly arrived personnel, particularly recruits and class "A" school graduates, will need special consideration and careful indoctrination. This is important, and it deserves the personal attention of the commanding and executive officers. Recruits are graduated in a state of mind that needs to be seen to be appreciated. They have been taught patriotism, respect for themselves and others, and exemplary conduct and are eager to join their ship and become part of the active Navy. If they join a crew whose morals are suspect, whose love of their ship, Navy, and country is low, and whose language and appearance mark them as poorly disciplined, the shock and disappointment can be devastating. These young recruits need not be pampered, but they must be encouraged to maintain their high standards.

MONTHLY TRAINING PLAN

MONTH OF **MARCH 1986**   TRAINING GROUP **B-DIVISION**

SUNDAY	MONDAY	TUESDAY	WEDNESDAY	THURSDAY	FRIDAY	SATURDAY
						1
2	3 B9 -1200# AUX STEAM SYSTEM BT2 HOTEL	4 EMOW ORAL BOARDS	5 B35-FO XFER AND STORAGE BT2 GOLF	6 BT L/L ORAL BOARDS	7 B38 - ABC SYSTEM BT1 DELTA	8
9	10 842 EOSS USE LT WILCOX	11 MMOW ORAL BOARDS	12 B46-COLD/HOT CHECKS BTCS ALFA	13 BTOW ORAL BOARDS	14 B45 MLOC PROCEDURES LT WILCOX	15 LIGHT-OFF UNDERWAY AM 3/17 FOR MTT
16	17 B50 HEATSTRES, BT2 FOXTROT	18	19	20	21	22
			UNDERWAY ENGINEERING MOBILE TRAINING TEAM VISIT → PQS EVOLUTIONS & CASUALTY CONTROL DRILLS			
23	24 BT2 LAYUP	25 EOOW ORAL BOARDS	26 B48 - EEBD BT1 ECHO	27 MM MESS ORAL BOARDS	28 B40 - VALUE MAINTENANCE BTCS ALFA	29
30	31					

SUBMITTED BY: W.W. Wilcox, LT USN
B. DIVISION OFFICER

APPROVED BY: J.P. Jones, LCDR, USN
CHIEF ENGINEER

Fig. 8-3. A monthly training plan should be detailed enough to give the division an idea of what to expect, who is responsible for the training, and how it all fits into the scheme of underway events.

Training Records

It is important that you set up a comprehensive record-keeping system, one that will show at any instant the exact status of all phases of training. The training officer and department head might well keep the long-range (annual and quarterly) training plans, the monthly training plan, and the record of exercises, trials, and inspections required by the type commander. On small ships this might be done with one set of records, but on a larger one an overall record might be required, with additional records kept by heads of departments.

The senior watch officer should keep records of deck watchstanding officer and enlisted assignments and qualifications and deck watchstanders' courses and training record. Similarly, the chief engineer should keep the same records for engineering watchstanders, and the communications officer should maintain records for the communications and coding watch. The division officer should keep a record of drills and instructions, formal school training, and a personnel record. The chief or leading petty officer of each rating should keep a record of practical factors completed and a Personnel Qualification Standards progress chart.

The foregoing record program is only a minimum; you will find additional records desirable, depending upon your ship type. Record forms and the recommended software to manage your training program should be readily available from your type commander.

The *SORM* provides an example of a simple and workable non-computerized training record system (however, software tools have been employed on all ships to save time in training administration and management). The *SORM* discusses the use of the following standards:

1. Quarterly training plan
2. Monthly/weekly training plan
3. Annual employment schedule
4. Indoctrination training
5. Record of personnel advancement requirements
6. General military training
7. Division officer's personnel record form

A well-established system of training records will be of great value. For you, it will provide an instant overview of the state of training of your crew. For your officers and petty officers, it will be both a reminder of past accomplishments and a record of tasks still pending. It may seem at times like useless paperwork, but you will find in the end that your training program will be no better than its records.

Mariner Skills Logbooks

A specific training record that has been formalized in recent years is the Mariner Skills Logbook. As part of the surface warfare community's effort to develop, assess, and sustain proficiency, commander, Naval Surface Forces, established the implementation of the Mariner Skills Logbook as an experience tracking tool. The logbook was implemented in 2018 as a hardbound book with preformatted sections that allow an individual to capture their experiences gained during each watch, special evolution, and simulator training exercise. By documenting bridge time, simulator time, and special evolutions, from both a qualitative and a quantitative aspect, follow-on training can be tailored to each officer and shaped to increase the individual's proficiency as a mariner. Commanding officers are responsible for implementing the Mariner Skills Logbook on their ship and establishing a wardroom culture of meticulous documentation of their experience. The CO is required to submit a detailed end of tour report for each individual's logbook to Surface Warfare Officer Assignments (PERS-41).

Personnel Qualification Standards

In earlier days, junior officers and senior petty officers had ample time to train and qualify junior petty officers and nonrated personnel personally. Following World War II, however, the steadily increasing sophistication of ships, submarines, and aircraft, and the ever more rigorous demands placed upon their personnel, combined to require a formalized system of training for personnel. This system is known as Personnel Qualification Standards (PQS). It is now the heart of the training program, and we will, therefore, discuss it in detail.

In essence, PQS is a written compilation of the knowledge and skills required for a sailor to qualify for each watch station, to maintain a specific equipment or system, or to perform as a member of a given team. It is a qualification guide, one that asks the questions trainees must answer to prove their readiness to perform a given task. It also provides a record of progress and final certification. PQS is an *individualized* learning process. Trainees have the complete program in their hands. The supervisor serves as both a source of assistance to the trainee and a quality control over the learning process by certifying the completion of each step.

Standard lesson plans are provided by bureaus and offices, training commands, and type commanders. They provide a detailed, step-by-step breakdown of the requirements of each task and watch.

The PQS system does not completely replace normal division training. Rather, it is the key element of that program.

PQS UNIT COORDINATOR'S GUIDE

Every commanding officer should be familiar with the *PQS Unit Coordinator's Guide* (PQS 43100-1M). It begins with an introduction to the purpose, format, and organization of the system. It defines PQS words, phrases, terms, and responsibilities. The main portion of the handbook discusses theory, system, watchstanders, and implementation of the system.

PQS BOOK

The PQS book is the individual PQS manual carried by each learner. It is a record of the completion of each item required for qualification for a task.

A typical book/qualification contains the following items:

- *A final qualification page*, identifying the long-term goal. Final commanding officer certification is placed on this page.
- *A qualification summary*, giving the subordinate qualifications necessary to achieve total qualification within the specialty.
- *An introduction to fundamentals* (100 section), which is a record of completion of the various fundamental requirements for qualification. It is the basic knowledge needed to understand the specific equipment or duties.

- *An introduction to systems* (200 section), which is a record of completion of the various systems requirements for qualification. In this section, each qualification standard breaks down the subject equipment or duties into smaller, more easily understood sections called systems.
- *A watch station evolution section* (300 section), giving all the various duties that a trainee must complete to achieve qualification. The goal of this section is to guide the trainee in categorizing, analyzing, and performing the step-by-step procedures required to attain qualification.

Properly administered and used, the PQS system is a valuable adjunct to your training system. Let your crew know that you support it and demand progress, and they will produce corresponding results. Inspect it personally during the Division in the Spotlight review. See appendix 3 for an example.

Routine Drills

You may think that after completing unit-level training you can forget drills and exercises for a while. This is not the case. Drills must be as much a part of your ship's daily routine as instruction, exercises, and inspections. Refresher training just gets you into the swing of things.

Drills are conducted to prepare a ship's crew to meet any conceivable requirement or contingency. The basis of drilling is ship's bills, each of which is designed to meet a particular contingency. Your ship's bills, as we have said before, must stem from the basic bills in the *SORM*. This publication contains sample bills in four categories: administrative, operational, emergency, and special. Type commanders augment these with additional and modified bills unique to their types.

Those bills requiring action by the crew also require *drill*. Drill allows those in authority to determine that qualified personnel are assigned, that requirements of bills are correct, and that equipment is in working order and on hand. Once this is established, repeated drills produce a set of automatic responses that will carry over under the most stressful conditions. All personnel should be able to perform their part even if wounded, in the dark, or in the presence of chemical and biological agents or nuclear fallout.

Once individual teams, such as damage control teams or gun crews, are organized and drilled, you may shift emphasis to larger groups, such as boat-loading teams or missile-firing teams, culminating in exercising the ship as a whole. Drills must be repetitive, thorough, and short. Obviously, drilling of a prize crew can be done infrequently, but the fire party must be drilled often and thoroughly, and it is important that this be done for each section.

This is of special importance during overhaul, when daytime debris and welding sparks may be smoldering at night in spite of the best efforts of your fire watches. You will sleep better if you require the CDO to report to you each day when under overhaul that he or she has mustered and instructed the fire party.

General quarters is the most important underway drill. If you make general quarters frequent, interesting, and as short as possible, it will be most productive. A good procedure is to plan a short battle problem for each drill, followed by imposed damages that will require the execution of various bills, such as nuclear attack or collision.

In all your drills, remember that modern ships depend on internal communications (IC) systems. If you have a real collision, however, you

Fig. 8-4. Frequent and thorough damage-control drills will prepare your crew for any eventuality—collision, fire, or war damage.

may find a ship's bow in the middle of your IC panel with no means of communications left to you except word of mouth and messenger. Condition your crew to this and other unpleasant outcomes. When USS *Cole* was attacked, the crew resorted to using messengers to physically pass messages between controlling stations. Try it. You may have to be even more inventive. Make repetition work for you, not against you. Simple repetition induces boredom, but repetition tempered with imagination produces both rapid response and the ability to react to the unusual. *Adaptability* will make you a winner in combat.

Exercises

By dictionary definition, *drilling* is "instructing thoroughly by repetition" and *exercising* is "training by practice." These terms are frequently used interchangeably, but in this discussion, we will adhere to the proper meanings.

Exercises, then, are used to put the knowledge given by instruction and ingrained by drilling to a more practical use. A telephone talker is *instructed* on how to use a battle telephone, *drilled* in its use by transmitting and receiving many made-up messages, and then *exercised* in its use by manning and using the telephone when the gun battery conducts a firing exercise.

EXERCISE DIRECTION

Major exercise programs are set forth in the fleet exercise publication (FXP) and the allied exercise publication (AXP) series of tactical publications. Key publications include the following:

> FXP 1, *Antisubmarine Warfare Exercises*: establishes tactics and procedures for conducting submarine and antisubmarine exercises, with criteria for evaluating results
>
> FXP 2, *Antiair Warfare Exercises*: presents procedures and tactics for conducting aircraft exercises, as well as criteria for evaluation
>
> FXP 3, *Strike Warfare, Antisurface Ship Warfare, Intelligence, Electronic Warfare, and Command, Control, and Communications Exercises*: provides exercises for all types of surface ships and guidance for observers in evaluating them

AXP 1, *Allied Submarine and Antisubmarine Exercise Manual*: establishes tactics and procedures for conducting allied anti-submarine exercises, with criteria for evaluation

AXP 2, *Allied Maritime Above Water Warfare Exercise Manual*: contains standard seamanship, gunnery, torpedo, and miscellaneous exercises for use by North Atlantic Treaty Organization navies in training their forces for participation in allied operations

TYPE COMMANDER'S SUPPLEMENTS

Each type commander issues a publication modifying or supplementing the FXP series. Where FXP 3, for instance, sets forth the goals, scoring, observation requirements, and reporting for a surface ship gunnery exercise in general terms, the type commander describes these criteria in exact terms for each type and subtype of surface ship. In the case of the surface type commander, the *SFTRM* (CNSP/CNSL 3502.7A) promulgates the certification exercises, repetitive exercises, and advanced exercises and required frequency in a single reference, with amplifying guidance available in the Training and Operational Readiness Information Services system.

EXERCISE DESIGNATION SYSTEM

A self-translating, short-titling system is used to designate exercises for ease in communications. A typical title is Z-24-G. *Z* means an exercise for surface ships, *24* is a particular exercise, and *G* means it is a gunnery exercise.

ADVANCED AND INTER-TYPE EXERCISES

Advanced and inter-type exercises are usually conducted by unit commanders using a written operation order or a letter of instruction (LOI). The operation order is used for more complicated exercises and can be quite lengthy. The LOI system is used when the unit has a standard operation order already in existence or when the exercise is relatively simple. The LOI can be nothing more than a schedule of exercises.

Advanced exercises are usually given self-descriptive titles, such as amphibious fire support exercise (FIREX), surface warfare advanced tactical training (SWATT), composite training unit exercise (COMPTUEX), or fleet readiness exercise (FLTEX).

A FIREX is a shorter exercise designed to exercise ship and air portions of the fire support system of an amphibious force. Exercises are limited to areas where firing and bombing may be conducted.

A SWATT is a multiship, multiplatform, multiwarfare event led by the Naval Surface and Mine Warfighting Development Center consisting of approximately one week in port of academic and fleet synthetic training and two weeks under way for advanced tactical training using the Plan, Brief, Execute, Debrief methodology.

A COMPTUEX is an integrated phase exercise that is arranged to combine available naval forces (usually from a strike group) as well as available joint forces to maximize employment of assets most efficiently. It often serves as a final assessment before a task force–level group deploys, and it usually lasts multiple weeks.

A FLTEX is a fleet problem type of exercise in which available forces are split in half and exercised against each other. Forces involved can be quite large, often including all those available and due for advanced training or deployment. They usually include units of all types. Extensive advanced planning is required, and pre-sail and post-exercise critiques are always held. These fleet exercises continue to evolve and have been called fleet problems, fleet battle problems, or large-scale exercises.

Larger fleet exercises are occasionally scheduled. Each of these is different, and their planning, preparation, and execution can run into months.

It is Navy policy to include underway replenishment in each of the above exercises, using whatever replenishment units are available. It is such an integral and important part of our operations that unit commanders and commanding officers should make every effort to keep ship skills at a high level. If service force units are not available, replenishment and other alongside maneuvers should be scheduled using other units of the exercise force.

Inspections

Inspections are a means of ascertaining the state of battle readiness, administration, preservation, and training of your ship and its crew. Inspections can be divided into two categories: those that you make, or cause to be made, under your authority as commanding officer (internal inspections); and those imposed on you and conducted by higher authority (external inspections). We will treat internal inspections first.

INTERNAL INSPECTIONS

The longest-established inspection in the Navy is the weekly captain's inspection. Article 0808 of *U.S. Navy Regulations* directs you to hold periodic inspections of the material of your command to determine deficiencies and cleanliness. If the command is large, you are permitted to designate zones and delegate assistants to inspect them, alternating the inspections so as to cover the entire command at minimum intervals. This has become known as the "zone inspection" and is generally held on a designated weekday (on a recurring weekly basis) according to the command's preferences.

Weekly inspections offer you an excellent opportunity to impress your policies on the crew. When you inspect, tell them what you expect, what is wrong, and, more importantly, what is right. This is also the perfect time to teach those on your ship how to inspect to meet the Navy's standard. If they know the standards as well as your expectations, then they will give it to you. It is also wise to require your XO to make a daily topside and living space inspection to see that proper cleanliness and maintenance plans and techniques are being used. The surest incentive for daily work is the knowledge by those doing it that it will be seen *every* day. Be circumspect about making daily inspections yourself, though, for too much "presence" can undermine the confidence and authority of your division and petty officers. They expect the XO, but they don't expect you. When you *do* inspect during the week, consider confining your efforts to trouble areas or special projects. This is a time to show interest, to bestow praise if warranted, but not to find too much fault. If you do find errors, have the XO correct them privately later. You must presume that the XO, the division officer, or the leading petty officers would have found the fault in due time if you had not preempted them. Doing this helps to build trust throughout the levels of the chain of command also.

You can make other internal inspections by means of boards. You can form a board or group to inspect any aspect of your administration.

However, the *SORM* requires you to form certain boards that, in effect, make inspections even though they may be called audits. The most important are the following:

> *Controlled Medicinal Inventory Board*: conducts quarterly inventories of all controlled medicinal items except for bulk stock carried in a stores account
>
> *Hull Board*: inspects the hull, tanks, free flood spaces, outboard fittings, valves, and appendages at times of drydocking and prior to undocking
>
> *Flight Order Audit Board*: inspects and audits to ensure that all requirements concerning hazardous duty pay are met as per instructions
>
> *Monies Audit Board*: inspects to determine that all government properties and monies are accounted for and are properly protected and disposed of; that personnel adhere to regulations and instructions; and that irregularities are corrected. The board audits disbursing cash verification, post office funds, imprest funds, recreation funds, and mess treasurer/wardroom officer accounts.
>
> *Precious Metals Audit Board*: audits precious metals in the custody of the dental officer
>
> *Ship Silencing Board*: assists the commanding officer in the development and execution of long-range plans for reducing the acoustic signature of the ship

The best approach to internal inspections is to perform a weekly Division in the Spotlight. See appendix 3 for an example.

INSPECTIONS BY HIGHER AUTHORITY

Over the years, higher authorities have formulated and imposed more and more outside inspections, though there has been an effort to consolidate multiple inspections that review the same or similar material. In World War II a Training Command was created, and refresher training was established, because of the large number of ships being commissioned, the relative inexperience of many commanding officers, and the preoccupation of type commanders with wartime operations. After World War II, the use of formal inspections remained high as administrators sought a substitute for wartime motivation. The intent was that competition, in combination with graded inspections, would be an incentive to superior performance. In more recent years, the number of inspections has been scaled back.

COMMAND INSPECTIONS

Command-wide inspections have for the most part been incorporated into the Optimized Fleet Response Plan schedule for all units. Type commanders provide guidance for inspection timing and execution and have consolidated inspections to execute them once per training cycle. For surface ships, readiness evaluations provide an overarching framework for completing inspections and assessments in the ship's training cycle.

You would be wise to completely understand the requirements of your TYCOM-directed inspections in order to organize and administer your ship to pass any inspection at any time. The checklist requirements are not that difficult, though there will always be differences of opinion as to interpretation. The biggest problem, mostly found on small ships, is that in time of busy employment, or when shorthanded, personnel may let required records and procedures lapse. You will have to make it clear that just the reverse should happen: the *routine* should be done in a *routine fashion* so that on any day, the records are in inspection-ready condition. The records setup and administrative procedures are designed to keep people (and your ship) out of trouble, not in it. A properly administered ship can pass a command inspection at any time.

Should you fail an inspection or assessment, sit down in the wardroom with your administrative personnel and test the advice given above against the record. Ninety percent of the time you will just have to start doing what you should have been doing all along. The other 10 percent of failures probably will fit within Murphy's Law or some variation thereof. It is up to you and your XO to keep your administrative personnel's energies directed where *you* want them. Do so before the inspection, and you will pass; do so after a failure, and you will quickly become satisfactory.

MEDICAL READINESS INSPECTION

The Medical Readiness Inspection is a graded event conducted by the regional medical representative to provide the unit commander, ISIC, and TYCOM an assessment of the readiness of the medical department and its ability to accomplish its mission. This inspection determines the qualifications and state of training of personnel, the adequacy of medical procedures, both peacetime and wartime, and the completeness of medical material allowances. It is usually conducted during the integrated phase of the OFRP from 120 to 90 days prior to deploying.

ENGINEERING READINESS

The ship's ISIC—with support from the Afloat Training Group and Engineering Assessments Pacific/Atlantic—conducts engineering assessments and training. Engineering training and certification requirements demand close attention and constant assessment. Guidance for engineering training and certification is issued by the various TYCOMs (such as that found in the *SFTRM*) and should be carefully reviewed. While specific terms and the details of assessment and certification processes continually evolve, there are many general aspects that remain timeless.

In the interest of verifying that steam, diesel, and gas turbine propulsion plants in conventionally powered ships are safe to operate and also to promote improved engineering training and readiness, including program evaluation, drill criteria, and standardization of procedures, the following actions are performed on a regular basis:

1. Examination of propulsion engineering personnel to determine their state of training and qualification; appropriate engineering Personnel Qualification Standards used to evaluate the level of qualification of all propulsion plant personnel.
2. Witness and evaluation of the conduct of propulsion plant drills and evolutions, employing the installed Engineering Operational Sequencing System (EOSS) as a guide.
3. Inspection of the material condition of the propulsion plant to ascertain its state of readiness, preservation, and cleanliness.

4. Review and evaluation of the administration of the ship's engineering department and the completeness and accuracy of all ship's records relating to propulsion.

There are two basic types of engineering assessments and certifications. The first is the light-off assessment (LOA), conducted prior to lighting off the first fire in any boiler (or first light-off of a main or auxiliary gas turbine) during a regular overhaul, major conversion, fitting out availability, or restricted availability in excess of four months (120 days) in length. In the case of new construction ships, the LOA will be conducted following delivery and prior to initial light-off by ship's company. The second type of assessment supports a unit's engineering certification (mobility-engineering [MOB-E] 1.4), which is a required element of the basic-phase engineering mission area certification.

The *SFTRM* details the specific requirements for LOAs under the varying circumstances described above (new construction or availabilities exceeding 120 days). In general terms, the LOA is a sequential, multi-part process. First, Engineering Assessments Pacific/Atlantic assess the adequacy of the administrative/operating procedures directly related to the propulsion plant and the capability of shipboard personnel to safely operate and maintain equipment, systems, and spaces—for example, logs and records, liquid programs, hearing and heat stress programs, equipment tag-out procedures, and training.

The second part is verification that the engineering damage control equipment meets required standards in accordance with the Joint Fleet Maintenance Manual and that the crew is able to successfully conduct a Main Space Fire Drill.

The third part is verification that the propulsion plant is in a material condition that supports safe operation. Associated auxiliaries are included in the examination—that is, ship's service and emergency electrical plants, air compressors supporting propulsion plant operation, and any other equipment located in the propulsion spaces and/or normally operated by propulsion personnel.

The final step is a determination of whether engineering personnel have the knowledge and skill to operate the plant safely. For a satisfactory finding, the ship must present at least two qualified watch sections with the proficiency to support safe auxiliary steaming. However, simple evaluations—boiler water and feedwater, fuel sampling and analysis (as applicable), and casualty control walk-through drills—may be conducted at the discretion of the examiners.

During MOB-E 1.4, those areas discussed above under the requirements for an LOA will be examined. In addition, there will be an evaluation of propulsion plant casualty control drills. EOSS will be the basic guide in evaluating the conduct of equipment light-off/securing and casualty control drills. While TYCOM instructions will clearly lay out the specific requirements in detail, inspectors generally will require demonstration of the capability of at least two watch sections to safely support underway steaming. Additionally, a ship will be required to have a training team that is capable of self-training—that is, Engineering Training Team members proficient in training and assessing watchstanders and watch teams in the control of routinely encountered casualties.

Prepare for these examinations as TYCOM and the assessments direct. Drill often and prepare well, and you should have no trouble. Fail to do so, and you will be putting your sailors at risk, and you will require additional oversight by the ISIC.

BOARD OF INSPECTION AND SURVEY

U.S. Code, article 8674, directs the Secretary of the Navy to designate boards of naval officers to examine naval vessels. INSURV is given those basic duties. The president of the board, assisted by the other members and by permanent and semipermanent sub-boards as designated by the Secretary of the Navy, is required to do the following:

1. Conduct acceptance trials and inspections of all ships and service craft prior to acceptance for service
2. Inspect each naval ship at least once every three years, if practicable, to determine its material condition; and if it is found unfit for continued service, report this to higher authority
3. Perform such other inspections and trials as directed by the CNO

Higher authority schedules INSURV inspections. Article 0850, *Navy Regulations*, provides one other means of scheduling an INSURV inspection.

If you feel that the condition of your ship, or any department therein, requires an inspection by INSURV, you may request it through official channels. This does not occur very frequently.

In 2019, the CNO directed that INSURVs be conducted every three years, which coincides with one fleet response plan cycle. Changes to U.S. Code 10 in 2020 additionally directed that ships shall be examined with minimal notice provided to the crew of the vessel. Staffs responsible for scheduling inspections usually seek to do so when they best fit for the individual ship so that it allows time to translate those deficiencies either found or confirmed by the board into yard work requests. An INSURV-confirmed deficiency gets top attention from all the intermediate authorities who act on or make recommendations regarding your requests.

Preparations for INSURV are discussed in the *Naval Sea Service Command Technical Manual* as well as Navy and INSURV instructions. The primary aim of the INSURV inspection is to determine the condition of your machinery and equipment and then to recommend steps

Fig. 8-5. Intense training and frequent inspections give U.S. submarines superb readiness and performance.

necessary to correct deficiencies and return unsatisfactory items to a satisfactory condition. This means it will be necessary to inspect the inside and all working parts of boilers, pumps, turbines, and other pieces of machinery. The president of the board will tell you in advance which machinery is to be opened. If the carrying out of these instructions leaves you without propulsion or auxiliary power, you must make arrangements with your type commander or other administrative authority to have your ship placed in a safe mooring condition and furnished with necessary services while it is undergoing inspection.

Your engineering records will also be an important item of the inspection. Make sure your 3-M system is up to date and that all records are complete and accurate.

Finally, most members of the board feel that a good indication of the condition of the engineering plant and its past maintenance is the cleanliness and preservation evident to the eye. This does not mean that your spaces must be spotless. It means that machinery must be clean, lubricated, and immaculate, and it should work as designed.

NUCLEAR PROPULSION EXAMINATION BOARD

A propulsion examination board for nuclear-powered ships is established by OPNAVINST N3540.3D. The boards, one in each fleet, are maintained within the organizations of commander, Pacific Fleet, and commander, Fleet Forces Command (the fleet commanders), and assist them in ensuring that naval nuclear-powered ships are operated by qualified personnel in accordance with approved procedures. The commander, Naval Sea Systems Command, and the director, Division of Naval Reactors, Department of Energy, provide technical assistance to the fleet commanders and to the boards.

Each board has a senior member (captain) who has served as CO of a naval nuclear-powered ship and usually also has an engineering officer. Deputy senior members have the same qualifications, and other members are nuclear power–qualified, both submariners and nuclear surface warfare officers. Normally four members constitute an inspection team for a submarine, eight members for an aircraft carrier.

The responsibilities of the board are to

1. Examine personnel assigned responsibility for supervision, operation, and maintenance of the propulsion plant to determine their state of training
2. Witness and evaluate the conduct of propulsion plant drills
3. Inspect the material condition of the plant to ascertain its readiness, preservation, and cleanliness
4. Review and evaluate the engineering (reactor) department administration and the completeness and accuracy of all records relating to the propulsion plant
5. Evaluate the ship's proficiency in daily operations

The board gives the following types of examinations:

Pre-critical reactor safeguards examination of nuclear-powered ships prior to initial criticality of a newly installed reactor core, including new construction ships and ships completing refueling.

Post-overhaul reactor safeguards examination prior to initial reactor operation after an overhaul without refueling but lasting more than six months. The board will ascertain the state of training of the propulsion plant crew, the adequacy of administrative procedures, and the material readiness of the propulsion plant and spaces as they affect impending reactor operations and propulsion plant power range operations. Appropriate evolutions and casualty drills may be conducted as part of this examination.

Operational reactor safeguards examination (ORSE) of ships in an operational status. These are conducted no more than one year after the last pre-critical or post-overhaul examination, and thereafter at intervals of approximately one year, as close to the anniversary as practicable.

Radiological control practices evaluation of those reactor support facilities in tenders authorized to handle radioactivity associated with naval nuclear plants. This evaluation is conducted at intervals not exceeding a year. For tenders in overhaul, if the yearly interval will be exceeded during overhaul, an evaluation will be conducted before the end of the overhaul, after work in the nuclear support facility is essentially completed.

An ORSE is conducted on each nuclear-powered ship (and each of the crews of a fleet ballistic missile submarine) at approximately one-year intervals, and more frequently if the fleet commander or the director, Division of Naval Reactors, so desires.

Following examination, the board submits a written report to the appropriate fleet commander and to the director, Division of Naval Reactors. It submits reports of corrective action in the same way. If the board finds the ship unsatisfactory, it submits its findings by immediate precedence message. The ship is then returned to port and shut down. The sequence of actions following such a finding is quite involved and will not be described here. Briefly, though, the crew is retrained until all discrepancies have been corrected. The ship is then reexamined and, if satisfactory, the restrictions are lifted. Obviously, failure has personal consequences for the commanding officer.

Annual Competition

In peacetime, annual competitions are a means of attaining and maintaining battle and administrative readiness by using the stimulation of competition. The intra-type competition was established in 1953 by the Secretary of the Navy's Instruction 3590.1. It provided for payment of prize money to enlisted members of the crew from the Marjorie Sterrett Battleship Award Fund for attaining certain scores in battle practices. Qualifying crewmen wore *E*s on their jumpers, and ships attaining certain scores displayed *E*s on gun and director mounts. In later years, the competition was expanded to an intra-type battle competition conducted in accordance with OPNAVINST 3590. Present regulations authorize type commanders to make awards to ships, submarines, and aircraft for attainment of certain standard scores in overall battle exercise competition. The criteria include performance of individual gun, missile, and department crews, including departments such as communications, engineering, damage control, and minesweeping—by functional area—and culminate in ship awards. *E*s of various colors are authorized for display on ships, weapons, and assault boats, and the Efficiency "E" ribbon is worn on the uniform.

The Admiral Arleigh Burke Fleet Trophy was established in 1961 for the ship or aircraft squadron in each fleet achieving the greatest improvement as measured by the criteria of the Battle Efficiency Competition.

Other annual competitions include the Battenberg Cup (top Atlantic Fleet ship), the Spokane Trophy (top combat readiness in the Pacific Fleet), the Arizona Memorial Trophy (top strike ship in the fleet), and the Ney Award for the best general mess.

The annual competition is a powerful stimulus to your crew. The display of an *E* ribbon on the uniform or the *E* on gun, sail, bridge, or stack is highly prized in the fleet.

Final Fleet Preparation for Deployment

Following completion of integrated and/or sustainment training, you will most likely have to begin preparing for deployment. Your preparation may be short in the event of crisis or may take several months if scheduling permits. The final period of preparation will vary and will be listed in the annual employment schedule.

WRITTEN REQUIREMENTS

In some cases, the ship you will relieve will forward you a "turnover letter" (message or email). This should give you an insight into the small day-to-day matters of preparation. The larger areas will be taken care of by your type commander's checklist and by the large packages of operation plans and orders you will receive from your future chain of command. Much of this information is available on command websites and "collaboration at sea" sites. Between the turnover letter, the predeployment checklist, and the operation plans and orders, you should have all the written guidance you'll need. The rest of your preparation is making sure you have achieved the necessary training and qualifications, personnel, material, and supplies and are in a state of readiness adequate to carry out the tasks set forth in the written requirements. To do this, you will need to carry out the following detailed preparations.

PREDEPLOYMENT CHECKLIST

Obtain a checklist from your type commander as early as possible. When you can answer all its questions satisfactorily, you are ready to deploy. The chances are that you will have to carry out many of the following tasks.

Equipment Calibration: Have all of your equipment that requires calibration checked as completely as possible. This includes magnetic and gyrocompass systems, sonar equipment, communications equipment, radars, electronic countermeasure equipment, and missile and gun battery alignment. Verify that the calibrations will last through your expected period of deployment.

Logistics: Obviously, you should be at 100 percent of allowance in all areas. Top off all your consumables before sailing. Make sure the key items in your allowance are sighted by responsible officers or petty officers.

Advanced Training: Your type commander will schedule you for advanced training. Additional advanced training is usually possible during transit to forward areas. The type commander will work closely with the fleet commander responsible for assisting in your preparation, and you can expect to participate in exercises appropriate to your type. Cruisers, destroyers, and carriers will take part in anti-air warfare, anti-submarine warfare (ASW), and anti-surface warfare (ASUW) exercises, among other events. If time permits, they will also take part in an amphibious exercise. Submarines will be worked up by their type commanders and will participate in advanced exercises where possible. The goal, of course, is to prepare your ship or submarine for forward deployment with the Fifth, Sixth, or Seventh Fleets or for independent missions—with Fourth Fleet, for example, conducting counternarcotics operations.

Predeployment Reports: Type commanders will require periodic progress reports and briefings on readiness. You may consider this extra reporting, but if you look at it objectively, you will find that the report will be a help to you as well as to the type commander in monitoring your progress.

Crew Briefings: You will need to schedule many briefings for various groups of your officers and crew and some for all hands. These will range all the way from review of operations orders for officers to cultural and drug abuse briefings for the entire crew. Working out this schedule without interfering with other preparations can be challenging for your executive officer.

Training Data Management

The Naval Tactical Command Support System and its subset, Relational Administrative Data Management (RADM), serve as automated means of tracking training. From general shipboard administration to training, PQS, schools management, and, ultimately, watch bill generation, RADM is the method required to track training and qualifications on most ships, but it has its drawbacks. As data management tools continue to proliferate, new methods and systems for automating the tracking of qualifications and creation of watch bills may become available.

You should take a good look at your entire training (and administrative) process shortly after taking command and ensure that your programs are running as smoothly as possible. Powerful automated time-saving tools are available, but they're only as good as the quality of data in them. While your training officer will be a key player in this critical area, be alert for ways to improve the overall administration of your training programs. Nothing is truly automatic.

The Captain's Role in Training and Inspections

We started this chapter by saying that training of your combat team and the related skill of passing inspections with them were at the very heart of your command responsibility. In what practical ways can you accomplish these key objectives?

First, you must show your people that training matters deeply to you. The most effective means of doing this is to personally and enthusiastically participate in every element of shipboard training. Naturally, your executive officer is the nominal head of training for your organization, but it should be clear to everyone that the XO is operating with your direct charter and under the philosophical guidelines that you establish. This can be done through your written command philosophy, via your reviews with the XO and DHs following the planning board for training, during wardroom or ready room discussions, informally as you react during the day-to-day situations that present themselves, by what you say on the 1MC or at meetings, and how you structure the schedule of your ship, submarine, or squadron.

A related aspect of your role in training is the recognition that you are the ship's chief mariner (or airman) and tactician. No one else on board will have your breadth of skill and experience in these areas. You should personally be part of the training process in these two important areas. This must include getting on your feet in the wardroom or ready room and teaching your officers what you know of tactics, shiphandling (or airmanship), and maritime operations. You should also be involved in every aspect of drills and discussions involving tactics, particularly in the CIC in surface ships. Don't become a mysterious force who suddenly descends into drills or exercises, wreaking havoc and then vanishing to your stateroom or the bridge; rather, you should be part of the planning, practicing, and executing of what your team is learning to do throughout the training cycle.

In the crucial area of relations with outside entities, it is wise to establish a few basic guidelines regarding training and inspections. The first and most frequently observed problem area is the occurrence of conflicts between your team members and the inspection party, assessment group, or chain of command at the staff level. Your team is justifiably proud of their own way of doing business and their own experience. This can cause conflict with outside experts who have different (and generally better, frankly) methods of accomplishing certain tactical, navigational, or material feats. The best way to approach this potential problem is to train your team to accept the methods and suggestions of the outside experts, but to also quickly and privately express their reservations up your organization's chain of command. A good approach to take is that *only* the CO (or possibly the CO and XO) is permitted to "argue" with the inspectors. This will ensure that there are very few arguments at the deckplate level, which—when they do occur—can and often do lead to bad feelings and emotional reactions. Naturally, when your team really does have either the *right* answer or even a *better* answer, you should plead the case strongly. But remember that the inspectors, although occasionally irritating in their manner, have a wealth of knowledge, resources, and experience; perhaps more importantly, they have the luxury of devoting all their time to the particular issue at hand—be it how to run a computer-assisted dead reckoning tracer, fire a torpedo, or perform aircraft maintenance. They will be right far more often than not, and if it is simply a matter of preference, your team is usually well served in the long run to opt for the "suggested" improvement. You can lose the war even while winning some very small battles in the world of training and inspections. Be perceived as the cooperative organization that "listens to experience" whenever possible.

One thing every command must do to ensure a coherent approach to training is to publish a training plan, get it out to the team at least monthly, and include a list of active plans to pass upcoming inspections. This document, often called a Command Plan, is really a top-level management tool for the commanding officer. It should be promulgated with your signature. Use it to track upcoming key events, particularly training and inspection evolutions. By glancing at it, you should be able to see what all the upcoming command-level training and inspections are over the next twelve months, along with the lead responsibility, and the date of the published Plan of Action and Milestones (POAM). This will cue you to have the XO set up a review at appropriate periods. For example, if you are in command of a destroyer with a final engineering certification coming up in six months, you should be meeting with the engineering team to review that POAM about every two weeks. The upcoming certification event in two weeks may demand a review every couple of days while final milestones are accomplished. With the OFRP cycles of training, this is often more difficult to sort out than it was when inspections were discrete events. Nonetheless, you should be able to use the Command Plan to ensure that the "big ticket" items are all covered.

A real skill for a CO is running a POAM review. You should insist that the XO assemble all participants in a clean, well-lighted wardroom. Everyone should have a complete copy of the POAM in front of them. When all the players are in place, you are called in and the review commences. Either the XO or the department head responsible for the evolution should run the actual meeting. Listen carefully as each task is reviewed, and ensure that it is fully accomplished. This is an excellent opportunity for your prior experience and personal skills to come to bear, as you "ask the second question" and request to actually "see a copy of the reference." Your personal interest will generally ensure a high level of enthusiasm on the part of your team. This is also *your* chance to see exactly what *you* need to be doing to support the effort: calling the local repair facility to bump up the priority on a key job, working with the chief staff officer at the squadron to facilitate delivery of a key part, obtaining more trainer or simulator time for your combat tacticians, finding an extra practice torpedo at the weapons station for the exercise. The influence of a call from a ship, submarine, or squadron CO is very high in every Navy port. Use your calls sparingly, but remember that the squeaky wheel really does get greased more often, and when you are in the crunch—with the exercise or the inspection looming close to the hull—you are expected to roll up your sleeves and pitch in. BUPERS didn't send you to your ship to sit in your stateroom detached from the action. Never underestimate what you can accomplish in a few polite phone calls that start out with, "Hello, this is the captain of *Daniel Inouye*, and I was wondering if . . ."

9

Independent Operations

A man-of-war is the best ambassador.

—Oliver Cromwell

I wish to have no connection with any ship that
does not sail fast, for I intend to go in harm's way.

—John Paul Jones, letter to le Ray de Chaumont, 1778

Joining the Fleet for Initial Independent Operations

In every commanding officer's tour, one highlight is the opportunity to take your ship, submarine, or aircraft squadron out of a period of inactivity—perhaps owing to a yard period, a postdeployment leave and upkeep period, an industrial availability, or initial construction—and join the fleet. While your efforts during a stand-down, construction, or repair availability are important, they are certainly not as professionally fulfilling as taking your command and heading out to sea. In this chapter, we'll discuss the kind of independent operations you will conduct after initially joining the fleet, as you prepare for the more complex fleet and joint operations to come.

Discussions with the Wardroom, CPO Mess, and Crew

Emerging from a period of time in port, whatever the reason, is a good time to review with your entire team the basics of the command's philosophy. You should determine the most important aspects of your "message" at each level in your command—that is, what you need to say to the wardroom or ready room, to your chief petty officers, and to your crew. While the message must obviously be consistent, it should be varied as appropriate to these three audiences. You may want to meet in a sit-down session with the wardroom or ready room, and then have an all-hands call with the entire command. Alternatively, you may choose to meet with each level of the crew separately, perhaps with the E-6s, E-5s, and E-4s, and then the E-3s and juniors. Doing so will encourage more discussion and questions. Another approach possible in larger commands is to use the installed closed-circuit television systems and go out initially to everyone at once, then follow up with smaller discussions with the officers and chiefs.

At a minimum, you must do three things in the "coming back online" discussion: outline the upcoming schedule, focus your team on safety, and lay out some specific goals for your command. The first thing, discussing the schedule, is your easiest task, and you can generally help by using some simple graphics—perhaps a calendar laying out the next six to twelve months. You should reinforce the schedule information by providing a monthly "command plan" that outlines your schedule and goals as well as ensuring that the information (in an unclassified format) finds its way into the command newsletter mailed (and emailed) to the families. It is not a bad idea to keep the schedule updated in the plan of the day and plan of the week as well. Focus on the positives and the challenges in the schedule and let everyone see how excited and enthusiastic you are about it.

Your second goal at this point should be to focus everyone's attention on safety. For obvious reasons, many serious accidents and mistakes occur when a command has not been operational for some time. This message is a challenging one to deliver without being boring or appearing to simply preach to the crew. You should try to incorporate some real-world examples of commands who have experienced problems at a similar point in the operational cycle; include some specific things you want to have done (e.g., safety briefs on station prior to all evolutions, written plans for complex evolutions, pre-briefs for certain situations, and post-action critiques); and try to incorporate some human interest in the presentation. Let everyone know that your top priority during the initial time at sea is to come back to port with a safe crew and working equipment.

The third major portion of your message at this point should be a discussion of your goals for the command over the upcoming year. These should be discussed at a high level but should be specific in character. As an example, "We want to operate smoothly during COMPTUEX" doesn't say much to the crew, but if you say, "During the COMPTUEX in October, we want to shoot over 95 on the naval gunfire range, score hits on 100 percent of our missile shots, and conduct every UNREP [underway replenishment] safely in less than sixty minutes," you have painted a far more specific picture. The introduction of "metrics" tightens your message and more sharply conveys your goals. It reduces ambiguity and aligns efforts among the crew. You should also mention some of the awards and competitions you are interested in, such as the Spokane Trophy on the West Coast, the Battenberg Cup on the East Coast, the Ney Award for food service, the Battle Efficiency E, and the Topgun Award. Try to select goals that are realistic and attainable by your command, and make an effort to get the entire crew, regardless of rate or pay grade, involved in the process.

In addition to those minimum points of discussion, you may choose to discuss many other things at this stage of your command's life cycle, including specific personnel issues (advancement, retention, good order and discipline, and fraternization); policies on drug or alcohol use; ideas about family support and community responsibility; command atmosphere; current events and the world situation that might affect your command's schedule; or any other particular point of importance to you and your team. You should also make an effort to look back over the activity that has kept your command from operating at sea (construction, repair, stand-down) and identify those individuals who worked hard to maintain the readiness of the organization.

Getting Back in the Saddle

The first underway period after an extended period away from operations is always a little exciting. Take some time before it happens to go over the ways you as the CO can make it smoother. Here are a few ideas.

Conduct a fast cruise. Whether you are in command of a ship, a submarine, or an aircraft squadron, having a period of time when your organization shuts down the phone lines, bars outside contact, and completely focuses on doing what you need to do to operate safely at sea has immense value. This can be a complex three-day affair, complete with watch bill changes, drills, exercises, communications drills, and all the panoply of actually going to sea, or it may be as simple as a two- to three-hour series of lectures, discussions, and rehearsals. There is also a range of options between these two courses. You and your leadership team can best decide what to do based on the needs of your command. Whatever you choose to do, insist that a formal schedule be developed and distributed under your signature and that your XO is driving the problem.

Pick a good time to get under way. While this is not always something within your control, it is generally better to select a morning departure at a reasonable hour, preferably no earlier than 0900; an ideal first under way is usually around 1000. This gives all your people plenty of time to get to work, park the car, have a decent breakfast, attend to final details, and get on station. Trying to jump under way at 0600 the first time out simply fails the common sense check.

Start with the basics. As you build the schedule for the first underway period, set yourself up for success. Pick out some drills and exercises that are neither complex nor dangerous. Single-ship operations, low complexity day flights, and basic drills should be the order of the day; there is no point in beginning day one with a dawn UNREP and moving into a gun shoot. As you succeed throughout the day, building familiarity, get on the 1MC and let your people know how quickly everyone is moving up the learning curve. Let confidence grow by remembering to crawl and walk a little before you break into a run.

Go easy for the first few hours. Everyone (including the CO!) needs to reacclimate to a moving environment, and about 40 percent of the crew will be at least somewhat seasick. People tend to make mistakes in a period of initial under way as a direct result of the tiredness and headache that can afflict many of your crew, even if it doesn't develop into a full-fledged case of "mal de mer." Virtually everyone will recover fully by the evening meal, but the first eight hours can be rough. Recognize this and give the team a chance to simply get their "sea legs" back.

Don't take outsiders. Avoid taking assist teams or inspectors if possible. A few yard workers may be unavoidable, but hold the presence of anyone outside the command to an absolute minimum. This is not the time to invite the commodore along for a navigation check ride.

Keep your sense of humor. Losing your temper, or permitting those in the organization to do so, seldom has any positive impact. People are almost always trying very hard to do the right thing, and yelling at them only decreases the chances that they will succeed. Be reasonable and sensible in your expectations and recognize that things will improve rapidly. Don't be afraid to laugh at the not-dangerous but funny occurrences that will inevitably be a part of that first day at sea.

Keep Seniors Informed

In all of the independent operations about to be discussed, one principle is all-important: *keep the chain of command informed.* You will find specific requirements for reporting in NWP 1-03.1, *Operational Reports*, which summarizes the reports required. Part II of NWP 1-03.1 promulgates movement report requirements for reporting locations and movements of Navy ships and aircraft, Marine ground units, and VIPs. Details include preparation of forms and reports and responsibilities of movement report centers and officers. Amplifying orders to NWP 1-03.1 will also be issued by administrative and operational commanders above you.

The array of requirements might sometimes be bewildering, but the aggregate demand is to *keep them informed.* Even if your ship is very small, you will have the communications equipment to reach your seniors, and they in turn will be in instant contact with superiors all the way to the White House, if necessary, via the chain of command. This is especially the case with our practically continuous access to the Internet and email. In these days of critical international situations, a single ship halfway around the world may find herself involved in search and rescue, asylum, visit, board, and search, or other events of interest to the chain of command. You will find that *how* you describe what you are doing is often as important as *what* you are doing. Indicate the who, what, when, where, how, and why of what is happening. If you can forecast the next event, do so. Tell them when you will report next. Try to include everything you might want to know if you were a senior commander. Additionally, understand that timeliness is essential. Don't withhold initial reports for additional details; these can be covered in follow-up briefs. Circumstances will almost always change following the "first report."

The Chain of Command

The old days of truly independent operations—when naval vessels disappeared into the South Seas for a year or so without being heard from—are gone. Even the pre–World War II shakedown cruise to foreign ports is no more. Today, a ship on independent operations and even ballistic missile submarine (SSBN) submerged patrols are firmly a part of the chain of command.

NDP-1, *Naval Warfare*, describes the basic command organization, the chain of command of the shore organization, and the dual lines of authority to the operating forces. You should master this publication. Note that the CNO, as such, has no operational authority. He or she is, however, in the administrative chain of command. If you are discussing a developing asylum case with your chain of command, you will have to keep these distinctions straight. Fortunately, the battle watch captains at the group and fleet levels will have a good grasp of these relationships. NDP-6, *Naval Command and Control*, is a simplified discussion of command and control matters and should be of great assistance to you.

Preparation for Independent Operations

You may, at times, be detached suddenly from your fleet assignment and ordered to proceed on independent ops. If this occurs, there is little you can do to specifically prepare. Either you are ready or you aren't. As a minimum, though, information and lessons on a wide variety of past operations *are* available electronically via reach-back. Your chain of command will assist in getting you connected to these resources. If you are given advance warning, however, or are going on a scheduled cruise, there is much preparation to be done.

If you did not do so before deploying, or if your independent operation begins from homeport, start with personnel preparation. Be sure you are up to date on inoculations and dental work and that all of your sailors have taken care of their financial affairs. Consider family issues, working with your command master chief and ombudsman. These are all important elements of predeployment preparations.

If you have the opportunity, top off logistically before departing. This means fuel, ammunition, provisions, and spare parts. It also means many smaller but equally important items that you have been used to getting from supply sources. Things that gave you little concern before will suddenly loom large. From postal supplies to ship's store items, particularly everyday necessities, such as razor blades and toothpaste, will all be needed for long underway periods. When you reach port, your supply officer will also need to know supply procedures for letting provision contracts, if none are in force for that port. You will be fortunate in this regard if your ship is big enough to warrant the assignment of a Supply Corps officer. A line officer who is doing this job will need help and your patience.

When you have a few minutes, have your XO survey the language abilities of your crew. Find out which of your officers and crew are qualified to act as interpreters and which can help with a smattering of a language. Compile a list and keep this handy, as you will need their help in search and rescue (SAR) operations, in rendering assistance at sea to vessels in distress, in contacts with merchant vessels, during port visits, and on other occasions.

Special Submarine Preparations

Submarines normally operate independently, providing exceptional training opportunities for our submarine force. For the fast attack force, independent ops provide training conditions not unlike wartime operations. In both SSBNs and SSNs, deployed operations are as independent as any command today, with the commanding officer given much latitude in decision-making.

SSN deployed operations are usually announced through the chain of command some nine months or so prior to deployment. As a surface counterpart does, the submarine CO will review in detail the administrative and logistical requirements prior to the deployment. In addition, the SSN commanding officer will review NWP 3-21, *Fleet Antisubmarine Warfare*, in detail in order to indoctrinate the wardroom and crew thoroughly in tactical procedures to be conducted while on station. As in all operations, in-depth planning is the key to success. During a notional nine-month preparation period, the SSN commanding officer will also be offered the services of the various training commands and technical agencies. Failure to accept their training offers can result in missed opportunities once deployed.

Given the demands on manpower, training deficiencies must be identified and corrected early in the preparation period. The tactical equipment a submarine carries must be used effectively to carry out its mission. If its personnel cannot support the technology, they must be either trained or replaced. There is too much at stake to deploy to a forward area when mission success probability is lessened by lack of experience or technical ability.

The final process in preparing an SSN for deployment is the deployment workup and certification by the squadron commander. NWP 3-21 is your guide in preparing for these events. Throughout the workup, stress the importance of the mission to the crew. Conduct all preparations as if the ship were deploying in time of war. If you conduct your training and preparation in this spirit, your ship will be successful during its truly *independent operation*, and every sailor will relish the experience.

SSBN preparations are similar to the SSN workup, except that the off-crew trains in homeport without the ship. The successful SSBN captain will set training goals for the crew and for each individual and will monitor progress toward these goals throughout the off-crew training period.

Fig. 9-1. Independent duty has its challenges, but as you head off on your own, you will enjoy your command independence to the utmost.

Movement Report. Whether in a submarine or a surface ship, the movement report is probably the single most important report you will make on independent ops. The movement report system is responsible for your continuing safety when you are operating alone. The movement report system is designed to provide all necessary authorities with a dead reckoning position for all units at any time. If, because of weather, engineering casualty, or other reason, your progress along your track varies at any time by more than four hours—one hundred miles for carrier operations, two hours for submarines—you must submit a report of change. NWP 1.03, *Operational Reports*, describes the entire movement report system. Be completely familiar with it. Now, as a matter of routine practice, all ships request both tailored weather forecasts and Optimum Track Ship Routing services when filing their initial movement reports.

Mail. A movement report provides information to appropriate naval area postal officials, who then verify the routing information on file. You must still, however, submit separate mail routing instructions to the appropriate fleet commander.

Fig. 9-2. The Navy's mail service is outstanding, but it will only be as good for your ship as your routing instructions.

Underway Independent Operations

Presumably, you are as ready now as prudence and a good forehanded group of CPOs, division officers, and department heads can make you, and you are probably headed for a foreign port visit. During your transit to this port, or while on a simple independent operation, many things can happen. When you were part of a task group, you could expect the task group commander to assist in resolving emergent issues. Now *you* are in charge. To assist you, we will review some of the most common challenges you can expect to face. Good planning prevents these challenges from turning into crises.

WEATHER

The challenge most likely to strike is heavy weather. Prepare your ship by reviewing your heavy weather plan and making sure all hands know how to implement it. Check your bill against the standard heavy weather bill found in the *SORM*. At a minimum, your bill should include all the points given there. If you carry out your bill properly and ballast correctly (if so configured), you should be able to handle any heavy weather situation if you maneuver your ship correctly. One exception might be if you command a very small ship. Small ships can reduce risk by early avoidance of the dangerous portion of storms; in some cases, they are safer than larger vessels.

A *good* ship captain always knows what the weather *is* at any moment. A *very good* one also knows what the weather *will be*. An *outstanding* one also knows what the weather *might be* in the future. The most important factor in surviving heavy weather is the captain's ability to recognize its existence, its probable movement, and its development.

Your studies of weather should start with the basics of worldwide weather formation and then proceed to the patterns of your particular area. A good text is *Weather for the Mariner*, published by Naval Institute Press. The piloting instructions for your area also cover local weather patterns and storm tracks.

These studies will enable you to interpret most weather predictions and weather advisories. The information in these messages will tell you what the weather is now, both near you and over a wide area. It will also tell you what the weather *probably* will be, based on past history of weather development and movement and using the skills of highly trained meteorologists.

This is not enough to ensure your safety. You will remember from your shore duty listening to the evening television weather program providing a forecast of fair weather and then walking out to the first tee in the rain. Forecasters—while good—simply cannot forecast with complete accuracy. At this point in the study of meteorology, the movement of weather masses is not completely predictable, even with the finest computer systems and most sophisticated mathematical models. The precise movement of air masses over the irregularities of land and island chains is particularly unpredictable. Movement over the open seas is somewhat more uniform and therefore somewhat more predictable. The point here is that you cannot place the safety of your ship in the hands of a meteorologist, no matter how skilled. In the final analysis, he or she must *guess*, and you must always take this into account. You must learn enough about the science of weather—and, more importantly, the homely, practical knowledge of close-in weather prediction—to know when the forecast you received is wrong or when the weather is refusing to follow it. The Naval Meteorological and Oceanographic Command has a wealth of helpful environmental products—both instructional and forecast-related—available via its website. These can be used for both wardroom professional training and daily weather briefs aboard your ship. Don't forget that meteorological detachments can also embark in your ship during independent operations. These highly skilled individuals can provide tailored environmental support for your operations, navigational planning, and training. Requests for their services are usually made via the chain of command.

Weather for the Mariner is technically correct, provides as much depth as you will need, and is written in a readable style. It covers the general theory of weather, the generation of worldwide weather, and the standard patterns of weather to be found throughout the world. It is relatively short and nonmathematical, and its photographs and illustrations will help you make local predictions.

Fig. 9-3 A hurricane off the coast of Florida.

TROPICAL CYCLONES

The most dangerous weather disturbance you will encounter is the tropical cyclone. This type of storm is known as a hurricane in the Atlantic area and as a typhoon in the Pacific. Ships of all sizes are in for trouble during hurricane or typhoon season, which lasts roughly from July to December. There are also tropical cyclones in the Southern Hemisphere, which rotate clockwise instead of counterclockwise, as in the Northern Hemisphere. These storms are given different names, such as the Indian Ocean cyclone and the Australian willy-willy, but are essentially the same.

To learn more about these dangerous and unpredictable disturbances, read the chapter on weather disturbances in *Weather for the Mariner*, particularly the section on precautions and disengagement. Another good text is *Heavy Weather Guide*, also published by Naval Institute Press. You,

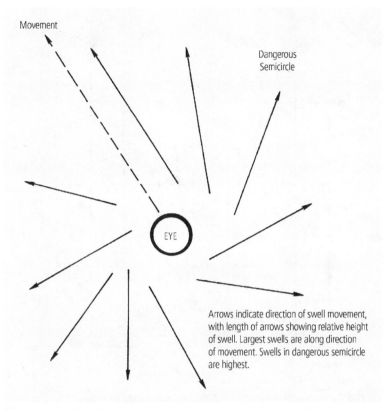

Fig. 9-4. Swell directions and heights surrounding a tropical storm.

as commanding officer, are the final authority on the safety of your ship, and as such, must know both her capabilities and her limitations as well as the environment she will travel in—wind, water, and storm. In this age of worldwide satellite weather observation and reporting, you will have advantages that World War II commanders and ship COs never had. You should have ample warning of typhoon and hurricane formation, movement, and prediction.

This said, we will now quickly review our storm precautions. In essence, a hurricane or typhoon is a large mass of water-laden air, rotating counterclockwise (in the Northern Hemisphere) around an eye of low pressure from twenty to fifty miles in diameter. As one approaches the storm center, air pressure decreases gradually until one enters the eye, when it decreases dramatically. The whole mass is hundreds of miles in diameter

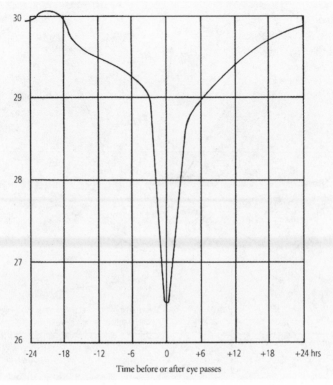

Fig. 9-5 . Barometric indication of movement of a typhoon
or hurricane over a ship or station.

and moves forward at speeds of up to fifty miles per hour. Occasionally it will remain stationary, though, and may even back up for short periods before resuming forward movement. Rotational wind speeds in the right-hand semicircle (looking along the direction of movement) are added as vectors to the forward speed. Rotational wind speeds in the other semicircle are subtracted from the forward speed. Hence, the right-hand semicircle, with its higher wind speed, is known as the "dangerous semicircle," and the left-hand semicircle is known as the "safe semicircle." The direction in which the storm lies from you can be predicted fairly accurately by looking back along the direction from which the swells are coming. The storm center will be within a few degrees of the direction of swells, as indicated in figure 9-4. Distance away can be predicted roughly by the speed with which the barometer is falling. A sudden drop to very low levels indicates the center is near, as indicated in figure 9-5.

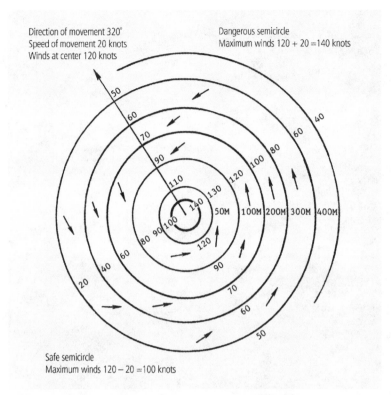

Fig. 9-6. Wind directions and speeds to be expected in a typhoon or hurricane with eye wind speeds of 120 knots and a speed of advance of 20 knots.

Wind speeds of more than two hundred knots have been experienced in hurricanes, and seas can be mountainous. Ships, particularly destroyers and smaller ships, must avoid being caught broadside in the troughs of the seas. Hurricanes and typhoons form in tropical latitudes and move west. As they progress, they tend to head more northwesterly and finally recurve to the northeast. Predicting the exact track is very difficult.

It is interesting to note that with only primitive prediction services from 1920 to 1940, the ships of the Asiatic Fleet never suffered any serious damage from typhoons. During this period, hundreds of typhoons of great violence swept through the Philippines area but never managed to catch any of the thirteen old destroyers of the Asiatic Fleet. The reason was that the commanding officers of these ships soon learned to use some simple rules of typhoon prediction and avoidance that had been handed down from captain to captain. You will want to review the more complete

Fig. 9-7. Hurricane winds of one hundred knots. Tops of long swells are flattened, but the direction of the swell is still apparent and helps to locate the center of the storm.

rules in *Weather for the Mariner*, but it is interesting to note how simple they can be made and still be effective. The following rules were taped to the bulkhead of the emergency cabin of the commanding officer of an Asiatic Fleet four-stacker (in which the emergency cabin was also the chart house):

1. If the barometer falls below 29.50 inches start worrying.
2. If the barometer falls below 29.35 *really* worry.
3. If you are in port, hoist in all boats, move to typhoon anchorage, put a second anchor down, and be prepared to steam at anchor.
4. If you are at sea watch out for long swells. The direction from which they approach is within 15 degrees of storm center.

5. Observe the direction of the wind. In the Northern Hemisphere the storm center will be 120 degrees to the right of the direction from which the wind is blowing.

6. Never try to outrun or pass ahead of a typhoon unless you are very close to its path. If you can, avoid the dangerous semicircle (left side looking toward eye.)

7. If the wind shifts clockwise you are in the dangerous semicircle; if it shifts counterclockwise, you are, if in the Northern Hemisphere, in the safe semicircle. If the wind direction stays steady and the barometer continues to fall, you are directly in the path. Bug out to the west as fast as you can.

8. In the southern Philippines most typhoons are moving in a northwesterly direction. By the time they reach the northern Philippines, friction of land masses and their natural tendency to curve to the northeast will change their direction of movement to northeast. One in ten will continue northwest to the China coast.

9. If you cannot evade completely, take the following actions:

    a. In dangerous semicircle bring wind on starboard bow. Make all speed possible.

    b. In safe semicircle bring wind on starboard quarter. Make all speed possible.

    c. If directly ahead of storm bring wind 160 degrees on starboard side. Make all speed possible, slowing as storm approaches. As eye approaches wind will decrease and then shift to opposite direction as eye passes over you. Keep turning to port to keep sea astern. Do *not* get in troughs.

    d. If behind storm go anywhere you want to go. Hold divine services if you feel sufficiently grateful.

The same instructions taped to the bulkhead of the sea cabin of a more modern destroyer enabled its commanding officer to leave the Third Fleet formation in the second typhoon experienced by Admiral Halsey's fleet and survive easily with no casualties or damage. Others were not as fortunate.

Fig. 9-8. The calm inside the eye of a hurricane.

Fig. 9-9. If the typhoon is astern and headed away from you, make best speed and hold divine services.

Hurricanes in the Caribbean and the Gulf of Mexico follow similar patterns and can be handled with the same rules of thumb. The island chains of the Caribbean and the large land masses surrounding the Gulf of Mexico influence storm buildup and movement differently from the western Pacific, but in both areas, simple principles of physics apply. Water areas add to storm energy and water content; land areas subtract from them. Storms move more easily over water, and the greater friction of land slows that portion of the storm passing over it. Storms, therefore, veer in the direction of that portion of them passing over land. As they pass over land, rainfall increases, energy lessens, winds decrease, and forward movement slows. The reverse happens if the storm passes out to sea again.

Keep your radars operating. Radar information can define storm center position and will show its movement accurately. This is of great assistance when maneuvering close to the storm's center. Antennas may be damaged by high winds, but you must balance a few thousand dollars' worth of repairs against the safety of your ship.

FRONTAL SYSTEMS

Most of the area of the Earth, both sea and seacoast, over which you will operate lies in the northern midlatitudes. The weather of this area is dominated by frontal systems. You should have a good understanding of what fronts are and how they form, travel, interact, and dissipate. They will control 90 percent of your weather. *Weather for the Mariner* has an excellent discussion of this subject, written in an understandable style and accompanied by photographs and diagrams.

There are two principal types of frontal systems, cold and warm. When moving in an orderly fashion and not otherwise influenced, they produce predictable weather. *Weather for the Mariner* contains a set of tables showing weather you can expect at each stage of the approach and passage of both cold and warm fronts. When they are occluded (which occurs when a cold front overtakes a preceding warm front), the occlusion literally lifts up the boundaries of both fronts, and weather becomes much more violent and unpredictable. Fronts can also be thrown off their orderly progression from west to east by low- and high-pressure cells, which can cause them to stall and remain stationary, to change direction, or to speed up. As with hurricanes and typhoons, weather prediction with frontal systems is sometimes educated guesswork. Still, an educated guess is better than an ignorant one. A small investment in the study of frontal weather systems can pay big dividends. A modern naval vessel is not usually vulnerable to frontal storms if properly moored or anchored in port or if well handled at sea, but ship's boats can suffer if not properly secured or hoisted early enough.

LOCAL STORMS

Other forms of local storms can be dangerous. The williwaws of the Aleutians, the Santa Anas of southern California, and the sandstorms of the Red Sea and the Persian Gulf must be understood and prepared for. The onslaught of local storms is usually sudden and without warning.

Fog is to be expected in various parts of the world at certain seasons. Check piloting instructions and your low visibility bill before entering such areas.

When thoroughly prepared for the vicissitudes of weather, though steaming peacefully under fair skies, you can concentrate on preparing for other emergencies.

SEARCH AND RESCUE

After heavy weather, the challenge you will most likely encounter will be some form of search and rescue. Spend a little time reviewing your responsibilities in this area. They stem from *U.S. Navy Regulations* and are spelled out in article 0925, Assistance to Persons, Ships, and Aircraft in Distress.

You are required, as far as you can do so without serious damage to your ship or injury to your crew, to proceed with all possible speed to the rescue of persons in distress. You must render assistance to any person found in danger at sea and must give all reasonable assistance to distressed ships and aircraft. Should you be so unfortunate as to collide with another ship, you must render assistance to that ship and her crew and passengers. As you would expect, you must report all SAR action to the chain of command as soon as possible.

Article 0925 ends with the reassuring statement that the accounting for rendering assistance and making repairs pursuant to the provisions and directions of the article shall be as prescribed by the comptroller of the Navy. These instructions are somewhat complicated, but they do provide for your reimbursement. Maintain a good count of blankets, crew's clothing (if you command a small ship and do not have ship's store clothing to use), food, and other equipment and supplies used in rescue operations. Your crew and your ship will be repaid. You are enjoined specifically, however, *not* to effect repairs to a merchant vessel in distress or in collision with you unless in your capacity as senior officer present you feel such repairs are necessary to save lives or to prevent the merchant vessel from sinking. If you do provide such assistance, you must report the cost of labor and materials in your subsequent report.

Now that you know what you *are* supposed to do and what *not* to do, a review of *how* you will do it is in order. The *SORM* contains sample bills that when implemented enable you to meet most requirements. Chapter 6.3.14 provides for the rescue and assistance detail. This bill provides for rescue of survivors of plane crashes, ship sinkings, and other similar accidents. Chapter 6.3.15 describes a rescue of survivors bill and provides procedures for rescuing large numbers of survivors from the water. Chapter 6.4.2, the aircraft crash and rescue bill, is a specific bill for the purpose of rescuing aircraft survivors. There is no specific bill provided for submarine rescue. If you are requested to assist a surfaced submarine, treat it like any surface ship in distress. If it requires a tow, the submarine CO will be careful to warn you what underwater portions of the submarine to avoid while passing the line. If it is submerged, you will have to try to find it by sonar search. If you are not so equipped, there will be help on the way soon. In the meantime, you can search the area for evidence such as smoke flares or a communication buoy. Ships equipped with sonar or underwater telephone can communicate with the submarine. The submarine may also have a wire antenna system, which may be usable for radio communication if it is undamaged and the water is shallow enough.

REFUGEES

Refugee situations in both Southeast and Southwest Asia, the Mediterranean, the Caribbean, and elsewhere present a problem that will likely persist. If you are transiting these areas, you may encounter small boats and even fair-sized freighters loaded with refugees. These unfortunate people may have gone for days without food and water and will present all forms of sickness and physical disability. A small ship may be hard pressed to provide the medical care and space that they will require. This kind of contingency is not uncommon in the forward numbered fleets, and there will be annexes to the standard fleet operation order telling you exactly what to do, what reports to make, and how to get help. Your standard bills will suffice unless you are overwhelmed by sheer numbers.

The standard naval warfare publications are implemented by the fleet commanders. They have SAR annexes to their standing operating plans. The commanders of the numbered fleets also have such annexes. With all of these publications and the fleet plans appropriate to your area and chain of command, you have all the guidance you will need as to what to do. Your bills will tell you how to do it.

The remaining element of SAR is *when* to do it. You may simply run across someone at sea in need of help. If so, your course of action is obvious. However, SAR incidents in which you will be involved will usually be initiated by someone else. The communications plan under which you will be operating will require that you guard the international distress frequency (in addition to other coordination circuits). You will hear calls for assistance directly on this frequency. Report these calls up through the chain of command, stating what action you intend to take. You will have to make a judgment as to whether you can reach the scene in time to help and whether your mission will permit you to divert. The chain of command will know the location of other forces available and will provide guidance swiftly. You may also receive direction from a senior who has information through other means than the distress frequency, such as by aerial sighting or via a third party. In this case they will have information regarding available forces and will issue appropriate orders.

MAN OVERBOARD

One of the most common SAR efforts is a very short-range one: that of recovering a man overboard. If you are part of a formation, finding someone else's sailor becomes a problem of avoiding other units nearby, maneuvering in accordance with directions from CIC or by visual observation, and bringing the sailor aboard. Since we are discussing independent operations in this chapter, we will concentrate on the problems of a single ship.

The *SORM*, chapter 6.4.5, contains a bill that covers training, responsibilities, actions, and many other details of man overboard procedure. You should, of course, have a complete man overboard bill patterned after this bill and adapted to your ship type. CIC and bridge watch personnel should be well qualified and instructed and exercised frequently at drill.

The one area in which the standard bill is weak is in maneuvering advice, particularly for small ships. Lowering a boat for recovery is feasible less than 50 percent of the time at sea. Thus, the usual method of recovery for small ships is by maneuvering close to the sailor, then throwing a heaving line with a float over the bow or side or by sending a qualified rescue swimmer over the side with a line attached (especially if the sailor in the water is weakened or incapacitated, which is usually the case).

There are many methods of returning your ship to the person's location. The three most widely used methods are the Williamson turn, the Anderson turn, and the Y turn. Regardless of the method you use, an immediately established, meticulously kept CIC dead reckoning plot on a two-hundred-yard scale is mandatory. If your special maneuvering method fails, CIC will be assisting you with bearings and ranges to the man in the water based on their plot.

The Williamson turn is illustrated in figure 9-10. This maneuver can be used by any type of ship, including carriers, cruisers, destroyers, submarines, amphibious ships, and single-screw vessels. As the diagram shows, it is well adapted for use when the exact time a sailor fell overboard is not known, since after making the turn you can continue back along the previous track indefinitely. Its disadvantage is that it takes a long time to execute, and the ship moves so far from the sailor that sight of him or her may be lost. Practice making the turn with your ship, for variations in maneuvering characteristics may require some adjustment.

The Anderson turn, illustrated in figure 9-11, was developed in 1952 by the CO of *Richard B. Anderson*, Commander W. P. Mack. It was promulgated to the destroyers of the Pacific Fleet and tested extensively by them both before and after promulgation. It was designed to be used by twin-screw destroyers, and it is still widely used by them with slight variations adapted by ship type. Its main purpose is to bring the ship back to

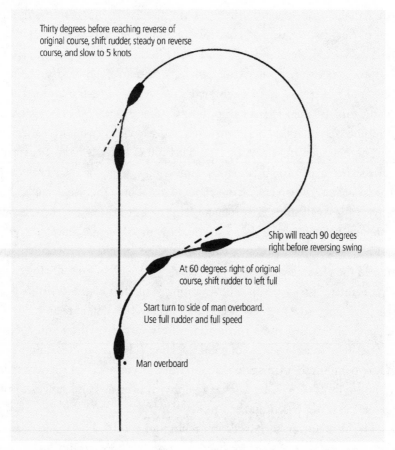

Thirty degrees before reaching reverse of original course, shift rudder, steady on reverse course, and slow to 5 knots

Ship will reach 90 degrees right before reversing swing

At 60 degrees right of original course, shift rudder to left full

Start turn to side of man overboard. Use full rudder and full speed

Man overboard

Fig. 9-10. The Williamson turn can be used with modifications by any type of ship. If a sailor is overboard to port, reverse the procedure shown.

the sailor in a short time in cold weather or reduced visibility. The ship is kept as close as possible to the person, and the maneuver ends with the ship stopped and its bow usually within fifty to one hundred feet of the sailor. The average time for the turn is three minutes and forty-five seconds, well within survival time in cold water. The Anderson turn also provides a simple set of maneuvering instructions readily mastered by inexperienced OODs. After the sailor is overboard and the initial orders are given to commence the turn—in the case of a sailor overboard to starboard: right full rudder, port ahead full, starboard stop (or alternatively, starboard back one-third to accelerate the turn)—the OOD has about two minutes to give the necessary orders to make sound signals,

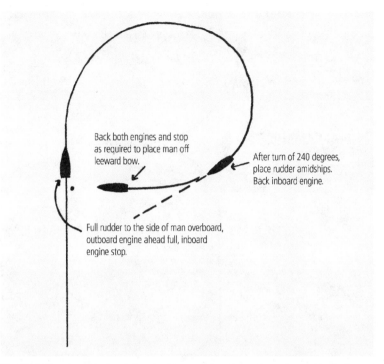

Back both engines and stop
as required to place man off
leeward bow.

After turn of 240 degrees,
place rudder amidships.
Back inboard engine.

Full rudder to the side of man overboard,
outboard engine ahead full, inboard
engine stop.

Fig. 9-11. The Anderson method of recovering a man overboard is designed for use in cold weather, low visibility, or rough weather. Average time to complete the maneuver is about three minutes and forty-five seconds.

pass the word, notify the captain, and otherwise prepare for recovery. The next step is a simple order, given when the ship has swung 240 degrees, to bring the rudder amidships and back all engines one-third. The third and equally simple order is to stop all engines when way is off. The ship can then do further maneuvering, if required. One destroyer, in an actual recovery, sent the boatswains mate of the watch and a messenger to the forecastle. They made the recovery using a line over the bow in three and a half minutes.

The Y turn, illustrated in figure 9-12, is intended for use by submarines but may be used by any type. It permits the submarine to stay as close as possible to the person without losing sight of them. This is important because of the submarine's low height of eye. This method is not adapted to low visibility, and for some surface ships, backing into a heavy sea can decrease control. Of all types, the submarine is best able to back into wind and sea because of low freeboard and small sail area.

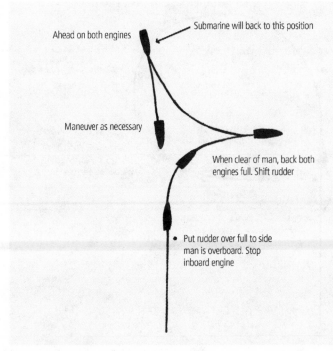

Ahead on both engines

Submarine will back to this position

Maneuver as necessary

When clear of man, back both engines full. Shift rudder

• Put rudder over full to side man is overboard. Stop inboard engine

Fig. 9-12. The Y-turn method of man overboard recovery is designed for submarines.

There are other recovery methods in use, notably the racetrack method, described in the *Watch Officer's Guide*, published by Naval Institute Press. This method is designed for use in column, but in our opinion the Anderson turn is superior for this purpose.

You must experiment with your own ship to find out which method is best and to determine what modifications you should make to the standard methods.

ASYLUM

Our asylum policy stems from the case of Simas Kudirka, a seaman serving in a Soviet fishing trawler off Martha's Vineyard. A Coast Guard cutter was alongside the trawler conducting a routine search for compliance with fishing regulations when Kudirka came topside, jumped over to the deck of the cutter, and asked for asylum. The trawler captain then asked that he be returned. The Coast Guard captain asked via radio for instructions from higher authority and was told to allow the return of Kudirka. A party from the trawler was then allowed to board the cutter, bind and gag the man, and return him to the trawler. A subsequent investigation found serious errors in the proceedings and violations of strict standing instructions. Guilt assessed and punishment made are history and are relatively unimportant to this discussion. What is important is for each CO to fix the proper asylum procedures in their mind.

As a result of the Kudirka incident, *Navy Regulations* now has much more specific instructions regarding asylum. Article 0939 states that any person requesting asylum on the high seas shall have it granted and shall not be surrendered except at the personal direction of the Secretary of the Navy or higher authority. When in a foreign port, a request for asylum shall be granted only in extreme humanitarian cases, such as pursuit by a mob, in which case the unit involved is technically providing "temporary refuge." Such protection can be terminated only by the Secretary of the Navy or higher authority. A request by foreign authorities for return of a refugee will be reported to the Chief of Naval Operations by immediate precedence message. However, though the person must be protected, the regulations state clearly that they shall not be *invited* to seek asylum.

The information and direction in article 0939 should be adequate to handle any situation regarding asylum either ashore or afloat.

HARASSMENT

Harassment by foreign forces may occur. The most common means of harassment are direct or close aboard overflights by aircraft, ships coming close aboard or shadowing closely astern, and shadowing by surveillance ships, either naval ships or trawlers. Harassment occurs most frequently when U.S. ships or groups of ships are engaged in exercises or other pursuits of technical interest to other forces, such as missile test firings. They may try to interfere in any way possible. Harassment can occur in areas of contested maritime jurisdiction as well as in widely recognized international waters. While you are on independent duty, you may be overflown by long-range reconnaissance aircraft or approached by other vessels. Take pictures and video, carefully document the encounter, and report the incident to the chain of command.

ATTEMPTED BOARDING OR CAPTURE

This sounds like something out of the nineteenth century, but it is an occurrence that has happened previously and must be discussed. We hope that *Pueblo*-style incidents are no longer possible, but they must be considered and planned for.

The 1968 *Pueblo* incident is well known. There are many opinions regarding the action taken by Commander Lloyd Bucher, the CO of *Pueblo*. The official opinion, as expressed by the findings of the Board of Investigation, was, in simplified form, that his actions were incorrect. The final action of the Secretary of the Navy in setting aside these findings is not pertinent, since the rationale for doing so was based on factors extraneous to the principles involved. The opinions expressed as to what action Bucher should have taken range from approval—with the rationale that resistance was useless and fighting the ship to the end would have resulted in the loss of many of the crew and the ultimate capture of any survivors—to the other end of the spectrum—that he should have had his guns ready (and not covered in iced canvas) and should have fought to the end.

The latter is the opinion held by most naval officers. Their reasons are best expressed in article 0828, *Navy Regulations*, which states straightforwardly and unequivocally that you shall not permit a ship under your command to be searched on any pretense whatsoever by any person representing a foreign state, nor shall you permit any of the personnel within the confines of your command to be removed by such person, so long as you have the capacity to repel such an act. If force is used in an attempt, you are to resist to the utmost of your power. This leaves no room for doubt. You are to resist *to the utmost*.

CROSSING THE LINE

Several ceremonies, including crossing the line, may be necessary if operations cause you to cross the equator or the international date line. The crossing the line ceremony can be as elaborate as you and an enterprising and inventive crew want to make it. *Naval Ceremonies, Customs, and Traditions* contains a history of the ceremony and a sample scenario to help you make plans for your own. The ceremony of crossing the international date line is also described, and this too has a special certificate.

Other ceremonies can be held for those visiting the Arctic and the Antarctic and for those who become golden shellbacks by crossing the intersection of the equator and the international date line.

Review current directives and closely monitor the proceedings to ensure that an enjoyable and safe time is had by all. Remember that participation is voluntary, and be mindful that hazing—which has no place in any ceremony—is strictly forbidden aboard U.S. Navy vessels. From start to finish, senior enlisted involvement and leadership are critical to success in these events.

Visits to a Foreign Port (Single Vessel)

TAKING A PILOT

As you approach port, your next challenge will be taking a pilot. *Navy Regulations*, article 0856, covers your responsibility with regard to pilots. This article states that they are merely advisers. Pilots do not relieve you or your officers of any responsibility for the safe handling of the ship. The one exception is the Panama Canal, where the pilot has control of the navigation and movement of your vessel. (The Suez is *not* an exception.) However, there have been occasions in the Panama Canal when COs took over from the pilot in the lake and channel sections to avoid grounding and had their actions subsequently upheld. Nevertheless, be sure you are prepared to support your action if you relieve a Panama Canal pilot.

You may allow the pilot to handle your ship much as you would the OOD, but you must maintain your own navigational plot and make sure that your helmsman and engine order telegraph operator are alerted to respond to your order if and when you feel it necessary to take over the conn. You may also simply use the pilot as an adviser and keep the conn yourself. Many pilots do not speak good English, and you will have to stand by to clarify their orders. Also, foreign pilots are accustomed to merchant ships and tend to give orders in their parlance. "Ahead slow" can be interpreted as "ahead one-third." Be careful with "ahead full" if you are a destroyer type. The pilot doesn't *really* want twenty-plus knots, so be sure you settle ahead of time as to what they want when they ask for "full." They generally are thinking about ahead standard, or fifteen knots. Orders to the helm may not be familiar to you, but these can be interpreted fairly easily.

To avoid confusion, especially in something as important as conning orders and ship characteristics, have handy a template of the ship, clearly illustrating major dimensions, such as length, draft, masthead height, number of shafts, and a general sense of the ship's underwater form. Include basic features, such as your hull-mounted sonar, and what it draws. Ideally, these dimensions should be noted in both feet and meters. Additionally, your engine bell schedule, clearly denoting standard speeds and associated shaft revolutions per minute, is helpful as a quick graphic summarizing your propulsion plant's capabilities. These elements, combined on a portable photo-engraved placard, for example, will go a long way in conveying your ship's characteristics in one glance—cutting through language barriers and any misperceptions the pilot may have about your ship.

PRATIQUE

Pratique is a French word meaning "the privilege of going ashore." The port health officer may board you either with the pilot or shortly after you are berthed. Remember that you are quarantined until they declare otherwise. U.S. Navy ships can request, and often receive, "free pratique," and this is usually arranged prior to arrival via the logistics request process.

Navy Regulations requires that you comply with all quarantine regulations for your port and that you cooperate with the local health authorities and give them all health information available subject to the requirements of military security. As international coordination continues to build in an effort to prevent the rise of pandemics, understand your part in that process as a sovereign vessel representing the United States. Quarantine will remain in effect, as far as you are concerned, as long as you have doubt as to the sanitary regulations or health conditions of the port—and, from the health officer's point of view, if you have a quarantinable disease aboard or if you came from a port or area under quarantine. You must not conceal such conditions. Assuming that none of these problems exists, you will be granted pratique.

If, during your stay in port, a quarantinable condition arises aboard ship, you must hoist an appropriate signal to notify port authorities and the chain of command.

BOARDING OFFICER'S CALL

A boarding officer will call on you at the first opportunity. Occasionally he or she will board with the pilot or by separate boat as you are proceeding up the channel, but most frequently just after you anchor or moor. In some ports, he will have to wait until after pratique is granted. If there is another U.S. ship in port senior to you, a boarding officer should still be sent to you with information and instructions. If you are senior, the other ship should send a boarding officer to you to ask when it would be convenient to turn over the SOPA files and duties and for the commanding officer to call.

The more likely possibility is that you will be the lone U.S. ship in port. If so, the boarding call will come from at least one of several authorities. If there is a U.S. naval attaché ashore, he will usually call or send someone from his office. If there is no such naval presence, the consul or a representative will call. If there is a naval command of the host country, either ashore or afloat, it will usually send a representative. The mayor or a representative may call.

In any event, there will be one or more persons who will welcome you and your ship and from whom you can obtain information necessary for the implementation of your responsibilities as SOPA or for your own ship if you are alone.

Relations with U.S. Governmental Officials Ashore

Early in your port visit, and on the occasion of your boarding call, you will make contact with U.S. governmental officials ashore. The exact organization and size of the U.S. mission will depend on the rank of its head. If the port is the capital of its country, the mission will be headed by an ambassador. This official is appointed by the president and is his or her personal representative to the head of state. If the port is not the capital, the mission will be called a consular office and will be headed by a consul. If the city is large, this individual will be a skilled and seasoned member of the U.S. Foreign Service. If the port is small, the mission will be headed by a consular agent appointed by the secretary of state. The consular agent will usually be a local business professional, not necessarily a U.S. citizen, whose primary duties will involve administration of shipping affairs.

Your duties as SOPA will probably require that you visit the mission frequently. A short description of the people you will meet will help you to seek the right persons to solve your problem. The ambassador, if you are involved with one, may be a political appointee with no previous diplomatic experience. He or she will, however, be a person of individual achievement and probably will be knowledgeable and communicative.

If not a political appointee, the ambassador will be a career member of the Foreign Service. The Foreign Service is the sixth federal service and is a professional corps of men and women specially selected and trained to carry out the foreign policy of our nation in day-to-day relations with other countries. There are approximately eight thousand members serving abroad in three hundred posts in one hundred countries. Foreign Service officers have a basic designation known as their "class," which establishes seniority for internal purposes. They also hold a title, which is their assignment. You will also encounter Foreign Service staff officers and employees who are clerks or staff assistants as well as other administrative personnel. Local nationals will be employed in supporting roles as well.

You will enjoy your relations with the embassy or mission personnel. They will be anxious to help and will in turn ask for your help in furthering the good image of the United States in the port. This can be pursued with community relations projects, arranging ship tours, and through personal interaction with local governmental and business people. Your point of contact in the consular office or embassy and their collective country team will be instrumental in arranging these events, meetings, and calls.

The Statesmen's Yearbook, published annually by St. Martin's Press, is a compendium of information about foreign countries, including descriptions of each, starting with the name of our ambassador and other U.S. governmental officials in that country, and covering the culture, religions, economy, demography, and other aspects. A study of the write-up for each country before you visit will be of great help.

Duties as SOPA

Once you have anchored or moored your ship and have received pratique, customs clearance, and your boarding call, you must get on with your duties as SOPA. These are covered in *Navy Regulations*. You might wish that all you had to do was look out for the safety of your own crew and ship, arrange liberty, and look forward to a pleasant visit, but this is only the beginning. As SOPA, you are the representative of your country and your Navy in that port, and you can be called upon to execute a great many duties.

SECURITY

Your first duty is to look out for the *safety of your ship*. Ensure that you have a safe mooring, access to weather reports, an assigned typhoon or hurricane mooring if applicable, a method of recalling your crew, and adequate internal security, including sentries, watches, locked limited-access doors, and if anchored out, proper boat landing and securing facilities. Think through the details of your force protection plan rigorously, asking yourself whether you've foreseen all potential contingencies. Ensuring a secure berth requires detailed advanced planning, including coordination with host nation officials. With this done, you can turn to your next priority, liberty arrangements.

LEAVE AND LIBERTY

Article 0921 of *Navy Regulations* requires you as SOPA to regulate leave and liberty in conformance with any orders you may have, such as from a fleet commander or a local U.S. military authority. If you have no specific guidance or authority, issue your own, having due regard to information obtained from local officials as to vice and dangerous areas and local curfews.

SHORE PATROL

With the privilege of leave and liberty goes the requirement to establish a shore patrol. Article 0922 of *Navy Regulations* requires that a shore patrol be established whenever liberty is granted to a considerable number of persons, except in an area that can absorb them without danger of disturbance or disorder. The purpose of a patrol of officers, petty officers, and noncommissioned officers, if Marines are embarked, is to maintain order and to suppress unseemly conduct. An additional, though not specifically stated, reason is to provide for the safety of your crew ashore. This article goes on to require that the senior shore patrol officer communicate with the chief of police or local officials and make such arrangements as may be practicable to aid the patrol in carrying out its duties. Such duties would include providing assistance to your crew in their relations with police and local courts, including release to your custody.

With regard to the first requirement, which infers a patrol only if the liberty area cannot absorb your crew, it is wise to establish a small patrol even though your ship is small and the port is big. Any sailor getting into trouble usually ends up at the police station, and it is good to have a representative there even though no street patrols are thought necessary.

You must, of course, obtain permission from local authorities to land the patrol, and if permission is denied, you must restrict the size of liberty parties accordingly. Overseas, the patrol must not be armed, but some countries will permit them to carry nightsticks. In addition to standardized training for all those assigned to shore patrol, a reminder to warn the members of the patrol that they may not indulge in intoxicants at any time when assigned these duties is helpful.

PROVISIONS AND SUPPLIES

Presumably, your supply officer will be off attempting to obtain fresh provisions and stock for your ship's store consistent with supply chain guidance. The officer should check first with the U.S. military force present or with the embassy or consulate to see if any contracts exist for this purpose. If they do, paperwork and time spent are very much reduced, and they can get on with ordering. If not, the supply officer will have to go through the time-consuming process of soliciting bids, awarding contracts, and then placing orders. Even these longer processes will be worthwhile, though, for the fresh produce will be welcome, and the "exotic" ship's store stock can be sold at sea to produce added profits for recreation funds.

CALLS

All of these above-mentioned responsibilities sound complicated, but they actually proceed together and do not take too much of your time. Your personal occupation this first day will be to find out from the boarding officer which calls you should make and to get on with arranging them. Since we have assumed that there are no other U.S. ships present, your attention will be ashore first. Article 0911, *Navy Regulations*, requires that the SOPA preserve close relations with the diplomatic and consular representative of the United States. You must consider requests, recommendations, and other communications from such individuals, although the final responsibility for your acts as SOPA is yours. You should call on the ambassador, if there is one, or the consul at the earliest opportunity.

Article 0912, *Navy Regulations*, requires that you communicate with foreign civil, diplomatic, and consular officials through the local U.S. diplomatic consular representatives. You are not *required* to communicate or call, but it will be helpful if you have time to do so.

You should make arrangements through the embassy or consulate to call upon senior governmental officials of the host country.

If there are host country military forces present ashore, ask the advice of the embassy or consulate regarding calling.

If there are host country naval forces afloat, arrange a call on their SOPA. They will probably already have sent a calling officer to see you with the boarding officer.

If there are other foreign naval vessels present, use your own judgment about calling. Allied commanding officers will probably receive you enthusiastically. When you ask by message to call, you may not always receive an answer, but in many cases you will receive a warm invitation. If you are invited, by all means go; you will learn a lot.

You and your officers may receive invitations to use military messes and civilian clubs ashore. If so, arrange to have one or more of your wardroom officers call at the messes and clubs and leave cards. A letter of thanks after departure is also in order. Wardroom-to-wardroom calls are common in the British, Canadian, and Australian navies. This is a fine custom, and your officers will enjoy it. They can expect a generous welcome, and any time after noon, often one with alcohol. A word to your officers on what to expect would be wise. Commonwealth officers are long conditioned to handling liquor on board ship. Their mess will have an open bar, but if observed carefully, it will be noted that even though they may drink *often*, they do not drink *much* at a time. They will always be ready for duty. American guests, however, may sometimes be plied with strong drinks in the spirit of hospitality. Your young officers will do well to follow their hosts' example. Don't drink *too much* and stick to the soft stuff if possible.

Finally, read articles 1240 through 1249 of *Navy Regulations*. These cover in great detail your responsibilities regarding calls in a foreign port and fill in some of the details omitted in the preceding summary of calls.

HONORS AND CEREMONIES

Honors and ceremonies can be particularly important to foreign navies. We often tend to play them down, under the theory that sheer power is the most important ingredient of any navy. Many foreign navies value the careful and exact carrying out of ceremonies and honors, which they look upon as indicators of a respectable navy. We can perform in this area too, and we should. *Navy Regulations*, chapter 10, sets forth the honors and ceremonies required in foreign ports. Careful study of them and instruction of your quarterdeck crew, boat crews, officers of the deck, and signal gang can ensure that your ship excels.

By now, your initial duties will have been completed, and your calls will be well on their way. You will also have taken care of all the miscellaneous duties of the SOPA. Try to get ashore for a little personal recreation and sightseeing before the rest of the social routine closes in on you. You will soon be receiving return calls and accepting invitations ashore. These will lead in turn to the possibility of scheduling lunches aboard to return hospitality. Some ships provide guided tours and a reception aboard the last day before leaving port as a convenient way for all hands to return favors.

This is an appropriate time to suggest that you research the *Supply Manual* and appropriate type and fleet directives to find out what source of funds you have to help defray entertainment costs. A little research and a few message requests will "pay off."

There are many other occasional but important duties that you will fall heir to as SOPA. If there are other ships present, you will be responsible for the coordination of all the foregoing actions for all ships. You

Fig. 9-13. A ship is evaluated, particularly in foreign ports, by the smartness of its quarterdeck, the manner in which it renders honors, and its conduct of official ceremonies. Here, USS *America* prepares to enter Sasebo as its new homeport.

must also take command if concerted action is necessary for mutual defense or for safety against weather, and, in any case, in overseeing the smart execution of your force protection plans.

USING MILITARY FORCE

With regard to the use of military force within the territorial waters of another nation, articles 0914, 0915, and 0916 of *Navy Regulations* are very specific. When injury to U.S. citizens is committed or threatened in violation of a treaty or international law, the SOPA must consult with diplomatic or consular representatives if possible and shall take such action as is demanded by the gravity of the situation. In time of peace, action by U.S. Navy personnel against any other nation, or against anyone within the territories thereof, either an actual use of force or a threat to use force, is illegal unless as an act of self-defense. You are required to exercise sound judgment and to assert this right only as a last resort.

LANDING FORCES FOR EXERCISE

In a more peaceful vein, you may not, in a foreign country, land a force for exercise, target practice, or funeral escort unless permission has been granted. You may not land a force to capture deserters. You may not conduct target practice with guns, torpedoes, rockets, or missiles at any point where these can enter territorial waters.

MEDICAL AND DENTAL ASSISTANCE

With regard to rendering assistance, you are required by article 0924 to render medical and dental assistance to persons not in the naval service when such aid is necessary and demanded by the laws of humanity or the principle of international courtesy.

MARRIAGE ABROAD

While you are attempting to relax, you may find the interlude broken by some of your other SOPA duties. One of them might occur when one of your officers or sailors conducts a romantic campaign ashore and comes to you asking to be married. Fleet regulations will cover the subject; refer first to them. If your ship is big enough to have a legal officer, you are in clover. If not, you or one of your officers will have to visit the embassy or consulate to determine the local laws and to help your sailor fill out the necessary forms. Hopefully ardor will cool when they see the paperwork difficulties and delays, or, if not, they will take charge and get them done without involving too much of your time.

MARRIAGE ABOARD SHIP

If still in the ball game, your sailor may ask to be married aboard ship. This matter is regulated by article 0716, *Navy Regulations*. This article is somewhat peculiarly phrased. It starts out by flatly prohibiting you from performing marriage aboard ship. Next, in a rather awkward and negative way, it states that you may not *permit* a marriage to be performed aboard ship when outside the territory of the United States, but it then gives certain exceptions. The ceremony must be in accordance with the local laws and the laws of the state, territory, or district in which both parties are domiciled and must take place only in the presence of a diplomatic or consular official of the United States who has consented to make the certificate and returns required by the consular regulations. From the tenor of the article, it can be assumed that the Secretary of the Navy takes a negative view of marriage performed aboard ship. Be very sure you want to do so before going through the bureaucratic necessities involved. Your sailor will probably be just as happy being married ashore.

In summary, you as commanding officer *cannot* yourself conduct a marriage ceremony aboard ship. A chaplain, if you have one or can borrow one, *can* perform a marriage ceremony aboard if you comply with article 0844.

SOPA FILES

The boarding officer, if a U.S. naval or consular person, will probably have delivered to you the SOPA file of previous visitors. It will be of help to you. Update it and return it to the same person or to the senior U.S. commanding officer remaining in port after you depart.

PEOPLE-TO-PEOPLE PROGRAMS

Fleet commanders require ships to conduct people-to-people and community relations programs. You may also want to conduct one independently. You will find that your crew will be responsive and even enthusiastic if it is suggested that they visit orphans ashore or invite them aboard ship, donate food to the poor, or take other, more innovative action. Your crew will do best if they are allowed to initiate the kind and amount of response; be sure that you check any proposed actions with embassy or consular officials ashore before carrying it out. Your actions should be consistent with larger government efforts, and you will avoid possible embarrassment to both of you if there is a political situation ashore that only the embassy or consular staff is aware of.

Hopefully, as part of your pre-overseas movement preparation, you will have been told about the various programs such as Project Handclasp, which provides materials and gifts such as toys, food, and supplies for less fortunate foreign nationals. The best material you can have, however, is the enthusiasm and friendliness of the American bluejacket.

Fig. 9-14. Community relations are an important part of the captain's job. They help build confidence in and admiration of the entire Navy—not just your own ship. Here, the commanding officer of USS *Ashland* interacts with visitors from Malaysia.

CONDUCT OF OFFICERS AND CREW

Navy Regulations requires you to instruct your enlisted personnel as to their conduct ashore. They will clearly stand out from the locals when in their uniforms and even in their civilian clothes, and they will bear the brunt of any criticism for misconduct ashore. It is especially important, and many times overlooked, to instruct your junior officers as well. In fact, because of their neat haircuts, clean clothes, and generally excellent appearance, they will be recognized in every port. Counsel them to use the utmost discretion, particularly in public places, and to conduct themselves as they would in their own hometowns. Foreign ports offer every kind of vice known to man. Your officers must lead the way in setting a good example in practicing restraint, if not abstinence.

Article 0917, *Navy Regulations*, enjoins you to uphold the prestige of the United States. Impress upon your officers and crew, when in foreign ports, that it is their duty to avoid all possible causes of offense to the inhabitants; that due deference must be shown by them to local laws and customs, ceremonies, and regulations; that moderation and courtesy

Fig. 9-15. American bluejackets are our country's best ambassadors. Prepare them to carry out this role by thorough briefings on the culture and current events of the area to be visited. Here, two sailors talk with Australia's prime minister.

should be displayed in all dealings with foreigners; and that a feeling of goodwill and mutual respect should be cultivated. Your crew will represent our country well if you have instructed them.

SHIP'S BOATS

Article 0855, *Navy Regulations*, states that ship's boats shall be regarded as part of their ship in all matters concerning the rights, privileges, and comity of nations. In ports where war, insurrection, or armed conflict exists or threatens, you must have an appropriate and competent person in charge of each boat and take steps to make the nationality of your boats evident at all times. This translates into flying a flag whenever the boat is away from the ship and having a boat officer or competent petty officer assigned. On some occasions, the coxswain, if rated and competent in your eyes, may be enough. A deck chief petty officer is appropriate in most circumstances, particularly in small ships with few officers. The rank or rate of your boat officers is purely a matter of your judgment of their competence and the seriousness of the situation ashore and afloat.

ADMIRALTY CLAIMS AND REPORTS

If a U.S. naval or merchant vessel collides with or otherwise damages a foreign vessel or pier in the port where you are SOPA, you will have certain responsibilities with regard to processing claims against the United States and rendering consequent reports. Article 0926, *Navy Regulations*, states that you shall process claims in accordance with the procedures set forth in the *Manual of the Judge Advocate General*. If you have a legal officer assigned, you will be fortunate. If not, you seek legal assistance from your chain of command. You have limited authority to institute legal proceedings against a foreign vessel in a collision case. However, the manual points out that the matter is within the primary cognizance of the Department of Justice. In view of your limited legal knowledge and experience and short time in port, you will do well to heed this advice and leave it to the professionals.

RELATIONS BETWEEN THE SOPA AND THE SOP

In a few foreign ports, but in many U.S. ports, you will find U.S. military forces ashore. This brings up the subject of the relations between you, as SOPA, and the senior officer present (SOP) ashore. Article 0901, *Navy Regulations*, states that in a locality within an area prescribed by competent authority the senior officer present shall be the senior line officer of the Navy on active duty eligible for command at sea, who is present and in command of any part of the Department of the Navy, except where both Navy and Marine Corps personnel are present on shore and the Marine Corps officer is senior. In such cases the officer of the Marine Corps shall be the senior officer present ashore.

Article 0903 then gives the senior officer present the authority to assume command and to direct the efforts of all persons in the Navy Department present, when, in his or her judgment, the exercise of authority is necessary. The authority must be exercised in a manner consistent with the full operational command vested in the commanders of unified or specified commands.

The import of these articles is that you must maintain close liaison with the SOP ashore. Commanding officers afloat tend to continue the independence they exercised at sea when they are in port. While you are still independent in certain matters, you must recognize the limitations upon you. Article 0930 specifically states that you must refer all matters affecting the afloat units under you to the senior officer present, either Navy or Marine Corps, ashore. This officer will not, however, expect literal interpretation of the requirement.

In the event that you as SOPA are senior to the SOP ashore, you must take other considerations into account. Article 0930 describes your general duties and states that as the common superior of all commanders of all naval units in that locality, except such units as may be assigned to shore units by competent authority, you are responsible for matters that collectively affect these commands. You are charged not to concern yourself with administrative matters within other commands, except to the extent necessary to secure uniformity and coordination of effort. You will assume command of all units of the operating forces of the Navy present in case of emergency or enemy attack.

Article 0932 then elaborates on relations with commanders ashore on the level of the commandant of a naval district. You are not likely to be senior to such a commander and will not be concerned with this problem.

POWERS OF CONSUL

If you are in a foreign port small enough not to have a consul, you may be required to exercise powers of consul. Article 0934, *Navy Regulations*, states that when upon the high seas, or in any foreign port where there is no resident consul of the United States, the SOPA has the authority to exercise all powers of consul in relation to mariners of the United States.

Article 1244 gives you the authority to issue rations to destitute sailors and airmen. The supply officer making such issue shall do so pursuant to an order in writing from you and shall procure receipts for such supplies in accordance with *Naval Supply Systems Command* references. Article 0848 permits you to receive distressed sailors on board for rations and passage to the United States provided they agree to abide by *Navy Regulations*. You may also accept merchant seaman prisoners for transport provided that the witnesses against them are also received or adequate means are adopted to ensure the presence of such witnesses at the place where the prisoners are to be detained. Article 0926 states that you may not authorize repairs to a merchant vessel in collision with a Navy ship unless the exigency of war or national defense so requires. You may, however, authorize or perform repairs to save lives or prevent sinking. If you do so, you must submit a report of repairs, including labor and material costs, and a certification as to why repairs were undertaken. In these unique cases, your chain of command will be available—via email if necessary—to provide advice and guidance.

PROTECTION OF COMMERCE

Today, when the mission of the Navy seems to all of us to be the maintenance of the national security of our country, we tend to forget that historically the Navy was created to protect commerce. Article 0920 will remind you that you are required, while acting in conformity with international law and treaty obligations, to protect, insofar as it lies within your power, all commercial craft of the United States and to advance the commercial interests of your country. This has particular relevance today as we see the rise of piracy in certain areas around the world, such as the waters off eastern Africa and in the Strait of Malacca.

INTERNATIONAL LAW AND TREATIES

Article 1125 requires that in your relations with foreign nations, and with governments and agents thereof, you shall conform to international law and to the precedents established by the United States in such relations. You are separately enjoined to report to higher authority any violation of international law or treaty both by U.S. citizens and by foreign nationals and their governments. Your reports in these matters should go to the fleet commander and the Chief of Naval Operations and, as a matter of courtesy, should also be reported to the local ambassador or consul via the U.S. defense or naval attaché as appropriate.

NWP 1-14, *Law of Naval Warfare*, presents and amplifies international law as related to naval warfare and legal restrictions on methods and weapons. It provides guidance on the legal status of ships, aircraft, and personnel engaged in naval warfare and the actions permitted against them under international law. The legal divisions of the sea and air are described, as are areas in which belligerent naval operations are permitted and the restrictions on belligerents in neutral jurisdiction. Those treaties that are the principal sources of the laws of naval warfare and the U.S. armed forces code of conduct are presented in appendices to this publication.

FOREIGN CIVIL JURISDICTION

The U.S. Senate, in giving its advice and consent to the North Atlantic Treaty Organization (NATO) Status of Forces Agreement, resolved that safeguards would be provided to protect persons subject to U.S. military jurisdiction who are to be tried by foreign authorities. In implementing the resolution, the Department of Defense directed that in each unified command, the commander would designate within each member country a "commanding officer" to ensure that such safeguards are provided. Both major fleet commanders also have issued instructions on this subject. This practice was first started to cover the needs of NATO members but has now been enlarged to extend the same protection to all U.S. personnel serving abroad, as far as is possible.

Local SOPA regulations should normally cover the basic procedures for dealing with a foreign jurisdictional problem, but in small ports, where such regulations may be sketchy, you will have to take steps on your own. You should first require your officers and those of any other U.S. ship in port to report to you instances where personnel have become subject to foreign jurisdiction. When this occurs, you should request a waiver of criminal jurisdiction and release of the person involved. Do so through the standing shore patrol organization, if one exists, or through your own patrol. Notify your next senior in command and other seniors as high as necessary to reach one who has authority to convene a general court-martial. Make sure a U.S. observer attends the trial. This should be one of your own officers if you are still in port. Otherwise, ask the consul to observe and report to you. You should advise and assist the person concerned, helping them to retain counsel, paying the trial expenses, and paying bail. You may pay for these contingencies. The act of July 24, 1956 (10 U.S. Code 1037), authorizes the Secretary of the Navy to employ counsel and pay counsel fees, court costs, bail, and other expenses required for representation before foreign tribunals and agencies of any person subject to the Uniform Code of Military Justice. In all cases, message reports up through the chain of command are required, with the judge advocate general an information addressee.

U.S. CIVIL JURISDICTION

Article 0822, *Navy Regulations*, prohibits you from delivering personnel serving under you to U.S. civil authorities except as provided by the *Manual of the Judge Advocate General*. Study it carefully and abide strictly by its provisions. There will probably be a large ship or station nearby where you can seek legal help. This same article authorizes you to permit the serving of a subpoena or other legal process as provided by the *JAGMAN*. There will frequently be occasions where your sailors will be detained by civil authority ashore. Usually you can seek legal help from other naval sources. Make every effort to see that your sailors get help. If possible, one of your officers should appear at the jail and in court.

PUBLIC RELATIONS

Public relations is a major personal responsibility of every commanding officer. We discuss it in this chapter on independent operations because it is most likely to be a challenge when you are operating independently. You will have to deal with both the positive and negative aspects of public relations in any situation that develops, not only with your own ship, but with regard to any situation involving the Navy or the United States. This translates as follows: If something *bad* (negative aspect) happens, you will have to explain what happened and what is being done to correct the situation. Further, if something *good* (positive aspect) *doesn't* happen in the normal course of events, it will be up to you to *create* some positive situation, such as a people-to-people program or a press tour of your ship, so that the U.S. Navy will be seen in a good light.

When you are operating independently, this responsibility will devolve upon you. When you are operating under another commander, it will be your responsibility to assist in the unit's public relations effort and at the same time to carry out your ship's responsibilities even though you are part of a larger unit. In other words, public relations is always a concern for, and a responsibility of, every commanding officer at all times.

Your basic guidance for public relations is the *Department of the Navy Public Affairs Policy and Regulations.* It covers every aspect of public relations, which, by definition, is the total of your relations with the public, including your relations with the press, families, members of Congress, and other groups. *Public information* is a limited part of public relations, involving the giving (or withholding) of information to the various media (television, radio, newspapers, and magazines) and to those parts of the public who either want it or who, in your judgment or the view of the policies and regulations, should be exposed to it. The manual will tell you how to approach the mechanics of public information. Fleet commanders will also have specific guidance, and their staffs are always available for advice.

Your public affairs officer is responsible to you for carrying out the ship's public affairs program. The *SORM* outlines the PAO's duties, responsibilities, and authority. In describing this officer's organizational position, it states that the PAO reports to you via the executive officer. This is certainly organizationally correct for all of the other ship's officers, but for the PAO, there are exceptions. Public affairs officers at all levels, from the White House to the Secretary of the Navy's office to your ship, must have direct and rapid access to the commander. Put your PAO in the prescribed organizational box for normal routine, but if you want to avoid unnecessary problems, make sure that the PAO and the executive officer both understand the PAO's authority to consult with you and to advise you directly. He or she should, of course, fill in the XO at the first opportunity after seeing you. As noted above, your PAO must be well connected with the public affairs personnel in your chain of command.

Now that you understand this, you are ready to consider a few simple rules that will help keep you out of trouble. First, don't be afraid of reporters. They have an important job to do and will ask frank and sometimes probing questions. Treat their questions as opportunities to get across the points that you want to make. You do *not* have to answer every question. You may decline to answer and give a reason for not answering, or you may simply move on to the next question. Second, if you have bad news to present, give it all at once and as fully and frankly as you can. If you don't, and it comes out piecemeal, the effect on the media will be to intensify and prolong the negative atmosphere. Third, if you want to tell

Fig. 9-16. Visitors observing operations at sea will carry away a good impression of the Navy. Here distinguished visitors observe an F-35B Lightning II aircraft preparing to take off from USS *Essex*.

a positive story about your ship's or crew's activities, carefully prepare a release, give it your personal attention, and make sure your public affairs officer gives it to the press and other local media at a time that allows them to meet their deadlines.

This may seem like a lot of detail to devote to this subject, but we want to underline the increasing importance of telling the Navy's story to the public. The public and Congress must know what the Navy does and what it needs and must feel a personal relationship with us. It is your responsibility to produce these results, and you must take part personally and enthusiastically in the public affairs program, afloat, ashore, and overseas.

ASYLUM

Earlier in this chapter, we outlined the requirements for a commanding officer to respond to asylum requests at sea. The same requirements exist in port and are covered completely in article 0940, *Navy Regulations*. Be conversant with them. If an incident occurs, it will happen quickly and without warning. Your actions should be both informed and automatic.

The Rewards of Independent Operation

As your port visit draws to a close, you have, we hope, carried out your social responsibilities, fulfilled your duties as SOPA, looked out for the many and varied interests of your Navy and your country, withdrawn your shore patrol, paid all of your ship's bills, and squeezed in a little personal recreation and sightseeing. Now you are more than ready to get under way. Both independent duty and being SOPA are rewarding experiences, but they are also demanding. Rejoining the fleet or visiting your next port with other, bigger ships will now have a sweeter taste than ever.

As you steam quietly out of the harbor and set course to rejoin, take time to recall the contingencies you either met or avoided on your independent duty. You can return to your unit secure in the knowledge that you have met the same physical challenges mastered by generations of mariners as well as some more modern administrative challenges they never dreamed of. The commanding officer of a naval vessel is truly "a mariner for all seasons" and fits Theodore Roosevelt's description of the individual who dares great things:

> The credit belongs to the man who is actually in the arena, whose face is marred with sweat and dirt and blood; who strives valiantly; who errs and comes short again and again; who knows the great enthusiasms, the great devotions, and spends himself on a worthy cause; who, if he wins, knows the triumph of high achievement; and who, if he fails, at least fails while daring greatly, so that his place will never be with those cold and timid souls who know neither victory nor defeat.

When returning to the fleet, you are part of a larger team. You will have the protection of this team and will face an array of different challenges. Independent duty places upon you, and you alone, the responsibility for meeting challenges with determined, positive action. Accept responsibility; enjoy it. It is what your profession is all about.

10

Forward Operations and Combat Philosophy

> Whosoever can hold the sea has command of everything.
>
> —Themistocles (524–460 BCE)

> War teaches us to lose everything and become what we were not.
>
> —John Milton

Your Role in Our Nation's Armed Forces

Having taken your ship, submarine, or aircraft squadron through training, inspections, and independent operations, it is time to discuss the truly critical importance of how to best integrate your command into the Navy–Marine Corps team and the larger organizations of joint task forces, interagency operations, and coalition warfare. We will conclude with some thoughts on the unique character of combat operations.

Naval Strategy, Planning, and Operations

Every commanding officer in today's world should be familiar with basic naval strategy, operational art, and tactics. While a detailed discussion of all of this is beyond the structure of this volume, a few key points are worth highlighting.

First, you should make an effort to be conversant with the basic Navy and Marine Corps doctrine publications, which provide a great deal of the philosophical underpinning to our nation's approach to sea power.

As background, these include . . . *From the Sea*, the initial document that appeared in 1992 and shifted naval focus to the littoral region following the end of the Cold War; *Forward . . . From the Sea*, which continued the discussion through the mid-1990s; and most recently, articulating our current focus, *A Cooperative Strategy for 21st Century Seapower*, written in 2007 and updated in 2015 in collaboration with the U.S. Marine Corps and Coast Guard. The 2015 update reflects a balance of enduring core capabilities—from building and maintaining maritime security, to sea control, forward presence, and power projection, adding *all domain access* to assure appropriate freedom of action in any domain as our Navy responds to crises and, if necessary, fights and wins our nation's wars. This most recent document is available at http://www.navy.mil/local/maritime/150227-CS21R-Final.pdf. Additionally, two of the most fundamental naval doctrine documents are NDP-1, *Naval Warfare*, most recently published in 2020, and NDP-5, *Naval Planning*, published in 1996. These two relatively concise publications provide an excellent overview of sea power's application to modern warfighting and the basics of planning for naval operations.

Second, remember that the United States is a maritime nation that relies on transoceanic trade. Our primary Navy–Marine Corps missions of all domain access, strategic deterrence, sea control, power projection, and maritime security will always be required given the global nature of U.S. interests. In your dealings with the public, seek to make the point that the sea services (the Navy, Marine Corps, and Coast Guard)—often in conjunction with our friends and allies—all conduct maritime operations in the world's oceans and littorals as part of fundamental U.S. strategy while also supporting international norms. As additional context, the *2018 National Defense Strategy*, noting the increasingly contested competitive advantage of the United States and its armed forces, declared the return of great power competition. In the Indo-Pacific, China's continued rise and its considerable naval expansion and assertive activities and a resurgent Russia's attempt to undermine NATO unity are challenging the global maritime primacy the United States has enjoyed since the Cold War.

Third, the increasingly joint and combined character of all operations is an important component to our approach as a Navy–Marine Corps team. Since the 1986 Goldwater-Nichols legislation, all of the services have sought to work more closely together in meeting the complex demands of national security. You will find that virtually every aspect of your command's operational activity will have a joint component to it, and you should be alert to improve your ship's, submarine's, or squadron's ability to integrate and perform well in joint operations. In preparing for joint operations, you should review the publications discussed below as well as the terms discussed in the glossary following this chapter.

Fourth, you will find that interagency activity is an important and challenging part of your role today. In addition to working with the other services in joint operations, your command will interact with an extraordinarily wide range of interagency actors. A few of the ones you will most frequently work with include the Department of State, the Department of Homeland Security (Coast Guard and the Federal Emergency Management Agency), the Department of Energy, the Central Intelligence Agency (CIA), and the Department of Justice (Drug Enforcement Agency). You may also work with private voluntary organizations and nongovernmental organizations (NGOs). Virtually everything you need to know about interagency activity can be found in an excellent joint doctrine publication, Joint Publication 3-08, *Interagency Coordination during Joint Operations*.

Finally, be aware that there is an increasing emphasis on coalition warfare throughout all forward deployed areas today. Since the end of the Cold War and the collapse of the Soviet bloc, the formerly bipolar character of the global environment has become far more fluid, allowing ad hoc coalitions to form to deal with emerging situations. Prime examples of this include the coalition formed in 1990–91 to defeat Saddam Hussein's attack on Kuwait, post-9/11 operations in Afghanistan that concluded in 2021, and operations in Iraq that continue to this day. The multinational efforts of Combined Task Force 151 off the coast of eastern Africa contribute to maritime security in their daily fight against piracy along vital international trade routes. Additional coalition activities have been conducted throughout the world in a wide variety of locales from Africa to Southeast Asia.

Welcome to the Joint World

Since joint operations are by far the most common form of activity today for your command, we'll provide more detailed instruction for preparing for them. To understand the position that your ship, submarine, or squadron plays in the world of joint operations, you must first comprehend the language associated with it. There are several key publications that should be mastered, including the "bible" of joint operations, *Joint Warfare of the Armed Forces of the United States* (Joint Publication 1) and *Joint Operations* (Joint Publication 3–0). These short, easy-to-read publications are available on the Internet at jcs.mil/doctrine/joint-doctrine -pubs/. We'll review a few key concepts and actors first. They are very basic, but you must hold them in mind as you review the joint world.

Unity of effort requires coordination among government departments and agencies within the executive branch, between the executive and legislative branches, between NGOs, and among nations in any alliance or coalition.

The president of the United States, advised by the National Security Council, is responsible to the American people for national strategic unity of effort.

The secretary of defense is responsible to the president for national military unity of effort for creating, supporting, and employing military capabilities.

The chairman of the Joint Chiefs of Staff (CJCS) functions under the authority, direction, and control of the National Command Authorities (NCA) and transmits communications between the NCA and combatant commanders and oversees activities of combatant commanders as directed by the secretary of defense.

In a foreign country, the *U.S. ambassador* is responsible to the president for directing, coordinating, and supervising all U.S. government elements in the host nation except those under the command of a combatant commander.

Commanders of combatant commands (COCOMs) exercise combatant command (command authority) over assigned forces and are directly responsible to the secretary of defense (although much communication goes through the CJCS) for the preparedness of their commands to perform assigned missions. These are the four-star officers who run the armed forces day to day on operational missions. In accomplishing the missions your command will undertake, it is important to know they often do so by forming *joint task forces* (JTFs) to conduct operations.

All joint force commanders, be they COCOMs or lower echelon commanders, have the authority to organize forces to best accomplish the assigned mission based on their concept of operations. The organization should be sufficiently flexible to meet the planned phases of the contemplated operations and any development that may necessitate a change in plan. A JTF is a joint force that is constituted and so designated by the secretary of defense, a combatant commander, a subordinate unified command commander, or an existing JTF commander. A JTF may be established on a geographical area or functional basis when the mission has a specific limited objective. Of note, your carrier/expeditionary strike group is also a joint task group.

With those basics in mind, you are ready to do some reading in the joint publication library. As you read through these materials, you will be helped by immediate familiarity with terms defined in the glossary following the end of this chapter. In addition to the many joint publications available on the Internet, you should use the Joint Chiefs of Staff Portal site to review the current Navy strategic and tactical publications.

Naval Warfare and the Principles of War

A very fundamental publication that should find a permanent place on your desk is NDP-1, *Naval Warfare*. If there is a "bible" for naval operations at sea, this is it. Derived from the long-standing Naval Warfare Publication 1A, this document lays out, in clear, systematic prose, the reason the U.S. Navy exists. You should be conversant with it for several reasons. First, it is an excellent summary of what naval missions you will be called upon to undertake. Second, as commanding officer, you must be able to articulate to your crew their role in the defense of the United States as part of the Navy–Marine Corps team. Third, when your duties bring you to interact with both the American public and the international world, you must be an articulate, informed spokesperson for our Navy–Marine Corps team.

One key section of this brief and easy-to-read publication includes a discussion of the principles of war, which are summarized here:

Objective: Direct every military operation toward a clearly defined, decisive, and attainable objective.

Mass: Concentrate combat power at the decisive time and place.

Maneuver: Place the enemy in a position of disadvantage through the feasible application of combat power.

Offensive: Seize, retain, and exploit the initiative.

Economy of force: Employ all combat power available in the most effective way possible; allocate minimum essential combat power to secondary efforts.

Unity of command: Ensure unity of effort for every objective under one responsible commander.

Simplicity: Avoid unnecessary complexity in preparing, planning, and conducting military operations.

Surprise: Strike the enemy at a time or place or in a manner for which the enemy is unprepared.

Security: Never permit the enemy to acquire unexpected advantage. Protecting the force increases our combat power.

These principles of war, identified by Clausewitz and validated in battle for centuries, should be considered in every aspect of your command's employment.

Other key sections in *Naval Warfare* include a discussion of the Navy and Marine Corps roles in today's potential combat scenarios. The publication focuses on Navy–Marine Corps involvement in command, control, and surveillance; battlespace dominance; power projection; and force sustainment. These twenty-first-century naval warfare concepts are balanced with a discussion of enduring naval roles in deterrence, forward presence, sealift, and joint operations. Taken together, the material in *Naval Warfare* is well worth sharing with your wardroom as part of general discussions of strategy and tactics.

Planning

In many ways, the key to your command's operational success lies in the effective execution of planning, and you, Captain, are the chief planner for your command. Your operations officer will be a great help to you, but only the CO can bring the right mix of operational experience, depth of tactical knowledge, and hard-won perspective to the table.

An excellent resource for you in your role as planner for your command is NDP-5, *Naval Planning*. It is not a detailed, "nuts and bolts" guide to planning; rather, it is a general overview that will refresh you on the key elements to bear in mind as you sit with your ops boss and other key planners and put together exercises, tactical engagement plans, and your battle orders. In it you will find a discussion of the basic planning principles: relevance, clarity, timeliness, flexibility, participation, economy of resources, security, and coordination. Each and every time you plan an event, whether it is a complex missile shoot, a multiday transit, or a dependents' cruise, you should methodically work through each of the principles of planning. Is the plan clear? Have we most effectively applied resources to the event? Is there flexibility (i.e., a Plan B and a Plan C)?

Naval Planning also includes a discussion of the linkages between our own Navy–Marine Corps team planning and the larger joint world. It discusses the three types of joint operation planning: campaign planning, deliberate planning, and crisis action planning. Reviewing this portion of the publication and keeping these separate processes in mind will be helpful as you work your ship through strike group and joint operations.

Finally, *Naval Planning* also includes a good discussion of the Maritime Tactical Messages used to standardize the general operating instructions—for example, Operational General Matters, Operational Tasks (OPTASKs), and Operational Status messages. All of these are structured in formats compatible with the Joint Operation Planning and Execution System, which drives the joint world. You will also see a discussion of Marine Corps planning, which is important for today's world of combined carrier strike group (CSG), expeditionary strike group (ESG), and amphibious ready group (ARG) activities. The Marines use a six-step planning process as well as a Rapid Response Planning Process, which is also increasingly in use by Navy units.

Study this publication and keep a copy handy in your "desk load." Your ops officer will want to keep equally familiar with NWP 5-01, *Naval Operational Planning*, which contains a more detailed, format-oriented discussion of the same topics. For your level of participation at the command level, though, NDP-5 is perfect.

Interagency Operations

An area of increasing emphasis in which your command may find itself playing a role is interagency operations. Examples of scenarios that will require interagency coordination include humanitarian assistance, natural disaster relief, noncombatant evacuations, migrant control, and many others. The key definition of interagency operations is simply that they are activities requiring the active participation of more than one governmental organization.

Some of the typical partners with whom you may work in the world of interagency operations are the Departments of State, Treasury (Drug Enforcement Agency), Commerce, Energy, Homeland Security (the Coast Guard and the Federal Emergency Management Agency), and Justice (Federal Bureau of Investigation), as well as the CIA. You may also find yourself involved with international actors, including the United Nations, allied civilian and governmental organizations, private voluntary organizations, NGOs, and a host of others. While a discussion of each of these organizations is beyond the scope of this work, there is an excellent two-volume publication that should be on every CO's desk: Joint Publication 3-08, *Interorganizational Cooperation*. In it you will find solid information about each of the organizations you may come in contact with, the command relationships, the organization of a Civil-Military Operations Center (now evolving into "coordination" centers in practice), and many of the other details of conducting joint operations.

In the course of your workups for forward deployment, you will conduct several exercises with interagency challenges embedded in them, typically a noncombatant evacuation operation (NEO) and possibly some type of humanitarian response.

Forward Deployment Preparations

As the commanding officer, you will be deeply involved in every aspect of deployment preparations. One of the most important things you should do is help your command leadership focus on the potential challenges for the deployment.

The first and perhaps most important tool is the predeployment checklist, provided by your type commander or ISIC. It typically starts about 180 days prior to cruise and contains a detailed series of hundreds of specific items your team should accomplish—everything from dental surveys to the loading of storerooms, from preparation of required reports to ensuring that the right communication crypto is on board. Take the time each month to sit down and review progress on the checklist with your XO and department heads.

You should be personally helping your officers, chiefs, and sailors focus on the tactical and operational challenges ahead. Brief each group on your ship about the upcoming deployment at about the ninety-day point, focusing on the fact that your cruise will entail "real world" operations. Discuss likely scenarios for employment of your unit, with frequent references to the front pages of the newspapers. The odds are greater than 50 percent that any given forward deployed Navy unit will participate in a crisis of some kind, and about 70 percent are often involved in either an NEO, United Nations sanctions–related action or the provision of humanitarian assistance and disaster relief. These are dangerous, challenging evolutions involving every person in your crew, which needs to understand how important their cruise is to the national security of the United States. Your personal involvement should be part of that understanding.

Also, ensure that your families are well taken care of in the deployment preparations. You should form a separate "family team" composed of the command master chief, XO, supply officer, chaplain (if assigned), legal officer (collateral duty), and other individuals in the crew or squadron who have an impact on family support activities. They should be working closely with the Navy Family Services Center, the command ombudsman, and the chairperson of the Family Readiness Group. Meet with them frequently and monitor their progress. They should set up predeployment briefings for the families, arrange support mechanisms in the homeport, line up services (such as United Through Reading), ensure that the command ombudsman has a care line installed, and generally work to make sure that problems are headed off in the homeport. Every sailor whose family has a problem while you are forward deployed will sap the combat efficiency of your unit, and anything you can do to stop problems before they happen will make you more capable while forward deployed.

Another important aspect of making a forward deployment is encouraging all the members of your team to think about how they can best improve themselves during the six months. They should have ideas and goals for self-improvement, with appropriate support from the command. Physical fitness is a great place to emphasize self-improvement, and the addition of new workout equipment before cruise is a must. Set up a means for your sailors to work on educational self-improvement as well, through the numerous online opportunities for both professional and general education (bandwidth permitting). Have a strong educational service program in place, and your personal attention to the entire area of crew goal attainment will pay dividends. Self-improvement is one of the most powerful motivators for individuals. Challenge your crew to grow and develop, then provide the opportunities for them to do so. *This investment process forges winning teams.*

Finally, specifically articulate your goals for the command as a whole on the cruise. Naturally, you should start with safety and mission accomplishment. Then think about what innovative tactical concepts your command should best pursue. Set a goal that each department complete a draft tactical memo, for example, or ask each division to complete one major project that will improve the command in some way during the six-month period. And don't neglect the good your command can do in various ports around the world. Painting orphanages may seem a little bit of a cliché, but it is a very real and tangible way for your sailors to light a candle of hope in an occasionally dark and turbulent world. Beyond that, there are numerous "capacity building" initiatives in every area of responsibility (AOR), and fleet commanders will have an array of theater support and cooperation priorities with which a proactive crew can synchronize. All of these initiatives are areas in which your personal involvement will have a positive impact on forward deployment for your command.

Another major aspect of forward deployment preparations is the workup period in the Optimized Fleet Response Plan. Most Navy ships, submarines, and aircraft squadrons currently deploy with either a carrier strike group (named after the CVNs, e.g., *Abraham Lincoln* Strike Group) or an amphibious readiness (or expeditionary strike) group (named after the large-deck amphib, e.g., *Essex* ARG or *America* ESG). Some units do deploy independently; these include the P-8A Poseidon squadrons, submarines conducting special operations, and small groups of ships deploying to the Fifth Fleet in the Arabian Gulf.

As part of your preparations for forward deployment, your command will be part of a designated *integrated* workup sequence, normally orchestrated either by Third Fleet on the West Coast or Second Fleet on the East Coast together with supporting commands, such as Strike Group 15, the Naval Surface and Mine Warfighting Development Center, and the Naval Aviation Warfighting Development Center. This workup sequence will commence when you complete the initial portion of the training cycle described earlier in this volume. When you "chop" from your type commander—after completing your *maintenance* and *basic* phases (COMNAVSURFLANT or COMNAVSURFPAC in the case of surface combatant, for example)—to Third or Second Fleet for *integrated* and *sustainment* phase training, you will begin a series of conferences, training exercises, war games, and at-sea exercises (e.g., COMPTUEX, FLTEX) culminating in a joint task force exercise (JTFEX) that is the "final exam" prior to deployment. This is a very strenuous and challenging exercise undertaken in the operational areas off the U.S. coasts and will put your command through its paces in terms of virtually every type of contingency you can expect to encounter on deployment. Observers and assessors will be stationed in the fleet commander's maritime operations center as well as aboard individual fleet units to observe the activity and to ensure that you are prepared for the rigors of forward deployment.

In terms of preparing for these evolutions, a good approach (to supplement the primary information avenue through your ISIC) is to seek the advice of a ship that has recently completed the predeployment portion of the OFRP workup cycle and can give you a blow-by-blow description of the training packages they experienced. While the thrust of the

OFRP is to maintain a level of *continuous readiness* via *self-assessment* and *tailored training* unique to each ship, this kind of advance information on what to expect for integrated training will be helpful in shaping your preparations. You should build on the information you receive from a recent "graduate" and develop a sort of tactical plan of action and milestones that will ensure that your team is ready to go. Items in the POAM should include combat and operational training scenarios run within your lifelines, time for tactical training for all watchstanders, as well as in-port lectures on the sorts of operations you will encounter (ASW, ASUW, ballistic missile defense, and maritime interdiction operations training, for example). Set up dedicated blocks of time for your wardroom and CPO mess to prepare for the COMPTUEX, FLTEX, and the subsequent JTFEX. Brief the events for which you hold pre-exercise messages, OPTASKs, and LOIs; go over the known portions of the schedule of events; discuss your own battle orders and command philosophy; review shiphandling and formation steaming issues; and conduct safety briefs. Each of your department heads and division officers should be encouraged to perform similar briefings for their individual portions of the command. This is all about thinking through the myriad details of how you will operate and fight when deployed.

Forward Deployed Operations

It is a proud and exciting day in every CO's tour when you forward deploy. You can look forward to six months of dedicated training, operations, port visits, and challenges. Whether or not you face a real-world crisis, you can take pride in the knowledge that your deployment is a significant factor in U.S. national security policy, beginning with the significant deterrent value every U.S. CSG, ESG, and independent deployer makes.

Each of the three forward deployed fleets has a different set of challenges, and as you transit from Third and Second Fleet AORs into the forward world of Sixth, Seventh, and Fifth Fleets, you should be working to ensure that your entire team is well briefed and ready for anything.

A good place to begin is by conducting a daily operations brief. This can be done in the morning, at noon, or after the evening meal. A good approach seems to be around 1800, after everyone has had dinner but before the mid-watchstanders and the late-night fliers need to be turning in. Use a standard format for each brief, perhaps beginning with the weather, position, current intelligence, and upcoming events for the next twenty-four hours. This should be followed by specific briefs on any complex events as well as a "topic of the day" on an individual issue—perhaps an intelligence report on a new type of cruise missile tactic. As CO, you should try to be part of the briefing lineup every evening. Remember, you are the leading tactician and mariner or airman of your command. Get up every night and share a little of your experience with your team.

These daily briefs are an excellent place to provide training and information to your wardroom or ready room and combat team on the challenges in the individual theater. You will find yourself amid continuing crises on the Korean Peninsula and wondering about stability throughout the Seventh Fleet AOR, the challenges of littoral states in the Fifth Fleet AOR, and the complex Arab-Israeli interrelationship and potential dangers in the Sixth Fleet AOR—just to name a few issues. Your team should be up to speed on these and other major potential operational challenges. As broad background, they should have an appreciation for the threat, our allies, and neutrals in each region in which you operate. Their primary focus, though, must always be on maintaining the highest degree of tactical proficiency and how to employ your ship and its combat systems with complete precision.

Keep your team training, training, training throughout deployment. Meet the challenges as they arise, and keep a weather eye on the longer-range issues that might be bubbling in your current AOR.

Liberty Call

One of the most important jobs you will undertake is that of being a good ambassador for your country. The actions of your crew ashore are a direct reflection of the United States, and you must emphasize that to your crew. The days of tolerance for the "ugly American" are long since past, and public intoxication, creating disturbances, or interfering with the good order of a host nation will land your individual sailor in local jail and send your entire ship packing in the blink of an eye. A few keys to having a safe, productive liberty call overseas include the following:

Emphasize the message to the crew. Get on the closed-circuit television the night before every port call, go around to divisions at quarters, get on the 1MC, and do anything you can to get the word out that only good citizens are going ashore.

Use the liberty risk program. When you identify someone who is a potential problem, don't let him or her ashore. The forward fleet commanders all authorize a liberty risk program, which gives you the authority (and the obligation) to completely curtail or partially restrict the liberty of anyone you suspect will not be a good ambassador for the United States.

Offer good alternatives to the bars. Task your command master chief, chaplain, and welfare and recreation team to come up with athletics, picnics, tours, and other alternatives to "hitting the bars." Give your sailors good options, and in most cases, they will make good choices.

Be consistent in the treatment of any and all violators. This is particularly necessary in the case of an officer or chief who gets out of line, as the whole crew will be watching for equity in their treatment.

Keep the chain of command informed. The absolute worst liberty incident is the one the Sixth Fleet commander first hears about from someone other than you. Don't think you can hide a problem or incident that involves local police. Tell what happened, what you did to resolve the incident, and what you have done to make sure it doesn't happen again.

Televise the port briefs. Whenever you arrive in a foreign port, you will be greeted by a group of officials, including representatives from the senior navy people in the area, the U.S. embassy, and local officials. Have the XO quickly put together a fact-filled brief and present it to the crew before anyone leaves the ship.

Give everyone who goes ashore a "liberty safety card." This card should include the ship's phone number and location (in both English and the local language). Also insist that each person take a simple map of the area around the ship; these can be photocopied and handed out.

Insist on the buddy system. No one should go on liberty alone, ever.

Hold your chiefs accountable for their sailors' plans. Every CPO should have a clear idea of what his or her division is doing on liberty and be able to move people into more productive activities.

Avoid mass punishment. It doesn't work. On some few occasions overseas, commanders may deem it necessary to temporarily suspend ship-wide liberty to reinforce the imperative of crew-wide accountability for each other; this is different from mass punishment.

Does all of this sound a little threatening? It shouldn't. Almost all of your people want to go ashore, do a little shopping, find Wi-Fi, and have dinner and a couple of beers before returning to the ship. Your job is to facilitate that program, perhaps with a tour and a ship's picnic thrown in.

And it should go without saying: as the commanding officer, your behavior ashore must be above reproach, as must that of every leader in your command. Focus on this, and you probably won't have a problem to begin with. Enjoy your liberty call!

The Captain's Duties Ashore

One of the most interesting aspects of foreign port visits is your own participation in formal calls. These are normally arranged by the local navy representative, and they may range from no calls, as perhaps in a frequently visited port, such as Naples, to many, many calls in a high-visibility port, such as Cannes on the Fourth of July. If you are going on calls, it is wise to ask about the custom of exchanging gifts; these can range from a ship's ballcap or lighter to a bottle of Kentucky bourbon or California wine. Another nice touch is a framed photograph of the ship, a plaque, or an illustrated book from your homeport or region. Be prepared; think about this before you deploy, and you won't be embarrassed.

If you are in a port in which it is appropriate, you will likely obtain a rental car for official business. Be certain, however, that you are fully aware of the conditions for its appropriate use. In this day of careful scrutiny for ethics, you should check with a Navy judge advocate general in your chain of command if you have any questions or uncertainties concerning this issue.

Combat Philosophy

This portion of this book is the most important part of our discussion on the art of command at sea. In modern times, we are prone to think that a naval vessel is built and manned for a variety of reasons, ranging from protection and promotion of commerce to carrying out "presence" visits. All of these peacetime occupations are important, but they sometimes obscure the fact that navies exist primarily to protect national security. Even this description of the Navy's mission is not clear, for the phrase "protect national security" is often perceived as a euphemism. The plain, brutally frank truth is that naval vessels exist to *fight*. We must never forget this, even though we must always be aware of the other functions and responsibilities we are called upon to carry out.

EFFECTIVENESS FOR SERVICE

Effectiveness for Service is the title of article 0827, *Navy Regulations*, which states that you shall exert every effort to maintain your command in a state of maximum effectiveness for war or other service consistent with the degree of readiness prescribed by higher authority. Effectiveness for service is directly related to the state of personnel and material readiness.

Article 0851, Action with the Enemy, is equally low-key. Its first paragraph requires you to communicate to your officers information that might be of value to them should they succeed to command. The next paragraph then gets to the point: it requires you to engage the enemy to the best of your ability during action and forbids you, without permission, to break off action to assist a disabled ship or to take possession of a captured one.

These are the only words of advice to you in all of *Navy Regulations* regarding your conduct in battle. We can only assume, from the simplicity of the words and the restraint of the rhetoric, that this is deliberate and that this language must be fleshed out with advice handed down over decades by naval commanders and distilled from the naval tradition of centuries.

U.S. NAVY COMBAT TRADITION

The foregoing is a reasonable assumption and is certainly not contradicted by any written information or directives. Therefore, let us examine the U.S. Navy traditions of the past and recent additions to them during more modern times, from World War I to the Gulf War and beyond. These traditions are *use of the initiative, boldness and daring, tenacity, courage, aggressiveness, ingenuity,* and *the ability of our young junior officers and enlisted personnel to carry on and display their own initiative when their seniors are dead or incapacitated.* You, as a commanding officer, may add to these traditions or originate others, but you must never subtract from them.

The Athenians most prized in their naval officers and men high enthusiasm or spirit, courage, the ability to innovate or solve problems, and the willingness to work long and hard. Our own prized characteristics are, therefore, not new. We have also learned from the British, who have had centuries of a sound naval tradition. The qualities they prized most were courage, aggressiveness, tenacity, and coolness under fire.

Our own American traditions are outstanding. They have produced the world's finest naval officers, from John Paul Jones to Chester Nimitz. In between came such leaders as David Glasgow Farragut, of whom Admiral Mahan wrote,

> It is in the strength of purpose, in the power of rapid decision, of instant action, and if need be, of strenuous endurance through a period of danger or of responsibility, when the terrifying alternatives of war are vibrating in the balance, that the power of a great captain mainly lies. It is in the courage to apply knowledge under conditions of exceptional danger; not merely to see the true direction for effort to take, but to dare to follow it, accepting all the risks and all the chances inseparable from war, facing all that defeat means in order to secure victory if it may be had. It was upon those inborn moral qualities that reposed the conduct which led Farragut to fame. He had a clear eye for the true key of a military situation, a quick and accurate perception of the right thing to do at a critical moment, a firm grasp upon the leading principles of war; but he might have had all these and yet miserably failed. He was a man of most determined will and character, ready to tread down or fight through any obstacles which stood in the path he sought to follow.

Farragut's other characteristics are well known. He sought responsibility where others shunned it. Above all, he *liked* being a naval officer, as witnessed by his oft-quoted statement, "I have as much pleasure in running into port in a gale of wind as ever a boy did in a feat of skill."

We can learn from those nations that were our predecessors upon the sea, and we can benefit from studying and observing various countries and their cultures and traditions, but in doing so, we must maintain our own established, successful, and honored traditions.

USE OF THE INITIATIVE

Probably the most distinctively American naval tradition is the use of the initiative. There is a fine line of distinction between the use of the initiative and the display of boldness, daring, and aggressiveness. Fortunately, the enemy won't know the difference and will be at a disadvantage if you display any or all of these characteristics.

A dictionary definition states that *initiative* means to be the "first mover" and to have the ability for original conception and independent action. A commanding officer who takes the initiative is usually also being bold and daring, but not necessarily so. In any event, don't be too concerned about the exact description of what you are about to do. Just do it *first*. Taking the initiative should be a principal part of your combat philosophy.

BOLDNESS AND DARING

Charles Lindbergh had a fine feeling for boldness and daring. He said, "What kind of man would live where there is no daring? And is life so dear that we should blame men for dying in adventure? Is there a better way to die?" Still, the ideal is to be bold and daring and *not* to die. Even more ideal is to make sure the *enemy* dies and that *you* survive.

John Paul Jones epitomized boldness and daring. He sailed in fast ships and in harm's way and would not tolerate any captain or subordinate who was not equally bold. Boldness was his legacy to those who would follow in his footsteps.

Modern American naval officers have been equally daring. In the opening weeks of World War II, when the Japanese were overrunning the Philippines and landing large forces in Lingayen Gulf, Lieutenant

Commander Wreford "Moon" Chapple took his submarine, the *S-38*, into the gulf via a poorly charted and shallow side channel and for more than twenty-four hours did his best to attack Japanese ships. He was harassed and attacked repeatedly by Japanese escorts and was discouraged by the repeated failure of the defective torpedoes he was firing, but he managed to sink and damage some shipping and to slow the landing process markedly. His boldness was inspiring to those who were doing their best to hold the Philippines against overpowering odds.

Later, his contemporaries of Destroyer Squadron 29 conducted an equally daring attack on another Japanese landing operation, at Macassar in the Dutch East Indies. Four of these decrepit old ships steamed at twenty-seven knots in the dark of night through a cruiser and destroyer screen into the middle of the Japanese landing area and sank five Japanese landing transports and escorts with torpedo and gunfire. They made repeated passes at high speed until all torpedoes were expended and then retired under cover of darkness and their own gunfire without damage. This was the first such surface action for the U.S. Navy since the Spanish-American War.

Only boldness and daring made these efforts successful. You will do well to give those characteristics a prominent place in your combat philosophy. They are distinctively American in character.

TENACITY

Tenacity has been a characteristic of our Navy for years. Farragut's order to "Damn the torpedoes; full speed ahead" is a classic example of refusing to fear what *might be*. Don't be put off by small failures; instead, drive *tenaciously* forward. You, as commanding officer, will do well to emulate Admiral Farragut. Washington Irving once said, "Great minds have purpose; others have wishes. Little minds are tamed by misfortune; great minds rise above them."

Lest you think tenacity is an old-fashioned quality, remember the advice given in World War II by Commander "Mush" Morton, a superb submarine commanding officer, to Lieutenant Commander Richard O'Kane, who would go on to become an equally famed CO: "*Tenacity*, Dick, you've got to stick with the bastard until he's on the bottom." O'Kane did so, repeatedly.

In World War II, other naval officers continued this tradition of tenacity. Admiral Arleigh Burke's operations repeatedly demonstrated this characteristic. He believed in hitting the enemy hard and fast, delivering repeated blows until the enemy's will to resist collapsed. Admiral William Halsey was as tenacious as any officer who ever went to sea.

It can be argued that the Japanese were equally tenacious. They were, but it was a tenacity without purpose, almost fatalistic. They repeatedly lost large numbers of men, aircraft, and ships long after they should have known that a particular battle was a losing strategic or tactical situation. Tenacity of this kind, without the ability to change direction or to modify operations to suit changed conditions, is a losing cause. The Americans probed, jabbed, kept moving forward, but changed the direction of thrust and the magnitude of their efforts to take advantage of uncovered weakness and to avoid strong points. This kind of tenacity is one of our traditions.

"I have not yet begun to fight" is not a failure to hear the starting gun, but a stern statement of tenacity of purpose that has become a part, not only of the traditions of the Navy, but of the personal philosophy of combat of every naval officer as well. Preserve and use it.

COURAGE

Courage comes in many varieties, and it has been the mainstay of the combat philosophy of all peoples and services for centuries. It can be wasted, though, as it was in the charge of the Light Brigade at Balaclava, when the cavalry went to certain destruction, knowing that its effort was useless.

American naval officers and sailors have performed many courageous acts in our relatively short history. Unfortunately for history, the most courageous individual acts are seldom recorded and are known only to those who performed them. This is the most superb kind of courage—when one does one's duty in full understanding that no one else will ever know.

There are many kinds of courage, and some in new settings. In Vietnamese and Iraqi prison camps, our prisoners of war demonstrated new kinds of courage when they withstood to the death the torture by their captors.

Physical courage will be commonplace in the next war, given the moral upbringing and characteristics of our fellow citizens. You, as a commanding officer, will find the personal exercise of physical courage easy. The stimulus of command will make you forget your own personal safety. The more difficult assignment for you will be the proper exercise of moral courage. Situations calling for moral courage will not have the stimulus of combat. It will be necessary when you demand top performance from your officers and crew; take steps to correct or punish those who do not perform; make honest reports of your or your ship's failure, should such occur; and you are completely honest in all of your command relations.

Courage, then, must be part of your combat philosophy, expected and required of others, and you must demonstrate this trait automatically as commanding officer.

AGGRESSIVENESS

The aggressive commanding officer is one who wants to win so much that he or she *will* take vigorous action to attain the objective. The key is to determine the right and appropriate action and to pursue it to the utmost, but not to the point of foolhardiness or of being led into an adverse situation, such as an ambush. Normally an aggressive fighter has the advantage and will win unless the defender has had the time to arrange his or her defenses so that attacking becomes a disadvantage.

One key element of aggressiveness is speed of attack. Admiral Arleigh Burke was known for his high-speed attacks. Burke was usually in the middle of the enemy's formation before they had a chance to retaliate. There were only two adjectives in Admiral Burke's lexicon, *good* and *bad*. He held that the difference between a bad officer and a good officer was about ten seconds. Ten seconds of decision-making by a gunnery, torpedo, missile, or conning officer translated into three five-inch salvos, the firing of a torpedo spread by either a surface ship or a submarine, a missile firing, a battery-unmasking turn, or the performance of an evasive maneuver. Ten seconds can mean the enemy's destruction or yours.

The same comparison applies to commanding officers. Be *quickly* aggressive if you want to add surprise and confusion of the enemy to your attack plan. By Admiral Burke's standards, you are a *good* CO if you take advantage of the time given you by a good gunnery, torpedo, missile, or conning officer by making a quick (but correct) decision. Fritter it away with indecision, and you are a *bad* CO who will end up with holes in the ship or a forty-degree list. Speed of decision goes hand in hand with aggressiveness, and aggressiveness has always been one of the hallmarks of our Navy. Make it one of yours.

INGENUITY

Yankee ingenuity produced the fast-sailing schooners and clippers of the eighteenth and nineteenth centuries. Their design and speed were incorporated into the ships of our early Navy. Further ingenuity put speed and endurance into our steam-powered naval vessels and eventually produced the nuclear-powered ship and submarine with both speed and unlimited endurance. Industrial ingenuity gave our Navy superior armor, excellent major-caliber guns and fire control systems, missiles, computers, solid-state electronics, and a host of other improvements. Bluejacket ingenuity kept them operational in peacetime with shortages of money and spare parts and in wartime in spite of damage and lack of repair facilities. The American sailor, officer or enlisted, is without peer in mechanical ingenuity. Fortunately, the same characteristic extends to strategy and tactics. Formations for air defense, combined antisubmarine search-and-attack procedures, amphibious landing techniques, and submarine and aircraft attack tactics are but a few of the ideas pioneered by our Navy.

Our tradition of ingenuity is superb, and you can depend upon this characteristic of our officers and sailors to carry you through many difficult situations. You, as commanding officer, will also be called upon to exercise ingenuity. You will have to improvise tactics, communication plans, personnel reassignments, and emergency repairs of equipment and machinery to meet various contingencies of operations and battle. Ingenuity by a commanding officer can make a superb ship out of a commonplace vessel.

INITIATIVE OF JUNIORS

Our Navy has always excelled in using the initiative of our junior officers and enlisted sailors. Fortunately, this process comes naturally to citizens of the United States, where family and cultural environment generally foster initiative. It is a part of our way of life. By contrast, some other cultures discourage the initiative of juniors, and they suffered accordingly in wartime when seniors were killed or incapacitated. Their juniors were neither trained nor expected to take the initiative, and their ships rapidly lost their efficiency when damaged in battle. Our crews were able to take prompt and heroic measures after damage with little guidance.

Add to the natural bent of your officers and crew by encouraging them to display initiative in peace. Your efforts will pay for themselves some bleak day when your ship is heavily damaged or has internal communication problems. If you have prepared your crew, you will find the other end of the ship running just as well as if your orders had been received.

DECISION-MAKING

Now that you have decided on the elements of your personal combat philosophy, you should remember that "philosophy" never fired a shot. Only a decision starts the firing process.

The human brain is the finest computer ever made. Like a computer, it stores millions of bits of information. The results of your readings and study are all there, as are the distillation of your experience; your observations of the experiences of others; the Navy's traditions; your own personal characteristics; and, on a shorter time basis, the input from your senses—what you have most recently seen, heard, and otherwise observed. With all this information in your memory, and from your current observation, you will have to make your decision.

The proper way to make a decision is to take in all the facts that are available, meld them in your mind with the information already there, and then reach a *tentative* decision. In war, as in life, there is always additional information being developed and brought to your attention. Consider such information and revise your decision accordingly and continuously. Keep your mind open, however, until the moment arrives when a *final* decision is necessary. Then make it, announce it firmly and vigorously, and see that it is carried out instantly.

There are shortsighted persons who think that a commander should make a final decision early and stick to it. They feel that allowing change indicates poor decision-making ability. The exact opposite is true. This type of decision-maker is, to speak charitably, a fool who will end up on a large rock because early on he or she chose a course heading for it and refused to change direction.

An example from real life: A U.S. ship, steaming in wartime in an area of patchy fog, detected a radar contact approaching at high speed. A radio challenge produced no response. The decision-making process began. The CO decided *tentatively* to take the contact under fire, but he decided to wait until it cleared the fog patches before making a *final* decision. The contact appeared; it was a British destroyer with a defective radio.

Another, slower-paced example from the experience of Admiral Claude Ricketts, an outstanding decision-maker, occurred with respect to a mast case. The day before a supposed culprit was to appear at captain's mast, then-Commander Ricketts was asked by his executive officer what punishment he was going to assign the man.

"I don't know," said Commander Ricketts. "I haven't made a final decision yet."

"But, Sir," said the executive officer, "we have all the facts, and they indicate he's guilty. Let's get on with it."

The next day a surprise witness appeared, testified that there had been a case of mistaken identity, and the case was dismissed.

As they walked away from the mast area, Ricketts said with his usual compassion to a considerably subdued XO, "Don't make a final decision until you have *all* the facts."

A good decision, with all facts included, is vital to success, but *speed* of decision is also important, particularly in time of war. With a *tentative* decision always in your mind, you can produce a *final* decision quickly if circumstances require it. Don't be afraid of making a quick decision. If you have done your homework, it will be a good one. If subsequent developments show that it wasn't, remember that even John Paul Jones made a few bad decisions. Also remember that probably no one else could have made a better decision in the same circumstances. You are as good a commanding officer as the Navy system produces. It is true that the selection system produced a few failures in World War II and the two decades thereafter, but in more recent years the selection system has been tightened and improved to the point where only the very best officers are honored with command. If you are one of these, *humbly* remember that you have been judged to have all the attributes and experience needed to be a superb commanding officer. The rest is up to you.

LOSING YOUR SHIP

Now that you have decided that you will have a positive attitude toward your success in combat, it is difficult to consider the possibility of the loss of your ship. Nevertheless, thought must be given to it. *Navy Regulations*, as discussed in previous chapters, states positively and without equivocation that you will fight your ship to the end. There can never be a single thought about surrendering your ship, allowing boarding, or permitting capture or removal of your crew. The aftermath of the *Pueblo* incident reaffirmed this historical tradition of our Navy.

Once your crew is off the ship, you have discharged your responsibilities according to *Navy Regulations*. You are then free to leave, and you are *expected* to do so. Don't be burdened by nineteenth-century stories of captains going down with their ships. Most who did so were badly wounded, and only a few took this final step. The modern Royal Navy and the U.S. Navy long ago discarded any remnants of this tradition. There is no current regulation or tradition that prevents you from leaving your ship after you have discharged your duties, if you are absolutely sure that it is about to sink. You should, of course, remain in the vicinity until it goes under to prevent any enemy from coming on the scene and boarding her. If you have commanded well and fought well, the Navy will want to use your experience and talents again.

Put the thought of losing your ship behind you, and remember only the positive combat philosophy you determine to make your own and to import to your officers and crew. Hope that you do not have to demonstrate it, but decide that if you do, you will be bold, courageous, daring, tenacious, and aggressive, and that you will exercise the initiative with all the ingenuity you can muster. No one could do more.

The Captain's Role

A final thought. Never forget that you are the chief planner, tactician, and mariner or airman of your command. The reason young men and women join the Navy and aspire to command is not paperwork, administration, personnel management, or any of the other important—but somewhat mundane—things we do on a day-to-day basis.

They join to go to sea and operate ships, submarines, and aircraft in exciting and challenging ways. Let them see your enjoyment and professional skill in a profession that is at once historical, unique, important, and dynamic. Take advantage of the excellent tactical library in your ship, try new and different tactical approaches, drive your ship or aircraft with skill and enthusiasm, and you will truly live the words of John Paul Jones to his young crewmen: "Sign on, young man, and sail with me. The stature of our homeland is but a measure of ourselves. Our job is to keep her free. To that end, I call on the young, the brave, the strong, the free. Sign on, young man, and sail with me."

Sail safely, Captain. Godspeed and open water to you.

Glossary of Terms
Regarding Joint Operations

administrative control. Direction or exercise of authority over subordinate or other organizations in respect to administration and support, including organization of service forces, control of resources and equipment, personnel management, unit logistics, individual and unit training, readiness, mobilization, demobilization, discipline, and other matters not included in the operational missions of the subordinate or other organizations. Also called *ADCON*. (Joint Publication [JP] 1)

area of responsibility. 1. The geographical area associated with a combatant command within which a combatant commander has authority to plan and conduct operations. 2. In naval usage, a predefined area of enemy terrain for which supporting ships are responsible for covering by fire and by observation known targets or targets of opportunity. (N.B. Generally used today to refer to the theater in which operations occur.) Also called *AOR*. (JP 1)

armed forces. The military forces of a nation or a group of nations. *See also* **force**. (JP 1)

assign. 1. To place units or personnel in an organization where such placement is relatively permanent, and/or where such organization controls and administers the units or personnel for the primary function, or greater portion of the functions, of the unit or personnel. 2. To detail individuals to specific duties or functions where such duties or functions are primary and/or relatively permanent. *See also* **attach**. (JP 3-0)

attach. 1. The placement of units or personnel in an organization where such placement is relatively temporary. 2. The detailing of individuals to specific functions where such functions are secondary or relatively temporary, e.g., attached for quarters and rations, attached for flying duty, etc. *See also* **assign**. (JP 3-0)

boundary. A line that delineates surface areas for the purpose of facilitating coordination and deconfliction of operations between adjacent units, formations, or areas. (JP 3-0)

campaign. A series of related major operations aimed at achieving strategic and operational objectives within a given time and space. *See also* **campaign plan**. (JP 5-0)

campaign plan. A joint operation plan for a series of related major operations aimed at achieving strategic or operational objectives within a given time and space. *See also* **campaign**. (JP 5-0)

chain of command. The succession of commanding officers from a superior to a subordinate through which command is exercised. Also called *command channel*.

change of operational control. The date and time (Coordinated Universal Time) at which a force or unit is reassigned or attached from one commander to another where the gaining commander will exercise operational control over that force or unit. Also called *CHOP*.

close support. That action of the supporting force against targets or objectives that are sufficiently near the supported force as to require detailed integration or coordination of the supporting action with the fire, movement, or other actions of the supported force. (JP 3-31)

coalition. An ad hoc arrangement between two or more nations for common action. (JP 5-0)

combatant command. A unified or specified command with a broad continuing mission under a single commander established and so designated by the president, through the secretary of defense and with the advice and assistance of the chairman of the Joint Chiefs of Staff. Combatant commands typically have geographic or functional responsibilities. (JP 5-0)

combatant command (command authority). Nontransferable command authority established by title 10 ("Armed Forces"), U.S. Code, section 164, exercised only by commanders of unified or specified combatant commands unless otherwise directed by the president or the secretary of defense. Combatant command (command authority) cannot be delegated and is the authority of a combatant commander to perform those functions of command over assigned forces involving organizing and employing commands and forces, assigning tasks, designating objectives, and giving authoritative direction over all aspects of military operations, joint training, and logistics necessary to accomplish the missions assigned to the command. Combatant command (command authority) should be exercised through the commanders of subordinate organizations. Normally this authority is exercised through subordinate joint force commanders and service and/or functional component commanders. Combatant command (command authority) provides full authority to organize and employ commands and forces as the combatant commander considers necessary to accomplish assigned missions. Operational control is inherent in combatant command (command authority). Also called *COCOM*. *See also* **combatant command; combatant commander; operational control; tactical control**. (JP 1)

combatant commander. A commander of one of the unified or specified combatant commands established by the president. (JP 3-0)

combined. Between two or more forces or agencies of two or more allies. (When all allies or services are not involved, the participating nations and services shall be identified—e.g., Combined Navies.)

command. 1. The authority that a commander in the armed forces lawfully exercises over subordinates by virtue of rank or assignment. Command includes the authority and responsibility for effectively using available resources and for planning the employment, organizing, directing, coordinating, and controlling of military forces for the accomplishment of assigned missions. It also includes responsibility for the health, welfare, morale, and discipline of assigned personnel. 2. An order given by a commander, that is, the will of the commander expressed for the purpose of bringing about a particular action. 3. A unit or units, an organization, or an area under the command of one individual. Also called *CMD*. *See also* **combatant command; combatant command (command authority)**. (JP 1)

command and control. The exercise of authority and direction by a properly designated commander over assigned and attached forces in the accomplishment of the mission. Command and control functions are performed through an arrangement of personnel, equipment, communications, facilities, and procedures employed by a commander in planning, directing, coordinating, and controlling forces and operations in the accomplishment of the mission. Also called *C2*. (JP 1)

command relationships. The interrelated responsibilities between commanders, as well as the operational authority exercised by commanders, in the chain of command; defined further as combatant command (command authority), operational control, tactical control, or support. *See also* **chain of command, combatant command (command authority), command, operational control, support, tactical control**. (JP 1)

communicate. To use any means or method to convey information of any kind from one person or place to another. (JP 6-0)

component. 1. One of the subordinate organizations that constitutes a joint force. Normally a joint force is organized with a combination of service and functional components. 2. In logistics, a part or combination of parts having a specific function that can be installed or replaced only as an entity. (JP 4-0)

direct liaison authorized. That authority granted by a commander (any level) to a subordinate to directly consult or coordinate an action with a command or agency within or outside of the granting command. Direct liaison authorized is more applicable to planning than operations and always carries with it the requirement of keeping the commander granting direct liaison authorized informed. Direct liaison authorized is a coordination relationship, not an authority through which command may be exercised. Also called *DIRLAUTH*. (JP 1)

direct support. A mission requiring a force to support another specific force and authorizing it to answer directly to the supported force's request for assistance. Also called *DS*. (JP 3-09.3)

doctrine. Fundamental principles by which the military forces or elements thereof guide their actions in support of national objectives. It is authoritative but requires judgment in application.

general support. 1. Support that is given to the supported force as a whole and not to any particular subdivision thereof. 2. A tactical artillery mission. Also called *GS*. (JP 3-09.3)

joint. Connotes activities, operations, organizations, etc., in which elements of two or more military departments participate. (JP 1)

joint force. A general term applied to a force composed of significant elements, assigned or attached, of two or more military departments operating under a single joint force commander. (JP 3-0)

joint force commander. A general term applied to a combatant commander, subunified commander, or joint task force commander authorized to exercise combatant command (command authority) or operational control over a joint force. Also called *JFC*. (JP 1)

joint operations. A general term to describe military actions conducted by joint forces or by service forces in relationships (e.g., support, coordinating authority) that, of themselves, do not establish joint forces. (JP 3-0)

joint operations area. An area of land, sea, and airspace defined by a geographic combatant commander or subordinate unified commander in which a joint force commander (normally a joint task force commander) conducts military operations to accomplish a specific mission. Also called *JOA*. (JP 3-0)

joint staff. 1. The staff of a commander of a unified or specified command, subordinate unified command, joint task force, or subordinate functional component (when a functional component command will employ forces from more than one military department) that includes members from the several services. These staff members should be assigned in such a manner as to ensure that the commander understands the tactics, techniques, capabilities, needs, and limitations of the component parts of the force. Positions on the staff should be divided so that service representation and influence generally reflect the service composition of the force. 2. (capitalized as Joint Staff) The staff under the chairman of the Joint Chiefs of Staff as provided for in title 10, U.S. Code, section 155. The Joint Staff assists the chairman of the Joint Chiefs of Staff and is subject to the authority, direction, and control of the chairman of the Joint Chiefs of Staff and the other members of the Joint Chiefs of Staff in carrying out their responsibilities. Also called *JS*. (JP 1)

joint task force. A joint force that is constituted and so designated by the secretary of defense, a combatant commander, a subunified commander, or an existing joint task force commander. Also called *JTF*. (JP 1)

multinational operations. A collective term to describe military actions conducted by forces of two or more nations and usually undertaken within the structure of a coalition or alliance. (JP 3-16)

operational authority. That authority exercised by a commander in the chain of command; defined further as combatant command (command authority), operational control, tactical control, or a support relationship. (JP 1)

operational control. Command authority that may be exercised by commanders at any echelon at or below the level of combatant command. Operational control is inherent in combatant command (command authority) and may be delegated within the command. Operational control is the authority to perform those functions of command over subordinate forces involving organizing and employing commands and forces, assigning tasks, designating objectives, and giving authoritative direction necessary to accomplish the mission. Operational control includes authoritative direction over all aspects of military operations and joint training necessary to accomplish missions assigned to the command. Operational control should be exercised through the commanders of subordinate organizations. Normally this authority is exercised through subordinate joint force commanders and service and/or functional component commanders. Operational control normally provides full authority to organize commands and forces and to employ those forces as the commander in operational control considers necessary to accomplish assigned missions; it does not, in and of itself, include authoritative direction for logistics or matters of administration, discipline, internal organization, or unit training. Also called *OPCON*. (JP 1)

subordinate unified command. A command established by commanders of unified commands, when so authorized by the secretary of defense through the chairman of the Joint Chiefs of Staff, to conduct operations on a continuing basis in accordance with the criteria set forth for unified commands. A subordinate unified command may be established on an area or functional basis. Commanders of subordinate unified commands have functions and responsibilities similar to those of the commanders of unified commands and exercise operational control of assigned commands and forces within the assigned operational area. Also called *subunified command*. (JP 1)

supported commander. 1. The commander having primary responsibility for all aspects of a task assigned by the Joint Strategic Capabilities Plan or other joint operation planning authority. In the context of joint operation planning, this term refers to the commander who prepares operation plans or operation orders in response to requirements of the chairman of the Joint Chiefs of Staff. 2. In the context of a support command relationship, the commander who receives assistance from another commander's force or capabilities and who is responsible for ensuring that the supporting commander understands the assistance required. (JP 3-0)

supporting commander. 1. A commander who provides augmentation forces or other support to a supported commander or who develops a supporting plan. Includes the designated combatant commands and Department of Defense agencies as appropriate. 2. In the context of a support command relationship, the commander who aids, protects, complements, or sustains another commander's force and who is responsible for providing the assistance required by the supported commander. (JP 1)

tactical control. Command authority over assigned or attached forces or commands or over military capability or forces made available for tasking that is limited to the detailed direction and control of movements or maneuvers within the operational area necessary to accomplish missions or tasks assigned. Tactical control is inherent in operational control. Tactical control may be delegated to and exercised at any level at or below the level of combatant command. Tactical control provides sufficient authority for controlling and directing the application of force or tactical use of combat support assets within the assigned mission or task. Also called *TACON*. (JP 1)

transient forces. Forces that pass or stage through or base temporarily within the operational area of another command but are not under its operational control. (JP 1)

unified command. A command with a broad continuing mission under a single commander and composed of significant assigned components of two or more military departments that is established and so designated by the president through the secretary of defense with the advice and assistance of the chairman of the Joint Chiefs of Staff. Also called *unified combatant command*. (JP 1)

There are currently eleven unified combatant commands. All of them can be either supported or supporting commanders in a given operation, and all are warfighters. Six are geographic in nature, which means they are in charge of a specified area of the world: U.S. Africa Command (AFRICOM, headquartered in Stuttgart, Germany), U.S. Central Command (CENTCOM, Tampa, FL), U.S. European Command (EUCOM, Stuttgart, Germany), U.S. Northern Command (NORTHCOM, Colorado Springs, CO), U.S. Indo-Pacific Command (INDOPACOM, Pearl Harbor, HI), and U.S. Southern Command (SOUTHCOM, Miami, FL). There are also five additional combatant commands: U.S. Cyber Command (CYBERCOM, Fort Meade, MD), U.S. Space Command (SPACECOM, Huntsville, AL), U.S. Special Operations Command (SOCOM, Tampa, FL), U.S. Strategic Command (STRATCOM, Omaha, NE), and U.S. Transportation Command (TRANSCOM, Fort Scott, IL).

Unified Command Plan. The document approved by the president that sets forth basic guidance to all unified combatant commanders; establishes their missions, responsibilities, and force structure; delineates the general geographical area of responsibility for geographic combatant commanders; and specifies functional responsibilities for functional combatant commanders. Essentially the "constitution" of the armed forces, this document sets out the fundamental structure of the warfighting organization of the Department of Defense. Also called *UCP*. (JP 1)

Sample Turnover Plan

USS KING (DDG XXX) NOTICE 5060

Subj: CHANGE OF COMMAND TURNOVER PLAN

Ref: (a) USS KING NOTICE 5060

Encl: (1) Notional Turnover Schedule

      (2) Briefing Guidelines

      (3) Department Information Books

1. *Purpose.* To provide guidance for the preparation and execution of a smooth and thorough change of command turnover between Commander J. Barry and Commander J. P. Jones.

2. *Background.* Reference (a) discusses general duties, responsibilities and deadlines for the completion of key preparations for the change of command of USS KING (DDG XXX). In order to ensure that the transfer for the responsibilities of command is conducted smoothly and thoroughly, this notice provides detailed guidance for the preparation of presentations and briefings for the Prospective Commanding Officer (PCO) by Department Heads and special assistants. A notional schedule is also provided for planning purposes at enclosure (1).

3. *Action.* Each individual assigned responsibilities herein will be prepared to thoroughly brief the PCO on the subjects listed in enclosure (2) as well as such other matters as the Commanding Officer may direct or the PCO may request. Although enclosure (1) is a notional schedule to which specific dates will be assigned later, it should be followed as a guideline for the amount of time each briefer will have

with the PCO. Department Heads will also provide the PCO with briefing books containing at a minimum those items listed in enclosure (3) and will ensure their subordinates are aware of and prepared for any briefing topic under their cognizance.

J. BARRY

(1) Notional Turnover Schedule (Example Starting at Sea)

DAY 1:
0800—PCO call on CDS-21
0900—PCO meeting with CO
0930—Review draft relieving letter with XO/CO
1000—PCO Senior Watch Officer Brief
1030—PCO CSO/WEPS Brief and tour
1300—PCO/NAV Brief and tour
1430—PCO call on CDS-21 Deputy/CSO

DAY 2:
0730—Navigation Brief
0830—Sea and Anchor
0930—ESO
1000—NC1 Brief
1030—Keys with CO
1230—Live-Fire Exercise
1330—XO turnover
1500—Sea and Anchor

DAY 3:
0915—PCO ENG Brief and Tour
1100—PCO Meeting with IDC
1300—PCO OPs Brief and Tour
1430—PCO SUPPO Brief and Tour

DAY 4:
1000—Ceremony Rehearsal
—Admin Day

DAY 5:
0830—CO signs pertinent documents and logs
0900—PCO Meeting with CO sign relieving letter
1000—Change of Command/Reception
1230—CDR Barry Departs
1300—CO signs pertinent documents/release messages

(2) Briefing Guidelines

1. Each Department Head shall review the following with the Prospective Commanding Officer during the scheduled briefing times:
   a. Departmental Organization
   b. Personnel Status
   c. Material Status
   d. Certification and Qualification Status
   e. Overview of Equipment/Capabilities and Tag-Out Procedures
   f. SRA Package
   g. Inspection Preparations
   h. PQS Status
   i. CSMP/3-M Status
   j. Training (Teams, School Grads, Departmental/Divisional, etc.)
   k. Departmental Budget
   l. Status of Controlled Equipage
2. Each Department Head will conduct a tour of all assigned spaces with the PCO for familiarization purposes.
3. The Operations Officer shall be prepared to discuss/show PCO the following:
   a. Operations-General
      _____Departmental Doctrines
      _____Current Task Organization/Assignments
      _____OPREP 3 Reporting Procedures/Guide for CDO's
      _____Operational Security/INFO Security/Personnel Security Clearances
      _____Eight O'clock Reports
      _____OPREP/SITREP Procedures
      _____Top Secret/Secret Inventories
      _____Training and Schools Program*
      _____Long Range Training Schedule*
   b. Combat Information Center
      _____AIC and ASTAC Status
      _____Naval Warfare Publications Library TRAREP
   c. Electronic Warfare/Intelligence
      _____INTEL Publications
      _____INTEL Gathering Team/Camera/etc.
      _____SLQ-32 Installation
      _____SRBOC Certification
      _____SSES

    d. First Division

_____Weight Test Status

_____Helmsman Training/Qualification

_____Age of the HIGHLINE/TOW RIG

_____Status of Mooring Lines

_____Flammable Liquid Stowage

_____UNREP Gear

_____Paint Control and Inventory/Issue/Stowage Procedures

_____Boats and Boat Gear

_____Coxswain Training

_____Heavy Weather Bill

_____Helo Operations/Helo Gear

_____Respiratory Protection Program

_____Lead Control Program

_____LSE/HCO Training/Qualification

_____Lifeboat Certification Status

_____SAR Swimmer Status

    e. Miscellaneous

_____Short/Long Range Training Program*

_____Ship's Schedule*

_____Status of Inspections*

_____Status of exercises for competitive cycle*

_____Status of CCRs for mission readiness ratings*

*In conjunction with the ship's designated Training Officer

4. The Combat System Officer and Weapons Officer shall be prepared to discuss/show PCO the following:

    a. Combat Systems-General

_____Battle Orders

_____Departmental Organization/Smooth Logs

_____Physical Security Plan

_____Ammunition Allowance/NCEA

_____Eight O'clock Reports/Daily Combat Systems Report

_____Explosive Safety Review Results

_____Manning/School Status

    b. Antisubmarine Warfare

_____OBT ASW Exercises

_____SQS-53C Operation/Material Status

_____Towed Array Operation/Material Status

_____MMT Inventory

_____ASW Watch Stations/Qualifications Status

_____ASW Training Program

_____Noise/Source Levels

_____SVTT Status

_____XBT Inventory/Procedures

c. Electronic Material

_____Personal Electronic Safety Program

_____Combat Systems Control Procedures

_____Communications

_____LINK 11, 4A, 16

_____Surface Search Radar/IFF/TACAN

_____2M Certification

_____General Purpose Electronic Test Equipment (GPETE)

_____Antenna Photos and Fade Charts

_____NEC Status

_____TEMPEST Status

_____CASREP Status

d. Fire Control

_____FCS Operation/Material Status

_____Computer Suite Operation/Material Status

_____AN/SPY-1D Operation/Material Status

_____Dry Air System

_____M Cap

e. Ordnance/Missile

_____Missile Load-out Status/Offload Preparations

_____Pre-fire Checks for Guns

_____Harpoon Operation/Material Status

_____CIWS PACFIRE Procedures

_____Dud Procedures/Misfire procedures

_____Mag Sprinkler OPS/Procedures

_____Missile Deluge System

_____Small Arms Allowance/25mm Installation

_____Ammunition Handling Equipment

_____Small Arms Security/Inventory/Key Control

_____Magazine Temperature Reports

_____Explosive Safety Review Status

_____Small Arms Qualifications

_____Sensitive Ordnance Handling
_____Conventional Ordnance Handling and Certification Program
_____Weight Test Status
_____Night Vision Devices

f. System Test Officer (STO)
_____SERT Team
_____Departmental 3-M
_____CSTT Organization and Training
_____CSOSS Implementation/CSOOW
_____Combat System Maintenance Manual
_____Master Software Tape/Disk Control
_____ACTS Training
_____BFTT and Synthetic Training

g. ADP Security
_____ADP Program
_____Security/Software Control
_____LAN Operations/Security/Access

h. Communications
_____Message Processing Procedures
_____"PERSONAL FOR" Procedures
_____COMM Standing Orders
_____Last COMM Assist Team Visit
_____Routing/Releasing Procedures
_____General Message Files (NAVOPS/ALNAVS/AL-PACFLTS
/ALNAVSURFORS)
_____Secret Message/Procedures
_____Watch-to-Watch Crypto Material Accountability
_____EA Folder
_____Antenna Maintenance
_____Portable COMM Gear

i. CMS
_____Custodian/Alternate
_____Couriers
_____CMS Training
_____CMS Required Reading
_____Required Spot Checks
_____CMS Assist Visit Results
_____CMS Inspection Results

_____Last Draw

_____Next Draw

_____Results of Inventory

5. Supply Officer shall be prepared to discuss/show PCO the following:

_____Latest Weekly Reports

_____Line Items in SIM (Last Inventory)

_____CASREP Processing Supply Input

_____DLR Control/Remain in Place Procedures

_____Last SMA and Disbursing Audits

_____Financial Conditions of the General Mess, Discuss Mess Management

_____Daily Meal Sampling Form and Procedures

_____Ship's Store Financial Status/Operating Procedures

_____Ship's Store Stock Turn

_____Material Obligation Validation Program

_____Vending Machine Operation

_____FSA Procedures/CO's Mess

_____Laundry Procedures

_____Maint/Other OPTAR Procedures and Status

_____Ready Service Spares/MAMs Inventory

_____HAZMAT/HAZWASTE Management

_____Controlled Equipage

_____Organizational Issue Material

_____Plastics Management

_____Travel Claim Processing

_____Disbursing Accountability

6. The Navigator shall be prepared to discuss/show PCO the following:

_____ECDIS/Electronic Chart Certification Status

_____Electronic Chart System Procedures (Verifying Inputs, Datum, Accuracy)

_____Most Recent CO Chart and Publication Letter

_____Most Recent Notice to Mariners

_____Chart and NAV Publication Update Procedures

_____Most Recent Chart and Navigation Publication Inventory

_____Equipment Inventory and Accounting (Watch-to-Watch/In port)

_____Boat Compasses

_____Most Recent Swing Ship and Compass Card/Compass Log

_____Standing Orders/Navigation Standards and Procedures
_____Degaussing Folder (Location–Who Has Control–Last Results)
_____Deck Logs
_____Navigation Briefs/Procedures
_____Standard Watch-to-Watch Procedures
_____Night Order Book/Last Thirty Days
_____Harbor Chart on Bridge
_____Tactical Data Folder
_____Ship's Physical Characteristics (Diagram)
_____Letter of Designation of Navigator/Assistant Navigator
_____Sea Detail/UNREP Helmsman
_____Navigation Light Certification/SUEZ Canal Certification
_____Low Visibility (SUPPLY)
_____Special Sea and Anchor Detail Check-off List
_____SATNAV/GPS
_____MOVREP/OTSR
_____LOGREQ Procedures

   a. Admin Officer
_____Relational Admin (RADMIN) Procedures
_____TEMADD Funding (TADTAR)
_____Routing System
_____Postal Program/Last Audit
_____Registered Mail Handling
_____Service Record Access
_____Service Record Entries
_____ID Card Accountability
_____Inspection Status (Admin/Medical/Postal)
_____ADMIN Tickler

7. Engineer Officer shall be prepared to discuss/show PCO the following:
   a. Engineering
_____Logs and Records
_____Casualty Control/EOSS/Restricted Maneuvering Doctrine
_____Last Engineering Assessment Report-Status
_____Engineering Standing Orders
_____Tag-out Procedures
_____Welder Qualifications/Hot Work Bill
_____Engineering Drills/Training/ECCTT
_____Conditions of HP/LPAC Air Compressors

_____Main Drainage Systems Procedures
_____Oil Lab Inspection/Procedures/Records
_____LOQM Program
_____BW/FW Program
_____Docking Plan/Last Docking Report
_____Gas Free Engineer Letter of Designation
_____Fuel Consumption Curves
_____NEURS Reports
_____Fueling Bill
_____Boiler Inspection Status
_____Last Full Power Trials
_____Heat Stress Program
_____Site TV (Tape Security/Accountability)
_____Hearing Conservation Program
_____Shore Power Procedures
_____8 and 12 O'clock Reports/Light Off Orders
_____Gage Cal Program
_____Valve Maintenance Program
_____EOOWs and EOOW Qualification
_____Watch Bill
_____Technical Publications/NSTM's/Tech Library
_____Electrical Safety
_____Cathodic Protection
_____Degaussing
_____Asbestos
_____QA Program/Level One Material Control
_____Auxiliary Equipment Status/Problems
_____IC Systems/WSN-7

b. Damage Control
_____DCTT Organization/Procedures
_____Repair Party Organization/Training
_____Main Space Fire Doctrine
_____CBR Suits/Equipment
_____MOPP Level Training
_____RADIACS
_____SCBA Training
_____DC Plates/DC Book
_____DC Organization/DC Drills Under Way, In Port

_____In-port Fire Parties
_____SCBA Allowance/Location
_____DC WIFCOM
_____DC PQS Program
_____Emergency Egress Training

Other Briefing Guidelines

1. In addition to discussions with the Department Heads, the PCO will be briefed by the following personnel concerned with major collateral or administrative duties as indicated below:

    a. Executive Officer
        _____Personnel Status/LORTARP/Manning/TPU/Berthing
        _____Upcoming Visits/Commitments
        _____Planning Board for Training
        _____Ombudsman
        _____Discipline(XOI/Mast/ADSEPS)
        _____Liberty Policy (Briefs/Liberty Risks)
        _____Deployment Awards (NAM/CAPS)
        _____Evals/Fitreps
        _____Change of Command
        _____XO Memos

    b. Senior Watch Officer
        _____Officer Assignments/Watch Qualifications
        _____Officer Watch Qualification Procedures (Tests/Board)
        _____In-port Duty Sections
        _____CDO/ACDO Rotation
        _____Officer Training
        _____Surface Warfare Officer Qualification
        _____PQS Program

    c. Command Master Chief
        _____CMEO Program
        _____Professional Development Board
        _____CPO Review Board
        _____Commanding Officer's Suggestion Box
        _____Petty Officer Indoctrination
        _____"I" Division
        _____Sailor of the Quarter/Month
        _____Enlisted Surface Warfare Specialty Qualification
        _____Navy Rights and Responsibilities

d. Senior Medical Department Representative
_____Medical Organization
_____Accountability/Controlled Medicinals
_____Inspections/Food Service/Water/Sanitation/Hazardous Material
_____Medical Department Training
_____Sick Call Procedures
_____Treatment of Potable Water
_____Heat Stress/Hearing Conservation Programs
_____Medical Records
_____Dental/Shots
_____Daily Reports to CO
_____Medical Waste Handling
_____Supply/AMAL
_____Status of Inspections (Last conducted/Next due)

e. Command Career Counselor
_____Retention Program/Status
_____Guard III/Score/SRB Procedures
_____Status of Retention Team
_____Interview Procedures
_____HARP Duty
_____Submission of NAVPERS 1306/7

f. Chief Master at Arms
_____Discipline/EMI
_____Drugs, Alcohol, UAs
_____Current Cases
_____Liberty Cards/Liberty Risk Program
_____Lucky Bag
_____NIS Interface
_____Urinalysis/Chain of Custody

g. 3-M Coordinator/SMMO
_____PMS Accomplishment Rate Last 13 Weeks
_____Ship's 3-M Program/Reports
_____Last 3-M Inspection Results
_____CO's Spotchecks
_____CSMP
_____3M-PQS
_____IMAV Procedures
_____Job Sign-Off/QA

h. Safety Officer
_____Overview of Program
_____Reports
_____Last NAVSAFECEN Inspection/Assist Visit
_____Personal Injury Investigation
_____Safety Committee/Council
_____Safety Training
_____Tag-out Program
_____How You're "Getting the Word Out"
_____ORM Procedures

i. DAPA/Aftercare
_____DAPA Instruction
_____Program Overview
_____Reports
_____Current Status of Personnel

j. Legal Officer Brief
_____Unit Punishment Log
_____Mast Procedures
_____Appeals
_____Court-Martial Procedures
_____Cases Pending

k. Public Affairs Officer
_____Command Presentation
_____Welcome Aboard Pamphlets
_____Family Gram
_____News Releases
_____Tiger Cruise
_____FHTNR Program

l. Physical Readiness/Athletic Officer
_____PFA Program/Mandatory PT/Weight Control Program
_____Command Fitness Routine
_____Ship's Athletic Teams

m. Welfare and Recreation Officer/Treasurer
_____Status of Account/Upcoming Plans
_____Committee Makeup/Meeting Schedule
_____Programs for the Crew
_____Cruise Book
_____Inventory

n. Test Control/Educational Services Officer
_____Off-Duty Education
_____College Education Programs
_____Online Programs
_____College Credit/Equivalency for Professional Skills
_____Functional Skills
_____Exam Procedures
o. SRA Coordinator SMMO 3-M Coordinator
_____SRA Work Package

(3) Department Information Books

1. Each Department Head will provide the PCO, upon his arrival, with tabbed notebooks containing copies of the following documents (in order as shown):

Admin
- Nav/Admin Department organization/key personnel and manning deficiencies
- Most recent muster report
- Ship Manpower Document
- ODCR
- Prospective gains/losses list
- Wardroom social rosters
- Collateral Duties List
- List of Effective Instructions
- List of submitted/outstanding awards and Command NAMS/ CAPS remaining
- List of personnel in a disciplinary status or awaiting ADSEP or SPCM
- Most recent correspondence TICKLER and list of required reports
- Sea and Anchor Detail checklist
- USS KINGINST 3120.2 (USS KING'S DAILY ROUTINE)

A separate copy of the ship's SORM, the Commanding Officer's Standing Orders, and XO's memos will also be provided for the PCO's review along with a folder containing a copy of all pertinent change of command notices, the guest and announcement list, a COC pamphlet, a sample announcement, and a script.

Supply
- Supply Department organization, key personnel and manning deficiencies
- Most recent monthly report to CO
- 8 o'clock reports
- List of major SRA jobs
- Results of Controlled Equipment Inventory and all audits
- List of required inspections (last conducted/next due)

The Supply Officer will also provide the PCO with a folder containing a pad of blank paper, pencils/pens, a Welcome Aboard pamphlet, a ship's phone book, and an officer roster/telephone number listing (and whatever other touches he deems appropriate).

Operations
- OPS Department organization, key personnel, and manning deficiencies
- Current Plan of the Week
- Current SOE
- Ship's long-range training plan and projected cycle schedule
- 8 o'clock reports
- Copy of OPS CASREPS
- List of major SRA jobs
- Daily boat report
- List of required inspections, certs, qual (last conducted/next due)
- List of required exercises (last conducted periodicity, M rating, due by, grade)
- Officer watch qualification matrix
- Current underway watch bill/CDO watch bill

Combat Systems
- Combat Systems Department organization, key personnel, and manning deficiencies
- 8 o'clock reports
- Copy of CS CASREPS
- Daily Combat Systems report
- List of major SRA jobs
- Current ammo load out/NCEA

- Last OCSOT results
- List of required inspections, certs, quals (last conducted/next due)
- CO's Battle Orders

Engineering
- Engineering Department organization, key personnel, and manning deficiencies
- 8 o'clock reports
- Copy of Engineering CASREPS
- Daily Fuel and Water Report and Draft Report
- List of major SRA jobs
- List of required inspections, certs, quals (last conducted/next due)
- List of departures from specs
- Sample light-off orders
- Sample refueling/transfer of fuel checklist
- Sample ECC briefing form
- Fuel consumption data
- Copy of last full power report
- Copy of last Engineering Assessment/Certification with IOP Status

The Chief Engineer will also make the following documents available to the PCO: EDORM and the Main Space Fire Doctrine.

APPENDIX
2

Sample Change of Command Plan

USS KING (DDG XXX) NOTICE 5061

Subj: CHANGE OF COMMAND ON 20 JUNE 2010

Encl: (1) Script

       (2) Seating Plan

       (3) Personnel Requirements

       (4) Remaining Actions

1. *Purpose.* To provide a sequence of events for each speaker for USS KING (DDG XXX) Change of Command on 04 February 2021.

2. *Discussion.* Commander J. Barry, Commanding Officer, USS KING (DDG XXX), will be relieved by Commander J. P. Jones on 04 February 2021.

3. *Information.*

    a. All participants should assemble on the flight deck no later than 0830.

    b. Uniforms:

        (1) Officer/CPO: Service Dress Whites (medals and ribbons). Officers will wear swords.

        (2) E-6 and below: Dress Whites (medals and ribbons).

        (3) Guests: Appropriate civilian attire.

    c. Guests will arrive via brow on the flight deck, and official guests will arrive via the midships brow. The ship's quarterdeck will be midships, but a ceremonial OOD with a Boatswain and side boys will be stationed at both brows to pipe officials aboard. No one will be "bonged aboard."

J. BARRY

(1) Script for Commanding Officer, USS KING (DDG XXX)

Change of Command

****

20 June 2010

****Following participants muster in assigned areas at pier and on board USS KING.

0600   Reserved parking guards

0830   Band (fantail)

        Quarterdeck OOD with long glass, two POOWs, two MSGRS, Boatswain, and side boys

        —Fantail OOD, Two MSGRs, Boatswain, and side boys

        —Color guard (fantail)

        —Ushers and escorts (starboard amidships)

        —Main gate and road directors

0915   Ship's company fall in for ceremony.

0930   CO/PCO families/special guests assemble in the wardroom.

0930   Ship's company in place. Band commences music program. Program notebooks placed on lecterns.

        Commander Naval Surface Forces (CNSF) departs for USS KING. CDO awaits arrival of CNSF and informs CDR Barry when he arrives.

0945   CNSF arrives.

        CDR Barry goes to the quarterdeck to escort CNSF to CO's cabin. Quarterdeck OOD calls "Attention to port" (not using the 1MC, which would affect personnel on the pier), band continues to play.

        —Eight side boys and piped aboard

        Official party will proceed to Commanding Officer's in-port cabin escorted by CDR Barry.

0950   Escort families to flight deck (officer's escort).

0955   Mrs. Barry, the Commanding Officer's mother, and the Prospective Commanding Officer's mother are met by ship's company officers and escorted to their seats.

        [Flowers presented during CO's remarks to CO's mother and spouse verified in vicinity of podium].

        Chaplain escorted to platform and seated.

        Following personnel take positions on board USS KING.

—XO USS KING at master of ceremony lectern

—CMC seated to the right of the master of ceremony lectern

After guests are seated, music ceases.

0958

XO   "Good morning, ladies and gentlemen. Welcome to United States Ship KING change of command. In just a few minutes, the Commander Naval Surface Forces, Vice Admiral A. Burke, Commander Destroyer Squadron Twenty-One, CAPT Johnson, the Commanding Officer, USS KING, CDR J. Barry, and the Prospective Commanding Officer, USS KING, CDR J. P. Jones, will arrive. A gun salute will be rendered this morning to Admiral Burke. The ceremony will commence with the playing of the National Anthem, followed by the invocation offered by Chaplain East."

0958   Band strikes up appropriate music. (Playing time 2 minutes.)

1000   Band ceases to play. (Band plays Attention.)

XO   "Ship's company, Attention."

XO   "Will the guests please rise (for the arrival of the official party, honors to Commander Naval Surface Forces, Vice Admiral Burke, parading of the colors followed by our National Anthem) and remain standing until the color guard has posted."

During arrival of official party, the following will salute during honors:

—XO

—Chaplain

—KING fantail OOD

—Honors bosun/sideboys

—Formation leaders and guests in uniform

Personnel in ranks will not salute.

(When CDR Jones is at entrance to the air lock, XO announces)

XO   "CDR J. P. Jones, Prospective Commanding Officer, USS KING"

Or

"Commander, U.S. Navy . . . arriving . . ."

(Bosun's pipe through side boys)

CDR Jones walks through ceremonial quarterdeck. After passing through side boys, CDR Jones proceeds to and stands in front of designated chair.

(When CDR Barry steps through air lock)

XO   "CDR J. Barry, Commanding Officer, USS KING"
Or

"King . . . arriving . . ."
CDR Barry walks through ceremonial quarterdeck. After passing through side boys, CDR Barry proceeds to and stands in front of designated chair.
(When CAPT Johnson steps through the air lock)

XO   "CAPT Johnson, Commander, Destroyer Squadron Twenty-One"
Or

"Destroyer Squadron Two One . . . arriving"
CAPT Johnson walks through ceremonial quarterdeck. After passing through side boys, CAPT Johnson proceeds to and stands in front of designated chair.
(When Vice Admiral Burke steps through the air lock)

XO   "Vice Admiral Arleigh Burke, Commander Naval Surface Forces"
Or

"Naval Surface Forces . . . arriving"
Admiral Burke walks through ceremonial quarterdeck. After passing through side boys, the Bosun's pipe ceases. Vice Admiral Burke pauses and maintains salute until Ruffles and Flourishes and the gun salute are complete. Vice Admiral Burke then proceeds to and stands in front of his designated chair on the podium.

XO   "Parade the colors." (The band playing in the background.)
Note: Color guard on fantail starboard side. Parade to front of podium, wheel, face guests, dip flags for National Anthem.

XO   When colors are in place amidships: "Ladies and Gentlemen, our National Anthem."

Band   Plays National Anthem.

XO   "Color guard, post." Color guard proceeds to portside of fantail. "Side boys, post."

XO   "Chaplain East will now offer the invocation."

XO   "Will the guests please be seated."

Official Party
        Take seats. [Platform guests remove gloves.]

XO   "Ship's company, parade rest."

XO   "Ladies and Gentlemen, Commander J. Barry, United States Navy, Commanding Officer, USS KING."

CDR Barry

> Introductory remarks/Introduces Vice Admiral Burke, CNSP
> Remarks

XO   "Ship's company, attention."

CNSF Award presentation to Commander Barry

XO   "Ship's company, parade rest."

XO   "Ladies and Gentlemen, Commander Barry, United States Navy, Commanding Officer, USS KING."

CDR Barry

> Remarks. (Present flowers to CO's wife/mother during remarks.)

CDR Barry

> "I will now read my orders." Pause . . .

XO   "Ship's company, attention."

CDR Barry

> From: Chief of Naval Personnel Washington, DC
> To: Commanding Officer, USS KING
> Subj: BUPERS Order 0417
> When directed by reporting senior, detach from duty as Commanding Officer, USS KING, and report to Harvard University, Cambridge, Massachusetts, to the John F. Kennedy School of Government as a Federal Executive Fellow.
> (Signed) C. Nimitz
> Vice Admiral, U.S. Navy, Chief of Naval Personnel

CDR Jones

> Stands (Note: May also stand initially upon XO calling ship's company to attention.)

CDR Barry

> "Commander Jones, I am ready to be relieved."

XO   "Ladies and Gentlemen, Commander J. P. Jones, United States Navy."

CDR Jones

> From: Chief of Naval Personnel Washington, DC
> To: CDR J. P. Jones
> Subj: BUPERS Order 2076
> When directed by the Secretary of Defense, detach as his military assistant, and after a period of leave and training, report to Commanding Officer, USS KING, as his relief. Upon relieving,

report to the immediate superior in command, Commander Destroyer Squadron Twenty-One.

(Signed) C. Nimitz

Vice Admiral, U.S. Navy, Chief of Naval Personnel

CDR Jones

Turns to CDR Barry

CDR Jones

Salutes CDR Barry and states, "I relieve you, Sir."

CDR Barry

Returns salute and states, "I stand relieved."

CDS-21

Stands (Note: May also stand initially upon XO calling ship's company to attention.)

CDR Barry

Turns to CAPT Johnson, CDS-21, salutes, and states, "CAPT Johnson, I have been relieved."

CDS-21

Returns salute and states, "Very well."

CDR Jones

Turns to CAPT Johnson, salutes, and states, "CAPT Johnson, I have assumed command of USS KING."

CDS-21

Returns salute and states, "Very well."

XO   "Ship's company, parade rest."

XO   "Ladies and Gentlemen, Commander J. P. Jones, United States Navy, Commanding Officer, USS KING."

CDR Jones

Remarks.

XO   "Ship's company, attention."

XO   "Master Chief Smith, Command Master Chief, USS KING, representing nearly 300 crew members on DDG XXX, will now present to CDR Barry the ship's commissioning pennant."

CMC Smith

Salutes and presents the pennant to CDR Barry

XO   "Will the guests please rise for the benediction."

Chaplain

Benediction.

Band   Plays Navy Hymn softly in background.

XO "Retire the colors." (Note: If not already retired at the beginning of the ceremony immediately following their parade.)

Color guard

March from port to starboard wheel and order colors.

XO "Ladies and Gentlemen, the change of command ceremony is concluded. All guests are cordially invited to the reception on the pier. Will the guests please allow a few moments for the departure of the official party and distinguished guests."

Escorts Proceed to front row as the XO announces the reception and escorts Mrs. Barry, the Commanding Officer's mother.

Sideboys

Fantail OOD, Boatswain, and side boys post for departing guests.

Band Plays "Anchors Aweigh"/patriotic medley.

Official Party

Proceed fantail quarterdeck where side boys and honors boatswain's mate are in position. Proceed in order through side boys and off via the brow.

—Vice Admiral Burke

—CDR Barry

—CDR Jones

XO (Upon official party departure) "Ship's company, dismissed."

Upon completion of change of command program, ushers and escorts take posts and expedite official party, spouses, families, and distinguished guests to the reception. Ushers will direct guests to the reception via the fantail brow.

(2) Seating Plan

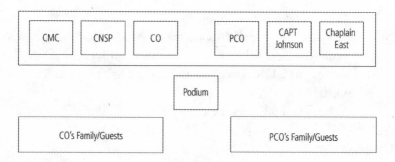

(3) Personnel Requirements
Quarterdeck

Midships	*Flight Deck*
OOD	OOD
(2) POOWs	(2) Messengers
(2) Messengers	(1) Boatswain with pipe
(1) Boatswain with pipe	(8) Side boys
(8) Side boys	

Ushers
    (4) Chief Petty Officers on the flight deck
Escorts
    (4) Division Officers on midships quarterdeck
CNSF Escort
    (1) LT with Vice Admiral Burke
Directors
    (1) CPO at the main gate
    (5) Personnel along the route giving directions
Parking Lot
    (5) Parking lot attendants
Pier
    (2) Gate guards
    (2) Brow directors
Communications
    The main gate lookout, (1) gate guard, the OOD at each brow, the CDO, the change of command coordinator, and the CDO will have walkie-talkies coordinating and tracking VIPs.

(4) Remaining Actions
1. Titivate ship—(All hands)
2. Reserve a truck for 02–05 FEB 2021—(SUPPO)
3. Report to base MWR for change of command materials NLT 1200 03 FEB 21, and set up flight deck—(Watch Bill Coordinator)
4. After RSVPs are received, reserve appropriate seating and make VIP cards—(Admin Officer)
5. After RSVPs are received, determine who will receive flowers—(Coordinator/XO)
6. Rehearse ceremony 1630 03 FEB 21 with CNSF's aide
7. Write commissioning ceremony watch bill—(Watch Bill Coordinator)
8. Determine and order required flowers—(Coordinator and SUPPO)

3

Sample Division in the Spotlight Program

PREBLEINST 1010.2D

USS PREBLE (DDG 88) INSTRUCTION 1010.2D

From: Commanding Officer, USS PREBLE (DDG 88)

Subj: DIVISION IN THE SPOTLIGHT

Ref: (a) U.S. Navy Regulations

       (b) OPNAVINST 3120.32D

       (c) COMNAVSURFORINST 3120.1

Encl: (1) Divisional Rotation and Program Review Summary

       (2) Division in the Spotlight Inspection Forms

1. Purpose. To set forth responsibilities and procedures for the Division in the Spotlight (DITS) inspection program.

2. Cancellation. This instruction is effective upon receipt and until superseded.

3. Background. References (a) through (c) refer to requirements and procedures which require the time, effort, and focus of various key personnel, including the Commanding Officer (CO), to conduct regular inspection and review of divisional spaces, programs, and personnel records. To ensure complete readiness of the ship and crew, the DITS program is established to maintain PREBLE in the highest state of material, personnel, and administrative readiness.

4. Action.

    a.   Executive Officer (XO):

       (1) Oversee DITS program and inspection debriefs.

       (2) Participate in zone inspection as required to assist the CO.

b. Training Officer (TRAINO):
  (1) Assist the XO in the DITS program.
  (2) Promulgate the sequence of divisions to be inspected.
  (3) Schedule DITS events in the Plan of the Week/Plan of the Day.
  (4) Maintain this bill.
c. Designated personnel are to conduct a thorough review and debrief of the following programs:
  (1) Personnel Inspection—Command Master Chief (CMC).
  (2) Training—TRAINO.
  (3) Maintenance, Material, and Management (3-M)—3-M Coordinator (3-MC).
  (4) Personal Qualification Standard (PQS)—PQS Coordinator.
  (5) Damage Control Readiness—Chief Engineer (CHENG).
  (6) Anti-Terrorism/Force Protection—Weapons Officer (WEPS).
  (7) Valve Maintenance—3MC.
  (8) Retention—Command Career Counselor (CCC).
  (9) Medical/Dental Readiness—Independent Duty Corpsman (IDC).
  (10) Electrical Safety—CHENG.
  (11) Workspace Safety—CHENG.
  (12) Compartment/Material Inspection—Cognizant department head.
  (13) Physical Fitness—Command Fitness Leader (CFL).
  (14) Information and Physical Security—COMMO and WEPS.
  (15) Personnel—Personnel Officer.
  (16) Enlisted Surface Warfare Specialist Review—ESWS Coordinator.
d. Department Heads:
  (1) Require division officers to report their readiness for DITS.
  (2) Review all zone program reviews from the previous divisional DITS inspection. Ensure corrective action on previous discrepancies is properly documented and available for inspection.
  (3) Attend debriefs for divisions within their department.
e. Division Officers (DIVOs) and Divisional Chief Petty Officers:
  (1) Ensure all spaces and programs are ready for inspection.
  (2) Report readiness status to department heads.
  (3) Present division for personnel inspection.
  (4) Designate recorders for both personnel and space inspections.

(5) Prepare and follow a preplanned route for compartment/ material inspection. Design this plan for efficiency, e.g., do not escort the CO to auxiliary room one, then aft to after steering, then forward to anchor windlass, etc.

(6) Assign the Petty Officer-in-Charge to present each compartment. Ensure all lockers, storage cabinets, and drawers are unlocked and open for inspection. The individual presenting the space will come to attention, salute, and state, "Good Morning/Afternoon Captain, [Rank] [Last Name], [Name] Division, Compartment [Number], standing by for inspection."

(7) Accompany the CO during the compartment/material inspection. Ensure the recorder has the previous zone inspection discrepancy list (ZIDL) on the left side of compartment folder and the new ZIDL on the right side of folder.

(8) Coordinate with program inspectors to ensure program reviews are complete prior to debrief.

(9) Collect all inspection results and deliver results to the XO via TRAINO prior to debrief.

(10) Review the inspection report, ZIDLs, and program reviews.

(11) Attend the DITS in/out brief.

(12) Correct DITS discrepancies. Annotate all discrepancies noted with appropriate corrective status, e.g., corrected, applicable JSN assigned, etc.

(13) Retain copies of the last four DITS inspection results.

    f.   3MC. Conduct 3M program review.

5. Procedures.

    a.   The ship is divided into divisions as summarized in enclosure (1).

    b.   The XO will approve division for DITS during weekly Planning Board for Training.

    c.   The one week DITS cycle will generally be conducted in the following sequence.

        1.   Monday:

            CMC's Uniform Inspection (at Quarters)

            CO's 3M Spotcheck

            Medical/Dental Records Review

            Personnel Records Review

            Career Counselor Review

            Info and Physical Security Program Review

2. Tuesday:
   CO's CSMP Review
   3M Review
   ESWS Review
   Training Review
   Personnel Qualification Program Review
   Damage Control Readiness Review
3. Wednesday:
   ATFP and Weapons Review
   Safety Program Review
   Electrical Safety Review
   Valve Maintenance Review
   Physical Fitness Review
   All Reports Due to DITS Division Officer*
4. Thursday:
   Zone Inspection
   Division Officer briefs outstanding items to Training Officer
5. Friday:
   DITS Out Brief
   Note: It is the responsibility of the DITS division to ensure that all reviews are conducted on time, but this does not relieve the program managers from the responsibility of conducting the reviews on time.

6. <u>Out Brief</u>.
   a. In the interest of expediency and brevity, inspectors should submit their findings via inspection form to the Division Officer and DITS Coordinator and debrief their significant findings during the out brief.
   b. The Division Officer shall follow up with the XO no later than 2 weeks after the DITS out brief to present the plan of action to correct discrepancies identified during DITS.

J. P. JONES
Distribution:
Department Heads
Division Officers
CPOs

Typical Divisional Rotation

Sequence	Division(s)
1	MP
2	OD
3	NX/NN/MH
4	CF
5	OI
6	CG
7	S1/S3/S4
8	E
9	S2
10	CE
11	IS
12	CA
13	R/ER09
14	A
15	CM
16	OT

Program Reviews

Program Review Summary

Division in the Spotlight Summary of Inspection
Compartment/Material Inspection Summary
Compartment/Material Inspection
Personnel Inspection
Training
3M
PQS
Damage Control
Retention
Medical/Dental Readiness
Electrical Safety
Workspace Safety
Physical Fitness
Information and Physical Security
Personnel
Valve Maintenance

1. Specific inspection checklists and forms for each program review category may be revised without requiring a change to this basic instruction.
2. All revisions will be approved by the XO.

APPENDIX
4

Standing Orders Guidance and Sample Standing Orders

Each ship's commanding officer produces a unique set of standing orders in accordance with guidance set forth by COMNAVSURFPAC/COM NAVSURFLANTINST 3120.3, Principles of the Commanding Officer's Standing Orders. Below are those principles and an example of how a ship may implement that guidance. Refer to the original reference above, for a complete description of all engineering-specific guidance. You should review your own ship's standing orders when you arrive and at least monthly thereafter.

GENERAL GUIDELINES AND CONSIDERATIONS
1. Considerations for Commanding Officer's Standing Orders
   a. Warfare publications, operating sequencing systems, and other instructions contain information specific to the operation and employment of ship systems for the accomplishment of assigned missions. However, this doctrine generally does not specifically address the day-to-day management of the ship's routines that form the foundation of safe shipboard operations. The standing orders should provide a compendium of processes and procedures to be followed by the crew on a day-to-day basis.
   b. Ultimately, the standing orders are the responsibility of the Commanding Officer.
   c. Standing orders are effective only if read and understood by the crew. Therefore, as a general rule, shorter standing orders are preferred. Additionally, concise directives should be favored over

long, flowing text. Commanding Officers would be well advised to remember that the target audience for their standing orders is typically petty officers and junior officers, not senior staff.

    d.   Standing orders must be current and relevant. Standing orders written to support equipment no longer aboard the ship or for missions that no longer apply will quickly cause the crew to assume the Commanding Officer has lost interest in their standing orders. Commanding Officers should establish a process such that the standing orders are regularly reviewed and updated, if necessary. Commanding Officers should take measures to ensure the standing orders do not duplicate or conflict with other ship's instructions, unless specifically desired and carefully considered as a point of emphasis.

    e.   Standing orders are an appropriate place to promulgate tripwires and expected action. For tripwires to be effective, watch teams must understand the parameter(s) that triggers the tripwire, must have a means by which the parameter(s) can be monitored, and must understand the context and intent of standing order tripwire procedures. Typical errors that reduce the value of tripwire schemes are:

        i.   Too many tripwires—watch teams simply can't remember and/or monitor desired parameters.

        ii.   Poorly defined tripwires—watch teams don't understand the Commanding Officer's intent and fail to identify the tripwire.

        iii.   Watch team–defined tripwires—watch teams pick tripwires on a selective basis, without the advantage of the Commanding Officers' experience and knowledge.

2.   Considerations for the Modification of Standing Orders

    a.   Following modernization of equipment, the Commanding Officer shall address new capabilities, limitations, and processes, and modify standing orders as appropriate.

    b.   User interface preference plays a real role in team performance. Watchstanders have a wide array of information, both processed (e.g., Combat Systems Fire Control Data) and raw (e.g., commercial radar returns). Additionally, most COTS systems offer multiple display options. While system doctrine can provide an explanation of display content and recommendations as to when such displays may be preferred, ultimately, the Commanding Officer shall provide guidance for the employment of those systems.

c. Effective standing orders must be sufficiently specific to be actionable. Increased specificity also demands a higher degree of responsiveness to changes in prevailing conditions. Individual Commanding Officers are best suited to ensure that standing orders are appropriate to the prevailing circumstances and responsive to changing operations, equipment, personnel, etc.

3. Considerations for Additional Topics to Include in Standing Orders

a. Default lineups for systems and communications layout (e.g., standardized communication speaker layout in the pilot house). Commanding Officers may also wish to specify default tactical decision aid displays (e.g., north up versus heading up displays on navigation radar repeaters).

b. Safety and/or maintenance requirements not otherwise specified but desired by the Commanding Officer.

c. Duties, responsibilities, and expectations of watches not otherwise specified.

d. Items not otherwise specified for which the Commanding Officer's permission is required.

e. Items not otherwise specified for which the Commanding Officer desires a report.

STANDING ORDER NUMBER 1
Responsibilities

1. *Commanding Officers Shall Address*:
   a. Commanding Officer (CO) Responsibility Statement
   b. Executive Officer (XO) Responsibility Statement
   c. Tactical Action Officer (TAO) Responsibility Statement
   d. Officer of the Deck (OOD) Underway Responsibility Statement
   e. Conning Officer (CONN) Responsibility Statement
   f. Engineering Officer of the Watch (EOOW) Responsibility Statement
   g. Navigation Officer Responsibility Statement
   h. Senior Watch Officer (SWO) Responsibility Statement
   i. Watch position relationships; at a minimum, the relationship between the TAO and the OOD and between the OOD and the EOOW.

    j.   Actions to take if watchstanders are unable to resolve a disagreement or clarify a discrepancy. At a minimum, include how disagreement between the TAO and OOD should be resolved.

    k.   That the presence of the CO or XO at or in the vicinity of a watch station does not relieve any watchstander of his/her responsibility for the proper conduct of that watch unless properly relieved. Watchstanders adhering to the principle of forceful backup make recommendations for the safe operation of the ship regardless of the presence of the CO.

2.   *Commanding Officers Should Address*:

    a.   Verbiage of 1MC announcements requesting the Captain's presence in a controlling station and notification of routine reports.

    b.   XO's responsibilities in the CO's absence.

    c.   Department Head (DH) Responsibility Statement(s).

3.   *Commanding Officers May Address*:

    a.   OOD underway weapons release authority.

    b.   Which individuals or watch stations have the authority to relieve a watch station. For example, the Navigator has the authority to relieve the OOD (written authority per reference (b)).

    c.   Emphasis on requesting relief from the SWO if any watchstander feels they are unable to stand a proper watch; e.g., too fatigued, illness, or physically/mentally unable.

STANDING ORDER NUMBER 2
The Watch

1.   *Commanding Officers Shall Address*:

    a.   How the sound shipboard operating principles will be incorporated into the execution of the watch.

        (1) Formality

        (2) Procedural Compliance

        (3) Level of Knowledge

        (4) Questioning Attitude

        (5) Forceful Backup

        (6) Integrity

    b.   The setup of the watch rotation and shipboard routine prioritizing circadian rhythms when feasible.

    c.   How turnovers will be staggered when feasible.

     d. TAO, OOD, and EOOW turnover instructions, including what spaces need to be toured and what information the oncoming TAO/OOD/EOOW must review prior to relieving.

     e. The importance of adhering to the Navigation Rules (commonly referred to as the "Rules of the Road"). Particular emphasis shall be placed on requirements for maintaining a proper lookout as well as the requirement to use all available means appropriate to the prevailing circumstances and conditions (i.e., using alidades or bearing circles to check bearing drift, visual lookouts, and surface-search radars).

2. *Commanding Officers Should Address:*

     a. Implementing the Plan, Brief, Execute, Debrief (PBED) process in day-to-day watchstanding and special evolutions.

     b. Emphasizing the importance of appropriate rest prior to turnover.

     c. Ensuring a complete exchange of information with the previous watch and include specifics.

     d. Addressing reasons to decline relieving the watch and to whom to report; e.g., SWO, XO, CO. List example reasons.

     e. Establishing standards for watchstanding on the bridge addressing topics such as the importance of a dark bridge at night, running a taut watch, alertness, presence of food and/or drinks, using the 1MC, striking of bells, etc.

     f. Actions for watchstanders during marine mammal encounters.

3. *Commanding Officers May Address:*

     a. Stating when turnovers require CO's permission and how turnovers are announced. Some may be in the space verbally such as the CONN; some may be over the command net such as the TAO.

     b. Establishing a requirement to conduct a formalized watch turnover brief with specified watch stations.

STANDING ORDER NUMBER 3
Conning and Maneuvering

1. *Commanding Officers Shall Address:*

     a. Adherence to and knowledge of actions or conditions that prevent compliance.

     b. Requirements for when maneuvering board solutions are to be calculated by both Bridge and Combat Information Center (CIC) watch teams for surface contacts meeting defined Closest Point of Approach (CPA) criteria.

    c. Standard Commands to the Helm/Lee Helm. Watch Officers should know the guiding principles and examples for the development of standard commands. Class-specific standard commands developed at a different echelon of command (i.e., squadron or group) may be incorporated to meet this requirement so long as the class-specific standard commands meet all the requirements in this instruction.

    d. Handling and propulsion characteristics specific to the ship.

    e. Process for the commanding officer to relieve the CONN.

    f. High traffic density situations that prompt the OOD to station additional watchstander(s) in the pilot house or in CIC. The bridge will inform the commanding officer when this additional measure is taken.

2. *Commanding Officers Should Address*:

    a. Providing example handling/propulsion characteristics which may include:

        (1) Turn diameter distances for various rudder angles and speeds.

        (2) Applicable order/speed/RPM/pitch combinations depending on ship class.

        (3) Locked shaft and Trail shaft limitations depending on ship class.

        (4) Surge rate for deceleration.

    b. Relationship with harbor pilots and the use of tugs.

    c. Preparing to steer toward "safe water" at any moment, and understanding a break-out plan if in formation.

    d. Baseline standoff distances and action in the event they will not be maintained such as the "3-2-1 rule" for maneuvering in the vicinity of a CVN or large deck amphibious ship and minimum standoffs for surfaced submarines.

3. *Commanding Officers May Address*:

    a. Procedures or requirements for specified maneuvering considerations, for example visually checking turns, using a formation diagram on a maneuvering board (i.e., in SCREEN KILO formations), and altering course from PIM for contacts.

    b. Quick math such as the 1/3/6 minute rules and the radian rule.

    c. Providing direction commonly derived from other references such as "Naval Shiphandling," "Knight's Modern Seamanship," "Naval Shiphandler's Guide," etc.

STANDING ORDER NUMBER 4
Required Reports

1. *Commanding Officers Shall Address*:
   a. Contact Report format and criteria that require the report. Criteria for the contact report should include the CPA distance that mandates the report, a minimum distance between ownship and the contact, or minimum time to CPA to make the report allowing adequate time for the Commanding Officer to evaluate the situation.
   b. Other reports, to promote organization and facilitate watchstander training; e.g., general, navigation, formations, engineering, special evolutions, occurrences.
   c. Including a statement about quickly developing situations or late detections of contacts, sometimes referred to as "pop-up" contacts, with the priority to take action and notify the CO as soon as possible with available information.
   d. When in doubt notify the Commanding Officer.
2. *Commanding Officers Should Address*:
   a. Format of the report, ensuring it suits the CO without becoming too cumbersome, complicated, or time consuming to complete. Example elements include:
      (1) Who is making the report
      (2) Time
      (3) Ownship course and speed
      (4) Type of contact (clarify if this means type per ROR or type of vessel; i.e., fishing boat or vessel engaged in fishing)
      (5) Source of contact information (hold visual/by RADAR/on AIS)
      (6) Relative position of contact (by numerical relative bearing or port/stbd bow/beam/quarter)
      (7) Range to contact
      (8) Course and speed of contact
      (9) Target angle of contact
      (10) Direction and rate of bearing drift
      (11) CPA range, bearing, time, and source or method of calculation
      (12) Type of situation or evaluation of hierarchy
      (13) Evaluation of risk of collision per USCG Navigation Rules rule 7

        (14) Intentions

        (15) Concurrence with CIC

3. *Commanding Officers May Address*:

    a. The following general reports:

        (1) Any information deemed significant for the CO to know, but not specifically mandated for report.

        (2) 12 o'clock reports (1200 position, magazine temperatures, fuel and water, draft, boat, muster, etc.).

    b. Navigation reports:

        (1) When passing within (specify range) of shoal water.

        (2) Discrepancies between charted depths and Fathometer readings.

        (3) Notification guidelines when off PIM/track by a specified range (ahead/behind/laterally) or time (ahead/behind).

        (4) Casualties, alignment errors, or maintenance discrepancies to navigation equipment (specify equipment).

        (5) Weather changes (wind speed, sea state, visibility, barometric pressure, dew point spread, temperature, etc.) with specific criteria.

    c. Engineering reports:

        (1) Equipment casualty that impacts ship maneuverability or safety of navigation.

    d. Other reports:

        (1) Reason for delays to commencement of an evolution.

        (2) Granting/requesting permission to proceed on duties assigned.

        (3) Detection of other military units (air, surface, or subsurface, regardless of nationality).

        (4) Whenever a watchstander declines to relieve the watch.

        (5) Conflicting interpretation of tactical signals, maneuvers, or situations that are not promptly clarified.

        (6) Injuries.

        (7) Loss of communications.

        (8) When queried, warned, or reprimanded on any communication circuit.

        (9) Formation reporting guidance to include changes in ordered formation composition, inability to maintain station, and the breakdown of units in company.

        (10) Marine mammal sighting.

        (11) Request for assistance from distressed mariners.

e. Designate when reports shall be made to individuals in addition to the CO. For example, make all navigation reports to the XO and Navigator, or make all contact reports to embarked Commanders in addition to the CO.

STANDING ORDER NUMBER 5
Commanding Officer Approval Items

1. *Commanding Officers Shall Address*:
   a. Deviating from standing orders, night orders, or orders from Commanders exercising OPCON/TACON of ownship or any approved procedure such as those contained in EOSS, CSOSS, PMS, Fleet Guidance, etc.
2. *Commanding Officers Should Address*:
   a. General
      (1) Discharging waste over the side.
      (2) Conducting casualty control drills.
      (3) Setting and securing the Restricted Maneuvering Doctrine (RMD).
      (4) Turnover of specified watchstations when the CO is present.
      (5) Securing from General Quarters.
   b. Engineering
      (1) When setting single valve protection to the sea, or any high energy or immediately dangerous to life or health (IDLH) system.
      (2) Main engine/prime mover startup (specify exceptions; for example, permission not required when inherent in another order such as setting maximum engineering reliability).
      (3) Tagging out specified equipment.
      (4) Rolling or stopping shafts.
      (5) Opening reduction gears.
      (6) Aligning installed drainage.
      (7) Transferring flammable liquids.
   c. Weapons/Combat Systems
      (1) Handling/transferring ammunition.
      (2) Testing magazine sprinklers.
      (3) Firing any weapon (reference exceptions granted for self-defense).
   d. Safety
      (1) Entry into IDLH spaces such as tanks, voids, spaces contaminated by toxic gas, etc.

    (2) Working on energized equipment (specify conditions).

    (3) Bypassing equipment interlocks or safety devices.

    (4) Personnel going topside after dark when under way.

    (5) Personnel going aloft or over the side while under way.

    (6) Exceeding heat stress risk stay times.

  e. Navigation

    (1) Securing navigation equipment (specify equipment; e.g., Fathometer, VMS, NAVSSI, GPS, INS, navigation RADAR, fluxgate compass, etc.).

    (2) Prior to closing within specified distance of land/shoal or prior to crossing a specified depth curve.

  f. Special Evolutions

    (1) Launching/recovering small boat.

    (2) UNREP permissions such as commencing the approach, tensioning/de-tensioning CONREP rigs, prior to receiving fuel or pumping to a receiving ship, etc.

    (3) Permissions associated with anchoring such as removing stoppers and letting go during anchoring.

    (4) Permissions associated with flight operations such as granting green deck, moving aircraft elevators, unfolding rotors, lowering nets, etc.

    (5) Permissions associated with well deck operations such as granting green well, vehicle movements, ballasting or deballasting, etc.

    (6) Permissions associated with mission bay operations such as opening or closing doors, crane and lift operations, vehicle movements, etc.

    (7) Permissions associated with streaming towed bodies.

STANDING ORDER NUMBER 6
Navigation

1. *Commanding Officers Shall Address*:

  a. Notification requirements and actions anytime the watch team experiences a conflict between expected navigation plan information and actual observations; e.g., Fathometer readings do not correlate to charted depths, unexpected presence of navaid, or absence of expected navaid, track appears erroneously close to hazard, etc.

    b.   AIS transmission requirements per Fleet Commander guidance.

    c.   Fix interval guidance as directed by Navy navigation regulations.

2. *Commanding Officers Should Address*:

    a.   Quantifying a high-density traffic area, taking into account ship and mission parameters, training and proficiency, and area of operations.

    b.   Equipment-specific guidance. For example:

        (1) Fathometer settings and corrected Fathometer soundings to account for hull projections such as rudders or a sonar dome.

        (2) VMS: including review of advisories and settings (e.g., Own-ship Safety Zone configuration, fix source precedence, etc.).

        (3) Use of the Emergency Navigation Laptop (ENL).

        (4) Navigation radar setup.

STANDING ORDER NUMBER 7

Restricted Visibility

1. *Commanding Officers Shall Address*: When to implement the provisions of the ship's tailored Low Visibility Bill per reference (c) within XX NM (specify range).

2. *Commanding Officers Should Address*:

    a.   Considerations for transmitting position via AIS.

    b.   Varying the timing of fog signals randomly (within 2 min intervals) to avoid sounding simultaneously with another ship, especially when closing a contact held on radar.

STANDING ORDER NUMBER 8

Man Overboard

1. *Commanding Officers Shall Address*:

    a.   The preferred method of recovery in daytime/nighttime and whether the man overboard is in sight or not.

    b.   Initial plotting responsibilities.

    c.   Off-ship reporting requirements (to include but not limited to: BTB emergency calls, sound signals, and operational reporting).

    d.   Guidance for special circumstances (to include but not limited to: towed body operations, wet well operations, flight operations—as applicable based on ship class).

2. *Commanding Officers Should Address*:

    a.   Securing use of Fathometer or active sonar (mission dependent).

    b.   Guidance on the use of smoke floats and life rings.

STANDING ORDER NUMBER 9
Anchoring
1. *Commanding Officers Shall Address*:
    a. Plotting and fix intervals per Navy navigation regulations.
    b. Required actions when actually dragging anchor or suspecting the ship is dragging anchor.
    c. Use of ship's nomograph for determining the minimum length of chain and the horizontal distance from the ship to the anchor for flat and sloped bottoms.
2. *Commanding Officers Should Address*:
    a. Additional actions in observed or anticipated inclement weather.
    b. Specified equipment configuration.
    c. Required reports while at anchor.

STANDING ORDER NUMBER 10
Restricted Maneuvering Doctrine
1. *Commanding Officers Shall Address*:
    a. Authorities for setting, maintaining, and securing from RMD.
    b. Conditions when RMD is required.
    c. Specific engineering plant deviations from normal operation procedures based on ship technical characteristics and references.
    d. Equipment configuration for RMD, tailored to meet their ship-specific needs.

STANDING ORDER NUMBER 11
Engineering/Maximum Plant Reliability
1. *Commanding Officers Shall Address*: Plant configuration for maximum engineering reliability and the conditions under which it should be set.

STANDING ORDER NUMBER 12
Steering Control
1. *Commanding Officers Shall Address*:
    a. Conditions when a Master Helmsman and Lee Helmsman are required.
    b. Conditions when after steering must be manned, and guidance for when the space is unmanned, regarding which watchstanders shall respond and their condition of readiness.
2. *Commanding Officers Should Address*:
    a. Equipment configurations based on specific operations.

b. Standard commands for transferring control between the pilot house and after steering.

STANDING ORDER NUMBER 13
Small Boat Operations

1. *Commanding Officers Shall Address*: Special shiphandling considerations for launching and recovering boats (e.g., creating a lee).
2. *Commanding Officers Should Address*:
   a. Minimum manning for small boats while maintaining requirements listed in references (b), (o), and (p).
   b. Requirements for the Boat Officer to receive a brief from the bridge team prior to launch that covers ensuing operations.
   c. Sequencing and associated permissions for launching and recovering small boats.

STANDING ORDER NUMBER 14
Flight Deck Operations

1. *Commanding Officers Shall Address*:
   a. Shiphandling restrictions based off of approved wind envelopes, polar plots, or other technical guidance based on ship class and aircraft specifications.
   b. Equipment configurations for both day/night and aided/unaided flight operations.
   c. Sequencing and associated permissions for launching and recovering aircraft.
2. *Commanding Officers Should Address*:
   a. Emergency situations and reporting responsibilities.
   b. Conflicts between the OOD and the aircraft commander.

STANDING ORDER NUMBER 15
Well Deck/Mission Bay Operations

1. *Commanding Officers Shall Address*: Delegated authorities and authorizations related to the conduct of well deck/mission bay operations.
2. *Commanding Officers Should Address*:
   a. Emergency considerations where safety of ship may preclude safety concerns of personnel and equipment in well deck or mission bay.
   b. Additional considerations based on the mission package capability and projected operating environment.

STANDING ORDER NUMBER 16
Towed Gear Operations
1. *Commanding Officers Shall Address:*
   a. Restrictions to maneuvering capability when deploying/retrieving or operating towed body (i.e., NIXIE or passive towed array sonar) per appropriate reference documentation.
   b. Emergency considerations for both ship control and towed gear recovery teams.
2. *Commanding Officers May Address:* Additional reporting and coordination instructions between the Bridge, Combat Information Center, and Sonar Control.

RESTRICTED MANEUVERING DOCTRINE GUIDANCE
Ref: (a) Engineering Operational Sequencing System (EOSS)
      (b) COMNAVSURFPAC/COMNAVSURFLANTINST 3540.3 (EDORM)
      (c) OPNAVINST 3120.32 (SORM)
      (d) COMNAVSURFORINST 3500.5 (Watchstander's Guide)
      (e) COMNAVSURFPAC/COMNAVSURFLANTINST 3504.1C (Redlines)

1. *Purpose.* The Restricted Maneuvering Doctrine (RMD) is a risk management tool that places a premium on ship maneuverability and safety at the potential cost of equipment. This established standardized RMD is written for a permissive, non-combat environment and, therefore, minimizes risk of possible equipment damage by setting the minimum requirements necessary to maintain effective ship control. The Commanding Officer retains the authority and responsibility to elevate readiness in light of the current threat environment and mission requirements; the Captain should amend the minimum engineering plant configuration requirements as situationally required to ensure adequate responsiveness to the tactical situation.
2. *Definitions.* RMD is to be set in those situations where ship's speed and maneuverability *must* be maintained for the safety of the ship at the risk of damaging equipment. Once the command decision has been made to set RMD, watchstanders are authorized to deviate from established casualty control procedures to ensure maneuverability is maintained. RMD will be set for the minimum amount of time required, and will normally be set during the following conditions:

    a. Sea and Anchor Detail (in port or under way).

    b. Operating in restricted waters or a high traffic area.

    c. Complex, close-in maneuvering situations or evolutions in close proximity to other vessels; i.e., connected replenishments (CONREP).

    d. Other special evolutions as required per the Commanding Officer's standing orders and battle orders.

    e. Unplanned:

       (1) If the Officer of the Deck believes an unsafe or dangerous situation is developing which can be mitigated by setting RMD.

       (2) When the tactical situation warrants, the Tactical Action Officer can direct the setting of RMD via the Officer of the Deck. Amplifying requirements and pre-planned responses will be delineated in the Commanding Officer's Battle Orders.

    f. Whenever the Commanding Officer deems it necessary.

3. *Responsibility.*

    a. *Commanding Officer (CO).*

       (1) CO will establish an RMD Policy informed by this appendix.

       (2) Approve any deviations to RMD.

    b. *Chief Engineer (CHENG).*

       (1) Review RMD for technical accuracy when required.

       (2) Advise the CO of any deficiencies of propulsion or ship's service electrical system equipment.

       (3) Incorporate the contents of this instruction into all qualifying boards for engineering supervisory watches, notably the Engineering Officer of the Watch/Readiness Control Officer, Propulsion and Auxiliaries Control Console Operators (PACC/A-EOOW), and Electrical Plant Control Console (EPCC) Operator as applicable.

    c. *Officer of the Deck (OOD).* Set RMD if the prevailing conditions or tactical situation warrant.

    d. *Engineering Officer of the Watch (EOOW)/Readiness Control Officer (RCO).* When in RMD, ensure that all orders from the OOD concerning the speed and direction of the ship are executed.

4. *Setting RMD.*

    a. When RMD is ordered, the OOD will direct all controlling stations (as per SORM) to set RMD:

    b. For Planned RMD, set briefed "Maximum Reliability" plant line-up as determined by the CO prior to setting RMD.

    c.   Have the word passed over the 1MC: **"SET THE RESTRICTED MANEUVERING DOCTRINE."**

    d.   Controlling Stations will announce over the controlling circuits: **"RESTRICTED MANEUVERING DOCTRINE IS IN EFFECT."**

    e.   Watchstanders will place "RESTRICTED MANEUVERING" placards and electronic status indicators (as applicable) at all ship controlling stations.

    f.   **"RESTRICTED MANEUVERING DOCTRINE IS SET"** will be entered in the Deck, CIC/CCC, CSOOW, and Engineering Logs.

    g.   All controlling stations will report to the OOD once all watchstanders have acknowledged that RMD is set and equipment is aligned per RMD/Maximum reliability plant lineup.

    h.   Once all controlling stations report RMD is set, pass the word over the 1MC: **"RESTRICTED MANEUVERING DOCTRINE IS IN EFFECT. DO NOT START, STOP, OR CHANGE THE STATUS OF ANY EQUIPMENT OR CONDUCT ANY PREVENTIVE OR CORRECTIVE MAINTENANCE WITHOUT APPROVAL FROM THE COMMANDING OFFICER."** and continue to repeat every 30 minutes.

    i.   <u>NO</u> PMS or corrective maintenance should be conducted during RMD, unless:

        (1) Specific permission is requested from the CO via the OOD.

        (2) Required maintenance in support of a special evolution that is briefed and approved by the CO prior to setting RMD.

    j.   <u>NO</u> new tag outs will be authorized without CO's specific approval during RMD.

    k.   <u>NO</u> ground isolation or troubleshooting will be conducted without CO's specific approval during RMD.

5.   *RMD is in EFFECT.*

    a.   A direct verbal order from the CO to the EOOW/RCO takes precedence over any other means of transmitting propulsion orders from the bridge to engineering controlling stations.

    b.   In the event of a casualty, EOOW will notify the OOD immediately of its effect on ship's speed, shaft revolutions per minute (RPM), electrical distribution and/or steering. If necessary, the

OOD will have to compensate for loss of ship's speed by increasing RPM or pitch on the unaffected shaft, particularly when alongside another ship.

    (1) CO has authority to direct action during RMD to direct casualty control

  c. The EOOW shall report any unusual condition or trend to the CO and OOD as early as practical to allow as much time as possible to maneuver the ship to safety or to prepare mitigation for a possible casualty.

6. *Secure from RMD.*

  a. When the special conditions that caused the restricted maneuvering situation to exist have passed, the OOD, with the approval of the CO, will direct all controlling stations to secure from RMD.

  b. All controlling stations will report to the OOD once all watchstanders have acknowledged the report.

  c. Watchstanders will remove "RESTRICTED MANEUVERING" placards and electronic status indicators (as applicable).

  d. The OOD must have the word passed over the 1MC: **"SECURE FROM RESTRICTED MANEUVERING DOCTRINE."**

  e. **"SECURE FROM RESTRICTED MANEUVERING DOCTRINE"** will be entered in the Deck, CIC/CCC, CSOOW, and Engineering Logs.

7. *Action.* All watchstanders will review this instruction monthly as determined by the CO. The content of this instruction will be prerequisite knowledge for all qualifying controlling stations, including, but not limited to: TAO/CICWO, OOD, EOOW/RCO, PACC, A-EOOW, Engine Room Operators (ERO)/Engineering Plant Technicians (EPT), Helm Safety Officer (HSO), Aft Steering, and Helm/Lee Helmsman.

STANDING ORDERS EXAMPLES
USS XXXXXXX INSTRUCTION ####.#

Subj: COMMANDING OFFICER'S STANDING ORDERS

Ref: (a) List applicable references

1. <u>Purpose</u>. This instruction promulgates standing orders for USS XXXXX. This instruction amplifies references (a) through (xx), which contain other information basic to the Officer of the Deck's (OOD) responsibilities.

2. Content. These standing orders include my directives encompassing the following topics and situations:
   a. Standing Order #1: Responsibilities
   b. Standing Order #2: The Watch
   c. Standing Order #3: Conning and Maneuvering
   d. Standing Order #4: Required Reports to the Commanding Officer
   e. Standing Order #5: Commanding Officer Approval Items
   f. Standing Order #6: Navigation
   g. Standing Order #7: Restricted Visibility
   h. Standing Order #8: Man Overboard
   i. Standing Order #9: Anchoring
   j. Standing Order #10: Restricted Maneuvering Doctrine
   k. Standing Order #11: Engineering/Maximum Plant Reliability
   l. Standing Order #12: Steering Control
   m. Standing Order #13: Small Boat Operations
   n. Standing Order #14: Flight Operations
   o. Standing Order #15: Well Deck/Mission Bay Operations
   p. Standing Order #16: Towed Gear Operations
3. Responsibility. As your Captain, I AM ON DUTY 24 HOURS PER DAY, and responsible for the safety of this ship at all times. I depend upon you and trust you to assist me in keeping our Sailors and our ship safe from harm.
4. Action.
   a. If there is ever any conflict between the Fleet standing orders, my supplemental standing orders or the night orders, bring the conflict to my attention immediately and take positive action to operate safely while we resolve the conflict.
   b. The Navigator will maintain the night order book and keep a copy of these standing orders in front along with a monthly Record of Acknowledgment sheet which will be maintained on board for one year. Each Sailor standing watch in a control station will read and acknowledge they understand these orders monthly by signing the Record of Acknowledgment. Supplemental night orders will be prepared nightly or as appropriate and reviewed by cognizant authorities prior to my signature.
   c. Recommendations for changes or additions to this instruction may be made at any time through the Navigator. The Senior Watch Officer and the Navigator are responsible for the annual review of this instruction.

d. All Bridge and Engineering watchstanders will review this instruction monthly. The content of this instruction will be prerequisite knowledge for all qualifying controlling stations, including, but not limited to: TAO, CICWO, OOD, SUWC, EOOW/RCO, CONN, JOOD, QMOW, Helm Safety Officer (HSO), and Helm /Lee Helmsman.

Commanding Officer

STANDING ORDER NUMBER 1
Responsibilities

1. Command Responsibility
    a. As the Commanding Officer, I am ultimately responsible for every action and inaction that occurs aboard this ship. Along with my trust and confidence in you as a watchstander in a controlling station, comes my expectation that you execute your duties to the utmost of your ability.
    b. **NEVER HESITATE TO CALL ME**. When reports are required, make certain I understand your report. In an emergency, concentrate on the safety of the ship and pass the word, "CAPTAIN TO THE (station)," on the 1MC. If a situation is not an emergency, and you are unable to locate me, do not hesitate to pass, "COMMANDING OFFICER, PLEASE CONTACT (station) FOR A ROUTINE REPORT."
    c. **DO NOT ABDICATE YOUR RESPONSIBILITY OR AUTHORITY**. As OOD, TAO, EOOW/RCO and CSOOW, you are in a position of special trust and confidence. You must act always for the safety of the ship and CALL ME IF DOUBT EXISTS.
2. Watch Relationships
    a. The OOD is my direct representative and is ALWAYS responsible for the navigational safety of this ship. The OOD underway is granted weapons release authority for crew-served weapons in self-defense. The Conning Officer (CONN) is responsible for issuing necessary orders to the helm and main engine control to avoid danger, to take or keep an assigned station, and to change course and speed following orders of proper authority. Normally a specified watchstander will be assigned as CONN, however whenever the CONN shifts to another watchstander, to the OOD,

or if I assume the CONN, it will be announced to all personnel in the pilothouse. Only one officer will have the CONN at any time and nothing absolves the OOD of their responsibility for safe navigation, regardless of who has the CONN.

b. The Tactical Action Officer (TAO) will be assigned during most underway operations, and is granted weapons release authority for weapons in defense of this ship. My Battle Orders outline the responsibilities of the TAO, but the assignment of a TAO does NOT relieve the OOD of his/her responsibility for the ship's safe navigation and operation. The TAO, or Combat Information Center Watch Officer (when the TAO is not present), is responsible to the OOD for navigational support as required in the NAVDORM. The Surface Warfare Coordinator (SUWC), in addition to their tactical responsibilities, is the primary surface contact management and contact avoidance watchstander and will make reports to the CICWO for contact management support.

c. The Engineering Officer of the Watch (EOOW)/Readiness Control Officer (RCO) will be assigned during all underway operations and in-port operations when the engineering schedule dictates. The EOOW is responsible for the safe operation of our engineering plant and will provide resources for power, propulsion and steering as directed by the OOD or TAO (in combat situations).

d. The Combat Systems Officer of the Watch (CSOOW) or equivalent will be assigned during all underway operations and in-port operations when the combat systems schedule dictates. The CSOOW is responsible for the safe operation of our Combat and Weapons Systems, and will provide resources for navigation, self-defense and offensive operations as directed.

e. If, at any time, these supervisory stations disagree in the safe operation of this ship, I am to be called IMMEDIATELY.

3. Command Relationships

a. Executive Officer. The Executive Officer runs the ship and is second in command. I trust the XO's experience and judgment implicitly, and the XO may relieve any watchstander in any situation when such action is necessary for the safety of personnel or equipment. The OOD is responsible to the Executive Officer for the execution of events contained within the Plan of the Day and will keep the Executive Officer advised of any changes that are required.

    b.   Senior Watch Officer. The Senior Watch Officer is charged with the supervision of the shipboard watch organization. Immediately notify the Senior Watch Officer if you or any of your assigned watchstanders are incapable of standing their watch or completing their duties.

    c.   Department Heads. The Department Heads are responsible for supplying the resources enabling successful execution of the ship's schedule. Keep the Department Heads informed of any changes you feel will affect our ability to accomplish our mission.

    d.   Navigator. The Navigator reports directly to the Commanding Officer with respect to the ship's safe navigation. The Navigator shall advise the OOD of safe courses and speeds to steer, however the OOD must evaluate each maneuvering recommendation with regards to the actual situation.

4.   Responsibilities

    a.   The fact that the Captain or Executive Officer is in a controlling station does not relieve the watchstander of the responsibility to maintain full situational awareness, and to forcefully and positively state his/her opinion and recommendations for the safe operation of the ship.

STANDING ORDER NUMBER 2
The Watch

1.   Conduct of the watch:

    a.   Ensure the watch is executed per the sound shipboard operating principles. These principles are:

        i.   Formality—Formality and the use of standard phraseology are important for clear understanding of your orders. Use it, and require all members of your watch section to do likewise. Additionally, address watchstanders by their watch station, billet, or rank/last name. Do not use first names or nicknames while on watch.

        ii.   Procedural Compliance—Established procedures are defined and approved written instructions from higher authority. It is your responsibility to know the procedure, understand the procedure, and execute as directed.

        iii.   Level of Knowledge—You must possess an in-depth knowledge of the systems you are operating so you can act with confidence and are able to recognize and correct abnormal conditions.

iv. Questioning Attitude—Apply critical thinking and be proactive. Expect to find conditions that require action.

v. Forceful Backup—Foster an environment of inclusiveness which values the input from subordinate watchstations. Have the courage to "speak out" and provide critical forceful backup when something is unclear or when improper actions are being taken. Communication up and down the chain of command is important, regardless of rank.

vi. Integrity—Be honest and truthful. Disclose mistakes, errors, and limitations. Confront others and adverse situations when firm adherence to the standard of integrity is absent or compromised.

   1. Ensure you are maintaining a proper lookout and use all available means such as surface-search radars and visual lookouts. When in visual range, take precise bearings using alidades or bearing circles to observe trends and validate bearing drift.

2. Prior to relieving the watch as a Controlling Station Supervisor, you shall:

   a. Ensure you and your watch team are rested and ready to perform your duties. To the greatest extent possible, we will use a watch rotation based on circadian rhythm and honor protected rest periods.

   b. Have a thorough knowledge and clear understanding of the shipboard material and operational status and any changes expected during your watch. You will visit all controlling stations, obtain a briefing by the station supervisor, and ascertain the tactical and technical understanding of scheduled evolutions and responsibilities. Seek amplification from myself, the Executive Officer, or the cognizant Department Head if you have any doubts.

   c. Ensure a complete exchange of information with the previous supervisor, to include:

      i. Tactical formation and organization, including our station and any unexecuted or expected tactical signals.

      ii. Awareness of the surface contact picture and intended course of action.

      iii. Ship-wide material condition, Condition of Readiness, Weapon Postures, EMCON status, and Engineering Plant Alignment.

      iv. Any special evolution scheduled during your watch and the status of preparations.

      v. Officers of the Deck will relieve on the hour specified on the watch bill, the JOOD will relieve 15 minutes prior to the OOD, the CONN will relieve 30 minutes prior to the OOD. TAO will relieve 15 minutes past the hour specified on the watch bill.

  d. The OOD will, specifically prior to turnover:

      i. Understand the ship's position, navigational plan, and overall equipment status and ensure it supports the tactical situation. If the situation cannot be resolved, call myself, the cognizant Department Head, and the Navigator.

      ii. Review the surface contact situation to ensure compliance with the Rules of the Road, safety with respect to the prevailing conditions, and adherence to these standing orders. A proper number of qualified lookouts will be stationed as appropriate.

      iii. If gear is streamed, to include NIXIE, review the scope of depth of the gear, comparing it with water depth along the intended track before relieving. Ensure the planned track allows for significant depth beneath the gear if the ship becomes adrift.

  e. The actual change of the watch shall be made with care and formality, as the relieving supervisor is completely responsible for the watch once he/she has relieved. The relief of all supervisors will be made formally in each space and also on whichever Net or channel is monitored by the greatest number of stations and personnel, e.g., the CO's Battle Net. If I am in the space, request permission to relieve the watch and report turnover to me.

3. Watch reliefs may be delayed due to the operational environment at any given time if introducing turnover would create an unsafe situation or endanger us. You may decline to relieve the watch if:

  a. The ship is out of station or off PIM without explanation or proper reports having been made, or if position cannot be adequately determined.

  b. The tactical situation is unclear.

  c. The previous watchteam has not adequately prepared for the turnover.

  d. The status of equipment found on your prewatch tour does not reflect the briefed status, and if the issue cannot be resolved.

  e. You are ill or otherwise physically incapable of standing the watch.

4. Should you decline to relieve, immediately inform me and the Senior Watch Officer. If the navigation picture is unsafe, inform me and the Navigator immediately.

5. We will incorporate the Plan, Brief, Execute, Debrief (PBED) process into not only planned special evolutions, but also day-to-day watchstanding. Conduct a formalized watch turnover brief led by the oncoming TAO and attended by the oncoming OOD, JOOD, SUWC, AAWC (or other specified watchstanders as required by the TAO) prior to the start of staggered watch turnovers. The focus of the brief should be lessons learned from previous watch, status of current and upcoming events, systems status such as weapons, comms, link, and any other controlling station priorities.

STANDING ORDER NUMBER 3
Conning and Maneuvering

1. I may relieve the deck and/or assume the CONN at any time. Normally, I will specifically inform the OOD of the duties of which he/she is being relieved; however, should I give a direct order to the helm or lee helm at any time, it will be understood that I have assumed the CONN and be so logged by the QMOW. If the OOD is in doubt as to the exact status in this regard, it is the OOD's responsibility to immediately clarify who has the CONN.

2. Maneuvering. When operationally feasible, take actions per USCG Navigation Rules and Regulations Handbook and notify me when this cannot be accomplished. Know where safe water lies and be prepared to maneuver toward it at every moment.

   a. Do not allow yourself to be distracted by lesser tasks during maneuvering situations, periods of high traffic density, or low visibility.

   b. Always look before you turn and verify the ship's response to your orders after you give them.

   c. Always maneuver per USCG Navigation Rules and Regulations Handbook and notify me whenever a situation arises where you believe compliance with the Rules of the Road is not feasible.

   d. Standard commands shall be issued by the conning officer in a clear voice with appropriate volume for the situation. (Provide examples.)

3. Contact Management

   a. All contacts with a CPA of 2.5NM or less will be closely monitored until they are past CPA and at a range greater than 10NM.

If there is a disagreement between the Bridge and CIC as to an impending situation, notify me immediately. Take frequent visual bearings on all contacts to ensure adequate bearing drift exists. If you are unable to meet these requirements due to high traffic density, the OOD shall notify me immediately.

b. When in formation, maintain an accurate, up-to-date formation diagram of all ships in company on maneuvering board. Maneuver independently to avoid contacts and give a wide berth to navigational hazards.

c. Maneuvering board solutions will be calculated by both the Bridge and CIC for all contacts with an initial CPA of less than 2.5NM.

d. Unless specifically ordered, maintain a minimum range of 2.5NM from a surfaced submarine or one at periscope depth. Observe a minimum distance of 3NM ahead, 2NM abeam and 1NM astern of an aircraft carrier or large deck amphibious ship.

e. Transits are planned to avoid hazards, optimize safety, and meet mission requirements. Altering course to facilitate safe passage with other vessels is acceptable, but do not leave track just to avoid making contact reports. If conditions warrant a potential change to the track, contact the Navigator to report those conditions and make a recommendation, i.e., contact density, traffic flow, unplanned hazards, etc., make the current track dangerous or impractical and a suitable alternative may exist. The Navigator will implement changes to the track per the Navigation Bill with my approval.

f. High traffic density situations should prompt the OOD to station additional watchstander(s) in the pilot house or request additional lookouts from the Senior Watch Officer to assist with contact management. The Bridge will inform me when this additional measure is taken. I may specify additional "on call" watchstanders on the normal underway steaming watch bill, but the OOD can call on any crew member to assist in maintaining the safety of the ship. Examples include:

   i. Shipping Officers

   ii. Additional OOD underway qualified officers

   iii. Department Heads

   iv. Any capable MOBOARD, Comms, or RADAR operator(s)

4. Formation Steaming

   a. If doubt exists, maneuver out of station, sector, or screen and into open sea room.

    b.   Signals received by radio or via the signal bridge will be simultaneously and independently broken by the Bridge and CIC. The Bridge will advise me if concurrence is not reached promptly.

    c.   If emergency action is necessary, regardless of reason, keep other ships in formation informed using radio circuits and visual signals.

    d.   While assigned a point station, maintain station within 2 degrees of bearing and 10% of range. For sector stations, remain within the designated sector. The Bridge will call me if we do not maintain station.

    e.   Upon receipt of an IMMEDIATE EXECUTE signal, take the required action (put over rudder, increase speed, etc.) as the Bridge informs me of the signal.

STANDING ORDER NUMBER 4
Required Reports

1.   I am always on duty. Call me if in doubt.

2.   Contact Reports

    a.   Notify me of any surface contact with a CPA within 2.5 NM. This report should be made before the contact reaches 6 NM. Contact reports shall be made in the following manner: "Captain, this is the (OOD/JOOD) with a contact report. The time is ___. We are on course ___° T at speed ___ kts. We have a (type of contact/AIS name) by (visual/radar/AIS), bearing ___ relative, off the (port/stbd, bow/qtr/beam) at ___ yards, on course ___ ° T, speed ___ kts. Target angle is ___ with (significant/good/slight) (left/right) bearing drift [or: "Is CBDR"]. By (radar/moboard) the CPA is ___ yards off the (port/stbd) (bow/beam/quarter) in ___ minutes. This is (overtaking/head on/crossing) situation and we are the (give-way/stand-on) vessel. My intentions are to: _____. This is/is not per the Rules of the Road. Combat (concurs/does not concur)."

    b.   In a fast-moving situation that requires quick action, the cognizant controlling station will report to me what you know immediately and supplement it when more information becomes available.

    c.   If a junior naval vessel requests permission to proceed on duties assigned, immediately grant permission and then the Bridge will inform me.

    d.   The TAO will notify me when other military vessels or military aircraft are operating in the vicinity, regardless of nationality.

3. General Reports
   a. All occurrences you believe deserve my attention.
   b. When you decline to relieve the watch.
   c. Conflicting guidance from higher authority contrary to these orders.
   d. Conflicting interpretation of tactical signals, maneuvers, or situations between any Controlling Watch Station.
   e. All significant material casualties and corrective action.
   f. All injuries to personnel. This will also be reported to the XO.
   g. Any abnormal condition or alarm that cannot be immediately cleared.
   h. When calling away the SNOOPIE team. If necessary, do not hesitate to set it first and inform me after.
   i. When setting the Low Visibility Detail. If necessary, do not hesitate to set it first and inform me after.
   j. Prior to alteration of the major engineering plant equipment or combat systems alignment not included in the night orders.
   k. Anytime you intend to discharge of waste not per Maritime Pollution Abatement Regulations.
   l. Prior to granting initial "GREEN DECK" for helicopter operations.
   m. Prior to loading, lowering, and launching small boats.
   n. While under way, prior to authorizing work aloft or over the side.
   o. Anytime a major evolution cannot be conducted on time.
   p. When a Flag Officer or Squadron Commander is embarked, make similar reports to him/her or his Staff Watch Officer per appropriate staff orders.
4. Weather
   a. Marked changes in the weather
      i. Sustained true wind of 25 kts or greater.
      ii. Wind speed changes of 10kts or more in one hour.
      iii. Increase in seas of 2 feet in a two-hour period.
      iv. Barometric pressure at or below 29.5 inches or a change in 0.04 inches in one hour or 0.10 inches in a four-hour period.
      v. If visibility changes significantly or reduces to less than 4 miles.
      vi. When temperature and dew point temperature are within 4 degrees of each other.
   b. If any unusual weather phenomena occrs.
5. Navigation
   a. When the ship's track will pass within 10 nautical miles of shoal water.

    b. Any time the ship's position is in doubt.

    c. When fixes plot outside the drag circle while anchored or there is indication of dragging.

    d. Whenever Fathometer soundings differ by 10 percent from charted depth, or when the ship is in less than 100 ft of water.

    e. When encountering any unexpected buoys, navigation aids, or hazards to navigation.

    f. When unable to maintain the Plan of Intended Movement or Speed of Advance.

    g. Any time navigation equipment or steering gear fails a special evolution preventive maintenance check.

6. Communication

    a. Significant tactical signals.

    b. Loss of communications on any maneuvering or warfare commander circuit for a period of 10 minutes.

7. Maneuvering

    a. Unresolved contact tracking conflicts between CIC and the bridge, especially when the bridge and CIC do not concur on course, speed, and CPA.

    b. If the ship deviates more than authorized in the night orders from the intended track to facilitate safe passage with another vessel.

    c. Report change of formation or station assignments or formation course changes immediately. Do not wait until the signals are executed to call me. Likewise, execute immediate execute signals and inform me as soon thereafter as practical.

    d. When in formation, report when we are off station more than 10% of range and/or 2 degrees in bearing; outside patrol limits; if unable to maintain station; if you do not understand the movement of the Guide or any other ships in the formation; or if any other unit is significantly off station and may present a problem.

    e. Breakdown of ships in company.

    f. When required to take immediate action to avoid risk of collision.

STANDING ORDER NUMBER 5
Commanding Officer Approval Items

1. Prior to conducting an evolution that could potentially place our ship and crew into a potentially high-risk evolution, we will discuss the

evolution in a formal brief (for planned evolutions) and conduct the necessary ORM to ensure its safety.

2. Unless otherwise given, obtain my permission prior to:

    a. General

        i. Deviating from standing orders, night orders, or orders from Commanders exercising OPCON/TACON or any approved procedure such as those contained in EOSS, CSOSS, PMS, or other Fleet Guidance.

        ii. Discharging waste over the side.

        iii. Conducting casualty control drills.

        iv. Setting and securing the Restricted Maneuvering Doctrine (RMD).

        v. Turnover of OOD, TAO, and CONN when the CO is present.

        vi. Securing from General Quarters.

        vii. Changing approved Watch Bills.

    b. Engineering

        i. When setting single valve protection to the sea, or any high energy or immediately dangerous to life or health (IDLH) system.

        ii. Main engine/prime mover startup (specify exceptions; for example, permission not required when inherent in another order such as setting maximum engineering reliability).

        iii. Tagging out specified equipment.

        iv. Rolling or stopping shafts.

        v. Opening reduction gears.

        vi. Aligning installed drainage.

        vii. Transferring flammable liquids.

        viii. Changing the electrical configuration of the ship.

        ix. Disabling installed Damage Control systems.

    c. Weapons/Combat Systems

        i. Handling/transferring ammunition.

        ii. Testing magazine sprinklers.

        iii. Firing any weapon (reference exceptions granted for self-defense).

    d. Safety

        i. Entry into IDLH spaces such as tanks, voids, and spaces contaminated by toxic gas.

        ii. Working on energized equipment.

      iii. Bypassing equipment interlocks or safety devices.

      iv. Personnel going topside after dark when under way.

      v. Personnel going aloft or over the side while under way.

      vi. Exceeding heat stress risk stay times as listed in OPNAVINST 5100.19 series.

  e. Navigation

      i. Securing navigation equipment (i.e., Fathometer, VMS, GPS, INS, navigation RADAR, fluxgate compass).

      ii. Prior to closing within 10 NM of land/shoal or prior to crossing the 50-fathom curve.

      iii. Prior to entering another nation's territorial waters.

      iv. Deviating from planned track more than 2 NM laterally or greater than 2 hours ahead or behind PIM.

  f. Special Evolutions

      i. Launching/recovering small boats as discussed in Standing Order 13.

      ii. Commencing the UNREP approach, tensioning/de-tensioning CONREP rigs, and prior to receiving fuel or pumping to a receiving ship.

      iii. Removing stoppers and letting go during anchoring.

      iv. Launching/recovering aircraft as discussed in Standing Order 14.

      v. Prior to streaming or recovering towed bodies as discussed in Standing Order 16.

STANDING ORDER NUMBER 6
Navigation

1. The safe navigation of the ship is the most important responsibility as a Controlling Station Supervisor. If there is any doubt in your mind regarding the accurate position of the ship or the ability to remain in safe waters, slow or stop as necessary until the issue is resolved, and the OOD shall call myself and the Navigator immediately.

2. The Navigator will perform duties as outlined in OPNAVINST 3120.32D (SORM) and CNSP/CNAP/CNSL/CNALINST 3530.4E (NAVDORM) as well as this standing order. Specifically, notify the Navigator when:

  a. You are in doubt about any element of navigation or the performance of any navigation watchstander.

  b. An expected aid to navigation is sighted 30 minutes or more ahead of schedule or not sighted within 15 minutes of expected time.

c. Any unexpected aid to navigation is sighted.

d. When fix intervals cannot be complied with the NAVDORM table below.

AREA	DISTANCE FROM LAND OR SHOAL WATER	GPS FOM	MAXIMUM FIX
Restricted Waters	Less than 2 nautical miles	FOM ≤ 2	3 minutes
Piloting Waters	2–10 nautical miles	FOM ≤ 4	3–15 minutes conditions warrant
Coastal Waters	10–30 nautical miles	FOM ≤ 6	15–30 minutes conditions warrant
Open Ocean (ERoute Navigation)	Over 30 nautical miles	FOM ≤ 7	30 minutes or conditions warrant

e. There is a malfunction of navigation equipment.

3. Whether using charts or VMS, take fixes per our ship's Navigation Bill. Although VMS continuously plots the ship's position, the requirement still exists to obtain a fix by an alternate source at least every third fix interval in restricted waters. Therefore, manual bearings and/ or ranges will be provided by the Bearing Takers and CIC RADAR Operator and entered by the ECDIS-N Display Operator at least every nine minutes in restricted waters. The fix interval can be reduced when prudent based on prevailing conditions and operational commitments.

4. Station the Navigation or Modified Navigation Detail when required, and ensure the details are set in a timely manner. The navigation detail will be set prior to entering restricted waters. The modified navigation detail will be set per the Navigation Bill.

5. Transmit AIS per Fleet Commander guidance while transiting any traffic separation scheme (TSS) and/or any high-density traffic area unless otherwise directed by the TAO.

STANDING ORDER NUMBER 7
Restricted Visibility

1. Reduced visibility requires increased vigilance on the part of the supervisory and controlling stations.

a. During reduced visibility, operational commitments will never override the safety of the ship. The speed of the ship will be determined as prescribed in the Navigation Rules.

b. Carry out, at a minimum, the procedures in the ship's Low Visibility Bill when surface visibility drops to 3NM. Execute these actions sooner if you consider it appropriate to ensure the ship is fully prepared to enter low visibility.

2. In reduced visibility situations, particularly in dense traffic areas, the safety of the ship may be enhanced by transmitting our position via AIS. Consult with the TAO, and call me if in your judgment AIS is necessary.

STANDING ORDER NUMBER 8
Man Overboard

1. During a Man Overboard under way, conduct the following actions concurrently:

   a. Throw a life ring and maneuver to recover.

      i. Man in sight: Prepare to conduct the recovery by the most efficient method for the prevailing circumstances. Ensure someone maintains visual on the man at all times until the recovery is complete.

      ii. Man not in sight: Prepare to conduct the recovery by the most efficient method for the prevailing circumstances. Employ all available means to locate the man, i.e., extra lookouts, electro-optical sights, night vision devices, additional units as necessary. The CICWO will give "expanding square" course recommendations if man remains unlocated.

      iii. Towed body deployed: Conduct a Racetrack turn and use the most efficient method of recovery available. Pass the word via the 1MC twice, "Man Overboard. Man the [insert towed body] detail." Operators will immediately cease any underwater transmissions.

   b. Ensure a smoke float is dropped as close to the man as possible unless there is a fire risk such as fuel on the water, e.g., in the vicinity of a crash site.

   c. Instruct all topside personnel to point to the man.

   d. Sound six short blasts.

   e. Notify ships in company and the OTC, and via VHF Channel 16 issue a "PAN PAN" if necessary.

   f. Pass "MAN OVERBOARD (port/stbd) SIDE. This will be a (small boat/shipboard/aircraft) recovery. All divisions submit muster reports to [insert station]" over the 1MC. Boat deck and foc'sle will automatically be manned.

    g. QMOW and/or CICWS shall mark the man on VMS and DDRT/DRT/CADRT.

    h. Break the OSCAR flag or energize pulsating red over red lights.

    i. CIC ensures any combat systems transmissions into the water and the Fathometer are secured (for an actual event only), mark the man, and report bearing and ranges to the Bridge.

STANDING ORDER NUMBER 9
Anchoring

1. While at anchor, the following precautions will be taken:
   a. All watches set forth in the NAVDORM will be manned and will:
       i. Ensure that a fix is taken on the Bridge and in CIC every 30 minutes (every 5 minutes if winds are greater than 25 kts) and compared for accuracy. If a fix falls outside of the drag circle, the VMS alarm activates, or you believe the ship is dragging anchor, immediately take another fix. If that falls outside the drag circle, immediately call the CDO and Navigator.
       ii. Guard all required circuits.
       iii. Ensure that the Fathometer is continuously energized.
       iv. If necessary, prepare to get the ship under way to reposition and anchor.
   b. A qualified CIC Watch supervisor will be in CIC and will:
       i. Guard all required circuits, including chat.
       ii. Maintain a radar watch to monitor nearby traffic and make a determination of risk of collision.
   c. An Anchor Watch will be stationed in vicinity of the anchor and will report status of the anchor to the Bridge/CIC every 15 minutes. The report should state the direction the chain is tending, the strain, and the amount of chain on deck (i.e., "the anchor is at twelve o'clock, moderate strain with 4 shots on deck").
   d. At anchor, each duty section will have a minimum of one Engineering Officer of the Watch. One main engine will be available for immediate start (< 15 minutes) and steering units will remain aligned for starting from the Bridge.

2. Required reports while at anchor include:
   a. All occurrences you feel deserve attention or whenever in doubt.
   b. When a change in Readiness for Sea status is directed by the Immediate Superior in Command.

c. When an increase in Force Protection condition occurs, or a Force Protection notification is received by the ship.

d. When severe inclement weather is forecasted or approaching.

e. When boating operations or liberty launches must be suspended.

f. When dragging anchor.

g. Upon parting of a line while moored.

h. Prior to aligning PWT (gray water) or sewage (black water) over the side.

i. Prior to transferring ammunition.

j. Prior to externally transferring fuel or oily waste.

k. Prior to starting engines or generators.

l. Prior to rolling shafts.

m. Prior to high-powered radiation of any element of the combat system.

n. When experiencing challenges with the defense attaché, husbanding agent, local or base police, etc.

o. Any liberty incident involving host nation police.

p. Notification that a Sailor has been hospitalized, reported to the emergency room, or has an urgent medical need.

q. Upon receipt of an AMCROSS message.

3. Reference the ship's anchoring nomograph for determining the minimum length of chain and the horizontal distance from the ship to the anchor for flat and sloped bottoms.

STANDING ORDER NUMBER 10
Restricted Maneuvering Doctrine

1. As noted above, Commanding Officers must tailor this standing order to meet their ship-specific needs.

STANDING ORDER NUMBER 11
Engineering/Maximum Plant Reliability

1. Due to unique configurations of engineering plants throughout the Surface Force, Commanding Officers must tailor this standing order to meet their ship-specific needs.

STANDING ORDER NUMBER 12
Steering Control

1. Due to unique configurations of Steering Control throughout the Surface Force, Commanding Officers must tailor this standing order to meet their ship-specific needs.

STANDING ORDER NUMBER 13
Small Boat Operations
1. The Boat Deck Safety Observer and the Boat Officer are the OOD's primary agents for safety during small boat operations.
   a. Minimum manning includes a Bow Hook, a Boat Engineer, and a Coxswain. The Bow Hook will often be manned by a SAR swimmer, and a Boat Officer is usually used. If two boats are to be used, and not in a lifesaving capacity, the second Boat Officer and SAR swimmer may be waived at the OOD's discretion. The Boat Officer will receive a brief from the Bridge Team prior to launch covering ensuing operations.
   b. The small boat operations checklist will be completed prior to requesting my permission to launch or recover boats.
   c. The OOD shall maneuver to create a lee for small boat operations. Inform the boat deck and the Coxswain if maneuvering is required to flatten the sea state such as when launching the small boat while the ship makes a slow turn.

STANDING ORDER NUMBER 14
Flight Operations
1. The Helicopter Control Officer (HCO) is the OOD's agent on the flight deck to ensure that all preparations are made correctly and that all aspects of the evolution are carried out safely.
   a. Set Flight Quarters in advance to permit thorough preparations, taking into account any alert or ready deck requirements.
   b. Complete the check-off list prior to helicopter operations.
   c. Deck status will be controlled by the OOD, with recommendations from the HCO. The OOD will inform me prior to authorizing Green Deck, and only when NWP 3-04.1 and NAVAIR 00-80T-122 environmental requirements have been satisfied for the applicable airframe.
   d. Maneuver the ship only during Red Deck conditions, paying special attention to polar plots and the status of the flight deck nets, especially during high-speed evolutions. Lowering and raising of nets will be at a safe speed for personnel.
   e. *AIRCRAFT IN-FLIGHT EMERGENCY.* Immediately pass the word "EMERGENCY FLIGHT QUARTERS" over the 1MC and the nature of the emergency, if known. Proceed at best

speed toward the known or last known location; if the helo is in our vicinity, immediately come to Foxtrot Corpen.

STANDING ORDER NUMBER 15
Well Deck/Mission Bay Operations
1. Due to unique configurations and missions required for Well Deck or Mission Bay Operations, Commanding Officers must tailor this standing order to meet their ship-specific needs.

STANDING ORDER NUMBER 16
Towed Gear Operations
1. Whenever towed gear is deployed, the ships effective dimensions increase in both length and navigational draft in proportion to cable scope. Manage the contact situation and track appropriately.
   a. While deploying, retrieving, or maneuvering with towed gear, follow guidance contained in the applicable technical manual.
   b. Use sternway only in an emergency.
   c. Navigational charts will be carefully monitored to ensure available water depth supports operations on the intended track.
   d. The TAO shall notify the OOD whenever cable must be paid out or retrieved. Towed body depth will be recalculated for the new tow length by both the CIC and Navigation teams using nomograms in the applicable reference.
   e. OODs will advise the TAO of intentions to change speed so that cable scope may be adjusted to maintain desired towed body depth.

5

The *Belknap-Kennedy* Collision

The following is the Chief of Naval Operations memorandum issued after the completion of the administrative and judicial processes incident to the *Belknap-Kennedy* collision.

2 October 1976
MEMORANDUM FOR ALL FLAG OFFICERS AND
OFFICERS IN COMMAND
Subj: BELKNAP/KENNEDY Collision
Encl: (1) Summary of Circumstances of Collision and Related
          Administrative and Judicial Processes

1. On 22 November 1975, USS BELKNAP (CG-26) was severely damaged in a collision at sea with USS JOHN F. KENNEDY (CV-67) which cost the lives of eight Navy personnel and injured forty-eight others. A formal investigation held the Commanding Officer and the Officer of the Deck of BELKNAP accountable for the tragic incident. The Commanding Officer was subsequently referred to trial by general court-martial which resulted in disposition tantamount to acquittal on all charges and specifications. The Officer of the Deck was also tried by general court-martial and, although convicted of three separate charges, was sentenced to no punishment. There has been some outspoken criticism of the outcome of the BELKNAP courts-martial. Much of that criticism reflects concern that the principle of command responsibility may have been imperiled as a result

of the BELKNAP cases. I want to here address that concern, and to assure each of you that resolution of the BELKNAP cases will not in any way jeopardize the concepts of command responsibility, authority, and accountability.

2. There has always been a fundamental principle of maritime law and life which has been consistently observed over the centuries by seafarers of all nations: The responsibility of the master, captain, or commanding officer on board his ship is absolute. That principle is as valid in this technical era of nuclear propulsion and advanced weapons systems as it was when our Navy was founded two hundred years ago. This responsibility, and its corollaries of authority and accountability, have been the foundation of safe navigation at sea and the cornerstone of naval efficiency and effectiveness throughout our history. The essence of this concept is reflected in Article 0702.1 of *Navy Regulations*, 1973, which provides in pertinent part that: "The responsibility of the commanding officer for his command is absolute, except when, and to the extent, relieved therefrom by competent authority, or as provided otherwise in these regulations."

3. To understand fully this essential principle, it must first be recognized that it is not a test for measuring the criminal responsibility of a commanding officer. Under our system of criminal justice, in both civilian and military forums, in order that a man's life, liberty, and property may be placed at hazard, it is not enough to show simply that he was the commanding officer of a Navy ship involved in a collision and that he failed to execute to perfection his awesome and wide-ranging command responsibilities. Rather, it must be established by legally admissible evidence and beyond a reasonable doubt that he personally violated carefully delineated and specifically charged provisions of the criminal code enacted by the Congress to govern the armed forces—the *Uniform Code of Military Justice*—before a commanding officer can be found criminally responsible for his conduct. Military courts-martial are federal courts and the rules of evidence and procedure applicable therein are essentially the same as those which pertain in any other federal criminal court and the rights of an accused, whether seaman or commanding officer, are closely analogous to those enjoyed by any federal criminal court defendant. The

determination of criminal responsibility is therefore properly the province of our system of military justice. The acquittal of a commanding officer by a duly constituted court-martial absolves him of criminal responsibility for the offenses charged. It does not, however, absolve him of his responsibility as a commanding officer as delineated in U.S. Navy Regulations.

4. When the results of the BELKNAP cases were reported in the press, many assumed that the Commanding Officer and the Officer of the Deck of BELKNAP had been absolved of all responsibility for the collision by the military judges that presided over their respective courts-martial and that the principle of command responsibility had thereby been imperiled. Soon thereafter I began to receive letters from concerned members of both the retired and active naval community. Much of this reaction was critical of the results of the two courts-martial and revealed a serious misunderstanding of the role of military justice in the naval service.

5. The responsibility of a commanding officer for his command is established by long tradition and is clearly stated in U.S. Navy Regulations. In the case of the BELKNAP-KENNEDY incident, the JAG MANUAL investigating officer determined that both the Commanding Officer and the Officer of the Deck of BELKNAP were personally responsible for the collision. CINCUSNAVEUR, the convening authority of the investigation, approved that finding on review, as did I, when I took action on the investigative report as CNO. BELKNAP's Commanding Officer and Officer of the Deck were thereby held to be accountable for that tragic accident.

6. Responsibility having been officially and unequivocally established, it then remained to determine what sanctions, if any, were to be taken against the two officers concerned. It goes without saying that documented professional shortcomings are appropriately noted in reports of fitness and that errors in judgment thus detailed are taken into account before the individual concerned is considered for assignment or promotion or entrusted with command. However, in this instance, it was determined that further official action was warranted. Accordingly, CINCUSNAVEUR issued a letter of reprimand to the Commanding Officer and recommended that the Officer of the

Deck be tried by general court-martial. CINCLANTFLT subsequently referred criminal charges against both the Commanding Officer and the Officer of the Deck to trial by general court-martial. As previously noted, the trial of the Commanding Officer resulted in disposition equivalent to acquittal and the trial of the Officer of the Deck resulted in his conviction. (Enclosure (1) is a summary of these administrative and judicial processes as well as a brief description of the circumstances of the collision itself.)

7. The imposition of the punitive letter of reprimand as nonjudicial punishment constituted a formal sanction against the Commanding Officer. The subsequent judicial resolution of his general court-martial in a manner tantamount to acquittal could not and did not vitiate the established fact of his accountability. It simply determined that the evidence of record was not legally sufficient to find him guilty of the criminal charges for which he had not previously been punished. In the case of the Officer of the Deck of BELKNAP, the court determined that the evidence of record was legally sufficient to find him guilty beyond reasonable doubt of all but one of the criminal offenses charged.

8. In summary, the Commander's responsibility for his command is absolute and he must and will be held accountable for its safety, well-being, and efficiency. That is the very foundation of our maritime heritage, the cornerstone of naval efficiency and effectiveness, and the key to victory in combat. This is the essence of the special trust and confidence placed in an officer's patriotism, valor, fidelity, and abilities. Every day in command tests the strength of character, judgment, and professional abilities of those in command. In some cases, Commanders will be called upon to answer for their conduct in a court of law. In all cases, they will be professionally judged by seagoing officers—a far more stringent accountability in the eyes of those who follow the sea. We in the Navy would have it no other way, for the richest reward of command is the personal satisfaction of having measured up to this responsibility and accountability. The loss of life, personal injuries, and material damages sustained in the collision of USS BELKNAP and USS JOHN F. KENNEDY serve as a tragic reminder of the necessity and immutability of the principle of command responsibility. The Commanding Officer and the Officer of

the Deck of BELKNAP have been held accountable for that terrible loss of men and equipment. The concept of command responsibility has not been eroded.

9. The JAG MANUAL investigating officer's report of the collision included a number of lessons learned and specific recommendations designed to ensure that corrective action is taken. I have directed that those recommendations be implemented expeditiously and some of you are now personally involved in that task.

J. L. HOLLOWAY III

SUMMARY OF CIRCUMSTANCES RELATING TO THE *BELKNAP-KENNEDY* COLLISION AND THE ADMINISTRATIVE AND JUDICIAL PROCESSES EMANATING THEREFROM

The following is a brief description of the circumstances of the collision and of the administrative and judicial processes that should help you understand why the principle of command responsibility in the Navy has not been eroded by the BELKNAP cases.

Collision

On the evening of 22 November 1975, elements of Task Group 60.1, including USS JOHN F. KENNEDY (CV 67) and USS BELKNAP (CG 96), were operating in the Ionian Sea. At 2130 BELKNAP and KENNEDY were in a line of bearing formation on course 200°, speed 10 kts, with the screen operating independently. BELKNAP was maintaining a station on a relative bearing of 200°, 4000 yards from KENNEDY. At approximately 2145 KENNEDY began preparations for the last recovery of aircraft, scheduled for 2200, and was displaying flight deck lighting for aircraft operations. KENNEDY transmitted her intentions to turn into the wind with a "CORPEN J PORT 025–12" signal. The signal was acknowledged in BELKNAP and KENNEDY's execute signal followed very closely thereafter. The OOD in BELKNAP planned to slow, allow KENNEDY to complete her turn in front, and then bring BELKNAP around to port to the new course and maneuver into station. The CO of BELKNAP was not on the bridge at the time this maneuver was commenced and it is not clear whether he was apprised of the signal before the OOD executed his plan of action. The OOD and CO had discussed two previous CORPEN J STARBOARD maneuvers and the CO had concurred in the OOD's intention to "slow and follow the carrier around" in both prior instances. However, a course of action in the event of a possible CORPEN, J PORT maneuver had not been discussed.

At about 2148 BELKNAP began to slow and ease to port as KENNEDY increased speed and came left toward the new course of 025T. Shortly thereafter the OOD in BELKNAP began to evidence first doubts as to the target angle of KENNEDY CIC, realizing that the CPA would be close, recommended that BELKNAP come right. That recommendation, however, was not acknowledged by the bridge. The OOD, becoming less and less sure of KENNEDY's target angle, summoned the CO to the bridge at 2156. Immediately prior to the CO's arrival, the OOD ordered left full rudder causing BELKNAP's head to swing left and prompting KENNEDY to signal "Interrogative your intentions" followed by "come right full rudder now." CO, BELKNAP, now on the bridge, recognized that his ship was in extremis, and ordered right full rudder, all engines back emergency. KENNEDY had also applied right full rudder and all engines back full and BELKNAP passed down KENNEDY's port side close aboard on an approximately opposing course (see attached diagram). However, KENNEDY's flight deck extension collided with BELKNAP's bridge, sheared off a large portion of BELKNAP's superstructure and knocked over the macks. Fire fed by aviation fuel from KENNEDY engulfed BELKNAP. A total of eight crewmen were killed and forty-eight injured in the two ships as a direct result of the collision. Damages exceeded $100,000,000.

JAG Manual Investigation

RADM Donald D. Engen, USN, was appointed by CINCUSNAVEUR to conduct a formal one officer investigation of the collision and to "fix individual responsibilities for the incident." The commanding officers and officers of the deck of both BELKNAP and KENNEDY were designated as parties to the investigation. The investigation was begun on 23 November 1975 and was completed on 31 December. The investigating officer determined that BELKNAP's Commanding Officer and Officer of the Deck were responsible for the collision and the ensuing personnel casualties and material damages.

The investigating officer recommended, among other things, that the Commanding Officer of BELKNAP be awarded a punitive letter of reprimand for his failure to ensure the safety, well-being, and efficiency of his command, as evidenced by his "failure to be present on the bridge ... during the initial maneuvers in a new station in close proximity ... to KENNEDY and his failure to assure the proper training of ... bridge team members." The convening authority, CINCUSNAVEUR, also determined that the Commanding Officer was responsible for the collision and approved the investigating officer's recommendation that a punitive letter of reprimand be issued. A punitive letter of reprimand was awarded to the Commanding Officer by CINCUSNAVEUR on 2 January 1976 for failing to secure a clear description of the Officer of the Deck's plan for the maneuver prior to its execution, for failure to assure himself that the Officer of the Deck understood the maneuvering requirements which should have been anticipated, and for failing to ensure that only adequately trained and competent personnel were permitted to assume positions of responsibility on BELKNAP's bridge team.

The investigating officer recommended that BELKNAP's Officer of the Deck be referred for trial by general court-martial for his failure to keep himself informed of the tactical situation, his failure to take appropriate action to avoid collision in accordance with the International Rules of the Road and accepted Navy doctrine, and his failure to make required reports to the Commanding Officer. CINCUSNAVEUR approved that recommendation and forwarded a charge sheet to COMNAVSURFLANT alleging violations of Article 92, UCMJ (disobedience of OPNAV Instructions and BELKNAP Standing Orders), Article 108, UCMJ (suffering the two ships to be damaged through neglect), Article 110, UCMJ (suffering the two ships to be hazarded through neglect) and Article 110, UCMJ (manslaughter).

Court-Martial of *Belknap*'s Commanding Officer

Notwithstanding the prior imposition of a punitive letter of reprimand on the Commanding Officer of BELKNAP as non-judicial punishment by CINCUSNAVEUR, COMNAVSURFLANT caused an Article 32, UCMJ, pretrial investigation to be conducted to inquire into the Commanding Officer's role in the collision. The pretrial investigating officer recommended that the Commanding Officer be tried by general court-martial on two specifications of violation of Navy Regulations and three specifications of dereliction of duty, all in violation of Article 92, UCMJ; one specification of suffering damage to BELKNAP and KENNEDY through neglect, in violation of Article 108, UCMJ; and one specification of suffering the two ships to be hazarded through neglect, in violation of Article 110, UCMJ.

COMNAVSURFLANT concurred in that recommendation and forwarded the sworn charges to CINCLANTFLT for consideration. On 12 March 1976, CINCLANTFLT referred the charges to trial by general court-martial.

At his request, the accused, Commanding Officer, USS BELKNAP, was tried by military judge alone. During the course of the trial that ensued, the two specifications alleging violation of Article 0702, U.S. Navy Regulations, were dismissed by the military judge on the ground that Article 0702 constitutes a guideline for performance and not an order to be enforced with criminal sanctions. Two specifications alleging that the Commanding Officer was derelict in his duty by failing to ascertain the specific maneuvers contemplated by the Officer of the Deck and by failing to ensure that only adequately trained personnel were permitted to assume responsible positions on the bridge watch were dismissed by the military judge on the ground that the Commanding Officer had previously been punished for those offenses by virtue of the punitive letter of reprimand imposed upon him by CINCUSNAVEUR. One specification alleging that the Commanding Officer was derelict in his duty in that he failed personally to supervise the Officer of the Deck during BELKNAP's maneuvering in close proximity to KENNEDY was dismissed by the military judge on the ground that it involved the same misconduct alleged under the charge of suffering the hazarding of the two vessels through neglect, and was therefore an undue multiplication of the charges.

As a result, the Commanding Officer was arraigned on one specification alleging that through neglect he suffered the two ships to be damaged by failing to personally supervise and instruct his OOD and JOOD and by failing to post a fully qualified bridge watch section, in violation of Article 108, UCMJ, and one specification of negligently suffering the two ships to be hazarded, also by his failure to provide personal supervision and training to his OOD and JOOD and by his failure to post a fully qualified bridge watch section. The Commanding Officer entered pleas of Not Guilty to these remaining charges and specifications. On 12 May 1976, following two days of testimony from eighteen Government witnesses, the military judge granted a defense motion for findings of Not Guilty as to both charges and their specifications on the ground that testimony of the witnesses failed to establish that the bridge watch was improperly qualified or that the Commanding Officer was negligent in not personally supervising and instructing his OOD and JOOD, and, therefore, that the evidence of record failed to establish a prima facie case that the Commanding Officer was criminally negligent as alleged.

Court-Martial of *Belknap*'s Officer of the Deck
Pursuant to the recommendations of the JAG MANUAL investigating officer, of CINCUSNAVEUR and of COMNAVSURFLANT, CINCLANTFLT referred the charges against the Officer of the Deck of BELKNAP to trial by general court-martial on one specification of failure to obey OPNAV Instruction 3120.32 by failing to keep fully informed of the tactical situation and to take appropriate action to avoid the collision, failing to issue necessary orders to the BELKNAP's helm and main engine control to avoid danger, and failing to make required reports to the Commanding Officer, and one specification of failure to obey BELKNAP Standing Orders to notify the Commanding Officer of a major course change order by the Officer in Tactical Command, both in violation of Article 92, UCMJ; one specification of suffering damage to the two ships through neglect, in violation of Article 108, UCMJ; and one specification of suffering the two ships to be hazarded through neglect, in violation of Article 110, UCMJ. At his request, the Officer of the Deck was also tried by military judge alone and entered pleas of Not Guilty to the offenses charged. The military judge found the accused Not Guilty of the specification alleging failure to obey BELKNAP's Standing Orders but found him Guilty of the remaining charges and specifications. Subsequent to presentation of matters in mitigation and extenuation, the military judge elected not to impose punishment on the accused on the ground that, under the circumstances, the conviction by general court-martial itself constituted an adequate and appropriate punishment.

Trial by Military Judge Alone

An additional misunderstanding of military justice which came to light in the aftermath of the BELKNAP courts-martial involves the concept of trial by military judge alone. As you are undoubtedly aware, every accused in a non-capital case tried by general court-martial or by a special court-martial presided over by a military judge has the unqualified right to request trial by judge alone. The military judge's ruling on such a request is final. This provision for trial by military judge alone is modeled after Rule 23(a) of the Federal Rules of Criminal Procedure. Unlike the Federal Rule, however, Article 16 of the UCMJ makes the accused's right to waive trial by court members independent of the consent of the Government. The Senate Report on the proposed legislation which ultimately became the Military Justice Act of 1968, makes it clear that this difference was generated by Congressional concern over the specter of unlawful command influence. Consequently, the election of the accused in the BELKNAP cases to exercise their right to trial by military judge alone and the granting of that request by the military judges in those two cases, was entirely proper under the law.

In any event, it would be well to remember that the concept of an independent judiciary is as essential to the administration of military justice as is the concept of command responsibility to fleet operations. Moreover, these two concepts are as compatible as they are essential. Strict adherence to one does no violence to the other.

A Commodore's Advice

Dear Commander Jones,

I was delighted to receive your letter of introduction last evening and hope you are finding the long command pipeline both useful and enjoyable. As the days draw you close to assumption of command, you will undoubtedly have many questions and I trust you will feel free to communicate with my staff. We are committed to ensuring that you receive the support that you and your ship require. I am confident that the DESRON 23 Little Beavers tradition will flourish as we form a new column in our squadron history. You will be a big part of that formation.

GENERAL THOUGHTS

Forget your last assignment. Focus now on your ship.

Not everything will go well—manage your schedule within your capabilities and scheme of priorities.

If you can't get everything done perfectly (and you can't), then accept the inevitable up front rather than giving your crew and chain of command the impression that life overwhelmed you.

Your crew will (amazingly, perhaps) accept as important what seems important to you—by your statements and questions, by what you appear to pay attention to, and by what you react to. If it's not important to you, then it will become increasingly less important to them. Think hard about what you'll shrug off as uninteresting.

Your first six months will be the most uncomfortable, your last three the most dangerous.

When bad things happen, waste no time wondering whether you ought to tell your boss—tell them what happened, how awful it was, and what you're doing to make things right. Don't force them to find out from somebody else. Understand from the beginning that there is no such thing as a ship in which nothing bad ever happens—if you try to give that wishful impression, nobody will trust you. Without trust from above, you'll never make a move on your own.

Avoid the "one-person band" syndrome. If you do your homework and engage your wardroom and chiefs mess (i.e., Planning Board for Training [PBFT], Integrated Training Team [ITT], etc.) in planning for upcoming events, you and they will know what to expect and can prepare for what will be required. Examples include tactical maneuvering (DIVTACs), underway replenishment (UNREPs), boat ops, and similar evolutions. From my perspective, the absence of micromanagement and reactive direction by the commanding officer indicates effective leadership, thorough training, and thoughtful planning.

Read the most recent edition of *Command at Sea*, from USNI.

Savor the small victories—the large ones are rare.

The first report is undependable.

Ask to see "Ref. A."

Sarcasm and subtlety are often lost on the easily confused.

Your crew expects you to be confident, professional, and a little mysterious and distant. You have no peers on your ship—get to know the other COs in your homeport and share your experiences and concerns with them.

Pay especially close attention to navigation, classified material, and public funds. Mind the weather. Know where your barrel is pointing before releasing the battery. Know where your helicopters and boats are. Know where your next load of fuel is coming from and when you'll get it. Let your officer of the deck (OOD) and command duty officer (CDO) know how to contact you in a hurry.

The more mature your ombudsman, the better.

Make going to sea an enjoyable experience by thinking hard about it beforehand—what can we do under way that we can't do in port? Not just drills or exercises, but unusual surprises like swim call, nighttime machine gun practice, topside movies, anything else you've done well on other ships.

Demand accuracy, currency, and formality in daily reports—if you don't feel that they tell you what you want to know when you want to know it, then change the system immediately. It can be useful to ask pointed questions based on daily reports from time to time, and especially to compare the supply department eight o'clock reports to those submitted by the line department heads.

Beware of radar-based overconfidence in fog.

Zone inspections have great potential as teaching evolutions and will reflect your interest in your ship's material condition and general readiness. Wear coveralls and make them dirty. Use a flashlight. Brief the inspection party beforehand and afterward. Track corrective actions.

People will judge your ship by its appearance in port and when you go alongside the carrier under way. Many believe there is no reason for a ship's sides ever to show streaks in port. Also keep an eye on the section of pier adjacent to your ship—it should be well policed and free of vehicles.

Most COs normally arrive on the ship each in-port day around 0800 and depart around 1700. Most make it a point to attend church services on board. Consider visiting the ship briefly each weekend and spending the night on board before getting under way each time. It is amazing how many interesting things you can find to do on those evenings before getting under way—observing the master light off checklist (MLOC), reviewing op orders, walking around the spaces to get a feel for the crew's state of mind and the ship's general readiness for sea, and getting settled in yourself.

You will be invited to many formal functions while in command—changes of command, retirement ceremonies, COs' breakfasts, waterfront all-officers meetings, etc. It would be a good idea not to gaff them off until you have a good sense of their relative importance in your home-port. It's hard to know how your absence (which will somehow be noted) will be interpreted.

Exercise a little reticence at your first couple of COs' meetings with your squadron or group commander: it's a good way to avoid developing a reputation for "knowing it all" in the eyes of your fellow COs who have been in the job a little longer.

Take pains to ensure that your casualty report (CASREP) list correlates well with your status of readiness and training (SORTS) status. Your chain of command will let you know otherwise.

Work closely with the Naval Criminal Investigative Service (NCIS) but remember that their priorities may be different from yours.

If you embark a unit commander, make it a wonderful experience for him or her.

Demand absolute adherence to Engineering Operational Sequencing System (EOSS) procedures, especially involving movement of fuel (in port, in particular), activation of educators, operation and testing of steering gear, and rigging shore power.

Make well known to the wardroom your expectations regarding attendance at social functions, personal behavior ashore, wardroom standards, and officer/enlisted relations. The earlier you establish your policies, the fewer will be your outrages. Don't tolerate poor food or service in the wardroom or in the general mess, particularly on holidays.

Demonstrate to your crew physical fitness, self-control, sobriety, a grasp of the big picture, commitment to their welfare, delight in their efforts, and a restrained sense of humor.

Ride in your boats. Often. In port and at sea. At night.

Exercise your rescue swimmers during man overboard drills.

Take pains to develop a strong, mutually trustful and friendly relationship with your chiefs. It will pay off in ways that you may never realize, and at times when you may very much need their support. On the other hand, if you have a bad chief in the mess, be merciless in doing the right thing.

Take a conservative dark business suit along with you whenever your ship leaves homeport. Keep a full seabag on the ship, regardless of the season and your schedule.

You've got to play the cards you're dealt as far as personnel are concerned. If an officer is weak, make him or her stronger. If you're becoming convinced that they just won't cut it, make your feelings known to them and to your chain of command early. Give the individual a fair shot at coming up to speed, but don't let them hurt your ship. Document the problem thoroughly and accurately and don't just pass the problem on to another command.

Look at holiday-period duty rosters with an eagle eye—where principle is involved, be deaf to expediency.

Insist that your Integrated Training Team thoroughly plan and conduct frequent general quarters exercises to maintain crew qualification at battle stations. Don't allow a comfortable condition III mentality to excuse your crew from rigorous and necessary combat training.

Use your judgment regarding the use of tugs and pilots—nobody else's matters very much.

Be very curious regarding the binnacle list. Take the time to visit every sick-in-quarters sailor every day. Ask questions of your corpsman and get a feel for how they're regarded by your crew. If it's not what you expect, obtain help from your squadron doctor.

Insist that your XO do messing, berthing, and sanitary inspections daily and independently from the IDC. Take a look yourself from time to time. Unannounced.

Climb the mast from time to time and crawl around in your bilges. Look behind and under things.

Keep your own files and ticklers on special items—such as investigations, congressional inquiries, etc. Don't expect your XO to be as perfect as you were, but ensure your standards are known and satisfied.

Make it your air department, not "the air detachment." Get an up-chit, go through aviation physiology and water survival training, and fly in your aircraft.

Think hard about message release authority. Are you trying to prove something by your policy? Demand absolutely professional and unemotional record traffic and voice transmissions from your ship.

Stay ahead of the exhaustion curve by taking naps in anticipation of all-nighters or whenever you feel it to be a good idea. Let the XO know if you need her on the bridge.

The XO stuff you learned in your last sea tour is still important, but you've got to try hard to let her take care of most of the detail stuff. Start out by seeing all correspondence, then reduce your personal routing as appropriate.

Let everyone around you see how much you enjoy your job. Keep your whining to yourself—they don't need to hear it.

When referring to your ship to outsiders, use "we" for good news and "I" for bad news.

Maintain your composure.

Relieving

If you are reporting directly to your ship as the commanding officer, send a modest but comprehensive letter to your commodore just before commencing the Senior Officer Ship Material Readiness Course (SOSMRC).

The commodore wants to know about your family as well as where you've been. Call the chief staff officer about a week later to ensure the letter arrived and provide any other information needed. This is also the time to send the letter of introduction your predecessor has been dreading but awaiting.

Depending on squadron standard operating procedures (SOP), you may want to report to the squadron a week before you arrive at the ship itself. You'll want to go through all the relevant principal's message files, meet the staff, and make calls around the naval station. You will find it useful to meet with the commanding officers at the Readiness Support Group (RSG), Ship Intermediate Maintenance Activity (SIMA), Fleet Training and Support Center (FTSC), Afloat Training Group (ATG), Naval Station (NAVSTA), Transient Personnel Unit (TPU), Naval Criminal Investigative Service (NCIS), the Brig, Base Ops, and any others that come to mind. Most of them have not met all the waterfront COs and will be delighted that you have taken the time to call on them. Some will be mildly insulted if you do not, some don't care—but you should do it anyway. Visit the harbor master and pilot station. Take the time to tour the channel and harbor with one of the pilots—particularly if the homeport is new to you. Local knowledge is priceless and is usually available only from pilots.

If you visit another homeport during your tour, have your ops officer call ahead of time to see about your paying a call on the group commander in that port, as well as the NAVSTA commander—you could save yourself a little embarrassment for having failed to do so. During your initial week with the squadron staff, you should also call on your group commander.

The ship should send a copy of the relieving schedule about a month before you arrive. If anything seems missing, let the CO know that you will want to witness that evolution, or see that document, or talk to that person. Don't wait until turnover week to identify something that's important to you if you can help it—enough will come up all on its own to fill the time.

Don't feel any great responsibility to protect your predecessor. If an item is important (and you'll know) and it's not the way it's supposed to be, then identify it as such. The chances are that your commodore already knows or expects that a problem exists—they expect you to be fair but critical of the ship whose command you have assumed.

As you inspect the ship, ask questions of your guides. You'll be amazed at how much your new crew will tell you that your predecessor may either not know or has forgotten. Issue no judgments until you have relieved, but ask questions and take notes. The word will spread quickly around the ship that you are interested, that you ask tough questions, that you are serious—or not. Try to visit every space in the ship before you relieve. Ask to see a recent underwater hull inspection. If one's not available, make every effort to schedule one prior to the first time you get the ship under way.

Three old rules for the new CO at the change of command ceremony: show up, stand up, wrap up. If your remarks go on for more than thirty seconds, you've overstepped the bounds of good manners and everyone present will know it. Remember, it's a great day for you but *the* great day for the CO you're relieving.

Schedule a call on your commodore for the week following the change of command. Go prepared with an agenda of initial impressions, a plan of action, and a list of goals, and be prepared for some heartfelt advice.

Never mention your predecessor's name again. Now it's your ship, warts and all, and your charge to make it as perfect as possible.

Potential post-relieving surprises: an inspection/assessment/assist visit in the week following the change of command, dings on screw blades, SWOs not qualified as officer of the deck underway (OOD), deck and engineering standard practices in direct variance with CO's Standing Orders, OODs unwilling to "bother" the CO with "routine" contacts well inside minimum reporting distances, OODs unwilling to maneuver the ship without specific direction from the CO, all-enlisted in-port duty sections (including "CDO"), and a long list of unofficial and unwritten "command policies." Some surprises take quite a bit of time and effort to unearth.

General Standards

3-M: Do all the maintenance requirements, do them perfectly. Apply a quality culture to maintenance and safety, insist on complete khaki involvement and attention to detail. Do several spot checks yourself every week. Pay particular attention to senior petty officer migration away from PMS, the electrical safety program (and the qualifications of the responsible officer), the tag-out program, calibration, and safety. Ask tough questions about the damage control work center–planned maintenance system (PMS) matrix (work center versus assigned fittings), and ensure your XO understands their responsibility for maintenance.

Combat Systems: Participate in oral exams for watchstanders, demand a realistic reading program, and institute a system of reinforcing formal training through professional watchstanding standards all the time. Go through PMS spot checks on combat systems–related equipment, test equipment, repair parts, maintenance assistance modules (MAMs), etc. Make DTEs a standard daily practice during routine ops. Demand superb performance from your systems all the time—take the time to ask the question that, as XO, you might have left for the chief staff officer (CSO) to figure out. **Consider that the captain's principal responsibility is to connect doctrine, systems, and people to success in battle**.

Run your hand over everything topside—if you feel salt or rust, get it cleaned or fixed.

Spot-check service records, medical records, training records, travel claims, classified material accountability records, and anything else you can think of.

Propulsion: Your watchwords are safety and reliability. Visit every main space every day you're on the ship. Take notes. Look deeply into the lube oil management program, firefighting, and training. Have your squadron staff engineers inspect your spaces and equipment quarterly, even if it does irritate your engineer. Give orals yourself to the engineering officers of the watch (EOOWs), electrical and propulsion plant operators, sounding and security watchstanders, and duty engineers. If a "qualified" watchstander fails a drill set, rescind his or her qualification. Be prepared to give the propulsion examining board (PEB) senior examiner a detailed tour of all your spaces (including all fire pump rooms) yourself. Assign your XO to help you out during the course of the inspection in terms of keeping an eye on the bridge, etc. Expect your commodore or CSO to ride for your ship's engineering certification. Become very familiar with your type commander's maintenance manual and engineering assessment instruction.

Logistics: Review your TYCOM Force Supply Instruction. Press hard on accountability, inventory control, maintaining the accuracy of your consolidated ship's allowance list (COSAL), financial management, supply department training, and all the other stuff you learned as an XO. Get close to the logistics management assessment (LMA) inspectors at the regional support group (RSG) and have them visit your ship about nine months before your LMA. Remember that some problems take an awful lot of manpower (and funding) to fix.

Cruise Missile Cert: Imbed yourself in the targeting process. You know a lot more about the subject than your best-trained TAOs. Be there for exercises and training sessions.

These remarks represent a few of my thoughts and experiences concerning destroyer command. I have not addressed combat operations or the issues covered during your pipeline training, but I have considered a number of matters that COs seem to deal with regularly. My intention has been to give you a few things to think about. In any event, the most important piece of advice I can give is this: **give the ship everything you've got—time, energy, thought, and care—and you will find real success and deep satisfaction in command.**

> Kevin Green
> Captain, U.S. Navy
> Commander, Destroyer Squadron Twenty-Three

Navy Professional Reading Program and Recommended Reading List

As a commanding officer, one of your most important duties is developing the *next generation*. Encourage the officers in your wardroom—and indeed the entire crew—to be readers. It is a rewarding and professionally enriching experience. From junior enlisted to the chiefs' mess, your wardroom, and your executive officer—both figuratively and literally, your reliefs—encourage professional development at every turn and lead by example with your own continuing education. The Navy Professional Reading Program, traditionally updated during the tenure of each CNO, is a helpful tool in this endeavor. The Navy Professional Reading Program web page can be accessed via https://www.navy.mil/CNO-Professional -Reading-Program/.

ADDITIONAL READING

Below are some suggested titles related to the profession of arms, the art and science of taking ships to sea, and national security issues:

Admiral Arleigh Burke: A Biography—E. B. Potter

The Art of War—Sun Tzu

Atlantic: Great Sea Battles, Heroic Discoveries, Titanic Storms, and a Vast Ocean of a Million Stories—Simon Winchester

Bull Halsey: A Biography—E. B. Potter

The Caine Mutiny—Herman Wouk

Captain Cook: Master of the Seas—Frank McLynn

Castles of Steel: Britain, Germany, and the Winning of the Great War at Sea—Robert K. Massie

Command of the Seas: A Personal Story—John F. Lehman

The Cruel Sea—Nicholas Monsarrat

Destined for War: Can America and China Escape Thucydides's Trap?—Graham Allison

Destroyer Captain: Lessons of a First Command—James Stavridis

Division Officer's Guide, 12th Edition—James Stavridis, Robert Girrier, Jeffrey Heames, Thomas Ogden

The Endurance: Shackleton's Legendary Antarctic Expedition—Caroline Alexander

The Face of Battle: A Study of Agincourt, Waterloo and the Somme—John Keegan

First to Fight: An Inside View of the U.S. Marine Corps—Victor H. Krulak

Fleet Tactics and Naval Operations—Wayne P. Hughes and Robert P. Girrier

Ghost Fleet A Novel of the Next World War—P. W. Singer and August Cole

The Good Shepherd: A Novel—C. S. Forester

The Guns of August—Barbara W. Tuchman

The Hunt for Red October—Tom Clancy

The Influence of Seapower upon History, 1660–1783—Alfred T. Mahan

In Love and War: The Story of a Family's Ordeal and Sacrifice during the Vietnam Years—Jim and Sybil Stockdale

Learning War: The Evolution of Fighting Doctrine in the U.S. Navy, 1898–1945—Trent Hone

John Paul Jones: A Sailor's Biography—Samuel Eliot Morison

The Killer Angels—Michael Shaara

Knight's Modern Seamanship—John V. Noel Jr., editor

The Mask of Command: A Study of Generalship—John Keegan

Master and Commander—Patrick O'Brian

Master of Seapower: A Biography of Fleet Admiral Ernest J. King—Thomas B. Buell

Military Strategy: A General Theory of Power Control—J. C. Wiley

Miracle at Midway—Gordon W. Prange

Mister Roberts—Thomas Heggen

Naval Shiphandler's Guide—James A. Barber Jr.

Naval Shiphandling—Russell S. Crenshaw Jr.

Neptune's Inferno: The U.S. Navy at Guadalcanal—James D. Hornfischer

One Hundred Days: The Memoirs of the Falklands Battle Group Commander—Sandy Woodward

On War—Carl Von Clausewitz

On Watch—Elmo Zumwalt Jr.

Pacific War Trilogy—Ian W. Toll

The Perfect Storm: A True Story of Men against the Sea—Sebastian Junger

Post Captain—Patrick O'Brian

The Price of Admiralty: The Evolution of Naval Warfare from Trafalgar to Midway—John Keegan

The Pursuit of Victory: The Life and Achievement of Horatio Nelson—Roger Knight

The Quiet Warrior: A Biography of Admiral Raymond A. Spruance—Thomas B. Buell

Red Star over the Pacific: China's Rise and the Challenge to U.S. Maritime Strategy, 2nd Edition—Toshi Yoshihara and James R. Holmes

The Right Stuff—Tom Wolfe

The Rise and Fall of British Naval Mastery—Paul Kennedy

The Rise of American Naval Power, 1776–1918—Harold and Margaret Sprout

Run Silent, Run Deep—Edward L. Beach

Sailing Alone around the World—Joshua Slocum

Sailing True North: Ten Admirals and the Voyage of Character—James Stavridis

The Sand Pebbles—Richard McKenna

Sea of Thunder: Four Commanders and the Last Great Naval Campaign, 1941–1945—Evan Thomas

Sea Power: The History and Geopolitics of the World's Oceans—James Stavridis

Sea Power: A Naval History, 2nd Edition—E. B. Potter, editor

The Ship—C. S. Forester

Six Frigates: The Epic History of the Founding of the U.S. Navy—Ian W. Toll

The Soldier and the State: The Theory and Politics of Civil-Military Relations—Samuel P. Huntington

Some Principles of Maritime Strategy—Julian S. Corbett

Thirteen Days: A Memoir of the Cuban Missile Crisis—Robert F. Kennedy

Two-Ocean War: A Short History of the United States Navy in the Second World War—Samuel Eliot Morison

The United States Navy: 200 Years—Edward L. Beach

War and Remembrance—Herman Wouk

Watch Officer's Guide, 16th Edition—James Stavridis, Robert Girrier, Tom Ogden, Jeff Heames

The Winds of War—Herman Wouk

With the Old Breed: At Peleliu and Okinawa—E. B. Sledge

For those who wish to expand their reading horizons even further, *The Sailor's Bookshelf: Fifty Books to Know the Sea* (Naval Institute Press), by Admiral James Stavridis, offers fifty diverse titles that will help any commander broaden his or her understanding of the sea. This book's excellent list of titles includes works that focus on the oceans and those who have explored them, and on sailors in fiction and nonfiction alike.

Index

Page numbers followed by an *f* indicate figures.

About the Authors

ADM James Stavridis is a retired four-star officer who led the NATO Alliance in global operations from 2009 to 2013 as Supreme Allied Commander, with responsibility for Afghanistan, Libya, the Balkans, Syria, counterpiracy, and cyber security. He served as Commander, U.S. Southern Command, with responsibility for all military operations in Latin America from 2006 to 2009. Admiral Stavridis earned a PhD in international relations and has published twelve books and hundreds of articles in leading journals around the world. He is Chair Emeritus of the U.S. Naval Institute Board and is a contributing editor for *Time* magazine and Chief International Security Analyst for NBC News. His latest book is *The Sailor's Bookshelf: Fifty Books to Know the Sea.*

RADM Robert Girrier served as Deputy Commander Pacific Fleet and Director of Operations for U.S. Pacific Command. He also commanded two carrier strike groups, a destroyer squadron, a destroyer, and a mine countermeasures ship. He holds master's degrees in international affairs, marine affairs, and public administration and is the coauthor of seven professional book editions, including *Fleet Tactics and Naval Operations*, *Watch Officer's Guide,* and *Division Officer's Guide,* as well as the previous edition of *Command at Sea.* Rear Admiral Girrier is President Emeritus of Pacific Forum International, an Indo-Pacific–focused foreign policy think tank, and founder and managing member of Strategic Navigation, LLC, providing consulting services for strategy and policy.

RADM Fred Kacher recently completed duties as Commander, Expeditionary Strike Group Seven, forward deployed to the Western Pacific. He was raised in Oakton, Virginia, graduated from the U.S. Naval Academy in 1990 with a degree in English, and holds a master's degree in public policy with a concentration in international relations from Harvard's Kennedy School.

Prior to strike group command, Rear Admiral Kacher served at sea as commodore of Destroyer Squadron Seven, forward deployed to Southeast Asia. Previously, he commanded USS *Stockdale* (DDG 106) and served as executive officer on USS *Barry* (DDG 52). Ashore, he has served as executive officer to the Supreme Allied Commander, Europe, as chief of staff to Commander, Naval Surface Force, and as lead speechwriter to the chairman of the Joint Chiefs of Staff. In 2006 he was selected as a White House Fellow. He has been the recipient of the Admiral Elmo Zumwalt Award for visionary leadership and the U.S. Navy League's John Paul Jones Inspirational Leadership Award during his command of Destroyer Squadron Seven. He is author of *Newly Commissioned Naval Officer's Guide* and coauthor of *Naval Officer's Guide to the Pentagon*, both published by the Naval Institute Press.

The Naval Institute Press is the book-publishing arm of the U.S. Naval Institute, a private, nonprofit, membership society for sea service professionals and others who share an interest in naval and maritime affairs. Established in 1873 at the U.S. Naval Academy in Annapolis, Maryland, where its offices remain today, the Naval Institute has members worldwide.

Members of the Naval Institute support the education programs of the society and receive the influential monthly magazine *Proceedings* or the colorful bimonthly magazine *Naval History* and discounts on fine nautical prints and on ship and aircraft photos. They also have access to the transcripts of the Institute's Oral History Program and get discounted admission to any of the Institute-sponsored seminars offered around the country.

The Naval Institute's book-publishing program, begun in 1898 with basic guides to naval practices, has broadened its scope to include books of more general interest. Now the Naval Institute Press publishes about seventy titles each year, ranging from how-to books on boating and navigation to battle histories, biographies, ship and aircraft guides, and novels. Institute members receive significant discounts on the Press' more than eight hundred books in print.

Full-time students are eligible for special half-price membership rates. Life memberships are also available.

For more information about Naval Institute Press books that are currently available, visit www.usni.org/press/books. To learn about joining the U.S. Naval Institute, please write to:

Member Services
U.S. NAVAL INSTITUTE
291 Wood Road
Annapolis, MD 21402-5034
Telephone: (800) 233-8764
Fax: (410) 571-1703
Web address: www.usni.org